A QUEER LECTIONARY

A QUEER LECTIONARY

(Im)Proper Readings from the Margins Year A

Edited by
Peter Carlson

Seabury Books
NEW YORK

Seabury Books
19 East 34th Street
New York, NY 10016
www.churchpublishing.org

Seabury Books is an imprint of Church Publishing Incorporated.

Cover design by Newgen
Typeset by vPrompt eServices, India

ISBN 978-1-64065-795-3 (paperback)
ISBN 978-1-64065-758-8 (hardback)
ISBN 978-1-64065-759-5 (eBook)

Library of Congress Control Number: 2024947709

TABLE OF CONTENTS

PREFACE

This all began as an online encounter, but then, so did my marriage.

If there is any more twenty-first-century way to start doing relationships or theology, I'm not sure what it would be (and, for that matter, what is theology but the attempt to articulate a relationship?). But years back, bc (Before Covid), I began posting my thoughts about the lessons from the lectionary each Sunday, because a good bit of what I heard in sermons seemed to me to be trying too hard to appease the status quo rather than to unsettle it. This is nothing new, of course, but it seemed to me then (and seems still to me now) that the job of theology was similar to the job of journalism, as expressed by Finley Peter Dunn's fictional character Mr. Dooley: to comfort the afflicted and afflict the comfortable. I know, by the way, that I am taking the original quotation wildly out of context, but it nonetheless makes a provocative point about theology.

I also realized that though I have, for perhaps obvious reasons, usually been a member of queer-positive (or at least queer-tolerating, which is *so* not the same thing) congregations, I was rarely if ever hearing sermons that were preached from a uniquely queer perspective—indeed, the sermons I heard were too often, in my arrogant opinion, watered down by trying too hard to be something for everyone, which seemed to reduce them to a sort of least common multiple that was neither hot nor cold, and frankly begged to be spat, lukewarmly, from my mouth, if not from G-d's. This led to a growing awareness of discomfort: not with my identity as a Christian, exactly, but with the fact that I felt as though I was being told that the holy texts of my tradition could only be read in certain ways, and more particularly that reading them through the lens of my queer, enfleshed experience was, if not outright heretical, at least discomfortingly problematic.

And so I started, pretty impetuously I admit, writing sermons based on my own readings of scripture—readings from and through my queer body. And I refused to be ashamed of that in-bodied perspective, because if there is anything that has completely confounded me about the Christian tradition, it's that we have become so viciously anti-body when, in fact, the central tenet of our faith is that G-d thought bodies were cool enough to want one. Seriously, folks: The incarnation (which *literally* means "enfleshment") is the foundation of our belief, but we've turned flesh, bodies, into a big theological *Ick*, and have rendered our physical pleasures and desires a source of perpetual shame, assuming that they separate us from the Divine. As a Christian, I will *not* go there.

I am convinced that our bodies are holy texts through which the Divine speaks to us, in which the Word continues to become flesh, just as we Christians believe that the *Logos* also became flesh in a particular time and place. I am convinced that our bodies—not in spite of the fact they are made of matter but *because* of it—that they, well, *matter* to G-d. And I am convinced that we can only read scripture meaningfully if we read it unapologetically in and through our enfleshed experience.

So I started writing, and posting online. And my sermonic ramblings seemed to be resonating with people. Apparently, like acting, tapping into the personal is what makes the art universal. And people began to suggest the possibility of gathering these sermons and getting them published.

I'll freely admit that, given my training as a medieval scholar of religion, the idea of putting together a sermon collection—something that was important, particularly in the ninth century, as Charlemagne worked to unify the Holy Roman Empire in partnership with the Church—was intriguing. And as time passed, the possibility of gathering my queer theological musings centered around the Revised Common Lectionary seemed more and more plausible, and I contacted Church Publishing with a proposal, to which the editors responded with some excitement.

And then Covid.

How many of our stories have some variation of that sentence as a plot device? Covid threw us all off balance, even if I don't agree that it was, as so many people claimed, "unprecedented" (I am, after all, a medievalist who knows exactly what the Black Death did to Europe, and I'm also a gay man who survived the 1980s, so trust me, I know for plagues). When we went into lockdown, I'll admit that, as an introvert, my first response was a hand-rubbing, "I have been training for this my entire life." I quickly realized, however, that even though I am introverted, I do a kind of "check-in" with colleagues and friends all the time: Seeing someone on campus, and waving to them, even if it was not a sustained interpersonal interaction, let me know that so-and-so was, at least, upright and alive. Ironically, checking in during lockdown ended up demanding far more intention and extroversion than I was prepared for, and it was exhausting.

Nonetheless, some good came of it. What Covid did for me was to test my pedagogical skills as education went fully online, and to provide me with the opportunity for deep reflection on my life and, perhaps more to the point for this book, my theology. And what I realized was that the world really didn't need one more book by one more white, (sort of) cis, gay man attempting to speak for Queer Theology. The very nature of queerness is rooted in the postmodern assumption that the varieties of individual experience matter, and that multiplicity in meaning is not a threat to truth, but an affirmation of its richness and complexity. And so I came to the realization that if this sermon collection were going to go anywhere, it needed to become an act of queer community rather than an act of an individual queerperson.

I got back in touch with Church Publishing, reworking my original proposal, and was admittedly surprised to discover that this new direction was if anything more exciting for them than the original. Of course, that meant that I had to find fellow queer theologians who were both interested in the project, and who had the time and emotional bandwidth to participate. This is when I began, really for the first time, to appreciate the gorgeous and rich web of queer life; not only was queer support for the work enthusiastic, I ended up being able to welcome fifteen additional queer theological thinkers into the project, allowing for multiple sermonic styles, multiple in-bodied readings of scripture, multiple ways of engaging with G-d. These people are lay and ordained; they are multigendered; they speak of lives at the intersections of race and ethnicity and gender and sexuality; they are disabled and temporarily able-bodied; they are cis and nonbinary and trans; and they are all transgressive. Indeed, they are part of that astonishing cloud of witnesses whose mission is to remind the church that queerfolx have glorious and priceless gifts to offer the Church, and that the Church should not be "all are welcome"-ing us, but should instead be *begging* us to share our charisms, which are fabulous and fabulously overflowing, like a drag queen's bustier.

What do we queerfolx offer? Well, to start, we can teach the Church a lot about picking up the cross and following Jesus, even when people say we're not doing that. We can tell you what it means to experience costly grace in the face of Jesus lovers who say Jesus does not love us. We can also teach you about finding joy and community in our clubs, even as we walk the Via Dolorosa together. We can teach you *a lot* about dying, and grief, and resurrection. We can teach you about what it means to live on the edges of respectability, and how much of a challenge it is to find a sense of dignity—the *imago dei*—in our bodies and souls even as the world tries to beat the image of G-d the hell out of us.

In other words, we can teach you Gospel.

I hope that's what you'll experience here: Gospel, Good News, as it is experienced by those who live on the gendered and sexual margins of society. Good News of liberation from the world's imprisonment, but also from the world's values. A Gospel of in-bodied, shamelessly incarnational theology. Good News that, even when our bodies finally give out (or are killed), proclaims to us that nothing as banal as death can erase or make meaningless our fabulous and glittering lives.

Good, Queer News indeed.

Some brief notes: The overall goal of this collection is to provide queer readings of the Sundays and major feasts of Year A in the *Revised Common Lectionary*. Some additional feasts have been included because contributors felt particularly inspired to write on them. In general, I have encouraged contributors to engage with all the readings; this has been done to lesser and greater degrees throughout. In the Sundays following Pentecost, there are two tracks: Track 1 works through books of the Hebrew Bible in a relatively continuous narrative; track 2 attempts to reflect themes in the Gospel reading for the day. I have largely left it to the contributors' discretion as to whether they would attempt to do both or only one. I found that less important than the fact that we are all, together, engaged in queer biblical theology.

I owe a debt of thanks to those who believed in this project from the start. My original editors were my readers on social media, who encouraged me, challenged me, and supported me, and I cannot ever repay the debt in full. Milton Brasher-Cunningham, my original editor at Church Publishing, was the first person who made me believe the idea of a queer sermon collection had worth and could become something real. Justin Hoffman, who has also moved on, took over from Milton, and helped me imagine more concretely what this volume could look like and what it could accomplish. Laurie Harting has, with Katherine Lim's invaluable help, shepherded the project through innumerable production details, allowing me a say in everything from fonts to cover art; and most recently, Carl Bromley has provided enthusiastic support in bringing the work to press.

In addition to those queer theological thinkers who have contributed to this work (in whose debt I will forever be), there are many fellow academics and laypeople and clergy and congregational communities that have provided encouragement and support for me as I have worked over the years to bring this project to publication. The Episcopal congregations and clergy of All Saints in Pasadena, Epiphany in Oak Park, and All Saints/Todos Los Santos in Oxnard have all been sources of community and joy, even when I introvertedly have not been a particularly good congregational member. My present and past colleagues in the Religion Department at California Lutheran University: Julia Fogg, Sam Thomas, Victor Thasiah, Rick Hankins, Jennifer Hahn, Khrystyne Wilson, Colleen Windham-Hughes, Rose Aslan, and Rahuldeep Gill (of blessed memory) all gave me confidence and space to pursue this outrageous book. And of course, my partners in the work of Miz Holy Spirit Thang: the fabulous queer contributors to this volume who know that good sermons require a level of vulnerability, of baring one's soul to strangers, and who nevertheless were not deterred from joining me on this queer venture. Finally, I am beyond grateful to The Spousal, Eric Kamm, who has been a constant reassurance whenever the voices of my conservative evangelical upbringing get loud in my head, telling me that my queer self does not have value, that I need to take up less space so as not to offend, that my experience of the Divine is less than valid. Without Eric, I would have given up on both myself and G-d years ago.

Peter Carlson,
Thousand Oaks, CA

Laus Deus Semper

INTRODUCTION

The Queerness of Space, Time, and Text

The B-I-B-L-E,
Yes, that's the Book for me!
I stand alone on the Word of G-d,
The B-I-B-L-E!

I grew up singing this Sunday school song both at my church in Wheaton, Illinois, and every summer at the Cedar Lake Bible Conference in northwest Indiana, where my family had a cottage. It's a rollicking, even somewhat martial tune, and I remember belting it out lustily, undisturbed in my youth by the implicit heresy of bibliolatry: worship of a book, rather than worship of the Divine Presence to Whom the book points. This, of course, is one of the great problems of modern Christianity (and, for that matter, it is one of the great problems of Rabbinic Judaism to which St. Paul regularly points in his letters): the confusion of a text with the Divine.

Wait! you may ask. Isn't the Bible G-d's[1] Word? Isn't it our only access to G-d? Isn't it, after all, the *Holy* Bible? Why are you dissing the Holy Bible, G-d's Word, calling my love of scripture "heresy"?

So many really great questions, and they need to be answered in this book, that strives to read the Bible as a holy text. So, briefly, yes: I, both

---

[1] You will note that I do not spell out the name of G-d. My husband is Jewish, and I have adopted the practice, as a way of honoring G-d's Name: a Name so holy that it would not even be spoken aloud or even spelled out. In fact, in the Hebrew scriptures, the four-letter Name of G-d is never written, but is marked by a kind of placeholder. It is traditional, when reading, to say "Adonai" (usually translated "Lord") or "HaShem" ("The Name," which I prefer). Throughout this volume, the contributors use a variety of ways of acknowledging the Divine, which include multiple pronouns or names, and it is important to recognize that our approaches are as individual as our queer theologies.

individually and as a committed Christian in the Episcopal Church, believe that the Bible is G-d's word, even if I believe that Jesus is in fact more definitively the *Logos*, G-d's True Word. In the liturgy of ordination in the Episcopal Church, priests declare, "I do believe the Holy Scriptures of the Old and New Testaments to be the word of G-d, and to contain all things necessary to salvation." I too, though I do not seek to be ordained, make this affirmation. The Sunday worship services based on the Revised Common Lectionary are *packed* with scripture; they include two readings from the Hebrew scriptures (one from the Pentateuch, the Prophets, or the Writings, and one from the Psalms) and two from the Christian scriptures (one from the Acts of the Apostles, the Epistles, or Revelation, and one from the Gospels). All of this is in addition to the passages of scripture that are included in the rest of the liturgy. In my daily life, I read the Bible regularly, expecting and receiving guidance and spiritual sustenance. I take scripture seriously and passionately, if not literally. The B-I-B-L-E is, indeed, a book for me (whatever others may say), and I read the texts because they contain the stories, the holy words, the *logoi* of my religious tradition.

But words, texts, are tricky things. Just when we think we've got hold of a meaning, it slips past us, like a cat skirting the edges of a room. How many of us have read a book, discovered that a friend has read it too, and in talking about it, wondered if we even read the same book? Discovered that we took entirely different things away from the same text? We need only look around to our fellow Christians to know that we do the same with the Bible, even though we might agree that it is the Word of G-d. Words are signs, they're symbols; they *point* to things, while they are not the things themselves, and we humans who use words are always, inevitably, struggling to determine what, actually, any given word is pointing at. Words are topsy-turvy. Words are slippery. Words are queer.

Postmodernism, in its rejection of a single, stable interpretation (of history, of literature, of words, of sex, of life), can appear unnerving and frightening in its willing and intentional instability. Queer theory, as a particular branch of postmodernism, takes that instability and adds to the mix our variable and unstable bodies, with all their gendered and erotic potential. When we use queer, postmodern lenses, we are tempted to think that meaning itself, and the authority to establish meaning, is up for grabs. This is uncomfortable. We humans ache for constancy, for someone simply to tell us what's what, that blue is for boys and pink is for girls. That there are only boys and girls. We need only look at fundamentalist religious communities that are so popular in every religious tradition to see this desire for constancy; they are the communities that provide easy answers, that reject a plurality of experience or interpretation. They are safe, and the only truly terrifying thing for these people is the dissenting voice or the alternative experience.

But we needn't fear multiplicity or diversity. Jacques Derrida, one of the great proponents of postmodernist thought, argued for the instability of meaning, speaking of an empty space between the mark and the thing that is marked—between the sign and the signified, between the word and the thing it attempts to explain. He sees in that space not chaos and horror but fertile potential, ripe multiplicity. It is not safe, if by "safe" we mean "comfortable" or "certain," because the empty space is uncharted territory, filled with awkward spaces where we are constantly looking for a foothold and not really finding one. Queerness, however, for all that it may seem unstable and awkward and dangerous, is ultimately a methodology rooted in hope and expansiveness. It is exploratory, scootching around the edges of the room like that cat, living in the margins, seeking always alternative ways of drawing lines between the sign and the signified, offering a new perspective from which to view meaning, and never rejecting the authority of one's own (in)bodied experience. Queerness is the manifestation of life on the edges, neither trying to achieve some stable (and ultimately elusive) center, nor to gain admittance to some imagined Inner Circle where at last we can rest. Queerness is by its very nature peripheral, active, alternative, nonbinary, and unsystematic.

And queerness is the very *heart* of the Christian tradition. Many of us have lost track of that fact, struggling to survive in a world that tells us to nail meanings down securely and to place ourselves at the center of everything, to be the focus of attention. Everything about Jesus and the movement he inspired is queer, because it rejects what the world says is important, right down to ways of thinking about space and time.

From an early age, I was fascinated by questions of time and space and our lives spent within them. When I was very young, and my older brothers and sisters would tease me (I was the youngest of seven; teasing was probably inevitable), I would simply close my eyes to end the torture—clearly, I had made them go away because they were no longer in my field of vision. This instinctively self-referential behavior led easily and inevitably to questions about self-reference: If I could not perceive something, did it exist? What did it mean, even, to say that something *does* exist? If it is out of my space, or my time, is it real? Is mine the only space/time that has reality?

It is probably no great surprise to discover that an author who influenced me since I was very, very young is Madeleine L'Engle. In particular, the questions that so many of her books raise about space and time and how we function in them have stayed with me, and I fiddle with those questions even today. They are essentially theological questions, at least in Christian terms, because they demand some account of the nature of G-d, both as creator of a universe in which the space-time continuum affects us all, and as a Divine participant in that universe. Space-time, it seems, are inseparable, and if we muck about with one, we're mucking about with the other. Space-time is a spectacularly queer concept, at the very least because it suggests that time is *not* a convenient two-dimensional line (in fact, our usual thinking about time isn't even fully two-dimensional, because it only moves in one direction). It also suggests that space is far more complex than the three dimensions which we usually affirm as its limits, and that it is instead haunted by the possibility of another, fourth dimension (time?), and another fifth (the tesseract of *A Wrinkle in Time*?), and another (Sixth? Seventh? How many dimensions might the Divine have?).

Early on in my conservative evangelical Christian world, I recognized the problem of placing the Incarnation too literally in either space or time with regard to the question of salvation and damnation: "What about the people who were born before Jesus, or who never got a chance to hear about him?" I fretted. I was thinking in soteriological terms that demanded a "personal relationship with Jesus Christ" (to use the customary evangelical formulation) without which a person would burn eternally in hell. While my soteriology has moved (and I hope grown) significantly since those days, I was fortunate to have parents who did not give me facile answers to difficult questions. They trusted that G-d, existing both within but also beyond the limitations of space-time, would somehow take our own creaturely, bodily limitations into account.

That's actually really queer thinking (wouldn't my parents be surprised!). It is a response that rejects an easy, sensible—in the literal meaning of being able to be perceived with the senses—binary of yes/no, right/wrong, saved/damned, and suggests that there is both a physical and a temporal space—a space-time, if you will—between the Incarnation and its meaning(s), between sign and the signifier, between the marker and the marked, between starting point and resolution. And in that space-time, a multitude of experiences can take place (or time) that could be salvific. Queerness insists on encountering both space and time in multiple ways that the world says are foolish; it seeks a marginal position both spatially and temporally and suggests that truth—or greater truth—can be discovered and proclaimed from that position. Queerness, then, insists upon encountering holy texts from the marginal positions that it inhabits.

The Seduction of Space

I spent, like many people, a large part of my youth longing to be a part of the in-crowd. I expended an incredible amount of energy trying to be cool, trying to be funny, trying to be smart, trying to be popular, trying to be "in." In retrospect, it was exhausting; to this day my siblings, who watched me work so hard at being extroverted and part of the cool group, remain skeptical that I am, in fact, an introvert, but that my paranoia of exclusion overrode my nature, forcing me into a performative mode. One of the great ironies of my youth, however, is that, based upon the world's standards, I was, by the very accidents of my birth, just about as "in" as a person could be. I was born white, gender-defined male, and essentially healthy, to loving parents, in a moderately wealthy Midwestern town, with a high-quality educational system, at a time when a high-quality college education (even at a private school) was still relatively affordable for those of us in moderately wealthy Midwestern towns. You could make a powerful case that I was destined from the womb to be successful. But there I was, still struggling to be in, because I felt out.

Of course, I can attribute a good bit of my outsiderliness to being gay, and trying to hide it, lest I be completely ostracized from my community (which was not, despite deeply loving and accepting parents, an unfounded fear). But it is only too clear that the fear of being an outsider is common to all of us, not just queers, or people of color, or the disabled, or transfolk, or women, because the world shouts at us in daily life and haunts us in our nightmares that we are in the wrong place if we are outside. "Loser! You're a failure, because you aren't in the Inner Circle!" We can tell ourselves with our rational minds that these words are false, but the very idea that there even *is* an "inside" is desperately seductive. The institutions of the world are everywhere evidence of this seduction, suggesting that insiderliness is the one essential element of success: varsity teams, fraternities and sororities, deans' lists, country clubs, promotion, reservations at exclusive restaurants, boards of directors, legislatures, SuperPACs. . . .

If only, we tell ourselves, we could get into *that* group, have influence among *those* people, live in *that* neighborhood, work in *that* company, have *that* corner office, we will have made it. The church is not immune from this seduction: If only (I told myself once upon a time) I were ordained, *then* I would be able to "do ministry." Our values in this world tell us that everything we do should be directed toward ensuring that we are at the center. Centrality—being "in"—is the only goal worth pursuing, and success can only be found at the center.

The Gospels preach something radically different. Indeed, the Hebrew and Christian scriptures alike teach that centrality is dangerous, though we often read the texts with a lens that ignores or actively discounts this teaching. Consider: It is perilously easy for us to imagine that Israel was a power player in the ancient world, since it is the focus of the Hebrew scriptures. But Israel and Judah were small, marginal countries that were frankly a little weird in their monotheistic tendencies, and they were constantly subjected to the whims of great, polytheistic empires that regularly trampled on them as they struggled to understand themselves in relationship to those empires and to their G-d.

Jesus himself was born to rather socially marginal parents in the thoroughly politically marginal province of the Roman Empire, as far away from Central Rome as Hadrian's Wall. He grew up practicing Judaism, which was a marginal religious tradition in the Empire. He was then marginalized even from his fellow Jews by preaching a prophetic message that asked them to reject all hope of worldly power—of centrality—and respond to the Roman Empire not with violence but with—well, it might almost be called disdain. His was a prophetic call to pay attention, not to the powerful and central, but the weak and marginalized, and to seek out a position at the edges of society and power, even if they were physically still located and entangled in sociopolitical power structures.

Jesus was asking his companions to be queer—to queer their very approach to life and to G-d. He invited his followers, not to the center, but to the margins, to reside with and *be* the outliers, the weirdos and freaks, the sexual perverts, the dehumanized. Certainly, Jesus was marginalized by circumstance; he chose, however, to move even more deeply into marginality by taking positions against the religious authorities of the day, by wandering around without a fixed home, by hanging out with All The Wrong People. He both literally and figuratively sought out the social and geographical margins, and performed his work, his ministry, there (without the benefits, I might add, of ordination by any centrally acknowledged religious authority). It is our job as modern-day Jesus followers to, well, *follow* him, and to resist the worldly seduction of the inner circle, of being with the power players, and to be willing—eager, even—to live marginal lives, practicing marginal ministry, with or without the benefit of centralized religious authority.

Holy spaces today continue to invite us into the margins. At the Cedar Lake Bible Conference, I can still visualize the words painted on the proscenium arch over the main worship space: "Come ye yourselves apart and Rest-A-While." This truncated version of the King James translation of Mark 6:31 always fascinated me. I didn't realize the context in my youth: Jesus's disciples have just tended to the body of John the Baptizer who had been murdered by the politically centralized Herod; they had been ministering to the needs of the people; and they were exhausted both by grief and by sheer physical work. And Jesus recognized the need to get away, to recharge. Who among us has not popped into a quiet church, or a secret garden, or a coffee shop, or a darkened stairwell, and discovered a sacred place apart, where they could rest a while?

At their best, church buildings function as holy, marginal spaces, inviting us to view the world from a different perspective, to participate in an "alternative lifestyle" (to co-opt a phrase thrown at queer folk by those who hate us). It is difficult work, though, to avoid being infected by the world. Too often, our churches are designed and/or used to establish Christianity's centrality rather than its marginality. Too often, we see pulpits as locations that express power rather than solidarity with the poor. Too often, our ritual space is designed to affirm whiteness, straightness, maleness, cis-ness, physical ability, and wealth, rather than to provide space to sit and listen to people of color, queers, women, othergendered, the disabled, and the poor. There are indeed Christians who think of church buildings and other gathering spaces in light of that marginality, that difference; they are asking how these spaces can reject centralized, worldly understandings of power and glory, and instead reflect the marginal experiences of the oppressed and the downtrodden.

Because our churches have so often failed at being marginal spaces, we must not really be surprised to discover that the marginalized have in in every time and place created their own holy spaces. Writing groups for women of color, Latinx street murals, trans or gender-nonconforming support groups, queer dance clubs, homeless camps, the Houses of drag ball culture—these are all sacred spaces, because they are spaces in which the marginalized need be nothing other than the very best version of who G-d created them to be, and to rest a while.

Perhaps—and I am risking much in suggesting this—the Church needs to abandon some of its own space, which we have been seduced into making so centralized, so worldly, so *un-sacred*, and ask humbly for admittance into the sacred spaces of the outsiders? I would wager that we will encounter G-d in those queer spaces, and that, in allowing our old self-understandings to die, we will have the opportunity to be resurrected to a glorious new, marginal life.

The Seduction of Time

Time is as seductive as space. And the first and most potent seduction of time is the fantasy that we can control it. My parents kept a remarkable number of mementos of our childhoods, and when my Mom died, I was surprised at all of the stuff they had saved: drawings, writing, report cards. In grade school, we were graded with an S, an N, or a U. Satisfactory, Needs Work, or Unsatisfactory. I don't think I got many Us, but my Ns were almost always related to my ability to focus and get things done in a timely manner. We have all, I'm willing to bet, fretted about "time management," convinced that time is, somehow, under our authority and able to *be* managed. If time were only a simple, two-dimensional thing, this might be within the realm of possibility, but time is a murkier, more complex, *wavier* thing than that, and trying to control it is kind of like trying to control a wave: You might be able to ride it, but you can't control it.

The world, however, tells us that time-control is essential. It encourages us both to dwell in the past, and to create for ourselves a successful future, and to freight the present with unrealistic and unsustainable modes of "productivity." The Church is infected by this thinking too, dwelling in an idealized faith history, fantasizing an idealized faith future, and fretting about a productive faith present. We are so worried about what the Church has been in the past, and what the Church will become in the future, that we are forgetting simply to *be* the Church in the present, and to be queerly present as Church. We must, as people practicing a queer faith, inhabit the margins of time as well as space: influenced by the queerness of the past, holding lightly our dreams of a queer future, and being utterly and fabulously queer as we dwell in the marginal moments of the day.

The seduction of the past is seen in our resistance to change, even though we know change is essential to the legitimacy of our moral platforms, and to our very survival. "But we've always done it this way" is probably the most common response to change I've heard, and it is the flimsiest of reasons, logically, for maintaining current modes of behavior. Don't get me wrong: Tradition matters, because it has brought us to where we are. History and tradition should inform our work, though, and not control it. Rituals that have lost their meaning have no place in any human institution, least of all the Church. Even our sacred texts need to be re-read, re-interpreted as the world changes around us. A past that continues to grip us and prevent us from seeing the world truthfully is a past that provides no place for queerness, for prophetic witness. And both the world and the church need queer prophets right now.

The seduction of the future is akin to the seduction of the past. In Dorothy Sayers's mystery novel *Clouds of Witness*, a character relates a pathetic story about a man who lived an intensely frugal life, leaving behind some noble (now turned sour) port wine that he had never drunk himself:

> The port was laid down by [his father], who died in 1860, when my client was thirty-four. He—the son I mean—was ninety-six when he deceased. He said no pleasure ever came up to the anticipation, and so he lived like a hermit . . . but planning all the things he might have done. He wrote an elaborate diary, containing, day by day, the record of this visionary existence which he had never dared put to the test of actuality. . . . An earnest Christian, he anticipated great happiness after death, but, as you see, he put the pleasure off as long as possible. He died with the words, "He is faithful that promised"—feeling to the end the need of assurance.[2]

---

[2] Dorothy Sayers, *Clouds of Witness*, London: T. Fisher Unwin, 1926. First HarperPaperbacks printing, 1995.

The story is not advocating frivolous spending but is a warning about refusing the joy offered us each day. We spend swathes of time preparing for a future that is not in our control, nor even remotely of our own making. Jesus's words "Do not care about tomorrow, for today has enough worries of its own" may sound lovely to us, but they are, we smile wryly, utterly unrealistic. I know that the world demands I fund my 401(k) plan, that I lay out a respectable retirement, and ensure that I leave a fat legacy for my legatees (or at the least not leave them my debt). It is far too easy for me to fret "sensibly" about the future than to live fully and queerly in the present.

But living in the present is not as easy as just paying attention to today. Remember Jesus's words: "Today has enough worries of its own." The present seduces us with its own allure: the temptation of *productivity*. I work in academia and have gone through the anxieties and outright panic attacks of a promotion review. The questions that every person going through this process asks themselves (and is asked by the academic tenure and promotion committee) are: Have I *done* enough? Have I *published* enough reviews/articles/essays/monographs? Have I *performed* enough service to the university? Have I *received* enough positive teaching evaluations?

Have I *produced* enough? Are my *products* sufficient unto the day?

Rarely, if ever, do we hear academic committees (or managers in corporations, or even our own brains, for that matter) asking candidates/employees/ourselves, Have you rested enough? Have you taken enough time for your family? Are you relishing what you do? What thrills you about your job, if anything? What connects you to your community? Do you feel like what you do is worthwhile? If not, what would or could you change? The only times, it seems, that we even ask ourselves these kinds of questions is when our lives and faith have smashed up against a crisis, when they have become unsustainable in their current, production-driven formats.

Corporations urge us to "work smarter, not harder," but not because they don't want us to work hard: The focus is *always* on productivity, which must never decline. The very idea of offering employees a minimum of four (or more) weeks of vacation a year is scorned in the United States as unproductive (which is, after all, another word for *unprofitable*). When we finally justify health care, it is not for the moral reason that people simply deserve to be healthy, but because "healthy employees are productive employees." Academia, for all its idealism, is infected by productivity-talk, and I buy into it. I regularly approach my day by asking myself how much I need to accomplish in it. In the summer months, if I am not teaching, I am driven to *justify* not teaching, reinforcing in my mind the siren song that I have no value if I am not producing (say, a book of sermons), if I am not productive. So I convince myself that I must spend my summer writing, or going to conferences, or designing syllabi for the coming semester(s). Even our sabbaticals, named (with deep, if not intentional, irony) after the Sabbath, on which Jews are required to rest from *all* their labor, must literally be defended to the administration as "productive." I was required in my sabbatical application to explain to my Provost what I would accomplish with my sabbatical time, how it would "benefit the university," and to pledge to provide a "talk" on What I Did During My Sabbatical. Sabbath? Cessation of labor? Hardly.

The Church, too, idolizes productivity: How many members are on the rolls? How many sick parishioners have been visited? How many communions/baptisms/marriages? How many converts? How many souls have been "saved"? All of these questions relate to what the late Gustavo Gutierrez would describe as quantitative soteriologies, concerned ultimately with numbers, rather than qualitative soteriology, which is concerned about what salvation actually *is*, particularly for the oppressed. We tend, unquestioningly, to value pastors of large congregations over small congregations, in great part because we assume that congregations are the type of community that is the only effective Christian presence in the world. Like so many things in life, we need only to follow the money to see what the Church values. We worship productivity as the God of the Present, even as the stories of Jesus, whom we believe to be G-d present in the flesh, warn us that productivity is an evil seduction indeed.

Past, future, and present: We need to inhabit time queerly. The first step in this process, I'm convinced, is that we need to stop thinking of time as a two-dimensional line, with a past, a present, and a future. Queer time does not bind itself to this restricted and restrictive understanding; rather, it views time as something far more fluid, in which we can dwell in past, present, and future all at once, each bearing witness to the others and in conversation with the others, and all the while living not at the center but in the margins of time. As queer residents of time (or as residents of Queer Time), we do not inhabit *a* time, but Time. When we try to centralize ourselves in a time, we encounter trouble: an uncritical devotion to the past; a desperate desire to control the future; a panicked attempt to produce enough in the present.

I have suggested that the Sabbath itself is queer, as a construct of Time. The Rev. Dr. Jay Johnson has spoken movingly of the queerness of the Ordo Calendar—the calendar that marks out, or orders, the patterns of the Christian year.[3] The Ordo, with its guaranteed times set aside for rejoicing, grieving, contemplating, atoning, and working (and its refusal to rush any of those things) is a reflection of Christianity moving intentionally outside of the world's "productive" time into queer time, beyond the seductions of past, present, and future *tense*, in all of its meanings. It reminds us that we cannot have the "productivity" of Easter resurrection without the anguish of dying—or the restfulness of being dead—in Holy Week. It reminds us to remember and re-member saints (who queerly countered the world's values) and to live like them. It reminds us that Ordinary Time is anything but Ordinary. It reminds us that we can take twelve whole days to celebrate a birth, and still not be done. It affirms Christ born, dead, resurrected, yesterday, today, and tomorrow. The Ordo provides us a way of moving out of the world's time zone (Central Time?) into the margins of Time, where life is lived and danced to different temporal rhythms: sitting in grief; toiling at our work/prayer; or even being utterly silly and frivolous, and dangerously unproductive.

Even so, we need to be careful as we rejoice in the original queer intent of the church year. The Ordo itself has often been centered, turned into a tool for productivity and efficiency. Time on the margins is time spent in witness both to the oppression that has sent the marginalized to those times zones, and to the fact that the marginalized may very well be creating "orders" that look and feel very different from those that the Church has established. If the Ordo becomes an ossified historical artifact, then it has lost the power to unsettle us, to turn us away from the world's Central calendar. It is no longer marginal time, and no longer queer.

The Lectionary

So what does all this space-time-continuum jabber have to do with the lectionary, with the texts that we read across the space-timespan of three church years? Certainly, our sacred texts are informed by space and time, even as and

[3] Jay Emerson Johnson, *Peculiar Faith* (Church Publishing, 2014).

because we read them in both space and time. The lectionary is not simply an assignment that we perform, like dutiful schoolchildren, to get good grades with The Teacher. Rather, as with the original intent of the church buildings, and the original intent of the Ordo, the lectionary is a *logos* invitation into the queer margins and multiple dimensions of space-time. The lectionary was *intended* to be queer: to invite us, textually, into the margins of living, where the centrality of the world is unsettled, put off-kilter, and decentered. Many Christians in their communities are intentional in reading scriptural texts in this way. The practices of *Lectio Divina*, the African Bible Study Method, and the *Comunidades Eclesiales de Base* are a few examples of encountering scripture in marginal ways and from marginal positions. In each case, every person encountering the text, but *especially* the person on the margins—the monastic, the colonized, the poor—has been given the Gift of the Spirit to read the words of G-d in such a way as to reveal G-d's care for the oppressed. They have been given the gift of reading the *Logos*—the Christ-Text—queerly.

For those of us who wish to recover this sense of the lectionary, I suggest that our work requires us to encounter the readings in both spatial and temporal margins, and at times even in the margins of the text itself. We must recognize not only the marginal spaces in which the texts were written, but the marginal spaces about which they speak, and the marginal people who inhabit(ed) those spaces. We must read them from the perspective of today's marginal spaces too. We must, in the best sense of postmodern literary theory, *deconstruct* and destabilize the received, so-called orthodox readings of these texts and read them in/from alternative spaces, and seeking to understand, or at least gaze in wonder, love, and awe at, the alternative, sacred spaces they reveal.

Space matters in our encounters with texts. I regularly teach an introductory course in religion at California Lutheran University. In one four-week block of time, we wrestle with questions of creation and creativity that begin (perhaps inevitably, at a school affiliated with a Christian denomination) with a reading of the creation myths of Genesis 1–3. One semester, I changed things up, and had the students meet for a class session at an outdoor classroom on campus called the SEEd Garden (Sustainable, Edible, Education), where we read the first three chapters of Genesis together. The ways in which the students understood the text was transformed simply by virtue of the space in which we read it. Reading stories about the first birds, for instance, as chickens squawk about your feet, provides an imaginative background that makes the stories *realer*; the cackling, scratching, and clucking inform the stories in new ways, and the wonders of nature help us understand, for instance, how the author(s) could have seen the cosmos as geocentric, even as we twenty-first-century folk condescendingly acknowledge that we are the inhabitants of a marginal planet in a marginal solar system, and hardly at the center of anything. *Where* we read the story—at the edges of the campus, rather than in a classroom where we tend to center the learning experience—quite literally queers the story, opening new, marginal ways of understanding. We enter into the story both as creatures and cocreators, seeing and questioning G-d's motives and our own.

I have mentioned that the Hebrew and Christian scriptures are stories told of and by marginal peoples, acting in marginalized ways, in marginal spaces, at marginal times, and (pay attention) beloved of G-d not in *spite* of their marginality, but *because* of it. Everything about the scriptures takes us to the very edges of life.

But we are too often guilty of centralizing the Hebrew and Christian scriptures by reading worldly authority into them; I suggest that this began in earnest with the co-option of Christianity by the Roman Empire in the early fourth century, and that Christianity itself quickly became drunk with imperial power. We have been able to continue believing that this power is divinely ordained, because Christianity has so effectively maintained it over the centuries. Our tradition has clung to and sacralized this power, though, to the detriment of the Beloved Community. Jesus made clear that his realm was not of this world: not a kingdom, but a Kindom[4] in which nationality, gender, age, and social status are united by equity. A Kindom maintained, not by the usual structures of political or financial power, but by the queer and unusual creation of loving relationships and fostering of marginal communities. When I do not read holy texts with this in mind, it is too easy for me to capitulate to the kingdoms of earth, rather than building up the Kindom of G-d on earth as it is in heaven. This capitulation happens when I try to centralize myself, to claim earthly power and authority. The residents of the Kindom are not central: They inhabit the margins, even as they stride through earthly kingdoms, rebuking their power.

---

[4] You will notice that, here and elsewhere, I take the "g" out of "kingdom," because, as an historian of the medieval period, I've got some serious issues with kingship as a model of government. When I take the "g" out, it also connects me theologically to the biblical idea that we are G-d's children, that we are, in fact, kin with G-d and with each other.

Reading the lectionary from a queer spatial perspective is not enough. We must also read our sacred stories from a temporally queer position. We can achieve this in part by holding before us both the fluidity and unity of past, future, and present as we read. As a historian it is perhaps not a surprise that I insist on the need to read scriptural stories in historical context. Christians who assume that the Bible has no contingent connection to the historical time or location in which it was written are refusing to acknowledge that humans and—yes, I will claim this—human understandings of the Divine change over time, reflecting our human experience of the universe and the role we play in it. I raise again the point of reading the creation myths, which assume a geocentric universe, in a time in which science has taught us otherwise. Poor Galileo! We hope that the Church would no longer imprison a man for suggesting a heliocentric solar system. But his experience tells us that scripture as the Word of G-d (and, indeed Christ as the *Logos* of G-d) is firmly rooted in time, even as it transcends it.

That transcendence is in some ways manifested as we hold not only the past but the future as we read the lectionary. Incarnation and resurrection, two foundations of Christian faith, are both rooted in hope, and hope inevitably looks toward the future. The apocalyptic future of St. John the Divine is often what we think of when we talk about religious futures, but a literal reading (if such a thing is even possible with such a fantastical account) prevents us from seeing the topsy-turvyness, the queerness, the marginality, of the story. When I read it, I see a vision, not of "bad people" going to hell and "good people" going to heaven, but of the inversion of worldly power and the decentering of worldly values. It is about queering everything we've been taught by the world; a centrifugal force that spins us away from the prison of the In Crowd out to the freedom of the margins.

Of course, even as we discern the historical context of a text, and even as we proclaim a hopeful future inspired by the text, we must needs still read the text in the present. Textual queer *presence*, though, can only be revealed by inhabiting or looking to those places and mindsets that are, in today's space and time, marginal. The scriptural texts speak of the marginalized: the widows, the stranger, the orphans, the sick, the imprisoned. Who today lives on the edges of worldly authority and power? Who are the folk who are "despised and rejected" of the world, whom G-d will establish as the "chief cornerstone" of the Church today? How can we, today, find within ourselves the marginalized experiences that speak Gospel, Good News, both to our own lives and to the dispossessed of the world?

Sometimes, we can do this by literally going to marginal spaces, like organic gardens or queer Latiné salsa clubs. But here is the important thing: When we go to those spaces, we must go not to *preach* the Gospel, but to *hear* it. We must die to our own centrality. Christianity teaches a costly grace (to use Bonhoeffer's phrase) that gives hope not by rejecting death, but by embracing it, and believing that death does not bat last.

I want to tell you a secret: Queerfolk can tell the world a lot about death.

We Queers have in both the past and the present (and likely will continue to have in the future) walked through the Valley of the Shadow of Death, and even if we are not strong enough to fear no evil, we can tell you about the resurrection promise that comes from refusing to have our voices silenced, our stories untold, even when we are threatened. We can teach the Church something about reading the lectionary from the margins.

James Cone argued famously that G-d is black, and that the white Christian's response to this proclamation must be to become black with G-d; and that praying for a cool summer, so the blacks in the ghetto won't suffer because of their lack of air conditioning is *not* how to become black with G-d. Too often, the Church has called from its white, straight, air-conditioned positions of privilege, proclaiming, "You're welcome here!" without bothering even to check if public transportation goes past their doors. Too often, the Church has assumed that its central location and central power structure and central viewpoint and central heating are Good News, even as we wonder why congregations are dwindling, and why our central physical spaces take up more and more of our budgets.

Queer theologians have followed Cone's example by proclaiming the Gospel Truth that G-d is Queer. I affirm this Gospel, this Good News, from my experience of the Divine within the physical location of my own queer body. I read this Gospel in the sacred texts of our tradition—both the Hebrew and Christian scriptures, but also in the in-bodied *Imago Dei* proclaimed by those scriptures. This book is a collection of sermon responses to the lectionary by a number of theological thinkers who represent a glorious and wild array of queer identities, all fully in-bodying the Image of G-d. They have Gospel—Good News—to proclaim, even if the Church does not yet have ears to hear.

Altar Call: *Just as I Am*

At Cedar Lake, altar calls were a regular phenomenon, rooted in the conviction that there was always at least one damned soul in the audience, finally ready to accept their morbid state, and turn to G-d's saving grace. Altar calls always, it seemed, were accompanied by the congregation singing *all* the verses (there were seven) of "Just As I Am," a hymn based on a poem written by Charlotte Elliott in 1835.

> Just as I am—without one plea,
> But that Thy blood was shed for me,
> And that Thou bidst me come to Thee,
> O Lamb of God, I come![5]

We would sing, and sing. And sing. If seven verses were not enough, we could go back and start over at a dirge of a tempo. I sometimes wondered if someone finally accepted the altar call and pretended to need saving just so we could go home. After all, I was pretty sure that everyone in the hall was attending church because they were pretty sure they had already been saved.

For all my cynicism, however, I still believe in the importance of an altar call—of a sacrificial coming forward—a coming *out*—publicly to make a commitment to Jesus and to the marginalized incarnation(s) of G-d. And I believe firmly that I need to answer that call today and every day, just as I am: a queer, introverted, big ol' homo, struggling and often afraid. To bring anything other than just as I am would be to present a worthless offering to the Divine.

In the seventeenth century, the metaphysical poet Henry Vaughan wrote a poem titled "The World":

> I saw Eternity the other night,
> Like a great ring of pure and endless light

---

[5] "Just as I Am" was written by Charlotte Elliott in 1835, first appearing in the high church magazine, *Christian Remembrancer*.

Vaughan's poem imagines eternity—fully encompassed, queer Time, past-present-future—as a ring of light. Earthly time in the poem, on the other hand, "like a vast shadow mov'd"—a one-directional, limited dimension, bound in and by darkness. Vaughan gives a haunting image of the "states-man hung with weights and woe" trapped in those limitations of earthly time, at the center of worldly power, where "Churches and altars fed him." Vaughan saw the centers of power, which we worship, as a vacuum: The center is, quite literally, nothing. Eternity, though, is a ring; it is at the margins; it *is* the margins.[6]

It is light.

The responses to the lectionary in this book are meant not be definitive or in any way orthodox, but exemplary: examples of readings from the margins that the contributors inhabit as queer Christians. I hope that they provide you with queer ideas to approach and experience our sacred stories from your own marginal perspectives. Our goal in encountering the sacred stories of Judaism and Christianity is to read the Divine *Logos* in and from the margins.

Because I believe that the margins are, ultimately, space-times of Divine Light.

---

[6] Henry Vaughan, "The World," accessed at poetryfoundation.org.

ADVENT

FIRST SUNDAY OF ADVENT

Dr. Peter Carlson

Isaiah 2:1–5
Psalm 122
Romans 13:11–14
Matthew 24:36–44

What with a date night, in which my spouse and I went to Paddy's in Ventura (*the* queer bar in Ventura County) that ended up going long past my bedtime, I didn't make it to church for the first Sunday of Advent; my soul is mightily stirred up in Advent anticipation nonetheless.

A mildly inebriated gent at the bar seemed to take a shine to us, and we had a lovely and earnest conversation, in which he made it clear to us that we, as Elder Queers, are the shoulders on which the younger generations are standing. In an act of classic self-abnegation (a gift of my gay childhood in a conservative Christian environment), I was inclined to pooh-pooh this as a kind of drunken sentimental hogwash, but upon more consideration I realized that, in fact, we are. I may not have been on the front lines of ACT-UP, or actually throwing a pie in Anita Bryant's face (I can dream, though), but I did learn to live as an out queer person, and I am a survivor of an epidemic that was utilized as a weapon to excoriate and demonize queers and, somehow, through it all, I did not lose my soul.

This morning, I awoke to news that a shooting threat had been made against four southern California universities, including the one at which I teach. This unnerving e-blast from campus safety was made even more disturbing because it came so close on the heels of the anniversary of the

Borderline shootings, in which a gunman opened fire during college night at a local country bar, killing students from several college communities, including mine. Violence is all around us.

And it has struck me that as a Queer Elder, as a teacher, and certainly as a Queer Elder Teacher, I am challenged to walk forward, once again, into the very real threat of danger, and somehow not lose my soul.

The vision of a glorious future in today's reading from the Hebrew Bible is a fantasy, clearly. The Prophet Isaiah writes so longingly of a time when swords shall be beaten into plowshares—when our weapons will be melted down and be made into tools for growing food in abundance and—glory!—"nation shall not lift up sword against nation, neither shall they learn war any more." It's a beautiful vision. But today, thousands of years later, even the most optimistic of us have become convinced that Isaiah's dream is just that: a bizarre, if pleasantly optimistic, hash dream, from which we wake every day to news of another act of violence, too much of it hitting far too close to home rather than comfortably far off in Ukraine or Palestine, or Yemen, about which we blessedly think we really don't have to give a shit.

The psalmist provides us with another vision of restoration, dreaming of a Jerusalem (not literal, surely, considering how war-torn that city is and has been) that is the abode of the Divine, in which nations together will find a way forward toward justice—echoing Isaiah's desperate hope. The psalmist seems to know, though, that this peaceable reign will not just happen magically: "Pray for the peace of Jerusalem," we are implored. "Peace be within your walls, and quietness within your towers." We must, it appears, pray for it, and that means we must work for it. As Pope Francis is rumored to have said, "First you pray for the hungry. Then you feed them. That's how prayer works."[1] First we pray for peace. Then we create peace. That's how prayer works. The psalmist closes with this final word to the House of the Divine: "I will seek your good." *Peace* is an active verb.

But creating peace is hard work, and I don't like it, because it's also dangerous. I'll freely admit that too often I and many other Christians expect Magic Jesus to fly in and fix everything, to "bring peace" as though peace is a Jell-O salad at a church basement potluck supper. Indeed, interpretations

---

[1] This is a common attribution, though I can find no source for the actual quotation among His Holiness's writings.

of today's reading from the Gospel of Matthew too often are influenced by Magic Jesus Theology, which is dangerous: Jesus is warning his followers, in disturbing and ominous language, that the "end of the age" is coming. Just before today's lesson, he explains that "many will fall away, and they will . . . hate one another. And many false prophets will arise and lead many astray [and] the love of many will grow cold." But after the terrifying signs and portents of The End, we read that, though heaven and earth may pass away, the words of the Divine will stand firm. This is supposed to make us feel better, by the way.

"But when, Jesus?" we ask. "*When* is this going to happen?" We are tired of war, Jesus. We queers, we black and brown folk, we abused women, we un- and underdocumented folk, we poor—we want to know when the swords that are still being used to kill us will be melted down to help make food for us instead? *When will there be peace in Jerusalem, Jesus?*

No answer. No one knows. Not even, apparently, Jesus himself.

And that's really uncomfortable, and if we pretend it's not, then we're really not doing justice to this passage in the Gospel. A big problem, though, is that in response to this discomfort too many Christians have decided that "belief" is enough, that they must simply wait, passively, for Magic Jesus to show up, like Superman, saving the day and making everything okay. And in the meantime, these Christians cling to their Bibles like swords, just in case they happen to run across a faggot who's trying to stay alive, threatening their precious belief.

In Paul's letter to the Christians in Rome, however, we are told in no uncertain terms that sitting around, and being alert (coffee anyone?), and "believing" isn't enough. Problematic as Paul's writings are for queer Christians (especially when interpreted from the context of a twenty-first-century understanding of gender and sexuality), he reminds us of something staggeringly important: We Jesus followers don't *bring* peace; we *make* it. How? Well, Paul tells us that we are to put on the "armor of light," and "live honorably as in the day."

This sounds lovely, doesn't it? Such a beautiful metaphor! But think again: Paul's comment is an outrageous and hilarious (and literally dangerous) joke: *Light is shitty armor*, and is incapable of stopping swords from running us through and killing us. "Light" did not keep the nails from ripping through Jesus's flesh in the crucifixion. "Light" did not save the victims of Nazi death camps. "Light" did not stop Dr. Martin Luther

King Jr. from being murdered by an assassin. "Light" did not protect all the beautiful queer lives who have died when people with access to deathsticks—guns—decided to walk into queer bars and start shooting. Armor of light? Ha!

Putting on the armor of light means that we are willing, metaphorically *and* literally, to beat our weapons into gardening implements, and start feeding others, even though those very others may still be clinging to their swords, ready to murder us. It means we must be willing to melt down guns and create art. Putting on the armor of light means that we are willing to stand in the face of danger, looking at it directly, and still create something beautiful in that very moment, whether it's dinner, a piece of art, or a relationship.

Advent is a daunting start to the church year, isn't it? It really has nothing to do with the festive trills of Mariah Carey only wanting me for Christmas, or the Grinch's heart growing three sizes. The calling of Advent is not a call to the malls, or to put up decorations, or even, more spiritually, to prepare for the fabulous and outlandish and insane story of the Incarnation of the Divine. No. The calling of Advent is to believe despite all the evidence to the contrary that plowshares are actually holier than swords, even if they cannot keep us from dying. The calling of Advent is a calling to live a life of peace—literally to *make* peace—that is so radical that even in the midst of righteous anger it refuses to engage in war and violence, it refuses to pick up weapons of earthly power. Advent is a call to live a life that is willing and learning, ultimately and often quite literally, to die to everything this world holds dear, including our own enfleshed bodies.

This, then, is how we prepare for the Advent of G-d. We don't wait for G-d to make peace. *We* make peace. We make it, every day, in our own actions, in our own lives.

This is how we do not lose our souls.

SECOND SUNDAY OF ADVENT

Dr. Peter Carlson

Isaiah 11:1–10
Psalm 72:1–7, 18–19
Romans 15:4–13
Matthew 3:1–12

At California Lutheran University, where I teach, we talk a *lot* about something that we call the "Culture of Nice." Let me be clear: Cal Lutheran isn't the only place where the Culture of Nice is endemic. You've all probably seen it at work: It's a culture in which being nice is given more authority and importance than being honest, and where, if you call out bad behavior and injustice, you're socially (or literally) demoted, considered to be Not Quite Our Type, Dear.

Don't get me wrong; I'm a big fan of courtesy, and of basic human decency (it's why, for instance, I let people tell me what their gender identity is rather than assuming I know it or have the right to tell them). But courtesy, fine a thing as it is, needs to take a back seat when fundamental human rights are at stake (I call this situation "injustice" or "oppression" in my lexicon). This is because courtesy's *only* job in an unjust system that is controlled by the oppressors is to perpetuate the systemic injustice. Let me explain further: Unjust systemic racism demands that black men turn themselves into ingratiating teddy bears so as not to appear threatening to white people who cross the street to avoid them anyway. Homophobia demands that I, for example, act the funny, campy queen so that I don't get labeled and shunned as a bitter angry faggot. Patriarchy insists that women who lead with high expectations and who expect the best from their team are, in fact, bitches. Cis-normativity insists on telling people what their pronouns and gender identities are. Ableism tells the disabled that complaining about lack of access is rude, when we can't even grudgingly adhere to the lowest expectations of the Americans with Disabilities Act.

So the Culture of Nice. Are you getting it? It's a problem.

In today's readings, the images of what the reign of G-d will look like that Isaiah, the psalmist, and Paul provide us are really Nice, aren't they? They're so, well, peacefulicious. So Lions-And-Lambs-Being-Nice-To-Each-Other. And that's lovely, it really is. Don't we all want that dream to come true? Don't we all want the vision of G-d's reign in Psalm 72, in which G-d rules the people righteously? Isn't it lovely that Paul reminds us of the fact that Christ has welcomed us?

Isn't that Nice?

But the thing is, it's not actually nice at all. These prophets who talked about G-d's justice were absolutely clear about what that justice will cost: It will cost us everything we have. And that's where truth-telling trumps niceness.

Proto-Isaiah, the first thirty-nine chapters of the book, is a book of poetic oracles, prophecies of judgement and, eventually, restoration. The prophet himself moans in the sixth chapter that he is "a man of unclean lips," who lives "among a people of unclean lips; yet my eyes have seen the Ruler, HaShem Almighty." You'd think that being chosen by G-d would be Nice. But Isaiah's very commissioning as a prophet, or messenger, for G-d is terrifying and includes, quite specifically, live coals burning his unclean lips off, as an act of purification. The passage we read today, from chapter 11, is probably familiar to many of us, because we hear it every year during Advent: "A shoot shall come out from the stump of Jesse; and a branch shall grow out of his roots. The spirit of HaShem shall rest upon him . . . His delight shall be in the fear of HaShem." The needy and the poor will be cared for, the wicked will be destroyed. Hunters will make peace with the hunted: wolves and lambs, leopards and goats, lions and calves, infants and cobras playing games together. "The earth will be filled with the knowledge of HaShem as the waters cover the sea."

It's so nice, isn't it? It's a beautiful, evocative dream, and we should, in fact, relish it. We are meant to do that.

But that should not stop us from taking a closer look, back at the beginning of the passage.

"Out of the stump of Jesse . . ." Not "from the tree of Jesse." This is a family tree that has been hacked to the ground and left for dead. Isaiah has been talking about the fate that Northern Israel suffered when it was destroyed by the Assyrian Empire, making it clear that it did not happen because G-d liked Assyria, but because G-d was punishing Northern Israel. Of course, the Judeans in the southern kingdom were fine with this. They escaped the wrath of Assyria, and assumed that their continued existence was due to (1) the fact that they were tight with G-d; and (2) that they had Jerusalem, and obviously G-d wouldn't swat G-d's own city, right?

Wrong, Isaiah is warning them. If you behave unjustly, then G-d's gonna whap you, too. G-d doesn't need Jerusalem to be G-d. You Judeans are treading on super-thin ice.

So, yes. There's this lovely passage in chapter 11, warming our hearts with a reign of justice and peace. But it's not "Nice." It's a small passage of hope couched in chapters of harsh truth-telling, which is, after all, what prophets are called to do. The hope is real. But so is the stump.

Psalm 72, too, is more than a bit deceptive. "Give the ruler your justice, O G-d, and your righteousness to the ruler's child. May they rule your people with righteousness and your poor with justice!"

Lovely. Like Isaiah, the psalm is describing an ideal realm—a kind of Utopia, which we should recall literally means "No Land." And in fact, it might seem that this land, this ruler, does not exist, considering the verb tense of the opening verse: "Give the ruler your justice, O G-d" (because the ruler apparently has not been given justice yet) that they "may judge your people with righteousness and your poor with justice." The entire psalm is written in future tense, articulating a dream that has not yet happened. In fact, in verse 17 (in the bits the lectionary skips over, which, as always, I encourage you to look up), we read that, *if* all these Nice things happen, "*Then* all nations will be blessed through the ruler, and they will call the ruler blessed" as the Book of Common Prayer reads, or, as the New Revised Standard Version would translate it, "May all nations be blessed in him; may they pronounce him happy." This is not something extant, but a bit of a pipe dream, hoping against hope for a happy ending to what is going on at the time.

Paul, in this passage from the book of Romans, provides us with more Nice, in this case the Niceties of Unity and Hope. This was probably something they needed to hear. Under the edict of Claudius in 49 CE, Jews (and presumably Jewish Christians) were expelled from Rome, though after his death in 54, they were permitted to return.[1] The bulk of Romans seems to be responding to the basic question that divided Jewish and Gentile Jesus followers: Do you have to be Jewish, and adhere to Torah, Jewish Law, to be Christian? Paul's answer, of course, is a resounding "no," and he spends the bulk of the book developing his doctrine of justification with G-d by faith, rather than works articulated in Torah.

Many early versions of Romans were only fourteen chapters long, suggesting that the bits we're hearing today were added at a later date. Whether original to the letter or not, Paul does indeed change focus here from a theology of justification to a request that all the Christians, whether Jewish or Gentile, get along. So as not to appear to dis the Hebrew scriptures by downplaying the Law too much, he reminds them that "whatever was written in former days was written for our instruction." It's not that Torah is *bad*, he's saying. In fact, it's basically there to teach us endurance, which we're going to need. "Welcome one another," he implores, because "Christ has become a servant of the circumcised . . . in order that he might confirm the promises given to the forebears, and in order that non-Jews might glorify G-d for G-d's mercy." Christ, Paul is reminding the people, was there for all of us, including Gentiles. To prove his point, Paul then cites several Hebrew Bible passages that talk about G-d caring for the aliens—an arguably more accurate translation of the Hebrew than "Gentiles."

But Paul concludes this passage, before changing the subject, by quoting the verse from the end of today's reading from Isaiah, asking that the "G-d of hope fill you with all joy and peace in believing, so that you may abound in hope by the power of the Holy Spirit." The reality is that as Nice as this is, the Roman Christians likely needed all the hope they could get. It's been a generation, after all, since Jesus died, resurrected, and ascended, and he still hasn't come back. In the meantime, we've got some Imperial powers that seem utterly unimpressed by our religion (indeed, in the mid-50s, Nero would start going seriously batshit crazy and start treating

---

[1] Jerry L. Sumney, "Reading the Letter to the Romans" in *Reading Paul's Letter to the Romans*, edited by Jerry L. Sumney (Atlanta: Society of Biblical Literature, 2012), 2.

Jerry L. Sumney notes that this may be oversimplified. He writes, "There is significant disagreement among scholars about the ethnic composition of the church in Rome and about its relationship to the Jewish community there." This does not negate the fact that Paul is, in this book, deeply concerned about the relationship between Jewish and Gentile Christians.

monotheists, Jews and Christians alike, really horrifically). Love you, Paul, but this Nice Hope is beginning to wear a little thin, if we're honest.

What intrigues me in these Nice Lessons is the final reading, from the Gospel of Matthew. Most of us have heard of John the Baptist, I'm sure. But John the Baptist makes a really refreshing change to the Culture of Nice that we've been gagging on. "You fucking brood of snakes!"

Whoa. Not exactly the way to win friends and influence people, John. Couldn't you be a little nicer?

No. John's message is clear: "Repent, for the reign of heaven is near." The reign of heaven is not, then, some cozy gathering, in which we all share afternoon tea and crumpets, whilst dressed attractively but comfortably, and share amusing stories. The reign of heaven is something for which, before it arrives, we'd damned well better repent of our injustices, lest we be, well, *damned*. And it's not only the message. John himself is a corker, too, isn't he? His coat of camel's hair, eating locusts and wild honey—I have an image of him shoving his fist into a beehive, oblivious to the stings of the furious insects. And screaming, always screaming: "Who warned you to flee from the wrath to come?" Wait. The reign of heaven is *wrath*? Jeepers . . . "Do not presume to say to yourselves, 'We have Abraham as our ancestor.'" G-d doesn't care about your ancestry! Remember that stump of Jesse you wanted to think was Nice? "Even now the ax is lying at the root of the trees!"

This is *not* a sky-blue-pink baby Jesus imagery that we're being offered in Advent. This is a world-upside-down-turning apocalypse, in which salvation will only be achieved by ripping up the whole shebang, by hacking down the trees of the current unjust systems, by burning chaff in unquenchable fire.

This Advent, this Coming of Something New, is not particularly Nice.

THIRD SUNDAY OF ADVENT

The Rev. Jeremy Whitner, MDiv

Isaiah 35:1–10
Psalm 146:4–9
James 5:7–10
Matthew 11:2–11

Queer Joy of Fulfillment

In our scripture readings today, we have four passages that speak to the image of prophetic queer joy and hope in a desolate land. The readings are telling us to have faith and maintain hope. We have a lot of waiting and suddenly things happen that point to a coming salvation. We have "joy fulfilled," as some would say. This is Joy Sunday after all. It is our moment in Advent to light the pink candle and momentarily celebrate the joy that comes from the presence of Christ. The trees are starting to be decorated if they aren't already. We start to feel the joy of Christmas. We suddenly lose the feeling that we are Scrooge and become Bob Cratchit. We start to experience joy beyond hope.

In some cases, it gives way to Queer Joy. Queer Joy is what we do as an LGBTQ community when we are happy despite circumstances. We celebrate living our lives to the fullest—even when there are difficulties that present themselves. We have that present under the tree for which we have been waiting. We have joy in the birth of something new. Even in the dryness and barrenness of these situations, we still find the joy that comes in fulfillment.

In our Hebrew scripture, we hear the words from the prophet of "second Isaiah." They speak to the possibility of beauty bursting out of the seams. The people of Judah have been taken to Babylon. In the chaos that is afflicting the people of Israel, the temple has been destroyed. The priests have been carried away to Babylon (picture Daniel and the fiery furnace). The sap is completely gone from the branches. The roots have dried up. Amid all that tragedy and sorrow, God says, "I will bring hope into this situation."

It isn't happening yet, but it will occur. God is going to create beauty and spontaneity in this desert. The Almighty will unlock this land's hidden potential. It's an oasis in the middle of a desert. In Hebrew the word for wilderness or desert is *midbar* (הַבְדְּמ־). In the mind of the Hebrew person, this word was the forty years of wandering of Israel's people, this was the desert before they entered the Promised Land. The wandering of the exile was an echo of that in the people's minds. A second important Hebrew word in this passage is *tiprah* (תָרְפִּת) or blossoming. In the Hebrew scriptures, it speaks to when something breaks forth. It is the verb, not the noun, so it is the action of the blossoming. It creates an image of that proverbial paradise breaking forth in a desolate landscape. It's Palm Springs in the middle of the Mojave Desert. In a way, it is a very sexual image of the fulfillment that is occurring. It suggests the romantic feelings that arise from the pure joy of happiness. When you have been going through a really dry spell romantically, and you see the perfect person from across the room. The sap starts to rise and other things start to rise as well. This passage from Isaiah is about having faith and maintaining hope. The Queer Joy says yes, despite all the bad activities of some in our society, the joy will come, and we will live our lives.

The psalm focuses on the happiness of liberation in a moment by people working to improve the situation of the oppressed. God's main concern is the justice and liberation of the oppressed. God is not a detached being sitting on a lofty cloud unconcerned with the plight of the poor. Just the opposite. Their main concern is the poor. This psalm tells us that liberation and justice truly come from God, and we are to work for it. We praise God even when the answer isn't in front of us. Even in dry periods of injustice, God is still there. God works for the good of the people. In verse 8, the word translated as "righteous" in the NRSV in Hebrew is the term *ṣad·dî·qim* (םקֶידַצ). The word for justice is *tzedek* (קֶדֶצ). When you make the word *justice* plural, you have the word *saddiqim*. The people who do justice are the righteous in the minds of the Hebrew people. Caring for the poor and practicing hospitality was paramount. There was no greater command. This was not for only Judaism, it was a cultural norm for the entire Middle Eastern culture at this time. It still is, as a matter of fact. This moment and reasoning resonates very much with the early queer movement for me. Marsha Hudson was out in the middle of the Gay Liberation parade speaking to help the trans youth who were on the streets at the time. The entire queer movement was a movement to help the wholeness of everyone and all of us. We could help fix everything else. People who do justice and righteousness are hope and salt for the earth. They shatter the darkness with light. Again, you see a consistent theme in today's readings: having faith and maintaining hope.

In our Gospel reading today, we have the people who followed and were baptized by John the Baptist asking Jesus if he is the savior they have been looking for. John the Baptist was the forerunner of Jesus. He spent his life preparing the way for the Messiah. They are looking for the next thing and wondering if Jesus is truly the Messiah. Jesus tells them that yes, he is. Look at the evidence, all the miracles that Jesus has done in a short time already. All the miracles and signs of life occur when the hope of God surrounds a situation. In verse 5 Jesus says, "Go and tell John what you hear and see: the blind receive their sight, the lame walk, the lepers are cleansed, the deaf hear, the dead are raised, and the poor have good news brought to them. And blessed is anyone who takes no offense at me." Jesus then praises the work of John the Baptist by saying in verse 11, "Truly I tell you, among those born of women no one has arisen greater than John the Baptist; yet the least in the kingdom of heaven is greater than he." Their belief has prepared the way for Jesus. These followers have kept the faith, and their hope is being rewarded. Imagine the impact this would have had on John's followers!

The true message we need to hear on this third Sunday of Advent is the message heard from James on this Sunday. This is one of the letters of the early church. In our passage today we have the statement to be patient in the waiting for the arrival of our God. We know Jesus comes. The author of James says (going one verse beyond our reading today):

> Be patient, therefore, beloved, until the coming of the Lord. The farmer waits for the precious crop from the earth, being patient

> with it until it receives the early and the late rains. You also must be patient. Strengthen your hearts, for the coming of the Lord is near. Beloved, do not grumble against one another, so that you may not be judged. See, the Judge is standing at the doors! As an example of suffering and patience, beloved, take the prophets who spoke in the name of the Lord. Indeed we call blessed those who showed endurance. You have heard of the endurance of Job, and you have seen the purpose of the Lord, how the Lord is compassionate and merciful

For the author of James, the early church is grumbling and complaining because the Apostles and first generations of the church are dying off. They are becoming disenchanted. They are wondering whether Jesus is coming back. They are wondering if the Gospels have a point if they can't see the kingdom around them. They are wondering if there is no hope, that there is just death. The author of James extols them to embrace hope when there is only desolation. Live into the vitality of life, the chance of newness. Again, our theme today: Have faith and maintain hope. It can be difficult, but that hope will be rewarded.

Our struggle in today's world is that we don't always see the fact that Jesus is already here. We argue over what Christ's coming back looks like and what that means for us today. Together, these passages point us to living and enjoying that space despite what the world says. We don't see the kingdom of God here before us. We have a hard time embracing the Queer Joy of the situation. Many days we feel like we are more frequently in the desert than the oasis. The dry spots are long and repeated in a world where greed and corruption seem to win more often than not. We have to remember, though, that Jesus has come. Jesus comes to us every day in moments we may least expect. Christ comes like blossoms in springtime, and the flirting on the dance floor beneath the thump thump of the dance beat. It is when we see the hope in situations where we haven't previously seen hope. It is when the sap starts to rise, and the spirits start to rise, and we feel more human in a world where they want us to be locked in busyness and strife. It is when we hope and live—despite fear. When we fully live our lives despite the people who want us to shine less; when we put on our gayest ensemble or whatever attire that makes us truly feel the most human and most fulfilled and walk confidently into the world—that is what our scriptures are telling us to do this weekend. Put on our best cha-cha heels and walk in every parade! Follow the example of all the queer ancestors who walked before us. Follow those who lived their queer joy!

Queer joy is created when we fulfill the kingdom here on Earth. Queer joy happens when we are not only aware of the paradise in front of us, but we create beautiful shiny things, in the blossoming. The struggle is that it is oftentimes hard to embrace hope when we are in the middle of the desert, so strive to embrace life and nurture hope. The vitality of life can cause the seeds we planted in the middle of cold winter to grow into new life with the coming of spring. We have to water them with our very nature. That is the call of both the psalm and our letter from James. When we don't see hope, we trust in God and work with God in all we do. We embrace the justice and love of God in all we do. May it be so!

FOURTH SUNDAY OF ADVENT

Dr. Peter Carlson

Isaiah 7:10–16
Psalm 80:1–7, 16–18
Romans 1:1–7
Matthew 1:18–25

O! Look! A virgin will give birth!

Okay, actually the Hebrew, *almah*, does not reference virginity at all, and it's the later Greeks (see Dennis MacDonald regarding the Homeric influence on the Gospels[1]) who bring Mary's sexual activity (or lack thereof) into the picture, with their longstanding mythological emphasis on virgin births and miraculous infancy narratives.

Reset:

O! Look! A young woman past puberty will give birth!

I know. It doesn't sound nearly as dramatic, or Christmassy, or even prophetic, does it? But seriously, folks—the emphasis on Mary's virginity, whether temporary or perpetual, is just one more example of how our society has constructed a "proper" femininity, isn't it, and how it controls women's bodies? Women past puberty giving birth is just ordinary, and not necessarily very submissive—they don't particularly demonstrate delicate female passivity in the face of an overpowering divinity of manfulness.

And now I'm going to let you in on really big a secret: Isaiah wasn't actually talking about Mary. Shocker!

---

[1] Dennis MacDonald, *The Homeric Epics and the Gospel of Mark* (Yale University Press, 2000).

I know, I know. I'm bucking, literally, centuries of interpretation here. But here's the important thing: It doesn't really matter. We humans are adept at meaning-making, at finding meaning in things that may in fact be rather arbitrary. And that's a good thing. It is important for Christians to be able to look back and read into the past the same yearning and longing and crying out that the Judeans were experiencing in the eighth century BCE. Whether Isaiah was thinking about Jesus, or just thinking a (relatively) few years into the future to the collapse of the northern kingdom of Israel under the onslaught of the Assyrian Empire? That detail is ultimately irrelevant. Look: Prophecy doesn't have to be about me, specifically, in order for the prophecy to be fulfilled in my life. Perhaps this is the single biggest lesson we can remember about the prophets: Their messages from God still apply, because our world still needs the prophetic. There is still injustice. Empires are still fucking us over. We will still stand the risk of getting killed if we dare to stand up for justice for the weak and the oppressed.

And the fact that we will still likely get killed? It still doesn't matter.

So, a young woman past puberty will give birth. Perhaps she is married; perhaps not. Perhaps we shouldn't be judging her either way. Perhaps men should stop policing women and allow them some bodily autonomy. But, and this matters, before that new child that the married or unmarried woman births knows right from wrong, imperial forces will be at work, destroying lives. It was true in Isaiah's time. It was true in the first century CE when Mary gave birth. It is true today.

The Psalms break our hearts, don't they, because they cry out at those imperial powers, those thrones, dominations. "O, HaShem, G-d of Hosts, how long will you be angry with your people's prayers? You have fed them with the bread of tears, and given them tears to drink in full measure."

And here's the kicker: "You make us the scorn of our neighbors; our enemies laugh among themselves." That's all kinds of appropriate as this nation has been all too willing to fall under the spell of demagogic blowhole asshats posing as politicians. The world is looking on, in hysterics, as they watch the collapse of this thing called democracy, that religion of which the United States has been the most aggressive and violent evangelistic force, going so far as to pretend that democracy was the reason we waged war in Iraq and Afghanistan. (Whether we approved of democracy in Central America, when they democratically elected Marxist presidents, is another matter of course.)

So. We are the laughingstock of the world, in no small part because we have spent so many years pretending to be the world's protectors, only to have the world discover that we are as, if not more, racist, bigoted, xenophobic, and utterly self-obsessed as any person or country we've dared to criticize across the decades. We *are* the derision of our neighbors around the world, Oh G-d—and what is worse is that our fellow countryfolk seem to be fine with that! How do we deal, Oh G-d?

We Christians have a shedload of work to do, but the problem is (if I can judge from my own experience) that we're cowards. Like Ahaz prompted by Isaiah, we refuse to put G-d to the test, even after G-d said, "C'mon. Test me." Trust me: Ahaz wasn't avoiding asking for the test out of reverence for G-d; he was refusing to put G-d to the test, because he was afraid of what G-d's answer would be. Probably we should all be afraid of G-d's answer.

Because what an answer! G-d does not say, "I will raise up Judah as a mighty nation, and they'll bomb the living shit out of (As)Syria." G-d does not say, "I will have you sell arms illegally across international borders so that humans can murder each other more effectively." G-d does not even say, "I will raise up a powerful organization called the United Nations, which will 'tsk, tsk' in the name of democracy when nations slaughter each other."

No. Here is G-d's response: "A woman will bear a child . . ."

Hope is found in the most unexpected and unreasonable and unruly places. It does not sit in the halls of thrones, dominations, powers, and principalities; it murmurs in the people. The ordinary people such as you and I. The ordinary people who are different, who are not good enough, who are not American enough, who are not Christian enough, who are not rich enough, who are not educated enough, who are not white enough, who are not male enough, who are not able-bodied enough, who are not straight enough, who are not cis enough, who are not US enough.

Even Paul (dear, misogynous Paul) is on the defensive at the beginning of his letter to the Roman Christians, because he's being accused of hanging around too much with *those* people, with those other weirdos who are Not Really Our Kind, Dear. "I really *am* an apostle!" Paul screams. "And I know this goes against everything the Jesus followers are saying back in Jerusalem, but I *know* Jesus loved Gentiles too!" It's not, Paul reminds the Romans, about observing obsessively the details of kashrut, or about literal circumcision, or about accidentally touching the scrolls of the Law with your hands. No, it's about eating to G-d's glory; it's about carving a sign of covenant on your heart; it's about dancing a tango with the Torah. And—and this is the kicker—outsiders can do that too! The Holy Spirit is messing everything up. *AGAIN.*

Just when you thought you knew how G-d operates, just when you think you're finally in the Inner Circle, the Outsiders become the focus.

And speaking of Outsiders, how about that Joseph? Today's account is from Matthew, where Joseph is about to "put Mary away" because he is a "righteous man" (does this strike anyone else as a completely horrific image of righteousness, or is that just me fretting over the warped masculinity of rape culture?), but then he is visited by an angel who tells him it's cool. What we see in this story is another overturning: an overturning of social constructions of masculinity and male power. I've always felt sort of bad for Joseph: He's pretty much the ultimate cuckold, who has absolutely no recourse, because his wife has been made pregnant by the *pneuma*, the Spirit of G-d, and really, can you ever get even with G-d?

But what's amazing about this story is that Joseph actually *isn't* cuckolded; he responds with extraordinary grace and refuses to cling to his manhood (as it were), as society has constructed it for him. He is willing (indeed, he is "man enough," if you will) to rethink what it means to be a man, to let go of the cultural norm that his wife was his property, existing to serve him, or to service him. Joseph redefines manhood and masculinity, letting go of his legal and sexual control, and realizing that, quite frankly, the last thing Mary needs is his manly, muscley protection. (Remember that Nasty Woman's Magnificat? That's not some helpless she-child, who needs a strutting cock to protect her, is it?) Rather, Joseph seems to recognize that what they might both need is companionship on what will undoubtedly prove to be a harrowing journey indeed.

So just as Mary gave us a new definition of what it means to be a woman, Joseph this week shows us a reconstruction of masculinity that is not bound up by fragile authority and domination, paranoid lest anyone find out that he has tiny hands, or a tiny . . . ego.

Once again, the prophets overturn all our expectations. Every bloody time we think we've got a handle on how the Divine works, Divine trips us up and shatters all our prized assumptions like so much inherited family crystal that we value more than the food that we serve in it. Through the prophets, Miz Holy Spirit Thang is fucking with us, folks, and we'd better learn to play that game, because that's how She operates. She will *always* surprise us and give us hope, if we look to something other than the world's values to find it.

THE INCARNATION OF G-D

NATIVITY OF OUR LORD

Dr. Pace Warfield

Isaiah 9:2–7
Psalm 96
Titus 2:11–14
Luke 2:1–14, (15–20)

Merry Christmas, and let's make the yuletide gay!

It's Christmas Eve, but I want to start this sermon with a story that doesn't take place on or around Christmas. Instead, I want to focus on the gay nature of the yuletide and talk about my first time going to a gay bar. I graduated high school in 2004, attending school in the suburbs of the Washington, DC, and Baltimore region. The queer movement was a much talked about object of conversation in church, culture, and political arenas, with headlines about the martyrdom of Matthew Shepard only six years previously, the *Lawrence v. Texas* Supreme Court decision that legalized queer sex throughout the country happening only one year before, and yet we were still two years before Lance Bass's infamous "I'm Gay" reveal in *People* magazine and another eleven years before the Supreme Court would rule in favor of same-sex marriages in 2015. Living in the 'burbs, I did not have much interaction with actual queer people. I knew I was queer, had known that about myself since I was in middle school and looking back could see signs from as long as I remember, but I was not out to my family and only out to a few friends. I felt that going to college would be my chance to finally be out, free from my parents and family, who at the time I thought would not accept me. Little did I know that a small

Lutheran liberal arts college in rural western Pennsylvania would not be the bastion of queer freedom I imagined it might be.

Even so, I started to find other friends and fall in with queer community. It was not until my sophomore year that our queer friend group truly solidified, and we started working on making a Gay-Straight Alliance while hanging, having fun, and learning in community who we were. And part of that learning experience, of course, involved trekking two hours south to Pittsburgh where, for all but a few of us, we would attend our first gay bar. It was early autumn, and I remember donning my gay apparel, then squeezing myself into my friend's sedan and traveling over the river and through the woods to Pegasus, at that point on the corner of Liberty Avenue and Strawberry Way, one of the most well-known gay bars in Pittsburgh. The bar at that point had been around for just under twenty-five years, had seen the rise of HIV/AIDS, and been home to performances by everyone from Divine to Kathleen Turner.

I am not sure what I expected. The bar was on the basement level of an older stone exterior city building. It was dim, darkly lit, but had enough strobing and flashing lights to see large groups of people dancing, talking, gathered at the bar. Some were sharing moments of physical intimacy, like making out in the corner, holding one another, even simple, small acts like holding hands. I saw gay and lesbian couples, bi couples, people of ambiguous gender, trans people, drag queens, and drag kings. The booming music flooded my senses.

I cannot quite put into words how that first time felt. There was a surreal disconnect with temporality; that is to say, I felt disconnected from the time and place of the present. Instead, I was transported to some queer space of in-between, where everything seemed to simultaneously go slower and faster than I expected. All of this was brought on by the sensation of being in a space made *for* me for once. There is a lot to say about how gay bars do not welcome all and especially how many cater toward white, cis, gay men with little space for trans, fat, disabled queers, and people of color. And yet, there was still something intangibly magical about finding myself surrounded by other queer folk. It came with a sense of safety, of awe, and the ability to relax into my own body in a way that is so hard to do in spaces dominated by cis straight people. It is an experience that so many white, cis, straight, and able-bodied people take for granted: the experience of being in a place made *for* you, where you can be safe and at home in your own body.

It may seem strange for me to begin my Christmas Eve sermon by talking about my first time going to a gay bar. But there is something going on in the Gospel passage for today that bears much in common with the feelings I shared about that experience.

The story we hear is likely a familiar one, one that we've heard year after year. The Gospel writer tells us that Mary and Joseph, who were engaged, had to journey from their hometown of Nazareth to the small town of Bethlehem, Joseph's family's ancestral home, for a census, about a seventy mile journey. Mary is pregnant, and we know from the first chapter of the Gospel that the pregnancy is a miraculous one; she is pregnant through the power of the Holy Spirit with the Messiah, the one that many see foretold in the prophecy of Isaiah we also heard today about the child born for us, the Prince of Peace, who will bring about justice for all people.

There is no room in the family house, so Mary and Joseph are left to sleep in the portion of the home reserved for animals. Typically, this would be the first floor of a family dwelling, while the second floor was meant for the household members and guests to sleep. And while there, sleeping among the donkeys and maybe even horses, sheep, and cattle, Mary gave birth to this child. She wrapped him tightly in a blanket to keep him warm and laid him in the cattle trough, the manger, for him to rest.

This story is already fascinating enough. A Prince of Peace, the child of God, the one foretold in ancient prophecies, the author of creation in human form, born in a small town to a laboring family, put in a cattle trough for his first night? And yet, the story gets even stranger, or queerer, to me.

The Gospel writer takes us to a new scene on the outskirts of town. There are shepherds who live in the fields with their sheep. While shepherds were an important part of the agrarian economies of ancient Judea, they were still considered outsiders to the hustle and bustle of city and town life. They would sleep out in fields with the herds to help ward off predators and prevent poaching of their animals. Sheep were very important in Judea, with their meat, milk, fat, wool, and skins all essential to food, clothes making, and other cultural and ritualistic purposes. Despite this central role in Judean culture, shepherds were outcasts. They were frequently seen as dirty and homeless. They lived off simple meals and sometimes lived nomadic lives, helping their herds of sheep travel great distances for food, water, shearing, and other needs.[1]

In the Gospel of Matthew's version of this story, a group of Magi figure out the auspicious birth of the Messiah through astrology and what follows is an account of political intrigue and betrayal involving the puppet ruler of Judea, Herod, plotting with the Magi. In Mark and John, we are introduced to Jesus through John the Baptist, a prophet who drew large crowds as he preached repentance and baptism.

But in Luke's version of events, Jesus isn't proclaimed first through a great prophet or the source of political scheming among kings and Magi. Instead, an angel appears to a group of shepherds, outcasts, on the outskirts of town among their sheep. You may have seen the "biblically accurate angel" memes across social media, these strange, mystical beings made of way too many eyes and wings. Luke's text doesn't specify what the angel looked like, but it is no wonder that the angel's first words to the shepherds are "Do not be afraid." This is followed by an announcement, "See—I am bringing you good news of great joy for all the people: *to you* is born this day in the city of David a Savior, who is the Messiah, The Lord" (Luke 2:10b–11, emphasis mine).

As if that is not strange enough, suddenly an entire host of angels, a host being a military term to mean a large army, appear in the sky singing glory to God and peace to humankind. After the angels fade away, the shepherds decide to leave their sheep behind in the fields and visit the child, which they find exactly as the angel had told them. They tell Mary and Joseph about the angels and about how the angels promised that this child is the Messiah. They then return to the fields, praising God and sharing with any they encountered what they had seen and witnessed. In the silence that followed, Mary treasured all she heard and pondered it in her heart.

It truly is an amazing story. But preparing for this sermon, what stood out to me the most is the angel's message to the shepherds: "to *you* is born this day." To you. This message is not directed at the Magi or King Herod as in the Gospel of Matthew. It's not directed to the Prophet John the Baptist. It's not directed to the priests and other religious authorities of the temple. The angel's message is directed to the shepherds, the

---

[1] Paul J. Achtemeier, ed., *The HarperCollins Bible Dictionary*, rev. ed. (HarperOne, 1996), 1012–13.

outcast, those living on the margins of Judean society. They receive the good news first, but not just good news that a messiah is born that will save the world, but that the Messiah is born *for* them, in particular. To you is born this child. The message is personalized and promised for the last, the least, the lonely, the outcast. For people for whom society is not designed, that is to whom the angels address their message and promise the Messiah child is born.

I have gone to a gay bar once on Christmas Eve, though. One of my partners at the time was a church musician, so he had Christmas Eve services to attend. This was one of the very few times in my life I did not have a job in a church, so I decided to take advantage of this and go with my dear friend to Annie's in Washington, DC, which I guess, to be fair, is not just a gay bar but a gay bar and steakhouse. The bar was much quieter on Christmas—this was in the 2020s and the world was different. Many queer people did have families and homes they could return to for the holidays. The bar was quieter than a typical night, but there were still plenty of people there. I noticed right away an older man, presumably gay, seated by himself at the bar examining the well-known David Willcocks organ scores to Christmas music while nursing a Budweiser. My friend and I imagined that he was a church organist at one of the many large churches in walking distance, coming for a quick drink before that evening's services. There were a group of drag queens hanging out by the end of the bar, some dressed in Christmas-themed outfits, one wearing a green velvet dress with glass ornaments affixed to it to appear like a Christmas tree.

I cannot help but think how similar this Christmas Eve gay bar experience was to that first Christmas. A mismatched group of people that don't quite fit in with the standards and expectations of cisheteronormative society, not to mention the church, gathered together for community. A group of people, people like me, sharing a dance, a laugh, or a drink.

How rare is it for something to be made for us, to be shared to us? How affirming is it when my differences and disabilities are not just acknowledged but welcomed and accommodated? So, just like that first Christmas two thousand years ago, in a gay bar one Christmas Eve, I finally understood the power of that promise. For you, for *us*, something new is happening. For us, in this time and place, we are known, seen, and loved by a God who is bringing about salvation for us and who is promising to live among us. That is truly a queer thing.

FIRST SUNDAY AFTER CHRISTMAS

Dr. Peter Carlson

Isaiah 61:10–62:3
Psalm 147 or 147:13–21
Galatians 3:23–25; 4:4–7
John 1:1–18

If there is anything that is abundantly clear to me throughout the entire season of the Incarnation, it is that spirituality is inextricably linked to physicality, even in the spectacularly spiritual-ooh-ooh Gospel of John. The collect of the day reminds us of the outrageous and even slightly creepy idea that words can take on flesh. It's perilously easy to forget that *incarnation* literally means "enfleshment." Incarnation. Carne. Flesh. Chili con carne. Chili with flesh. Carnal. Fleshy. In-fleshiness. So, really, when we look at this whole season, what we ought to see is not so much the romanticized Jan Gossaert oil painting *The Adoration of the Kings*, lush and gorgeous as that might be, but a flesh-and-blood baby, perhaps still coated in blood and vernix caseosa, fully in-bodied. The Incarnation is, in fact, nothing less than Divine Carnal Desire. Carnality and fleshiness—ideas that, ironically, Christians have for two thousand years been *terrified* of coping with in any kind of honest and practical way, are in fact the very goal of the Divine, and are the absolute, fleshy, *core* of our creed.

The *Logos* became flesh. What a bloody concept.

The Gospel of John, so very mystical, seems often to me to be written entirely as a grand spiritual metaphor: In the beginning, we read (in what is obviously an intentional reference to Genesis 1) was a *logos*—an idea, or word. And the *Logos*/Idea/Word was with G-d, and the *Logos*/Idea/Word was G-d (although the Greek could technically be translated "was a G-d," which is disconcertingly intriguing, isn't it?). The awkward and ironic thing is that words are the way we create and communicate meaning, and at the same time are imprecise symbols that elude strict meaning. Words, however clear they may seem to us, are ultimately themselves metaphors—signs that point to something else, with our recognition that the sign is absolutely not the same as the thing it signifies. So in the beginning, the Christian scriptures seem to be claiming, what existed was metaphor and imprecise meaning. And that metaphor and imprecision was G-d.

This is not, perhaps, very satisfactory—especially for a Myers-Briggs type J like me, who finds solace in labeling everything and knowing that those labeled things have a very particular place in my cupboards, or in my knowledge-bank. But John just dances on with the metaphor, paying no attention to my desire for taxonomic clarity. *Light,* John says. *The logos/idea/word is like light.*

More metaphor. Not that that's bad. Light helps us see—for those of us who are sighted, of course—and it becomes a marvelous (literally something to marvel at) metaphor for understanding and for spiritual sight, Spirit-sight, in-sight. But it's still metaphor. Words are *not* light, though they might function metaphorically as light. And even when we get to an actual human being in the story—John the Evangelizer, the Baptizer—we still see only a human who is testifying to something nonhuman, a metaphorical light, a "true" light that enlightens everyone. Indeed, it would appear that the Gospeler is not just being metaphorical, but consciously and intentionally rejecting literalness and physicality, snubbing "the will of the flesh" in favor of the will of G-d.

But—and talk about a flip-flop!—the very next verse follows all this metaphor, crying out those words that are so familiar to so many of us: "The Word became flesh and lived among us"! Indeed, we discover that it is that very fleshiness that has revealed the glory of the Divine, "full of grace and truth." Read this carefully, folks: In this shift from spirituality and metaphor to fleshiness, as it were, we really ought to sing a Gloria! about the fact that the Gospeler has described Fleshy Jesus as, quite literally, graceful. That is gorgeous. That is what the Gospel says.

I admit that I am fascinated that this enfleshment is contrasted to the Law by John in this passage. The Law, this writer is telling us, was a way of following G-d, of staying in relationship with G-d, and that is important;

the fleshfulicious Jesus, on the other hand, is light, and is consequently how we *see* G-d. You can know all the rules, John seems to be saying, but a relationship isn't just about obeying rules. It would seem, according to John, that G-d finally figured out that you can't be in relationship with an absent parent. And so G-d determines to make *Logos* fleshy, and visible.

We see this fleshiness even in Paul's letter to the churches in Galatia—a letter in which Paul is making the argument (either just before or just after the Jerusalem Council? whichever) that conversion of non-Jews to Christianity need not demand that Gentiles follow the legal code of Judaism (my own guess completely unsubstantiated by anything except Freudian penile anxiety is that it was less about the drama of giving up bacon as the fear of men, particularly, wondering if they had to have their bits snipped by a mohel in order to follow Jesus). The fact that Paul places such an emphasis on the fact that Jesus was G-d's child, "born of a woman"—on the fleshy, lived experience of Jesus—is remarkable and almost conflicted in a letter that is arguing against the fleshly requirements of Judaic law. It becomes clear to me that, for all that Paul is engaged in trying to make a bizarre Jewish sect comprehensible to cultures steeped in Greek dualism, in which Spirit = Good and the Material World = Evil, even Paul can't completely let go of the central fact of his religious belief that embodiment matters—that we have bodies, that the fact that we are made of matter, matters. That we (are) matter.

I can't really be surprised. After all, we can legitimately ask, if Paul hadn't been physically struck blind and physically cured, would he have converted? Paul may spend a lot of time in his Hellenistic thinking putting down material, legal things, but ultimately even he has to admit that Jesus was flesh, and peed and pooped, and probably even sprang an erection at times. And, therefore, that human flesh is something that mattered, because it *was* matter, even as it was divine.

Here, then, is the central, essential belief of Christian faith, without which one is not, in fact, a Christian: The Divine encountered us *in a body*. And in a parallel statement of belief, it is essential to remember that we encounter the Divine in our bodies. It really is that basic. So, if there is anything that this season of the church year seems to be teaching us, it's to stop being afraid of our bodies. It is, in fact, to recognize that *because* we encounter the Divine from within our bodies, our bodies can be read as holy texts. The Word, in our flesh.

O, Peter, you say. I have been raised in a culture that says bodies are vulgar, and sex is naughty, and we don't talk about poopoo peepee.

I get it. This is a tall order. We have centuries of fear built into our theology. St. Augustine of Hippo himself postulated (in a truly sinister way, let's be honest) that Adam and Eve were, in effect, genetically changed in the Fall, and that in this postlapsarian world, semen is the actual conduit for original sin. Men inject sin into women, who get pregnant with babies, and babies are therefore born prestained by sin. Sin, Augie argued, is an STI. He postulated that we're sinful, quite literally, because our parents banged.

But bodies aren't just sex scary; they're also scary because they're the source of so much angst, generally, for us: Our bodies get sick; our bodies age; the bones in our bodies break; sometimes the bones of our bodies are broken for us. Bodies—as Fleshy Embodied Jesus discovered—can be crucified.

It is an ongoing struggle for me to work at loving my embodiment, even if my body at any given moment is not behaving lovably. Diabetes, for instance, is a really sucky embodiment. And, quite frankly, I wish G-d had consulted me before designing knees. I could have pointed out some bugs that might have been eliminated had the Creator done a reworking following the test of the beta version. But this old, diabetic, achy body is the embodiment that I have; just as Jesus's body was the embodiment he had. That body: a Middle Eastern Jew born in Palestine, under an oppressive Imperial government that cared for nothing and no one except those in the top echelons of power; born while his parents were trying to get their legal documentation sorted out in a town away from their home; hunted down by the local Imperial regent, because some insane astrologers from the East were stupid enough to ask a sitting king where the new king was; growing up to learn carpentry . . .

I wonder if Jesus enjoyed his body? If he relished running through the streets with friends as a kid? What his favorite foods were, that maybe reminded him of home? If maybe he felt gawky and ungainly and confused when he went through puberty? Did his voice squeak as he read Torah? Did he get any awkward sexual urges? Maybe when he was changing the water into wine, he just wanted a glass of water. We know he occasionally was so tired he could sleep through a storm at sea. Surely when the woman who had been bleeding for twelve years, who obviously had body stressors of her own, touched his hem, Jesus physically felt the power leaving him. And certainly his body screamed in pain when he was whipped, beaten, and murdered by the Roman state.

I have to believe that Jesus's fully human incarnation, his enfleshment, was as real, as joyful, as painful, as physical, as mine. Not because mine is particularly special, but because mine, too, is fully human. So when I struggle with my flesh, with a body that simply isn't doing what the twenty-five-year-old version of it did, I try to remember that Jesus struggled with his flesh. Not in a "flesh is icky" way, but in a rather ordinarily embodied way. And when I am able to rejoice in my flesh, when my body feels the caress of my spouse's hand on the back of my neck, or relishes the strawberries that came from the farm that day, I remember that Jesus rejoiced in his flesh too.

Because if it's not matter, then it doesn't matter. If it's not flesh, then it's not Emmanuel, G-d with us. If G-d isn't literally flesh, with us, then we have no way to see the metaphorical Light.

FEAST OF THE CIRCUMCISION OF OUR LORD / THE HOLY NAME

Dr. Peter Carlson

Trigger Warning: offensive gendered, sexual, and racial terms
Numbers 6:22–27
Psalm 8
Galatians 4:4–7
or *Philippians 2:5–11*
Luke 2:15–21

It is amazing to me how often and effectively on this feast day we ignore the tradition of circumcision that Jesus's parents engaged in on the eighth day after his birth. Instead, we focus on the name of Jesus, forgetting that, in Judaism, the two are each a sign of covenant with G-d—and not two separate signs, but one indivisible covenantal promise of G-d With Us and For Us. Eight days after their child was born, Mary and Joseph had him circumcised in accordance with Torah (the Law) and at that time they gave him a name. The two rituals must happen together: The covenantal relationship with G-d will only work if G-d knows the name by which you are called. Names and relationships are intertwined beyond all comprehension. We cannot have one without the other. The collect, or opening prayer, in the Episcopal Church's Book of Common Prayer reads: "Eternal G-d, you gave to your incarnate Child the holy name of Jesus to be the sign of our salvation." Think about it: The name of Jesus is the sign of our salvation. If our salvation is not a relationship with G-d, then what on earth is it?

Names matter. And just as names matter, so do bodies matter. The tradition of the Israelites was to inscribe their relationship with G-d (whose Name is so holy that they don't even speak it aloud, or spell it out fully) on their very bodies, through circumcision. We can have important conversations today, of course, about whether or not circumcision is an appropriate thing to do to children who have no say in the matter, that does not alter the historical importance of connecting our physical bodies to a divine relationship; and this importance has been lost in Christianity to our detriment, despite that fact that Jesus Christ modeled that connection himself. He was circumcised and he was named: He was connected to the Creator, and the Creator knew by what name to call him.

In the passage from Numbers, we read a blessing that most of us within the Judeo-Christian tradition have probably heard any number of times: G-d spoke to Moses, saying: "Speak to Aaron and his children, saying, 'Thus you shall bless the Israelites: You shall say to them, Ha-Shem bless you and keep you; Ha-Shem make the divine face to shine upon you, and be gracious to you; Ha-Shem lift up the divine countenance upon you, and give you peace.'"

It's an ancient and powerful blessing. It is *not* Hallmarky sweetness and Thomas Kinkade precious. We know this because of what G-d says next: "So they shall put my Name on the Israelites, and I will bless them."

G-d's magnificent, overwhelming, unwriteable, unpronounceable Name is placed upon the Israelites in that blessing. And I don't know about you, but I'm pretty sure that's a helluva burden to carry. Moreover, that is the exact burden that is placed on Jesus on his eighth day out of the womb, when the local mohel, the person trained in the practice (Who was it? Surely they were still in Bethlehem? Did they have to hunt a mohel down? Was he kind? Bored? Annoyed with all the outsiders in town for the census?), performed the *brit milah*, the Covenant of Circumcision, thus ensuring that Jesus was a Jew, right down to his penis.

There's something astonishing about marking your relationship with G-d on your dick, on the bits of a body where a whole bunch of nerve endings are focused when you make love. If nothing else, it suggests that sex is, after all, something holy, rather than something wicked or naughty, as we've been trained to think. And thus, Jesus's foreskin was removed as a sign of his relationship with G-d, and he was named as a sign of his relationship with G-d.

I'll say it again: Names matter, folks. They hella matter. In the psalm we are reminded that G-d's Name is exalted in all the world, and that we are pretty much nothing in comparison, even if it seems at times that we have "mastery" over the works of G-d's hands. Even from the mouths of infants (the infant Jesus?) G-d's majesty is sung. G-d's Name is certainly exalted across the universe. Names, whether G-d's or ours, are important.

Jesus received his given name, and it connected him to G-d. And that's another thing about names, and why they matter: Names reflect kinship. My surname, Carlson, connects me biologically to others: my parents and other forebears, my siblings. But there are more than biological bonds, of course, and some of those bonds are even stronger than the biological. Who among us does not have "framily"—chosen folk who are close to us and with whom we share deep joys and sorrows? My husband and I live every day in deep gratitude for our framily, who support us in unimaginable ways, and who know who we are and how we should be called—they know our names. And when a couple marries and take the same name (whatsoever name that might be), is it not an indication of their commitment to the relationship? Indeed, my given name, Peter, connects me not only to its meaning, from the Greek word for "rock," but to other Peters in history, including St. Peter, with all of his frustrating foot-in-mouth tendencies (see the Transfiguration) and his stupid misogyny (see his response to Mary Magdalene after the resurrection), as well as with his leadership and openness to change (see his eventual willingness to accept Gentiles in the Acts of the Apostles). Sometimes, I'll confess, that connection is too alarming for comfort; like my namesake of the Gospels, I have a gift for tying heavy burdens for other people to carry.

The author of the Epistle to the Church in Galatia gets this: because G-d has entered into the world, enfleshed, embodied, as Jesus, with the covenant quite literally inscribed on his flesh. And in this fleshiness, our own relationship with G-d, our own enfleshed covenant, has changed: We are redeemed under the law, receiving adoption as children, kinship with G-d. We are children and even heirs of G-d's promise, right down to our genitalia, just like Jesus in today's Gospel: "After eight days had passed, it was time to circumcise the child; and he was called Jesus, the name given by the angel before he was conceived in the womb."

The very thought that there is a name that most truly Names Us, that has been ours to claim since before we were conceived in the womb? That is bloody mind-boggling. A name that is, quite literally, our birthright, the right of our birth.

The odd thing is that sometimes the names that our biological parents gave us, or that the world gives us, is not that Name. Sometimes misnaming is subtle. Using gender pronouns that don't apply. Assuming that equality means being able to be like me. Mansplaining in the guise of helpfulness. But often being called by the wrong name can be not only disheartening, but dangerous. How many of us have been damaged because we have been cruelly named by vicious and hateful people? Faggot. Bitch. Tranny. N-word. Paki. Cunt. These false names are harmful and often are quite literally fatal. We owe each other the love of learning others' names.

Names matter because they have power. At their best, they have the power to hold us in deep relationship with G-d, and also with our own selves, at our most essential. I am remembering Madeleine L'Engle's book, *A Wind in the Door,* in which Proginoskes ("I am a singular cherubim") helps Meg Murray figure out what her job, her vocation (her "purpose," in Cal Lutheran parlance) is. He tells her that he is a Namer, and that in his last job he was given the task of learning the names of all the stars. Meg, shocked, asks, "All of them?" Proginoskes says yes, all of them, because not many people know all their names, and it's nice to know that someone does. Meg then asks what it means to be a Namer, and Progo responds with this kicker:

> "When I was memorizing the names of the stars, part of the purpose was to help them each be more particularly the particular star each one was supposed to be. That's basically a Namer's job. Maybe you're supposed to make earthlings feel more human."[1]

Part of our journey, it seems to me, is to find our Name. That Name that seals the covenant between us, our bodies, and the Divine, so that when G-d calls one of us, someone will know which one They mean. That Name, whispered and shouted by angels before we were conceived, from the beginning of time. That Name that is Us at our most authentic, right down to our most private bits. That Name that, if it is (finally) known, will help us feel less lonely, and more complete.

My name is Peter. Will I be foundation on which others can build? Or will I be a boulder hurtling downhill to roll over others who are trying to find their names?

May the Great Name help me.

---

[1] Madeleine L'Engle, *A Wind in the Door* (Farrar, Straus, Giroux, 1973).

SECOND SUNDAY AFTER CHRISTMAS

Dr. Peter Carlson

Jeremiah 31:7–14
Psalm 84 or 84:1–8
Ephesians 1:3–6, 15–19a
Matthew 2:13–15, 19–23

I admit to feeling a bit sorry for the second Sunday after Christmas, because it gets something of a short shrift in the liturgical lifecycle: It only appears in years when Christmas occurs on a Wednesday, Thursday, Friday, or Saturday, and, quite frankly, when it falls on the day before Epiphany on the 6th of January, the more glamourous feast day often bumps it aside, like an unwanted pet dog that parents gave to their child as a Christmas present without realizing that it pees and poops and that their three-year-old isn't mature enough to care for it. It's also a Sunday when, to be honest, it's a little hard to get people to church, because they're not only recovering from the exhaustion of holiday parties with people they don't really like and Christmas dinner with family who they may love but who are still exhausting, they're also coming down from celebratory sugar highs and are probably thinking once again of their annual determination to go to the gym, not church. But here we are, not in the gym, honoring the second Sunday after Christmas, and trying to figure out what G-d might be trying to tell us when we're not really in the best emotional or physical space to listen. And it's a bit of a stewpot of lessons, I'll admit.

Christmas, of course, is a season of joy, right? Our carols have told us so: "O, tidings of comfort and joy, comfort and joy"; "Joy to the world!" How many of us have "joy" written *somewhere* on *something* in their boxes of holiday décor? Joy, indeed. But it might be helpful for us to make something of a distinction between happiness and joy, if you'll bear with me semantically for a moment. I like to imagine that joy is something deeper than happiness—that we can, if you will, find joy or be joyful, even in moments that we are not particularly happy; and we can be happy, if we are not in a given moment particularly joyful. Indeed, it is one of the gifts of queer people—and oppressed people generally—to be able to model finding joy in the midst of horror: Think, if you will, of the joy rising up in spite of slavery in the ancient spirituals, or the refusal to give in to despair in queer dance clubs, or the wickedly subversive humor that is unique to a twelve-step meeting. Sadness, frustration, and grief do not have to be barriers to joy, and in fact we can experience sadness, frustration, and grief at exactly the same moment we experience joy. The glory of the human being is that we are capable of profoundly complicated emotions.

The lessons for today seem to acknowledge that: Bad things have happened, or are happening in these lessons, just as bad things are very possibly happening in our own lives here and now. We come across the Judaeans in Babylon; we see the Ephesians caught up in disagreements; and Herod is after the Christ child. Even so, as we celebrate these twelve days of Christmas, we know that a child has been born. There is hope in the sorrow and frustration. There is space, indeed, for joy.

I dearly love the passage from Jeremiah, in great part because it is about as cheerful as this gloomy prophet gets. Remember, Jeremiah is the ultimate "I Told You So" prophet, whose dire and dismal prophecies resulted in the coining of the word *jeremiad*—a list of lamentations and woes. When grumpy recitations are called eponymously after you, you know you've got a pretty dour reputation. But chapters 30–33 take a turn from the sour attitude of the previous chapters and look forward, instead, with hope: the hope of restoration. And restoration in the bit we've heard today is proclaimed in a song of homecoming. Now, I remember when I decided to go back to school to get my MA and my PhD, and a friend at the television production company where I was working asked, the day after my visit to Claremont School of Theology, how it had gone. "It was amazing," I gushed. "I stepped foot on the campus and felt like I'd come home." She stared at me for a moment, blankly. Then, "Oh. Home is a good thing for you."

Home may not be a good thing for everyone, but it is absolutely a good thing for Jeremiah's audience. Home is, after all, the place from which they were wrenched, and long ago taken forcibly to Babylon, and the Judaeans dreamed of a return. They have, in their exile, been crying, "Save, HaShem, your people, the remnant of Israel," to which G-d responded through Jeremiah, "I am going to bring them from the land of the north, and gather them from the farthest parts of the earth." And look at who it is who is saved! Not the hale and hearty, but "the blind and the lame, those with child and those in labor, together; a great company, they shall return here." G-d is particularly interested in the outcasts, those who do not have the opportunities that others have had, even in exile. But look at the next line: "With weeping they shall come, and with consolations I will lead them back." It is important that we recognize that Jeremiah as speaking of a deep joy that does not pretend that the bad things have not taken place, or that the world doesn't often suck eggs, but that finds solace where it can, and the hope of homecoming, even though the return home may offer its own challenges, and rebuilding the country when they get there will not be easy.

It is just after this passage in Jeremiah that we run across the words "new covenant," which is a phrase that Christians have traditionally interpreted to refer to the promise of G-d in Christ. Jews, on the other hand, downplay the phrase (in great part because this is the only spot in the Hebrew scriptures where it appears), and instead think of it as a reaffirmation of the Mosaic covenant at Sinai. In both interpretations, though, we find a vision that embraces both joy and happiness: a time of singing, and a postdrought relief when "life shall become like a watered garden." At that time, we are told, "young women [will] rejoice in the dance, and the young men and the old shall be merry." This is a party, folks, that will outshine any New Year's Eve bash you've ever been to: The buffet will be enormous, and the dance clubs will be filled with people of all ages, getting down! It is important to note that this party doesn't pretend that the heartbreaking loss never took place, or that life will somehow be magically easy, but it is what J. R. R. Tolkien called a "eucatastrophe": that sudden something that changes the direction of the story, and ultimately saves us. Remember, Jeremiah is still speaking to people in exile; but even in their exile he is offering them the gift of divine eucatastrophe. G-d is going to turn things around and is offering them the opportunity to find joy in the midst of their current struggle to survive.

The psalm also speaks feelingly of finding joy even in the midst of trial, and of homecoming. Home here, however, is not specifically Judah, as would be assumed in Jeremiah, but is "the courts of HaShem." Granted, in a Jewish reading, we would likely assume that this means Jerusalem, since Zion is understood to be the house of G-d, but whether we think of this home as a literal or spiritual place, the imagery is powerful. "The sparrow has found her a house and the swallow a nest where she may lay her young by the side of your altars, O G-d of hosts!" Even the small birds have a home in G-d's house and are cared for by G-d; how much more do I long for such a home, and such care? It has been a long road, the psalmist tells us: They have gone through a desolate valley. It has been worth all the challenges of the pilgrimage, however, because a day in G-d's courts is better than a thousand in my own room, and to stand at the threshold of the house of my G-d, than to dwell in the tents of the wicked," as the Episcopal Church's Book of Common Prayer (which is rooted in the Coverdale translation of 1535) so beautifully puts it. This, then, is the deep joy that a renewed covenant with G-d offers. Not an easy life in the prosperous tents of the wicked, but a joyful life on G-d's doorstep.

I won't deny that I have more than a little trouble with the Epistle to the Ephesians, in no small part because the author, whether actually St. Paul or someone writing pseudopigraphically in Paul's name, spews a lot of language that seems to be pushing Paul's more-than-frustrating Platonic dualist theology of Bad Body / Good Spirit that he uses to try to get Christianity to make sense to an audience steeped in a Greek philosophical mindset. But as New Testament scholar Daniel Wallace suggests, in spite of all that dualism talk, the primary theme of this letter actually seems to be something along the lines of "Oh, for Christ's sake, *get along*![1]" And that's actually an important theme, because it's important to recall that Christianity in the first and second century CE was in some ways very similar to Christianity now: people unable to disagree on what it actually means to be a Jesus follower. Paul is reminding them that they are, in fact, children of G-d through the redemption of Jesus, and that's the really key point he's making.

I'm kind of sad that the lectionistas (my affectionate term for the people who developed the Revised Common Lectionary) didn't actually include

---

[1] Daniel B. Wallace, "Ephesians: Introduction, Argument, and Outline," bible.org, 2010.

all of the first chapter of Ephesians, because it finishes up with the fabulous affirmation that G-d "has put all things under Christ's feet and has made him the head over all things for the church, which is his body, the fullness of him who fills all in all." The word translated here as "church" is the Greek *ecclesia*, which (remember, we're talking to people steeped in Greek philosophy) in Greek history actually meant the gathering of the people who made decisions about a city's affairs. So it could be helpful to think of this word not so much as "church," which has a bucketload of baggage packed over the past two thousand years, but instead as "community." So Christ is head over all things for the community, which is Christ's body. And we must, during the season of the Incarnation (which, remember, means "enfleshment"), associate the (physical) body of Jesus with the (communal) body of Christ, in spite of (pseudo)Paul's attempts to spiritualize the fleshiness of embodiment. The Ephesian Jesus followers were clearly having trouble getting along, and may not always have been particularly happy in their affairs. Even so, the author of this letter is reminding them of things that are far more important than a group muddling along as though everything is copacetic: (pseudo)Paul is asking them to remember that they are, as a community of fleshy bodies, the body of Christ. The author is reminding them of "the hope to which G-d has called [them], what are the riches of G-d's glorious inheritance among the saints, and what is the immeasurable greatness of G-d's power for us who believe." This is a joy that goes far beyond happiness.

Eucatastrophe, we should note, not only does not change the horrors and sorrows of the past; it is also not a protection against dark forces attempting to continue wreaking havoc, even as the tide has turned, and hope for the future has been reignited. The story from Matthew's Gospel today shows how evil will continue to struggle against us, even when the eucatastrophic event has taken place. In Christianity, of course, that event is the arrival of a small child, in remarkably humble circumstances. In today's Gospel we hear of the departure of the three Magi, or stargazers (for full details, please attend services on January 6, the Feast of the Epiphany), and then jump to the part of the story that follows, in which Herod, enraged by the astrologers' civil disobedience (they didn't tell him where Jesus was), goes after all the newborn male children (echoes of the Pharaoh in Exodus). Joseph is warned in a dream about the upcoming, horrific murder of children—what is commemorated as the Feast of the Holy Innocents on December 28, and which our reading today skipped. Joseph, of course, is an old hand at dreams and angelic messages by now (remember, he was visited when Mary got pregnant, and told not to "put her away," as the phrase goes). An angel tells him to escape with Mary and their child to Egypt. Matthew, writing to a Jewish audience, wants to connect this to Jewish prophetic writings, and quotes Hosea: "Out of Egypt have I called my child." But reading this from a twenty-first-century perspective in which Christian Nationalism has disturbingly risen in popularity, what stands out to me is that Matthew is reminding us that Jesus, Mary, and Joseph were refugees, fleeing violence in their homeland, and needing to escape. Perhaps we should be grateful that Egypt apparently did not have strict immigration laws and deport those seeking asylum. Even after Herod dies, and they are able to return to Palestine, they cannot go back home, because Herod's son, who was just as awful, was now ruling Judea. So they settled in Nazareth, a backwater town, in order to fulfill another prophecy.

I sometimes wonder if Jesus was told about the massacre of children that was the result of his birth. I think of him carrying that burden, that deep sorrow, through his life, and like to imagine that it was one of the things that made him as compassionate toward outcasts as he was. What I am sure of, though, is that Jesus was a textbook example, as well as a model for us, of holding deep grief and deep joy in one's heart at the same time.

EPIPHANY

THE EPIPHANY OF G-D

Dr. Peter Carlson

Isaiah 60:1–6
Psalm 72:1–7, 10–14
Ephesians 3:1–12
Matthew 2:1–12

Yesterday evening I went out with the Spousal and a dear friend to have some drinks and support the Diversity Collective, a local organization that works to provide a variety of services to queer folk in Ventura County. Alcohol, bar food, and a room full of queers was, in fact, a perfect Twelfth Night—the last night of the Christmas season, which is also traditionally a night of revelry and hilarity (see Shakespeare's play of the same name as a delicious example). But Twelfth Night must needs pass, and Epiphany must needs arrive—a day and season of the church year given too little attention, nestled between the commercial pomp and twinkly ballyhoo of Christmas and the penitential circumstance of Lent.

Epiphany in our house means taking down the Christmas decorations, which is always a little bit elegiac, but it's also the day that the sages find their way to the Christ child, not just giving him great prezzies, but (almost incidentally, according to the scriptures) saving his infant ass from a power-hungry, violent tyrant.

The lessons for the Epiphany are actually pretty daunting, when you think about it. They start with Deutero-Isaiah, speaking to the remnant of Judah in Babylon; this is the origin of that spectacular poetry that always makes me play Handel's *Messiah* in my head: "Arise, shine; for your light has come, / and the glory of HaShem has risen upon you!" This vision, this metaphor of light piercing the darkness must have been startling to a people who had lived for, literally, generations in exile. And it's not just that the Judeans will be *in* the light; they will, if they follow G-d, *become* the light, and in so doing, attract others. The promise of Deutero-Isaiah is amazing: "Nations shall come to your light, and rulers to the brightness of your dawn." If they remember the covenant, they are being told, they will not just get to go home; they themselves will become a beacon to the world. Hmm. That sounds familiar in this country, for some reason.

Oh, yeah. "Give me your tired, your poor, your huddled masses yearning to breathe free . . ."

There are things to remember here, of course, lest we unproblematically assume that we (white, middle class, male, straight, American) are the inheritors of this promise: The first thing to remember is that building walls, a solution to immigration proposed by presidential administrations, is not the way to invite the tired, poor, huddled masses, or to be a light for the nations. The second is that Deutero-Isaiah is speaking to exiles: people who have literally been ripped from their land and forced to create an entirely new life, singing songs in a strange land. The prophet is *not* speaking to people (like most of us, frankly) who are comfortable, who already have (or think they have) light, but to those who are in the darkness, on the margins.

And as I think about it, it strikes me that exile is even more complicated than that. If exile is darkness, I need to remind myself that I can grow comfortable in the darkness; I can even *grow* in the darkness. There is a book on my shelf that dates back to the early days of gay liberation theology, by Christopher Glaser, entitled *Embracing the Exile*. I still refer to it occasionally, even though my own theological work has moved very intentionally out of gay liberation theology into queer theology. But the key to Glaser's work, and the thing I still go back to in wrestling with theological queerness, is right there in the title: *Embracing the Exile*. The challenge of Epiphany to me is that I find myself as a queer man having embraced the exile, living on the edge, in the odd, cool, vibrant, countercultural community that we queerfolx have built up at the margins and in the liminal places of the world. There is something really pretty fierce and fabulous about looking at the church from the position of an outsider and asking, "If your table does not have room for me, why should I beg acceptance? Why the hell would I want to be a part of that icy, exclusive club?

And (and this is really, really important) why should I or anyone else think that you have some kind of a hold on G-d, that you have conveniently gotten the final answer?" But we are even fiercer and fabulouser than that, because then we go and create our own tables, or perhaps create an entirely new ritual without any tables at all, that speaks to G-d's participation in our lives in the margins.

Those marginal places are dangerous, of course. I'm remembering the Ghost Ship community in Oakland that burned several years back, in which the lives of artists and other marginal folk were lost. Neighborhoods where poverty is rampant are inevitably more dangerous to live in, not just because of crime, but because infrastructure (the water in Flint, Michigan, anyone?) literally kills the residents. And then those of us in these marginal communities are often chastised or outright abused for remaining in them: Why don't you act normal? we're asked. Why don't you live somewhere better? Why don't you lift yourself up by your own bootstraps? Why don't you accept the way the world works and be part of it? The answers sing a protest song in my head:

> I'm *not* your kind of normal. I can't *afford* to live somewhere better. I don't *have* any fucking bootstraps. I can't make art/theology/love in the world that you want me to join.

So stop telling us why our community, which we have created on the margins because that's the only place we can live authentically, or where society/empire will even *let* us live, is wrong, is going to hell. We folks on the edges have created a new, a different world here, a world that survives not only in spite of, but in direct defiance of your world. We may be in your world, gurl, but we are most certainly not *of* it.

The Epiphany of G-d is a *promise* of a different world, isn't it? It's the promise of the outrageous reign of G-d's justice. And look at what the psalmist tells us G-d's justice looks like: "The ruler shall defend the cause of the poor of the people, give deliverance to the needy, and crush the oppressor." Other rulers will bow down, not because G-d's ruler uses military strength, but because G-d's ruler "delivers the needy when they call, the poor and those who have no helper." G-d's ruler will have "pity on the weak and the needy, and saves the lives of the needy. From oppression and violence he redeems their life; and precious is their blood in his sight."

Let's be clear: This is not a "normal" or even "sensible" government. This is not a government built on military might; this is not building walls to keep people out; this is not calling people who don't have spectacular sums of money (or who simply disagree) "losers." Once again, G-d has made absolutely clear what a righteous ruler looks like: It is the one caring for the least of us, for the oppressed, for the people who have been exiled. This righteous government is as much out of the mainstream—as queer—as I am. And it is unlikely to become real unless Christians begin to take up their positions, not at the center, but in the margins, at the edges, with the oppressed.

Paul knew for oppression. Literally blinded by the light, he was imprisoned for his work in the Roman Empire. Whether or not he is the author of the passage from Ephesians assigned in the lectionary, we are nevertheless being told what it means to follow Jesus: It means to be a literal prisoner of a tyrannical empire; it means recognizing that G-d's grace actually makes us servants (not in charge) of others. In this Ephesians particularly, it means recognizing that G-d's grace is in fact most recklessly extravagant among the most unexpected and undeserving of peoples: In the case of the author of Ephesians, this means Gentiles, non-Jews. The most unattractive people, according to the religious hierarchy, are now, according to the writer, "fellow heirs, members of the same body, and sharers in the promise."

Who are the most unexpected people who might be showing us G-d's grace in our society today? People of color? Trans, queer, gender-non-conforming folk? Syrian refugees? The working poor? Women? The innocent victims of political leaders' war-hard-ons?

In the scriptural tradition, it is always—ALWAYS—about those on the margins, away from the centers of power. That's where the Shekinah, the indwelling or breathing of G-d, sets up camp. That's where Miz Holy Spirit Thang blows Her disruptive, unruly wind. That's where the divine Fire Dance takes place, because Miz Spirit is burning down the house.

Our stories tell us that G-d entered the world, became embodied, enfleshed, in a most marginal and queer place: a barn—home to animals, animal fodder, and animal shit. We also read the remarkably improbable story of sages, astronomers whose job it was to read truth in the skies, coming to honor that queer, divinely human, humanly divine flesh, and to give gifts. But the key to the story is not that everything suddenly changes, and that the queer baby born to queer parents in a wildly queer family unit suddenly becomes the center, the main attraction, the normal: It is

Saint Lazarus (Saint Lazare) cathedral. The sleep of the Magi. Autun. France., Godong/Alamy Stock Photo

that, at the end of this story, that queer baby is *still* on the margins, *still* under threat from an empire that sees any challenge to its "normal" as a capital crime—and yet, everything does, in a way, change. So, warned in a very queer dream, as they slept (naked, spooning, three to a bed, in the kinky, queer medieval carving from Autun cathedral pictured here), the sages returned home by another, marginal route.

Follow the star, follow *Christ* to the edges of the world's acceptance, beyond the realm of propriety. It's a dangerous life, but it's where we're called to live and eat and sleep.

FIRST SUNDAY AFTER THE EPIPHANY

Baptism of the Lord

Dr. Peter Carlson

Isaiah 42:1–9
Psalm 29
Acts 10:34–43
Matthew 3:13–17

I have said, with enough regularity for it to become something of a tired trope that Old Doc Carlson tends to repeat in his classroom, that one of the key reasons Christianity fits me as a religious expression and mythic language of salvation is because its two primary sacraments are dinner and a bath.

Some people still think that I'm joking.

But think about it: Where better to see divine activity than in nourishment, whether in a protein bar wolfed down before I teach my next class, or in a huge vat of spaghetti and a bottle of cheap chianti shared by friends around a patio table? How better to feel the restoration of Holy In-Spiration than in a relaxing bath, or flopping into the waves of the ocean, or even bracing yourself to face the day in the stinging needles of a shower? Surely G-d is in these places! Or, if G-d is not, then where on earth could G-d possibly bother to be?

I freely confess to the heresy of being an omni-sacramentalist: If the sacraments are in fact defined truly as outward and visible signs of inward and spiritual grace, then the world presents us with sacramental glories that are, in the words that Annie Dillard gave us in *Pilgrim at Tinker Creek*, "strewn broadside with a generous hand."[1] And Sister Macrina Wiederkehr reminds me to look especially at the everyday: "Holiness comes wrapped in the ordinary. There are burning bushes all around you. Every tree is full of angels. Hidden beauty is waiting in every crumb. Life wants to lead you from crumbs to angels, but this can happen only if you are willing to unwrap the ordinary by staying with it long enough to harvest its treasure."[2]

Inward and spiritual grace is either locatable in everything and everyone, or in nothing and no one—and even as I type, I recognize that is an astonishing, even outrageous theological claim. We so desperately (or, to be honest, *I* so desperately) want to be assured that certain things (cilantro, for instance) and especially certain people (I name no names) I am not very willing to like are not, after all, vessels of the divine spark. I really, really want to believe that those I most despise are justifiably despised and despisable, because I am, I'm completely convinced, anointed by G-d with the Holy Spirit and power, like the Chosen One in the book of Isaiah. And if am anointed, then surely I get to determine those in whom the face of Christ can actually be seen, right?

Right?

In fact, though, the presence of the Divine is everywhere, if we can bring ourselves to see it. Deutero-Isaiah, almost certainly writing during the Babylonian Exile, had every reason not to see G-d at work; this G-d had, after all, allowed the Babylonians to overrun Judah and raze the temple in Jerusalem to the ground. I remind myself that biblical authors read history providentially: In other words, if something bad happened to the Israelites, it was obviously their fault (and, conversely, if something good happened, they had obviously done G-d a solid). But even if they acknowledged their own culpability in their being hauled off to another empire as prisoners of war, that doesn't mean it would have been easy for the Judaeans to see G-d by the waters of Babylon, or to sing their songs of praise in a strange land. There, without any of the treasured markers of either their ethnic heritage or of their covenant with HaShem, they were forced to see G-d not only in the ordinary daily experiences of exile, but even in a foreign language. And in today's reading, we find that the prophet *does* see G-d and, in fact,

---

[1] Annie Dillard, *Pilgrim at Tinker Creek*. Harper & Row, 1985, p. 20.

[2] Macrina Wiederkehr, *A Tree Full of Angels: Seeing the Holy in the Ordinary*, HarperOne, 2009, xiii.

sings a song in that strange land: In this lush, poetic "Servant Song," we can hear a haunting ballad of one who has been chosen, upon whom G-d's spirit will be poured, and who will be so gentle as not to bruise a reed, yet who will bring justice to all the nations.

It is interesting that this person will not simply restore the divine covenant that HaShem had established generations before with Abraham, and reaffirmed with Isaac and Jacob/Israel. Something is different now: It is not G-d's covenant with a people, but a *new* covenant, and the chosen person themself is it, *is* the covenant:

> I have given you as a covenant to the people,
> a light to the nations,
> to open the eyes that are blind,
> to bring out the prisoners from the dungeon,
> from the prison those who sit in darkness.

Imagine the hope that those words would have inspired in the exiles in Babylon! How understandable that they would have heard in these words a promise to them, that they would, as Deutero-Isaiah had said only a couple of chapters previously, find a straight highway across the desert, leading them home.

Home!

But they weren't home yet. They still had lessons to learn: to see the holy in the ordinary; to see G-d in the places that they least expected to find G-d. They had believed with every fiber of their being that their G-d dwelt by the Jordan River, and in the Holy of Holies in the temple of Jerusalem. They had yet to discover G-d in the Holy of Holies in Babylon, by the Euphrates. They had yet to understand, really and truly, that the Chosen One of this Servant Song was to be a light to all the nations, not just to them.

How could G-d be in such ordinary, unchosen folk? A profound question, indeed, that still drives me bonkers. I want so much for G-d to dislike the people I dislike, for G-d's voice, as the psalmist sings, to split "the flames of fire" and to "strip the forests bare." And I forget all too easily that G-d's voice is like thunder on the waters, whether they are the waters of the Jordan, or the waters of Babylon, or the waters of baptism. G-d's gonna trouble, the antebellum spiritual warns us, the waters. And when I forget these things, I don't see the sacredness in the bath. And then I doubt all too readily Peter's words from the Acts of the Apostles that G-d, in fact, shows no partiality. Surely, oh *surely* it is much more likely that G-d is partial toward *me*, because I at least am so maturely self-aware of my fucky-upness, and surely, *surely* G-d would find that at least worth of mercy, if not downright endearing?

We are all, I think, adept at believing that we ourselves, even in our worst moments, have at least a tiny spark of G-d's presence in us. But believing that people who do horrible things on a global scale are also created in the *imago dei*? That is some hard shit, and I avoid hard shit because I am theologically lazy and will not, as Sister Macrina encouraged, stay with it long enough to harvest the treasure. Dorothy Day is another person who knew how hard that shit is, when she reminded us of her priest's blunt statement that "you love God as much as the one you love the least."[3]

Dorothy Day has a gift for convicting me.

Chapter 10 of Acts is a story of visions: Cornelius's vision of G-d, granted him because he prayed and gave alms, and Peter's vision of the kosher and tref alike being delightful to G-d. Surely if a Roman centurion and "profane and unclean" food are acceptable to G-d, then G-d does not, in fact, show any partiality, and probably finds acceptable even the people I don't want to accept. I find it fascinating that Peter finds it important to assert that this grand theological message (and it *is* grand!) began "in Galilee after the baptism that John announced." And when we look at the bits of Matthew that come just before the Gospel reading for today, we see that "the baptism that John announced" was a baptism of repentance—of *metanoia*, a changing of the mind, or a turning around toward G-d, toward the discovery that we, too, are acceptable to G-d.

And that, of course, points out the Big Theological Conundrum of the Sunday that commemorates the baptism of Jesus: Of what on earth or in heaven had Jesus to repent? Why did he need to be baptized at all? Wasn't he already good with G-d, acceptable? Why might he need to change his mind? *Doesn't this entire story actually kind of mess with our assertion that Jesus is G-d?*

---

[3] Dorothy Day, *By Little and a Little: The Selected Writings of Dorothy Day*, edited by Robert Ellsberg (Knopf, 1983), 229.

Interestingly, what we get from Jesus, when John understandably balks at baptizing his cousin, is that it needs to happen in order to "fulfill all righteousness"—*dikaiosynen*—an interesting word that in my reading comes closer to justice. And then my ears perk up. Because justice is my theological love language. But it doesn't yet solve the conundrum: How does Jesus getting baptized fulfill all justice? I get how repentance does this—that turning of the mind, as it were, toward the hope of a just world, and the turning of our actions toward making that hope come true. But Jesus didn't need to repent or convert, did he? He had nothing to turn *from*, and was apparently already turned *to*.

And then I keep wondering: Maybe Jesus did, in fact, need to turn. To turn from the life he had been living before, with his family, with a job, in his home; to turn *to* the life of telling as many people as he could about a kind of Good News that wasn't exclusive to the temple in Jerusalem—as the Judeans had discovered centuries before in Babylon—and that radically opened up the Kindom of G-d to everyone that "Good Jews" cared about the least and hated the most: Roman centurions, Samaritans, widows, orphans, lepers, children. Even, presumably, Babylonians. Today, we can insert the outsiders of our society: the disabled who do not have access to public places and services; the trans and nonbinary kids who have nowhere to pee; the people of color trying to survive in society's structural racism.

And so Jesus did, in fact, convert. He turned, in the startlingly ordinary act of taking a dip in the river.

The extraordinary demands to be housed in the ordinary. The holy is encountered in a cup of coffee, the sacred in the prisons, and the salvific in the unhoused, reeking chap on the subway. Pay close attention: It might even be encountered in your own self, at your most ordinary, perhaps whilst taking a bath, when you suddenly hear that G-d is saying to you, "This is my child, my Beloved, with whom I am well pleased."

And you will turn, you will change your mind. And you will go out into the world, sharing that great and radical Good News with everyone, no matter how ordinary they might be, so that they might nurture the Divine Spark in their own lives too.

SECOND SUNDAY AFTER THE EPIPHANY

Dr. Peter Carlson

Isaiah 49:1–7
Psalm 40:1–12
1 Corinthians 1:1–9
John 1:29–42

I freely admit that I waffle over the idea of destiny, or fate.

I utterly renounce what I am convinced is the heretical doctrine of predestination—the idea that G-d is in control of everything, to the point that They know, before we are even born, whether we will go to heaven or hell. This effectively turns G-d into a monster, willing some of us to be born for the express purpose, apparently, of condemning us to eternal punishment, and acknowledging that our own lives, our own choices, can have no effect whatsoever in determining the outcome. If John Calvin is right, and this is how G-d acts, then G-d is, quite simply, not worthy of our love. This G-d is an abusive spouse, who harms us, and then shouts, "Look what you made me do!" I will have nothing to do with such a so-called divinity, and if that's what G-d is, then I'll willingly go to hell rather than pander to that kind of abuse.

But destiny? Fate? Those have a different quality, in my lexicon, from predestination. I know that in Greek mythology, human attempts to escape fate are useless; Laius, warned by an oracle that his own child will kill him, sends that child away in order to thwart the prophecy, but in doing so set in motion the very workings of the prophecy. But in my way of thinking, destiny and fate, unlike predestination, leave room for human will—for choice. We do not have to follow our destiny; it's just that our lives will be more fulfilling if we do.

This wrestling with fate seems to be what is going on in the readings today. Certainly, Isaiah speaks of a kind of destiny in the first words of the forty-ninth chapter: "HaShem called me before I was born, while I was in my mother's womb They named me." But notice the struggle just a few lines further on: "But I said, 'I have labored in vain, I have spent my strength for nothing and vanity.'" This passage, almost certainly written in the Babylonian Exile, was one of hope for the Israelites—hope that the covenant would be restored, that the exile was coming to a close, that they would finally be able to go home. The author voices the exhaustion that we've all felt when we are trying, simply, to do what we are called to do. How many of us have had moments in which we despair that our lives will ever mean anything, or even that we will have any idea of what it is, in fact, that we are supposed to be doing with those lives?

And Isaiah goes on to reveal that what the prophet once thought was their calling, "to bring Jacob back to G-d, and that Israel might be gathered to G-d," is in fact just the first part of their job. G-d says that this calling isn't enough (Wait, wut, G-d?), that "just Israel" is too small a group for the enormity of G-d's covenant: "I will give you as a light to the nations, that my salvation may reach to the end of the earth." The prophet's heart must have sunk a bit upon receiving this message.

In C. S. Lewis's book *The Horse and His Boy*, the main character, Shasta, has ridden with his companions desperately to let people know of an invasion from foreign armies. He has leapt from Bree, the horse he was riding, to save his companion Aravis from a lion, and is exhausted. It is at that point that he is told that he must continue running to meet the king of that land to let him know about the invasion: "Shasta's heart fainted at these words, for he felt he had no strength left. And he writhed inside at what seemed the cruelty and unfairness of the demand. He had not yet learned that if you do one good deed your reward usually is to be set to do another and harder and better one."[1] I imagine this must be how Isaiah felt. "Really, G-d? You've already given me the impossible task of saving the Jews—now I'm supposed to save everyone else, too? Fuck off."

---

[1] C. S. Lewis, *The Chronicles of Narnia* (Harper Collins, 2001), 272. *The Horse and His Boy*, © 1954.

It doesn't help, of course, that G-d's salvation is supposed to come, not through powerful connections, or military might, but through a rather pathetic prophet, "one deeply despised, abhorred by the nations, the slave of rulers." Even so, the final words remind us of the power of being willing to follow our destiny, of accepting our fate: "Rulers shall see and stand up; children of rulers shall prostrate themselves, because of HaShem, who is faithful, . . . who has chosen you."

Being chosen to do a good work that is harder and better than the last one we've just done offends all our sensibilities, and the psalmist recognizes that there are times when we are going to cry out to G-d in frustration and agony. But again, our trust in G-d must be the trust in a Divine who does not want what we think a god should want. We keep thinking G-d wants praise and glory from us—but this is actually really problematic, when you think about it. It suggests a G-d with some massive insecurities, desperate for adulation. But the psalmist gets it: "In sacrifice and offering you take no pleasure. . . . Burnt-offering and sin-offering you have not required." This is not an economic quid-pro-quo relationship with G-d, but a relationship of mutual love. You can't buy your way back into a broken relationship.

It is amazing how many people do not want to hear that message, though. The psalmist has proclaimed the righteousness of this relationship in the great congregation: "Behold, I did not restrain my lips. . . . I have not concealed your love and faithfulness from the great congregation." But this message that G-d loves others as much as G-d loves me is somehow spectacularly offensive, which explains the psalmist's pathetic cry at the end: "You are HaShem; do not withhold your compassion from me; let your love and your faithfulness keep me safe for ever." If your destiny is to make people aware that Divine Love is something much bigger than we can comprehend, you'll need all the safety you can get.

Paul, in the first letter to the Corinthians, seems to be hinting at the danger of accepting your fate. This opening passage of the letter is generally read with a great deal of hope and cheerfulness: "I give thanks to my G-d always for you" because the community at Corinth has received lots of spiritual gifts. But Paul also says that Jesus Christ "will strengthen you to the end"—implying that becoming a Jesus follower is far easier than being a Jesus follower. And indeed, the letter goes on to give the Jesus followers in Corinth all sorts of advice about how to be in community when we are each convinced that we are doing what G-d wants. We really do want to be blameless on the day of our Savior Jesus Christ, but it's so hard to do what we honestly feel we were called to do—to follow our destiny. Do not withhold your compassion from me, G-d!

The Gospel reiterates this sense of fate: We start with John the Baptizer, whose job is not to be a messiah, but to identify the Messiah. We know how he ended up because he followed his destiny: dead, with his head on a platter.

Of course, John is pointing, fatefully, at Jesus, a rather ordinary Jew but who, apparently, is "the Lamb of G-d who takes away the sin of the world," and upon whom the Spirit remained, the Child of G-d. I cannot help but think of the marvelous line, "The good news is there's a savior. The better news is that it's not me." I sometimes wonder if Jesus took on this naming, this destiny, willingly or if, like Isaiah, like the psalmist, he might have been a little more than mildly regretful that his fate was not simply to be a carpenter and live a quiet life, unremarked by the imperial forces of Rome. It can be really dis-easing to have your fate pointed out to you.

But the pointing goes even beyond Jesus, doesn't it, to Jesus's first companions. Two unnamed fanboys are tagging after him, and when Jesus turns and talks to them, asking what they want. They get tongue-tied, and finally sputter, "Um. Where are you staying?" (Be honest: This is a pickup line in a bar. I always imagine Jesus here in a leather jacket and tight jeans, because as a young gay kid, it was the bad boys who I thought were hottest.) And Jesus replies (with a sultry wink?), "Come and see." And they came, and they stayed.

And then one of those fanboys, Andrew, went to find his brother Simon to tell him about this hot savior: "We've found the anointed one!" and Andy dragged Simon along, and Jesus, who has apparently accepted his fate as savior/lover, pronounces Simon's fate: "You are to be called Cephas." A rock. Whether he was to be a rock causing others to stumble, or a foundation stone? That fate isn't clear yet in this passage, any more than the fate of Oedipus is clear when the prophecy is pronounced over him as an infant.

Names matter. Our true names are related to our fate. When we are named truly, then we can start living truly, living out of our most honest selves. This is why deadnaming our trans siblings is so dangerous—it keeps them from living into their destiny. Indeed, trans people model for us a job we must all do: the discernment of our authentic selves. Once we have found our names, we are well on the way to finding our destiny. And then we can start doing what we were called to do: to live, fatefully.

THIRD SUNDAY AFTER THE EPIPHANY

Dr. Peter Carlson

Isaiah 9:1–4
Psalm 27:1, 5–13
1 Corinthians 1:10–18
Matthew 4:12–23

More calling this week. Calling one and all! The Gospel relates the Matthean version of the calling of the disciples Andrew and Peter (in addition to James and John) by Jesus at the beginning of his ministry. But what is striking me in all of today's readings is not so much that we are called, as that we've really gotta start leaving things behind. When we agree to follow G-d's demands, it means abandoning so much that the world keeps telling us is important.

I don't know why I keep being surprised that the Hebrew and Christian scriptures keep telling me that the world's values are reprehensible. You'd almost think it was a theme, or something.

Proto Isaiah (Isaiah 9:1–4), you might remember, is a prophet from the southern kingdom (Judah) speaking to a people who have seen the northern kingdom of Israel smashed (or, at least threatened, at this time) by the Assyrian Empire. Speaking within a worldview that sees history as providential—that everything is not only directed by G-d, but that everything is a direct result of our behaving well or badly—it is perhaps only natural that Proto Isaiah would try to identify what Israel had done badly. In the same way, because Judah had not been decimated in the same way, he would need to explain what Judah had done well (or at least not as badly as Israel).

Once again, it all comes down to justice. He has just finished (in chapter 8) explaining that Assyria would rage over Israel like mighty flood waters, and that the floods will affect Judah as well. It will be a time of great dread. "But there will be no gloom for those who were in anguish," we find in today's reading. The glorious poetry is as refreshing as the news it brings: "The people who walked in darkness have seen a great light. . . . For the yoke of their burden, and the bar across their shoulders, the rod of their oppressor, you have broken." But it goes on beyond the day's reading, and we need to know what it says; this is not just lovely YumyumsJesusLovesMe that we'll all get to have because.

It is the shattering of worldly authority; it is, in fact, the utter destruction of that authority and everything it values. The very next verse, which I think should have been included in this lesson is, "For all the boots of the tramping warriors and all the garments rolled in blood shall be burned as fuel for the fire."

We will see a new kind of authority that does not rely on bombast, on arrogance, on violence—and the remnants of that military authority will be burned into ashes, so that finally a child can be born for us, who is named Wonderful Counselor, and who will establish the rule of justice and righteousness. If we are clinging to those militaristic interpretations of power, we cannot enter that new realm, it cannot begin. We MUST leave them behind. There's no room for bloodshed, for nation to rise up against nation, for gang to rise up against gang, for police to kill civilians, for consumers to destroy the planet. The zeal of HaShem, the G-d of hosts, has called us to something much more difficult than war and control. So Isaiah provides us with a vision of hope for justice, but reminds us that this hope can only be realized at a cost: We must leave behind everything we think matters.

The psalmist (27:1, 5–13) is hopeful, too, though a lot less certain, or providential, about why shit is happening. The words are glorious, but there's a note of desperation, isn't there? "Ha-Shem is my light and my salvation; whom then shall I fear?"

Well, for starters, howsabout that guy over there threatening to kill me because I'm gay? Or howsabout we fear that man whose own masculinity can only be affirmed by bashing a trans person? Or maybe, just maybe, we even might legitimately fear a president who suggests that Mexicans are rapists, Muslims are terrorists, and women are pussies to be grabbed?

Ha-Shem might be my light and my salvation, but fuck me sideways, there's still plenty to be afraid of in this world. Hide not your face from me, O G-d. Do not turn me away. I'm seeking your face, G-d. It's just really, really hard to see, because it's been covered up by a KKK hood. Or is that just a veil over the bread and wine?

Hearken to my voice, HaShem, when I call; have mercy on me and answer me. Do not forsake me, O G-d of my salvation. . . .

Sometimes our hope sounds desperate. We live in desperate times, and it is a dangerous thing to choose G-d over the world.

Once I get past the hilarity (and it IS hilarious) of Paul trying to remember who the hell he baptized in Corinth (1 Corinthians 1:10–18), we get to the crux of the matter as he berates the Christians in that town: We are not called to baptize.

(Um. What? Isn't that one of the sacraments that even Protestants think is a sacrament? Whaddya mean we're not called to baptize?)

Baptism is great, don't get me wrong. I have often said (and I'm not joking) that one of the reasons I'm a Christian is because our two most important sacraments are dinner and a bath. But baptism is not the center of what we are to do as Christians. Listen to Paul: "Christ did not send me to baptize, but to proclaim the gospel, and not with eloquent wisdom, so that the cross of Christ might not be emptied of its power."

We do not baptize; we proclaim the Good News, which is the insanity of the cross. Pain. Death. And not death or pain as some kind of bloodletting that G-d requires in order to satiate some divine, sadistic, vampiric thirst, but pain, suffering, and death that are the inevitable result of pursuing G-d's justice, and which run directly counter to the world's logic. The world says that the person who has the most stuff wins. The world says that violence brings peace. The world says that manipulation is power. The world says that control is victory. The world kills us, saying that it has ended us.

The insanity of the cross claims that the relentless pursuit of stuff keeps us from seeing and loving each other. The cross claims that peace only comes when we lay down our weapons and the will to use them, even when others are still wielding them. The cross dares us to discover that power is found in just and equitable relationships with each other and the earth. The cross says that victory is in the subjugation of our selfish will to G-d's righteous will. The cross tells us that death is only the beginning.

Jesus totally knew this—you can't read today's Gospel passage (Matthew 4:12–23) and not realize that Jesus knew exactly where his work would get him. In this reading, Jesus—as SOON as John was thrown into prison—steps into John's shoes, and begins preaching *exactly the same message that John preached*. We know, right here, that Jesus is absolutely clear about the likely outcome of what he was doing. And we see that he did it anyway. And and, we see what his message was: "The Kindom of heaven is at hand!" And and *and*, we see what that kindom is about:

First, it is about repentance. "Repent! For the kindom of heaven is at hand!" We suck at repentance, don't we? We suck at it because we've been told that we're special, and that we haven't really done anything wrong. (I'm not racist!) We've been told that G-d loves us. You know what? That's true. But while G-d loves us just as we are, G-d's love should, if we let it into our lives, be a light that shines on all the shit we've let pile up in the corners of this world. G-d's love is not some cheap grace (thank you, Bonhoeffer) that works as a get-out-of-jail-free card so we can keep knowingly fucking up. Relationships place demands on us, and G-d's relationship with us demands that we account for our fuckery, and *repent*. (This is not about false guilt, which tells us we should feel guilty about being gay, or about having bodies with sexual desires, or eating an egg. This is about not living into the justice of G-d's kindom. This is about loving things and using people, rather than the other way 'round. This is about confessing the evil that has been done on our behalf, and from which we benefit, even if we didn't actually do it.)

Second, it is about ordinary people, with ordinary jobs, being called to participate in things bigger than themselves. "He saw two brothers. . . . They were fishermen." This is not about presidents or army generals or corporate robber barons. It is about millions of women marching. It is about a girl in Pakistan named Malala Yousafzai who could not be silenced by gunfire to her head. It is about teachers who go each day to make lives better for students of all sorts. It is about the laborers who perform backbreaking work to get food to our tables. It is about a mechanic who knows that his work enables others to get to *their* jobs or take care of *their* kids, and takes pride in it. It is about you. It is about me. It is about us. G-d does love us, but that doesn't mean that we're anything special. But *that* doesn't mean, either, that we aren't needed.

Third, it is about leaving behind everything the world says is important: even, sometimes, our jobs and our families, if they stand between us (or others) and the vision of G-d's reign of justice and righteousness. It is certainly about being willing to leave behind those talismans that mark us, in society, as "successful" or "important." (Besides, we're not. We're ordinary, remember?) It is about killing the world's values in us, because they keep us from being in relationship with each other and with G-d.

Fourth, it is local. Start doing the work you are called to do now. Start doing it here. Right where you are. "Jesus went throughout Galilee, teaching in their synagogues." He didn't go to Jerusalem, the important city for the Jews. He certainly didn't go to Rome, the center of worldly power. He wandered around in the place he already belonged. That was dangerous enough.

Fifth (and this is essential), the Kindom of G-d is about the least of these. Jesus, like John before him, proclaimed the good news of the Kindom, and cured every disease and sickness among the people. Throughout the rest of Matthew, we see Jesus caring about the people no one else cared about. He handed out free health care. He talked to women and gave them authority and space to act on their own. He talked to immigrants and foreigners as equals. He treated the scum of the earth like royalty, and the religious leaders like scum.

And he did it all, knowing exactly what the likely result would be.

Isaiah, Paul, and Jesus were all speaking and acting under the threat of empire, under the threat of the world's values, and the world's understanding of what power is, and what it means to have worth as a human being. And all of them were pushing back hard against those values, and reminding us that our worth is found in our relationships with G-d and with each other. Our worth is found in our willingness to stand up for the least of these, or (better) to help them stand on their own, and let them have their own platform, their own voice, to give them space for their own grief, and their own hopes, and to cry for themselves, "Do not forsake me, O G-d of my salvation!"

Paul was right. Preaching this kind of whacko shit will lead to the cross. But that is the only destination that has any real value.

FOURTH SUNDAY AFTER THE EPIPHANY

River Cook Needham, MA ThM

Micah 6:1–8
Psalm 15
1 Corinthians 1:18–31
Matthew 5:1–12

As a disabled trans woman, who grew up in a high-control religious environment, I derive great pleasure from seeing people challenge the status quo and do things that are unorthodox. However, I have a rule that when people do eccentric things, they cannot harm another being. Behave outside the social norms all you want, as long as you are the only being liable for your actions. However, when another being is brought into the picture, I expect the people I am accountable to, and those that are accountable to me, to care for all those around them as best as possible.

As I write this sermon, a reality docuseries, *Chimp Crazy*, has been released recently over several weeks and has provided a significant and enjoyable supply of people acting in unorthodox ways to my life. Additionally, I am writing this sermon during the ecumenical Season of Creation. The Season of Creation is a time when Christian communities around the world and from many, if not most, branches of Christianity, make commitments and take action for the ongoing care of creation.

In the docuseries, the two documentarians follow the people involved in a court case brought by People for the Ethical Treatment of Animals (PETA) against Connie Casey, Tonia Haddix, and the Missouri Primate Foundation. As I watched the PETA lawyers and Tonia in court and in their day-to-day lives, the theme of justice captured me. Reading the texts we heard this morning, it was easy to imagine what the kindom of God might look like, what God's justice might look like, and what it might have to do with guilty pleasure reality TV.

In today's Hebrew Bible reading, God presides over a trial in nature as the prosecution, judge, and jury. They[1] ask the people of Israel what God has done to harm or otherwise injure them. Additionally, They tell the people what They do to preserve and care for them. God makes it clear that the overarching and sole responsibility for the human community is "to do justice, and to love kindness, and to walk humbly with your God."

Tonka, a chimpanzee housed at the Missouri Primate Foundation, has been exploited his entire life. At first, it was by his breeder, Connie Casey. Later in the series, Tonia Haddix exploits him by faking his death, chimp-napping him, and hiding him so that he remains out of a chimpanzee sanctuary. Tonia goes to great lengths to hide Tonka. First, she put him in a private zoo in Ohio. Then, she moved him to a relatively small cage in her basement at her home in Lake of the Ozarks, Missouri. The contrast between a God who cares for Their creation and an apex creature capturing and coercing companionship out of other creatures could not be starker.

The psalm reminds us about life and conduct on God's holy hill. This idyllic place reaches out from the world as it could be and offers up an image of a way the world could be better: a way of being categorized by honesty and forthrightness, where people care for the poor and do not extend or continue their exploitation.

In contrast to the beginning of the episode, at the beginning of the second episode, six out of seven chimpanzees that lived at the Missouri Primate Foundation were living life at a chimpanzee sanctuary, unencumbered by small cages. During the second episode, Tonia cries crocodile tears, holds up a bag of "ashes" that look very similar to a strawberry cake mix, and claims, under oath, that Tonka the chimpanzee is dead, and that her spouse and possible veterinarian cremated him. As soon as the Zoom court hearing is over, she leads the proxy-director Dwayne Cunningham to her basement, revealing the secret of this documentary—Tonka is alive and well, stuck in a cage, in her basement.

---

[1] For ease of reading, I capitalize They/Them pronouns when referring to the deity, and do not capitalize them when not.

As the church celebrates the Season of Creation, it is important to remember the command given during the first creation myth, to have dominion with the wild animals. Although we, as humans, are now predators, the initial idyllic setting for humans was a vegan life in the garden of Eden, a life that required no animals for food but rather allowed companionship between all creatures. The initial aim was not to imprison primates or any animals, but instead to have a peaceful cohabitation on the earth.

The New Testament reading takes us from the general concept of justice to what I like to call the upside-down kindom of God. This upside-down kindom of God turns the expectations of the then dominant culture and turns them on their head. The congregation I work for has an Upside-Down Talent Show many years. It happens sometimes between Ash Wednesday and Pentecost, usually on a Saturday or Sunday. It's been a year or two since they held one, but from what I remember of the name, it was a time to try out new things. Instead of expecting well-practiced perfection and excellence, the congregation gathered around to celebrate possibilities and potentialities of new skills, experimentation, and sometimes even failure.

In this text, we hear the upside-down kindom of God in the declaration that the message of the cross was foolishness for those "who are perishing" and the power of God to those who were being saved. In the Roman Empire, followers of Jesus were a small minority of the population, who at the time First Corinthians was composed had little to no institutional power. Instead, these followers of Jesus were viewed as a threat to be irradicated. Here, the author tells us again and again that this small minority experienced God's power. In contrast to the elite and powerful of the empire, who the text implies were not experiencing the power of God.

Now the power of God is something I imagine as possibilities and whispers of influence rather than some disappointed face in the sky that glares when we make a suboptimal decision. Said another way, I do not believe that God is an omnipotent planner who has designated plans and outcomes for each and every individual, group, and collective. Instead, I see God as a limitless force of influence for the goodness of each and every creature and the collective.

When I first watched the chimpanzees in *Chimp Crazy*, I commented to the person who had lovingly persuaded me to join in watching the show that Tonia (and Connie) operated with a worldview of omnipotence, and that it made me very troubled and uncomfortable. I noted that the chimpanzees were there for the humans' enrichment and enjoyment, and the chimpanzees' needs and desires were ignored and omitted.

From my high-control religious background that thrived on an omnipotent view of God, I learned that if I just acquiesced to the all-powerful man in the sky and let him do whatever he wanted, I would be safe and protected and thrive. This teaching left me vulnerable to adults as a child, and to the more powerful as I became a teenager and adult. Eventually, when the time came to escape the high-control environment, I was absolutely lost without some ultimate human or cosmic authority forcing their will upon me.

As I've grown older, these vulnerabilities that were embedded into my childhood, youth, and early adulthood development have pushed me to the point that it has become essential to me to queer the ways that power flows through the world. To see and understand that there is no man in the sky to acquiesce to, but rather experiences and options that I am influenced to participate in and experience. As humans we get to join with God as second-degree creators, shaping and forming our own experiences in our lives, our groups, and as the collective of creation.

This queer understanding of the power of God turns this paradigm of omnipotence that Connie and Tonia had over the chimpanzees on its head—not as an opposite, but rather as a critique that needs serious consideration to expand, shape, influence, and persuade the outcomes that we as a creation collective might experience. In this kindom of God, we stop holding omnipotent power over the chimpanzees, keeping them in cages in human homes, and instead let them roam free in ways that are safe for them and for God's good creation.

This understanding of the power of God, unlike the power of Tonia Haddix (and Connie Casey), is excited for all of the beings in this cosmos to experience freedom and choice and unfolding. With this understanding of both the power of God and Their initial aims, we can look further into the text.

In this text, Paul continues with this upside-down motif, reminding us that God chose the lowly, poor, and ordinary ways to enter the world, that God chose to reach out to the people held under the grasp of empire and in the clasp of poverty. Here, Paul argues that the wisdom of God can be heard, followed, and experienced most by those not concerned with conformity to the ways of empire, wealth, capitalism, and cisgender-heterosexism. Instead, these people hear and experience God's power and wisdom and put it into action.

This brings us to the Gospel text, where Jesus teaches specific ways that God's power turns the expectations of this world upside-down and welcomes in a world where people and their embodied realities are shifted and changed into something much better than expected.

In our capitalistic world, selling one's body for the financial requirements of life is almost a foregone conclusion. But in God's kindom, the poor and working-class people are not always going to want for enough to eat and to meet their needs. In the upside-down kindom of heaven, God has said that they would be the owning class.

In our modern world of aggressive and toxic positivity, that denies any emerging negative emotion, Jesus tells us that those who mourn, pointing out that sadness, anger, and fear are all part of a full emotional experience, belong. Not only do they belong, but they will be comforted.

In our modern world of influencers and success coaches and endless marketing of side hustles and special skills, Jesus tells us that the meek are not unworthy or failures. That not only do they belong, but that in the kindom of God, they shall inherit the earth.

The examples go on, examples of ways that the kindom of God influences and persuades people to live a life that is counter to empire. That is counter to the model of scarcity that so many of us as queer folks wrestle with daily. That is counter to the model of omnipotence that removes human agency and instead offers a new way for humans to participate in the creative process.

The upside-down kindom of God that Jesus proclaimed is not just good news for the humans who heard it two thousand some years ago. It is good news for you and me. When we watch trash TV, it helps us see the shortcomings of our world. When we fear and fret about paying rent, it shows us that there will be enough if distributed equitably. When we fear that our companions will abandon and leave us, the kindom of God shows us that there will always be companionship when we care for our neighbors and resist the powers that be.

FIFTH SUNDAY AFTER THE EPIPHANY

Dr. Peter Carlson

Isaiah 58:1–9a (9b–12)
Psalm 112:1–9 (10)
1 Corinthians 2:1–12 (13–16)
Matthew 5:13–20

I have a confession to make.

Sometimes? I don't much like some of the prophets. I don't much like Isaiah, or Micah, or Amos, or even Moses, or even—dare I say it?—Jesus.

They say such *freaking* irritating things.

They poke holes in my religious well-being.

They knock the wind out of me with a staggering right hook to the solar plexus.

They tell me that it's not about me, and that it's about the very least in the world, about everyone I'd rather not think about.

Take the passage from the book of Isaiah that we heard today, for instance. This is from a section of the book that scholars sometimes call Tri to-Isaiah, or Third Isaiah—it's prophecy that probably was being revealed following the return of the Judaeans from exile in Babylon, possibly when they were rebuilding the temple, and feeling like G-d had finally forgiven them all their sins, and they were back in G-d's good graces, and everything was just super-deluxe and hunky-dory.

And the passage starts so promisingly, doesn't it? "Shout out! Do not hold back! Lift your voice like a trumpet!"

(I like trumpets, don't you? Trumpets are great.)

But then you realize that this is a warning trumpet, not a trumpet of triumph: "Announce to my people their rebellion . . ."

(Oh, *not fair*! You got my hopes up! I thought we were good, G-d. What's the deal?)

"Day after day they seek me and delight to know my ways."

(Yes, G-d! Don't you love that? Aren't you happy about that? I seek you!)

". . . as if they were a nation that practiced righteousness . . ."

(Oh, ouch!, G-d! You mean we *don't* practice righteousness? But we work at it so hard! Seriously, G-d! What more do you want? Why do we fast, but you do not see? Why humble ourselves, but you do not notice?)

Indeed, I have a confession to make. I hereby confess in front of all of you that through Third Isaiah, G-d is speaking directly to me: "Look, you serve your own interests on your fast day, and oppress all your workers. Look, you fast only to quarrel and to fight and to strike with a wicked fist."

I confess that my religiosity is all too often in my own interests. I confess that my ooh-ooh-spirituality is a sham, because it's all about whether or not *I'm* one of the in-crowd, whether or not *I* will get into heaven, whether or not G-d loves *me*.

I confess that that is BAD theology.

Part of the problem that we face, if we're going to be searingly honest with ourselves, is that even if we can take criticism of bad behavior, we can't listen to critique of what we think are our best selves. Isaiah is driving a spike right through the heart of everything we think we're doing *right*. And having that stabbed to death is a grievous thing, indeed, isn't it?

Jesus is on the same vicious path today too. Probably lots of us have heard this passage before, haven't we? "You are the salt of the earth! You are the light of the world!" I love this passage—I feel so . . . *salty* when I read it. I feel so . . . *lightfulicious*. I feel so . . . *saved*.

But let's take a closer look: Jesus's words here are not compliments. They're not assurances. They're not actually very pleasant. This passage is part of the famous Sermon on the Mount in the Gospel of Matthew. And this passage follows immediately on the topsy-turvy insanity of the Beatitudes. Anyone know the Beatitudes? They're so lovely, aren't they? So . . . blessingful.

I'm going to suggest something here: The Beatitudes have a problem. They've been so completely whitewashed by our society that we can't even see what they mean any more. We need to reread them—closely—and see that they are a complete upheaval of the social order. Those who, according to Jesus, receive G-d's blessing are those who the world says are the least blessed. The losers. The ridiculous. The shameful. The clinically depressed. Those who do not make war. The weak. The version from Luke is a little more direct and ruthless than the Matthew version, but they're making the same point, aren't they? The world's values are not the values of the Kingdom of G-d.

So think, for just a moment, about the world we live in. How many of you strive to be weak at work? What the hell? If I'm weak at Cal Lutheran, I won't get tenure! Meekness is *not* one of the qualities that the Advancement, Rank, and Tenure committee look for, *trust me*.

So our passage today comes right after that social upheaval of the Beatitudes. Matthew is writing to a Jewish audience, and there's no doubt that Jews would see the significance of Jesus going up a mountain to talk about the Law (the Torah), just like Moses did, centuries before. But if Moses brought the law to the Israelites, Jesus reminded us what the law is actually about.

Anyone here ever read the Ten Commandments?

Have you ever noticed that only the first two commandments have anything to do directly with G-d? *Have no other gods before me, and don't worship any graven images*. Everything else is about how we live with each other. Don't take the name of G-d in vain (keep your word when you give it). Remember the sabbath day (practice self-care individually and as a community). Honor your parents. Don't kill. Don't screw around in your relationships. Don't take other people's stuff. Don't pervert justice. Don't covet other people's stuff. You might almost think that G-d is trying to tell us that religion isn't actually about G-d!

Or, to put it another way, that being G-dly means living in a world in which everyone is cared for equally, and justice is available to everyone, regardless of their marriage status, their socioeconomic status, their gender identity, their sexuality, their race, their ethnicity, their . . .

It is that Law of Justice, that Torah, that Jesus is talking about here. This is why Jesus finds it so important to remind us that he has not come to abolish the law or the prophets, but to fulfill them. That our behavior, he tells us, needs to be better than all those holy-holy-ooh-ooh-muckety-mucks preaching prosperity-theology, and it's-all-about-me-getting-to-heaven, and Jesus-loves-you-but-doesn't-expect-you-to-*do*-anything heresy.

We ARE the salt of the earth. We ARE the light of the world. And I am here to tell you today that those phrases are not meant to comfort us, but to challenge us. We are meant to be salt that preserves, not ourselves, but others. We are meant to be light, not so that we can find our own way, but so that others can find theirs. We are meant to be the savor, the beacons of G-d's greatest gift: the Law.

Jesus just got done telling us that the Law doesn't look like what we think it should look like. And when we go back to the book of Isaiah, we find out precisely what it *does* look like: It's not going to church and belonging to the right groups and occasionally indulging in a little charity that doesn't hurt us. That's what I call Country Club Religion, and Isaiah is tearing us a new one for practicing it. Those sacrifices that aren't really a sacrifice at all, the fasting that is meant to impress rather than to humble (what are you giving up for Lent, by the way?). All of that is only so much bull . . . poo.

The psalmist, in Psalm 112, reminds us of what righteous people look like:

> It is good for them to be generous in lending and to manage their affairs with justice. They will not be afraid of any evil rumors; their heart is right; they put their trust in HaShem. They have given freely to the poor, and their righteousness stands fast for ever (paraphrased).

And let's go back to Isaiah (and remember that Jesus told us that the words of the prophets still apply to us with staggering force today):

> Is not this the fast that I choose:
> to loose the bonds of injustice,
> to undo the thongs of the yoke,
> to let the oppressed go free,
> and to break every yoke?
> Is it not to share your bread with the hungry,
> and bring the homeless poor into your house;
> when you see the naked, to cover them,
> and not to hide yourself from your own kin?
> . . .

> If you remove the yoke from among you,
> the pointing of the finger, the speaking of evil,
> if you offer your food to the hungry,
> and satisfy the needs of the afflicted,
> *then* your light shall rise in the darkness,
> and your gloom be like the noonday. (emphasis added)

Then, you will be the light of the world and doing your job.

Being here in church is great. But Isaiah and Jesus are both reminding us today of the single most difficult lesson we have to learn as Christians:

It's actually not about you.

It's about the weakest in our world.

It is about the refugees fleeing violence.

It is about the grief-filled parents who mourn the loss of another child to gun violence.

It is about the poor who have no access to justice because it costs too much in this country.

It is about policing that protects some citizens but not others.

It is about the girls who are told that they should look pretty, because "pretty" is required to be successful as a woman.

It is about people who are bound to low-paying jobs without health insurance.

It is about residents who cannot obtain a quality education because of where they live.

It is about the trans woman murdered for trying to be the person she knows G-d has created her to be.

It is about the Hispanic worker criticized for broken English in a society that refuses to learn other languages.

It is about victims of sexual violence being asked what they did to deserve it.

It is about addicts, who have discovered an alternate reality that is more comforting than the one we want them to live in.

It is about the tired, the poor, the huddled masses yearning to breathe free . . .

It is political, if by political we mean having to do with the common good.

Be salt. Be light. But be them for others.

It's not about you.

SIXTH SUNDAY AFTER THE EPIPHANY

Dr. Peter Carlson

Deuteronomy 30:15–20
or *Sirach 15:15–20*
Psalm 119:1–8
1 Corinthians 3:1–9
Matthew 5:21–37

Even though I am not addicted to the more common things that we tend to think about when we think about addiction (you know: alcohol, drugs, sex), the twelve steps of AA have had a profound influence on my relationship with and my understanding of G-d, and on my understanding of myself as a Christian. An ex of mine was an alcoholic and in an effort to support him in the program, I would go to meetings with him, particularly on his sobriety birthday. And every time, I was astonished that a bunch of queer drunks seemed to have a better idea of what it meant to follow the teachings of Jesus than I did. In the process, they helped me a lot with my own addiction: which is the addiction to self-assurance, the need to be right, to be perfect. I finally admitted I was powerless over perfection, and that my life had become unmanageable. Fortunately, I've taken care of that now, and I no longer seek to be perfect.

That was a joke.

One of the most important lessons I learned from my addicted queer sisters-and-brothers-and-all-gendered-others was that my program is not your program, and your program is not my program. The lessons today seem to be screaming, "Work your program!" even as they remind us that our programs might actually be worked out in a multitude of different ways. The key is not to make every single person exactly like us, or to assume that what works for one person (or in one historical time) should work for another person (or in another historical time). The key is to stay sober. Or, as the One Big Fat Overriding Theme of scripture seems to put it, to stay in relationship with G-d and to stay in relationship with each other. Which are the same thing.

I love the reading today from Deuteronomy (30:15–20). Deuteronomy is kind of the Reader's Digest Condensed Version of Torah, giving the most important bits of Genesis, Exodus, Leviticus, and Numbers. Moses begins by reminding the people of their journey in the wilderness, and then reaffirms the necessity of obeying the Law, and instructing children in it, followed by the Deuteronomic Code itself: the popularly numbered 613 rules that G-d's people need to follow.[1] The fact that these are called "mitzvoth," which literally means commandment, but which implies blessing rather than burden, is important. The commandments, the Law, are a gift to help us stay in covenant with G-d.

It's easy and super-tempting to focus on the mitzvoth about sexual relations, of course (because, let's admit it, we love talking about sex, don't we?), without seeing the bigger matters, which are (1) justice and (2) the maintenance of the community of G-d's people—that G-d's community would last, and be true, and not become "polluted," if I might use that word, with the idolatry of the outside world. Out of the 613, a whopping twenty-four are about sexual intercourse, and most of those have to do with various forms of incest. Far more important, based on the raw data, are issues of how we treat each other, even if the other is "the stranger." Justice, in fact, is the single biggest issue that I see in the commandments: treating the stranger with equity; making sure the powerless are cared for first; ensuring that courts and judges are free from corruption; denouncing abuse of property rights; ensuring that the innocent are protected; care of the animals, even; contributing a portion of one's wealth to the common good (to G-d's work); to forgive debts every seven years so people can have a chance to catch up (can you imagine asking this of Citibank or Wells Fargo or Goldman Sachs?).

Seriously: Who we fuck is the least of our concerns today if we think we're supposed to be living a biblical life.

---

[1] The 613 mitzvoth actually were first identified by Maimonides in the Mishneh Torah, and this is not the only list, but I am in my thinking speaking the tradition back into the Deuteronomic Code.

So at the close of this section, Moses lays it on the line for the Israelites: "I have set before you life and death. Choose life." And just to remind you that choosing life is not actually about taking the land and prospering in it, Moses provides a potent summary of Torah: "walking in G-d's ways, and observing G-d's commandments, decrees, and ordinances. . . . Loving HaShem our G-d, obeying G-d, and holding fast to G-d." Paying attention to the stranger. Holding our judiciary responsible. Making sure the government is not corrupt. Ensuring that the least in our society are cared for first. We've just been told that this is what walking in G-d's ways means. We've just been told that to choose those things is to choose life.

The world wants us to think otherwise. The world tells us to keep our profits for ourselves, because we've earned them, by golly. The world tells us that the weakest in our society deserve everything they get (or don't get), and that it's their fault if something goes wrong. The world tells us that we can fuck whomever we want without consent, but with impunity, especially if we are men, because grabbing women by the pussy clearly is not anything that will get us into trouble, so it must be okay. The world tells us not only that we should prosecute debt, but that we should charge usurious interest, because we can. And it tells us that those who need loans the most (for education, for houses, for utterly destructive medical bills) deserve to have their entire existence at the mercy of international banks, because that's How Things Are And Banks Are Too Big To Fail.

The world tells us that we need to look out for Number One.

But the mitzvoth are not about taking care of Number One. They're not even about a personal relationship with G-d; they are about our communal relationship with G-d. You might almost think that we are in relationship with G-d when we are in relationship with each other, and care for each other, and see G-d in each other. You might almost think that seeking justice for each other is the same thing as seeking G-d. Hmm . . .

We will each pursue justice in our own ways. We all have issues about which we are passionate. I obviously have gender and sexuality justice on my list. Others might seek to increase food justice, or seek to ensure justice in our court systems, or in Congress, or in the Oval Office. Some might seek reproductive justice, or justice for un- or underdocumented immigrants, or racial or ethnic justice. All of these people are seeking to redeem humanity, to build the divine community, to follow the mitzvoth provided to hold us close in relationship with G-d. We are not all doing the same thing, but we are working toward the same goal. We are each working our own program.

Paul reminds us how important this is, when he addresses the divisions that are threatening to rupture the community of Christians in Corinth (1 Cor. 3:1–9). Each of the people there is so convinced that s/he/they has the right program, that s/he/they has found the answer to everyone else's problems, the fulfillment of everyone else's needs.

I am utterly guilty of this. I see problems in the world, and I am absolutely convinced I know how to solve them. Worse, I am convinced I know what others' problems are, better than they do themselves. I am so good at solving other people's issues. (Seriously. If the world would just listen to me, things would be so much better.)

But Paul is reminding us that our path is our path, and that we are all journeying toward something that is beyond our own individual doing, even as our individual work is essential. Do you belong to Paul? Do you belong to Apollos? Do you belong to Cephas? Great. Work that program. But if you see someone working a different program? If they're staying sober, then quitcher bitchin, gurl. Are they working toward justice? Give thanks, not piss-and-vinegar. "The one who plants and the one who waters have a common purpose." Keep that in mind. Eyes on the prize, folks: justice and mercy.

Cephas is not Apollos is not Paul. And who the hell cares? The key for Christians is Jesus, who reminds us how much is required of us. Jesus pushes us harder than ever when it comes to issues of justice and mercy, because he is reminding us that while the goal of the Law, the goal of Torah, always remains the same, the details might need to shift, based on who is most in need of G-d's justice. In today's passage from Matthew (5:21–37), he's still on the Sermon on the Mount mountain, and still channeling Moses, and still talking about the law. Only now he's really getting down to brass tacks. If you thought the Beatitudes two weeks ago and his harsh words last week were problematic, this week is gonna make you shit bricks.

"You have heard that it was said to those of ancient times, 'You shall not murder' and 'whoever murders shall be liable to judgment.' But I say to you that if you are angry with your sibling, you will be liable to judgment."

"You have heard it said, 'You shall not commit adultery.' But I say to you that everyone who looks at a woman with lust has already committed adultery with her in his heart."

Holy shit on a stick. Seriously? I mean, I know that Jesus just said last week that he came to fulfill rather than to abolish the Law, but it sounds like he's making it even harsher.

Actually, he is.

Here's the deal. What seems to be going on here is not that Jesus is substantially changing the Law, but that he is telling us how it is applied today. What is going on is that Jesus is reminding us that we ourselves are often the problem, not other people. We live in a world that to this day blames women for being raped, by asking what they were wearing, or how much they had to drink. Based on the kinds of punishments that have NOT been handed down for rapists in this past year, it would appear that the lower-case law agrees with this. And Jesus is yelling at us: "Look. You seem to be interpreting the Law in a way that allows you to treat women like shit! You can assault them and THEY get punished! You can divorce them in a society that leaves them socially helpless! I'm telling you that you should cut off your own over-fucking penis instead, you assholes! How dare you foist the blame for your own sexual power trip onto someone else?"

Seriously, folks. The Law is about being in relationship with G-d. G-d has, over and over again, made it clear that if we are to stay in relationship with G-d, we have to care for those who society has abandoned, rather than those who are abusing the weakest in society. If we are to stay in relationship with G-d, we must demand justice and throw ourselves into the fight.

And if my eye prevents me from doing that, I need to gouge it out. If my hand keeps me from seeking the Kindom of G-d, then I'd better chop it off. And if my dick is the source of my power, and I use that power to oppress, I'd fucking better hack it off my body. Better to stand in front of G-d with a disfigured body than to live in Gehenna with a proud erection.

Begin with confession. Begin by admitting what holds you back from seeking justice. Then work your program. You'll make mistakes. You'll fail miserably sometimes. But you'll get up and try again. Jesus has given us a vision of the Kindom, a vision of justice for all, not just for those who can afford it, or who look like us. Jesus has given us the spit and vinegar to keep fighting. You can do it, even if you have to do it without those body parts of you that you thought were most important. You in all your brokenness—the handless, eyeless, dickless you—are enough for this job.

I spend a lot of time reminding people, "It's not about you." Well, now it's finally about you.

I'll see YOU in the trenches.

SEVENTH SUNDAY AFTER THE EPIPHANY

The Rev. Melissa Campbell-Langdell

Leviticus 19:1–2, 9–18
Psalm 119:33–40
1 Corinthians 3:10–11, 16–23
Matthew 5:38–48

"For the wisdom of the world is foolishness with God." I like to think that queer Christians at our best are fools for Christ. We reject the wisdom of the world in favor of the greater wisdom of God. We don't just do this to be contrary, but sometimes it is just to survive. And today's readings really seem to bring this out again. Surely, it seems foolish that Jesus, talking to a poor population under the thumb of the oppressive Roman Empire, would suggest that they just "turn the other cheek" and otherwise allow themselves to be taken advantage of further. And this portion of Psalm 119 waxes lyrical about God's commandments, only for us to be reminded just how rigorous God's commandments can be in the passage from Leviticus.

God's commandments are not easily followed all the time. Generosity with resources and lavishness of spirit do not always come easily to us. We are all too quick to judge. And in the passage from Matthew, is Jesus really just telling folks to be trampled underfoot? Walter Wink has come up with a way of reading this passage that I think includes a lot of holy foolishness. He says that Jesus was trying to show a third way of dealing with the Powers That Be in the ancient world. He said that neither to respond passively or reactively and aggressively to the Powers That Be would be right for followers of Jesus.

Instead, Jesus is showing the followers a way to resist that completely undermines the power structure of the time. For example, about "turning the other cheek," he says that typically "You are probably imagining a blow with the right fist. But such a blow would fall on the left check. To hit the right cheek with a fist would require the left hand," and the left hand was ritually unclean. This would mean that the person hitting the left cheek would have the nose in the way, and thus would have to use the right fist.

Wink says that "only equals fought with fists" so "this act of defiance renders the master incapable of asserting his dominance in this relationship."[1] In this way, turning the other cheek becomes not the action of a victim but the victim's way of turning the situation around in order to reclaim his or her power.

About giving your coat and your cloak, Wink shares that the system of debt forgiveness often used someone's long outer cloak as a sort of collateral on a loan, which would then be returned every evening so the person had something to sleep with. He says: "A creditor has taken a poor man to court over an unpaid loan. Only the poorest of the poor were subjected to such treatment. Deuteronomy 24:10–13 provided that a creditor could take as collateral for a loan a poor person's long outer robe, but it had to be returned each evening to the poor man would have something with which to sleep."[2]

But in Jewish law, to be naked in front of another was to shame them, so he suggests that giving away your coat too is a way of not being constantly ground down by the oppressive law for debtors.[3] Taking off one's coat, in that time a sort of undergarment, leaves one more or less naked, and thus shames the creditor. Taking off one's coat takes back one's power. Once more, this is seen as a kind of nonviolent resistance to the Powers That Be.

About going the second mile, it was well known that any Roman soldier could command any subject person to carry his baggage for one mile. Now we may think of soldiers in our society as committed to protecting us, but

---

[1] Walter Wink, *The Powers That Be* (Bantam, 1998), 101–2.

[2] Wink, *Powers That Be*, 103.

[3] Wink, *Powers That Be*, 104.

at that point the soldiers worked for Rome and not for the subject population whom they mostly saw as free labor and people to keep in line.

Taking that pack a second mile could technically get the soldier into trouble with his superiors, because he could be seen to be breaking the military code.[4] Once more, Jesus suggests pushing back just a little bit against the law, but in a surprisingly generous way.

As Wink says, "The Powers That Be literally stand on their dignity. Nothing deflates them more effectively than deft lampooning. By refusing to be awed by their power, the powerless are emboldened to seize the initiative, even where structural change is not immediately possible."[5]

This makes me think of the Stonewall riots, and many other queer acts of defiance, in which queer people may have been aware that we might not immediately see change, but we still rebelled and pushed back in order to make our voices heard. We have sometimes experienced violence as a result, but those brave moments have paved the way for more recent expressions of queer joy to abound and for some forward movement in legislation, although some areas have also experienced a reversal of progressive policies that limit inclusion of our LGBTQ community.

Now some can take this form of pushing back against the Powers That Be and see it as a kind of unchristian way of shaming those in power, just pushing back in order to ridicule the other. But if there is truth in his way of reading Jesus's words, I have to believe that it is not in simply shaming the soldiers or creditors, but it is in helping them acknowledge at least two things, two things that bring us right back to why we treasure God's commandments: One is that the only true Power that we Judeo-Christians look up to is the one, true God. And the second is that God wants God's people to live into abundance for all.

In the same way, queer Christians never just fight back for our own good, but we do so because a world that truly includes us and embraces us is a better world for all. A world that refuses to see or include us is not only poorer for the lack of us, but is incomplete because we are part of God's good creation.

---

[4] Wink, *Powers That Be*, 106–7.

[5] Wink, *Powers That Be*, 105.

When you look at the Leviticus reading today, we are reminded that Yahweh is the Lord right left and center, it basically ends almost every line. This section is a reframing of the whole Decalogue, or Ten Commandments, with some special notes added for how to live morally, and front and center is the concept that the Power we are to look to first is the Lord our God, Yahweh.

When Jesus is asking the disciples to play with the notions of Power and Empire, he is not doing so just to be coy. He wants to point out that, although his followers are currently living under a very powerful reign, the Roman Empire has got nothing on the reign of God, and God's power is the ultimate Power that we are all subject to.

Additionally, God wants us to live into our fullness. God wants us queer Christians to live into our fabulousness. Not just in the future, but as human beings, right here and now. Not just when a future more enlightened time comes and we see more inclusive policies across the country, or when LGBTQ youth are not as at risk for suicide, but now. We know that God wants us to live into our fullness. Irenaeus of Lyon famously said, "The Glory of God is the human being fully alive."[6] God's yearning for human thriving is especially present in the Leviticus passage, where it talks about how we must not reap the edges of the field, but leave them for the poor and the alien (Leviticus 19:9–10). God doesn't just want those that own or work the land to eat, God wants those who cannot work or do not have an "in" in society to eat also.

And God wants those who feel like they are at the margins to know there is a place for them too. You are not alone. Your fabulous light needs to shine in order for this world to be a more complete place. A place that truly reflects the glory of God's good creation. There are other passages that speak to the same concepts of reaching out, not just to those that we like, but being generous with complete strangers. I believe this is part of it. God knows we need every single gift of every single person.

And God wants us to thrive. I remember the "It gets better campaign" a few years back aimed at encouraging LGBTQ youth and letting them know that life does get better, even if it is not all rainbows and sunshine all the time. We reclaim this promise when we remember that Jesus wanted to

---

[6] Irenaeus, *Adversus haereses* (*Against Heresies*), Book IV, chapter 20, paragraph 7: *Gloria enim Dei vivens homo.*

show through pushing back against laws that kept certain segments of the population down that there was a way to reclaim dignity and sanity in the midst of oppression.

And sometimes reclaiming that dignity means being a bit foolish by the world's standards. What is more foolish than going two miles when you just need to go one, turning the cheek when someone has just degraded you by slapping you, or giving someone your undergarment when you just were ordered to hand over your cloak? What is more foolish than a drag queen in full hair, makeup, and dress reading to children at the library? These are all silly by the world's standards, but they make a point.

They say, I am a human being, a beloved child of God, and though you can ask much of me, I can reclaim my dignity because the power I look to is the power of God in Christ. Christ is the cornerstone of my community, and of my day, and if you are not treating me in a way that honors my being fully alive in God, then I will show you up! I will show up in my fabulousness, and you just have to deal with it.

How can we live into being fully alive in Christ and sometimes being fools for Christ? One way to seek the reign of God in our midst is to see how we can advocate for others being unfairly trampled by our modern Powers That Be. How can we look out for elderly LGBTQ seniors who may need an advocate, or for trans and nonbinary youth who just need to use a gender-affirming bathroom but run into prejudices just getting their bodily needs met?

In all that we do, may we pray for Christ to be our foundation—in our church community, in our work, and in our family lives. I pray for God to show us a path of holy foolishness and unashamed fabulousness that allows us and all our neighbors to be fully alive in God!

EIGHTH SUNDAY AFTER THE EPIPHANY

Dr. Peter Carlson

Isaiah 49:8–16a
Psalm 131
1 Corinthians 4:1–5
Matthew 6:24–34

In season 4 of the brilliant television series *Northern Exposure*, Chris, the town's local DJ and long-haired free spirit who's done jail time, speaks to the entire (albeit very small) population of Cicely, Alaska, in the middle of the months-long winter darkness. It's an astonishing soliloquy, which begins with the reputed final words of Johann von Goethe: "More light!" Chris argues that ever since we climbed out of the primordial broth, we have all, like Goethe, been calling for "More Light!" listing one example after another of the roles light has played across the human story, from lighting caves and refrigerators to lighting football stadiums and books to reading secretly under the covers at night. But light, he notes, is not only literal; it is metaphorical and even spiritual. He turns to the poets, biblical and secular alike: The psalmist, breathing "Thy word is a lamp unto my feet." Dylan Thomas's villanelle, "Do not go gentle into that good night . . . Rage, *rage* against the dying of the light." Blessed John Henry Newman's prayer/poem, "Lead, Kindly Light, amidst th'encircling gloom, / Lead Thou me on!" And back to the Bible, in the prophet Isaiah, "Arise! Shine! For your light has come!"

And then he flips some switches, and the small, dark town is lit up. The people, having grown used to being in the dark, look about them in awe at Christmas tree lights, table lamps, chandeliers, neon signs, beer signs, fairy lights, patio lights, floor lamps . . . a wonderland of light, catching them all by glorious surprise.

As we come to the close of Epiphany, the season of light breaking into a dark world, we often find ourselves mildly depressed, because the cheery twinkling of the holiday season has been dimmed, and we find we still have to slog our way through the rest of winter's shortened days.

"More light!" we cry.

So it is disconcerting at best to have a set of lessons that seem to be saying that light is something we ought not to pursue, or at least not right now. Can we have too much light? The prophecies of the Suffering Servant in Isaiah speak despairingly of a people who will not or cannot listen to the promises of G-d; the psalmist brags about not messing about with things that are "too hard," like some 1950s advertisement in which the wifey speaks adoringly of letting the Man of the House handle Hard Things, like money. Paul, too, reminds us that there's a mess of things that are now hidden, and that we should not pronounce judgment, because we cannot see the things now hidden in darkness. Even Jesus is telling his followers that they worry too much, and they're trying to be in charge of things that are better left to G-d.

"You can't handle the light!" we are told.

The passage we hear today from Deutero-Isaiah is the second of four so-called Servant Songs, which speak of a suffering servant, called by HaShem, to guide the Israelites and indeed all the nations (the "Gentiles") back to G-d. The passage itself seems wondrously positive: G-d's promise that the prisoners shall be freed, and hunger and thirst will be no more, "for he who has pity on them will lead them." But just before this passage, the servant, whom G-d has chosen, is complaining to G-d: "I have labored in vain; I have spent my strength for nothing and vanity." Clearly the people of Israel are not trusting in the promise. And this is borne out at the end of our reading for the day: "But Zion said, 'HaShem has forsaken me, HaShem has forgotten me.'" I wonder if Zion is upset that G-d told the suffering servant that not only Israel, but *all* the nations, would be drawn to Them? "Look!" the Divine is saying—but they do not look. Perhaps it is because G-d's promise of redemption for all, not just for us, is too much light—more than we can handle.

"More light!" we cry.

"You can't handle the light," we are told.

The psalmist is doing a weird humble-proud in this Psalm of Ascent. Indeed, it is the assumption that this song is one to be sung or recited while on pilgrimage to Jerusalem that helps make it more understandable. Because it does, at first glance, read with a kind of "look how perfectly humble I am—am I not amazing?" quality. But when read aspirationally, it makes more sense. It sounds, in fact, like my own words to myself when I am settling in to meditate. "I'm breathing. I'm letting go of outside thoughts . . ." But still, there's this whole "I do not occupy myself with great matters, or with things that are too hard for me." I'll admit that as a college professor and theologian, I rather rejoice in tackling things that are hard, and trying to make sense of them. In fact, that's kind of my job.

Am I trying to take in too much light?

Can I handle the light?

Apparently not, Paul writes to the Jesus followers in Corinth. We are stewards, not of G-d's clarities, but of G-d's mysteries. And this is hard, especially in our world where we want answers—and, ideally, really clear-cut answers at that. (This at least partially explains the rise of fundamentalisms across religious traditions, by the way.) Be patient, Paul tells us; don't be over-hasty in looking for solutions. G-d "will bring to light the things now hidden in darkness and will disclose the purposes of the heart."

But right now? You can't handle the light.

And then Jesus. Totally aside from the really depressing reminder that I am not able to serve G-d if I am serving wealth (and there really is not any wiggle room in that statement, which sucks eggs for those of us who are comfortable at least in the moment), we are told "do not worry about your life, what you will eat or what you will drink, or about your body, what you will wear."

Oh, c'mon. It's as though Jesus is making a check list of all the things I worry about the most. My husband will tell you that I like to plan meals ahead of time. And as an elder queer, worrying about my body is simply reality: Is my blood sugar going to spike or plummet today? Are my knees finally going to give out? How's that cholesterol? Also, what can I do about this dad bod that seems gym-proof? Is sex still a realistic option, without pulling a muscle? And quite frankly, Dr. Bowtie has a reputation to keep up on campus, gurl. Don't tell me not to worry.

But Jesus continues: "Don't worry about tomorrow." Tomorrow is too much light.

We really do treasure light, don't we? Both literal light and metaphorical light—they matter to us so much and give us so much hope. Even aside from the problem of attaching too much literal meaning to light as metaphor (which literally can result in both conscious and unconscious discrimination against people of color), light is almost universally perceived as a good. A lamp unto our feet. Your light has come. I am the light of the world.

At the same time, we all know that the sun (the Son?) can burn our skin if we aren't careful, and staring at it can cause irreparable harm to our vision. The blue light from computers screens can damage our eyes. And DarkSky International reminds us that artificial light can actually negatively affect our health and warns us of the increasing worldwide problem of light pollution.

Too much light.

I sometimes wonder if these readings at the end of Epiphany are telling us to detox from the twinkling insanity of the winter holidays. They were great, the lessons seem to be telling us, but you cannot live on light alone. Humans need darkness; we need mystery too. Not everything needs to be clear. Besides: Lent is just around the corner, so you might want to start getting used to the darkness . . .

I find this message to be strangely comforting as a queer person, whose own body and spirituality are such that, even as I long sometimes for clarity and right-or-wrong answers, are stunning examples of complexity and mystery. I cannot explain, for instance, why on some days I feel moved to wear a pencil skirt and heels, when I usually am very happy indeed in the more traditionally masculine presentation of trousers, dress shirt, and a bow tie, or for that matter jeans and a tank. My gender presentation is ultimately fluid, or at least oozy, and it's something that I can't predict or quantify. I know this makes others uncomfortable, and believe it or not, I actually do really care about others feeling comfortable around me.

But then, mystery is at the heart of queer believers' experience. If nothing else, it is a mystery that so many queerfolx are willing to stick with G-d, considering how horrifically G-d's followers have treated us over the centuries. To this day, I can't really explain why I remain Christian, except to say, in mystery, that Christianity is my mythic language—its stories are the stories that help me imagine how I engage with the Divine and with the cosmos.

The thing is, LGBTQ believers are willing to ask those stunningly hard questions about why we continue to be believers, even if we do not have clear, light-filled answers. Or, even if we're not even particularly willing, we've nonetheless been *forced* to ask them. We queers are in fact stewards of the mysteries of G-d, and for that reason, we have the privilege of walking with other believers through those dark places when their religion seems to fail them, because we've already walked through that darkness. We are uniquely positioned in the Church to tell everyone else, as the safe, heteropatriarchal religious worlds begin to collapse around them, "It gets better," like the It Gets Better Project, which seeks to give hope to queer kids.

I have suggested in other sermons that coming to the queer margins of society can be important for the Church, because we sparkle out here. But I wonder, as I ponder the possibility of too much light, whether maybe it's not so much our sparkle in and of itself that is helpful. Perhaps our queer glint is a miraculous gift to the Church because, sometimes, the Divine Light itself is too great to look at, especially if we have chosen to live in the darkness of exclusive theology, if we are like Zion, bitching that G-d has forgotten us because G-d is willing to draw *all* the nations and ethnicities and genders and sexualities to Themself. Our sparkle can actually be salvific, because it is a bearable reflection of that overwhelming Light that people can't handle.

Our baptismal covenant asks us to seek out Christ in everyone around us. So if looking directly at G-d might prove to be too much light, let me suggest that you might helpfully look to the reflected light of the Queers in the Kindom, who have learned to glow and sparkle, even when faced with unfathomable mysteries of awkwardly gendered bodies and uncomfortable sexualities, those mysteries of which queers have been made the stewards.

I think you can handle that light.

TRANSFIGURATION SUNDAY

The Rev. Emily E. Ewing

Exodus 24:12–18
Psalm 2
2 Peter 1:16–21
Matthew 17:1–9

I remember it vividly. Sitting at my computer, typing out the words, rereading them, going back, deleting and changing, and tweaking and rewriting again.

And then finally, on February 14th, I wrote to my parents and my sibling, "In the spirit of loving myself more fully, and loving you more deeply, I need you to know that I am nonbinary, that I use 'they' and 'them' pronouns."

I don't know exactly why I was so nervous. They already knew I wasn't straight.

But I was still stuck in the space that our culture and our world has created that says that I am maybe a little too much. That maybe this is just one thing too far, and my whole self is too much. Too much for these people who know me so well. Or at least they think they do, and maybe they do, and maybe they know a version of me that is not quite my whole self.

And I think about that whenever I think about TRANSfiguration. In particular, not just because the name of the day has trans in it to make me smile and giggle a little, but because in today's readings we encounter, perhaps, a divine coming out up on those high mountains. In Exodus, the Becoming One invites Moses up to Them on the mountain to receive guidance on how best to be in relationship together, on what it means to be in relationship in this new way with the Divine Liberator.

In our Gospel, Matthew echoes Moses's journey as Jesus takes Peter, James, and John "up a high mountain, by themselves. And [Jesus is] transfigured before them, and his face [shines] like the sun, and his clothes [become] dazzling white."

And I can't help but ask is this Jesus's own coming out? Jesus's own moment with these three disciples who are closest to him?

He's been trying to get the disciples to understand who he is for a little while now. Just a chapter ago, Jesus asked his disciples, who do people say that I am? And then asked, who do you say that I am? And Peter came in fast as he always does and said, "You are the Messiah, the Son of the living God."

And Jesus affirmed Peter's response and then talked about what it means to be the Messiah. That the "he must go to Jerusalem and undergo great suffering." That he would be tortured and killed on the cross. And suddenly, Peter's proclamation that Jesus is the Messiah was not okay by Peter. Peter began to rebuke Jesus, saying, "God forbid it, Lord! This must never happen to you."

When Jesus was sharing who he was and what he was about, Peter didn't get it. He missed the mark and rebuked Jesus. It is a feeling that trans and nonbinary people know all too well. Trying to explain what it means to be nonbinary, agender, gender flipflop, not the gender everybody thought. And so Jesus rebukes Peter in that line that so many of us know so well, "Get behind me, Satan! You are a stumbling-block to me; for you are setting your mind not on divine things but on human things."

So no wonder Jesus might be a little bit nervous about sharing with everybody the full truth of who he is. At the end of today's Gospel Jesus even orders them not to tell anyone about the vision—about what happened. To save the truth, the full and deeper truth of who he is for later, "after [the Human One] has been raised from the dead." Maybe then they will get it a little bit better.

And so on this mountain, when Jesus is transfigured, it's a second try, a new attempt to share the full dazzling amazingness that is Jesus with these people who are so close to him.

And this TRANSfiguration echoes back to Exodus, to the Divine Liberator's coming out to Moses, giving Moses all the detailed instructions to hold an entire community in relationship with God. A relationship that will be broken by the time Moses returns down the mountain. Just as Jesus will be betrayed and abandoned by those he has chosen as family, as disciples. But Jesus persists with a courage and love for himself and for them.

Jesus brings Peter, James, and John up the high mountain where he is transfigured and dazzling, where Moses and Elijah appear, affirming Jesus's divine identity.

And again, Peter responds so quickly . . . and misses the mark. Jesus is dazzlingly revealed. And Peter says, "Hey, do you want me to set up the tents? We'll get a tent for Elijah, a tent for Moses, a tent for you. We'll just like camp out here." But that is not why they are there. They are not there to live on top of the mountain. They are there to know Jesus more fully.

It's easy to ask how Jesus could have been transfigured and then go back down the mountain and nobody notices. I think about it a lot. How changes and revelations can come about . . . and yet the world seems to keep turning, missing each insight and revelation. I think about it particularly as a transgender person, as a nonbinary person.

When I came out to my family, I didn't change. I might have dazzled a bit at finally having named my truth aloud for them, but I didn't change. Their perception of me changed. Their understanding of who I was changed, but I had always been me. I had never fit this binary of gender that we have created.

And as my family thought about it, they started to understand that. But it took time. They didn't quite respond like Peter. But they still don't always get my pronouns right. And each time they get them right or they correct themselves, it is an act of love. And each time I correct them, it is an act of love for myself and for our relationship.

So, each time Jesus tries to explain to the disciples again and again who he is, the fullness not only of his humanity, but his divinity, the full understanding of what it means to be the Messiah at work in the world, the reality of what happens to those who work and fight for justice in the world, the disciples, this chosen family, keep saying, "No, no, no, you're not going to die. No one's going to hurt you."

But Jesus knows us better than we are willing to admit.

And so Jesus keeps loving them. He loves them deeply enough to keep trying, to keep telling them and showing them. He loves them enough to take them to this mountain and show them the full brilliance, the glittery, sparkly, dazzling trueness of the divine in him.

It holds true with us as well, when we are in the presence of love, embodied in each person. When Jesus comes out to his closest chosen family, to Peter and James and John at the TRANSfiguration, he is inviting them into a more intimate relationship with him, to a way of understanding who he is.

And in the midst of that, the divine voice overshadows them in a bright cloud and says, "This is my Son, the Beloved, with whom I am well pleased; listen to him!" This proclamation echoes back to Jesus's baptism in Matthew 3, where the divine voice says, "This is my Son, the Beloved, with whom I am well pleased." Which echoes in our reading from 2 Peter, where Peter finally gets to give the accounting of his experience, to name the words of "the Majestic Glory, saying, 'This is my Son, my Beloved, with whom I am well pleased.'"

And I think about the ways that we are each Beloved. The parts of ourselves that sometimes we hide because we don't know if others will be able to appreciate them, will respect them, will love those parts of ourselves. Sometimes it's big and it's about identity and sometimes it's small and it's about something you care deeply about. An experience you had in your life. A joy or passion you care deeply about. And those are the places and spaces where the divine words from our psalm echo with God's words at the TRANSfiguration, decreeing to each of us, "You are my child; today I have begotten you."

Again and again we are reminded of Jesus's belovedness—and not only Jesus's, but our own as well. God calls us chosen, beloved, child.

This TRANSfiguration moment is a moment of openness, of realizing that those things that are so deep and secret, those things that are so important to who I am, to who you are, are precisely the things that God says are beloved: That God says we are chosen and begotten and special and a child of God.

And sometimes, those moments last the briefest of time, sometimes they last for forty days and forty nights as in Exodus, or for forty years or more. Those moments are glimpses now, but are meant to endure, to be everlasting, even as we descend back down the mountain and into a world that isn't the ideal we glimpsed in the TRANSfiguration. They are moments of intimacy, marked by Jesus's gentle touch and affirmation to the chosen ones. Their fear at hearing the divine voice claim Jesus overcomes them, and yet Jesus, who continues to invite them into this intimacy and care, comes and touches them, saying, "Get up and do not be afraid."

In the face of a world that is not as it should or could be, in the face of a world that will certainly chew Jesus up and spit him out—torture, abuse, and execute him, Jesus chooses gentle belovedness with his disciples. Even knowing their failure to understand, to act, to show up in the ways that he needs, Jesus comes to them, reassures them, and continues to journey with them.

But not without condition. Jesus doesn't let Peter, James, and John tell everybody what happened. That intimate truth is just for them, at least for now. When they walk down the mountain, Jesus orders them, "Tell no one about the vision until after the Human One has been raised from the dead." Because maybe then they might get it enough to be able to explain it to the next person, as we read in 2 Peter. But right now, they still aren't getting it.

They so miss the mark, in fact, that in the next chapter, the disciples ask Jesus, "Who is the greatest in the reign of heaven?" Because that's what we do. We try to figure out who is the greatest instead of recognizing when we are in the presence of greatness. We try to position and order and prioritize instead of resting in our belovedness and the divine belovedness of Jesus.

But Jesus never stops trying—never stops loving us, reminding us, bringing us back, creating those moments of intimacy and truth, the mountaintop moments where clouds and people dazzle. Those moments are when God tells all those we are in relationship with to listen to us, when God tells us to listen to each other, to listen for the deep truths about ourselves, about each other, to listen for that love in each person, dazzling, even in the dark.

Thanks be to God.

LENT

ASH WEDNESDAY

Dr. Peter Carlson

Joel 2:1–2, 12–17
or
Isaiah 58:1–12
Psalm 103
2 Corinthians 5:20b–6:10
Matthew 6:1–6, 16–21

Guilt, guilt, guilt, guilt, guilt, guilt, guilty-effing guilt.

Ash Wednesday, the beginning of the penitential season of Lent. The beginning (or the culmination?) of guilt.

As you might guess, I have a conflicted relationship with Lent, because I have a conflicted relationship with guilt in general. On the one hand, I was raised in a conservative evangelical Christian community where the ongoing theme of our guilty humanity was that bodies and sexuality were ever so ick and the root of all evil, and that queer bodies and queer sexualities were super ick and ultra-evil, and probably beyond redemption. This theological filth left a spiritual and psychological stain that I try to scrub off to this day.

On the other hand, I look around and see a stunningly self-focused society, in which conservatives and progressives alike seem to be focused on how "I deserve to be happy," and the parallel doctrine that, though I might publicly mouth concern for others, ultimately salvation is about me, dammit.

I'll be honest with you: the opening collect from the Book of Common Prayer doesn't really help much with my conflictedness. It starts with the hopeful statement about G-d: "You hate nothing you have made and forgive the sins of those who are penitent," but then moves immediately into the reminder that we shitty little humans are sinful and wretched. Don't know about you, but this isn't sounding like anyone is wishing us any sort of an easy Lent. The first twenty or so years of my life were spent believing in my queer wretchedness and lamenting of my queerness with a penitent and contrite (read, self-loathing) heart.

So here I am today, an Elder Queer, trying to figure out what it means to find some kind of synchronicity, or at least an uneasy truce, between my belief that humans are created *imago dei*, and that we are all also subject to a kind of wretchedness. And what it indeed means is that I struggle all the time with trying to figure out what things in my life *are* actually something of which I need to repent, and what are the things in which I need to learn to rejoice. And, perhaps oddly for a queer person, I turn to scripture; and I find, once again, that if I call myself a Jesus follower, then I must believe that the world's values have it all wrong, and that the Kindom of G-d is something distressingly topsy-turvy and, frankly, both comforting and discomfiting at the same time.

There are two choices for readings from the Hebrew Bible on Ash Wednesday, both of which reflect this awkward relationship between me, a miserable sinner and me, utterly worthy of G-d's love. The prophet Joel begins chapter 2 with, literally an alarm: "The day of HaShem is coming, it is near! A day of darkness and gloom, a day of clouds and thick darkness! Like blackness spread upon the mountains, a great and powerful army comes!" I am reminded of Tolkien's description of the Orcs swarming down the mountainsides and out of Mordor in *The Lord of the Rings*, and wonder if this is where the author found his inspiration. We don't know the historical context of the prophet Joel, but at whatever time it was written, this is, and is meant to be, a terrifying image and a dire warning to the people in Judah. The bits that are omitted are even more horrific: fire, and earthquakes, and enemies literally overrunning the city in an unstoppable force.

But then the text does a neck-snapping switchback: "Yet even now . . . return to HaShem your G-d, for G-d is gracious and merciful, slow to anger, abounding in steadfast love, and relenting from punishment." Gather everyone together for a communal repentance, Joel cries. Maybe—just maybe—G-d will change Their mind!

Spoiler alert: G-d does change Their mind, if for rather selfish reasons, because the repentance looks more like an accusation against G-d: "Do not make your heritage a mockery! . . . Why should it be said among the peoples, 'Where is their G-d?'" This doesn't sound like the Judeans are sorry, but are suggesting that their G-d will look weak if Judah is overrun. Is this, then, what our repentance should look like? A sly twist on justice, suggesting that if G-d actually gives us what we deserve, G-d will look bad?

A conflicted relationship with guilt and penitence indeed.

Deutero (Trito?) Isaiah also starts with a trumpety alarm, in which G-d is screaming at the prophet to scream at the people: "Announce to my people their rebellion, to the house of Jacob their sins!" And this is followed by the real kick in the ass: "Day after day they seek me and delight to know my ways, *as if they were a nation that practiced righteousness.*" This is like a direct hit on the solar plexus, because I like to imagine that I do seek G-d, and delight to know G-d's ways. Am I being told that G-d will not reveal Their ways if I am not perfectly righteous?

I'll be honest: This passage reminds me of people who glibly say "G-d bless America!" without considering what the blessings of G-d might actually look like, or what is required in order to receive those blessings. These are people who are dutifully in church every Sunday, going through all the right motions and saying all the right words, thinking to themselves, "Why do we fast, but G-d does not see? Why humble ourselves, but G-d does not notice?"

And they (I) do not hear when G-d responds, "Look, you serve your own interest on the fast-day, and oppress all your workers. Look, you fast only to quarrel and to fight and to strike with a wicked fist." And they (I) block ears when G-d makes it absofuckinglutely clear: "Is not this the fast that I choose: to loose the bonds of injustice, to undo the thongs of the yoke, to let the oppressed go free, and to break every yoke? Is it not to share your bread with the hungry, and to bring the homeless poor into your house; when you see the naked, to cover them?"

They (I) don't like to hear this because they (I) have worked *hard* for my house, and I obviously shouldn't have to share it with the lazy unhoused. And yeah, I hate injustice, but what control do I have over the system? I can't change it. I can't make CEOs guarantee equitable pay for the people in their companies who actually do the work—and besides, I have my retirement plan to keep up. And if the poor would just get jobs, they'd have their own bread and clothes, right?

Let's face it. Being a repairer of the breach sounds really exhausting, and I already have a place to live and enough to eat, and I think I'd rather just pretend that G-d thinks my comfortable Lenten penance is cool.

The psalm seems to want to reassure me too: I bless G-d, because G-d forgives all my sins and heals all my infirmities, and even redeems my life from the grave! G-d satisfies me with good things! G-d is totes the best, and removed my sins from me as far as the east is from the west! This is great! And there's none of that pesky crap about feeding the hungry or letting the unhoused into my home, which is such a relief! But there is toward the end (in the optional part that a congregation can choose to omit, interestingly), a more daunting element that brings us back to harsh reality: We are only dust. Our days are like the grass; we flourish like a flower in the field, but then we're gone and forgotten. And the only way we can avoid this extinction, to persist in HaShem's merciful goodness, is to keep the covenant and remember the commandments and do them. Not just the Big Ten, but those pesky commandments that Isaiah was accusing us of not following. So, G-d will do all these great things, but they are conditional: They are predicated on my caring for the least of these, and working to execute judgment for the oppressed.

And lest we think that "good things" are what HaShem satisfies us with, Paul, in his letter to the Jesus followers in Corinth, has a harsh reminder of what being reconciled to G-d involves: afflictions, hardships, calamities, beatings, imprisonments, riots, labors, sleepless nights, and hunger. Do not accept G-d's grace in vain, Paul warns. Do not be like the audience of Isaiah, who are going through all the motions, but not engaging in the hard work of repentance! Being reconciled to G-d is a life of holding queer contradictions together in our bodies: sorrowful, yet always rejoicing; poor, yet making many rich; having nothing, yet possessing everything.

Jesus captures this experience in contradictions when he warns his followers, "Whenever you fast, do not look dismal, like the hypocrites. . . . But when you fast, put oil on your head and wash your face, so that your fasting may be seen not by others, but by your Heavenly Parent." And Jesus pushes the admonition from Isaiah even further: Don't just help the poor; help them anonymously (and not for a tax deduction). Don't pray publicly so others can see how holy you are; pray in secret.

This is hard advice in a world where we are told that we, if we are virtuous, should stand up as models for others. Shouldn't we behave well publicly, so that others in our community might learn how to behave well too? Shouldn't I be trying publicly to counter the forces of Selfishness and America-First and The-Poor-Deserve-Everything-They-Get? How can I change systemic evil if I do not confront it loudly, and on the street corners, so that my confrontation may be seen (and hopefully imitated) by others? Should I not pray in public (or at least on social media) for the downfall of imperial or capitalist forces that seek to subjugate peoples? I have always said in my work that I am publicly and vocally queer because it makes the world a little bit safer for my students.

How do I fight for justice *in private*?

I really do think that the key to all this is that Jesus is talking about the role of piety, not justice. Piety is, quite literally, the quality of being religious or reverent. And, let's be honest: Jesus doesn't talk a lot in the Gospels about being religious or reverent. He talks about gospel—good news—which is freedom for the prisoner, hope for the poor, a space at the table for the sex worker, and, yes, a welcome into our homes for the inconvenient homeless. It's not about being religious or reverent; it's about pissing off the religious and the reverent.

And that, finally, gives me some hope. Because I'm not actually very good at being pious. I may not be very good at laying up my treasures in heaven (I checked the returns on my 401(k) again yesterday), but I can at least hold before myself a reminder that, when I pray my desperate and inadequate prayers in secret, G-d will see me in secret and reward me in secret. That reward might not be what I'd hoped for (in *The Horse and His Boy*, C. S. Lewis wrote of Shasta, "He had not yet learned that if you *do* one good deed your reward usually is to be set to do another and harder and better one"[1]), but I am absolutely certain that the good I receive, humble queer sinner that I am, is something that thieves will not be able to steal.

Ash Wednesday and Lent are moments of tension in the church year. We are dust and ashes. We are deeply loved. We need to repent of so much that we do. We do not need to repent of that which we are.

We must remember where our hearts are. Because that is where our treasure is.

---

[1] C. S. Lewis, *The Chronicles of Narnia* (Harper Collins, 2001), 272. *The Horse and His Boy*, © 1954.

FIRST SUNDAY IN LENT

The Rev. Phoenix Bell-Shelton Biggs (they/them)

Genesis 2:15–17; 3:1–7
Psalm 32
Romans 5:12–19
Matthew 4:1–11

Embracing Love and Redemption: "A Journey Through Temptation"

Loving Creator,

We come before you with hearts open and souls yearning for understanding. We acknowledge our intrinsic desire to be seen, loved, accepted, and welcomed.

We long for communities that sustain and nurture us, guiding us in love rather than judgment. Life presents us with challenges and temptations, striving to divert us from recognizing our inherent worthiness and separating us from your divine narrative. In our busy lives, we encounter numerous temptations—consumerism, productivity, addictions, and the sacrifice of our happiness for others.

Help us, dear God, to carve out moments for stillness and self-care. Allow us to realign ourselves with our values and remember who we are and whose we are. May we embrace our humanity and extend compassion and understanding to others.

During this season of Lent, we reflect on Jesus's forty days of fasting in the desert, facing temptation yet remaining grounded in your love. We see this as a metaphor for our own spiritual journeys, especially for those of us who are queer, nonbinary, and BIPOC Christians. Just as

Jesus emerged stronger, help us to view our struggles as opportunities for growth and resilience.

We confess the times we have succumbed to temptation and ask for your forgiveness. We seek your guidance to stay true to our identities and purposes, embracing our true selves in the face of societal and internal challenges.

As we journey through Lent, remind us of our worth as followers of your divine love. Help us to resist the temptation to conform to a world that does not fully embrace us. Let us find healing in the wilderness and emerge renewed, transformed, and ready to live lives that reflect your love and grace.

May we, as a beloved community, share our stories, support each other, and celebrate our joys and sorrows together. Let us embrace this season of reflection, repentance, and renewal, committing to lives that reflect your love.

We pray for strength and courage to face our temptations, stay true to our authentic selves, and grow in our spiritual journeys. May we find healing and wholeness, emerging from this season of Lent, ready to embrace the fullness of life you have created for us.

In your loving name, we pray. *Amen.*

We all have an intrinsic desire to understand our humanity and feel seen, loved, accepted, and welcome. We yearn for communities that sustain and nurture us, that guide and ground us, and embrace us in a spirit of love rather than judgment or temptation.

Yet, life always presents us with challenges and temptations. It constantly seeks to divert us from recognizing our inherent worthiness, striving to separate us from the divine narrative for which we were created. Every day, we navigate our busy lives, moving from place to place and meeting to meeting, and in the process, we encounter numerous temptations.

We are tempted by consumerism, which tells us our value is in what we own rather than who we are. We are tempted by productivity culture, which urges us to measure our worth by our output rather than our intrinsic humanity. We face temptations of addiction, in various forms, that offer fleeting escape but ultimately distance us from our true selves. Additionally, we are tempted to deny our happiness for the sake of another's, losing sight of the delicate balance between selflessness and self-care.

Let's face it: Our lives are busy. Many of us fall short in our daily efforts to fully acknowledge our humanity and that of others. We often neglect to give ourselves time for introspection or to cultivate self-compassion, leaving little to no space for the renewal of our spirit.

This space allows us to take advantage of opportunities for deep personal reflection and growth. We become disconnected from our true selves and our divine essence. It is crucial to carve out moments for stillness and self-care, to realign ourselves with our values, and to remember who we are and whose we are. Only then can we truly embrace our humanity and extend that same compassion and understanding to others.

It is the human need for such opportunities for deep personal reflection and growth that the season of Lent exists. Lent is forty days of reflection and repentance in the Christian calendar leading to Easter. It commemorates Jesus's forty days of fasting in the desert and often involves fasting, prayer, and acts of charity. Lent is a season that reminds us, challenges us, and invites us to slow down, reflect, remember, and cultivate our lives in accordance with the divine Love and God of our naming and understanding. It is a season where we are reminded of our worth as followers of God's Love. Lent is the season of naming how we have been tempted and tempted others as we reflect, grow, and respond in ways of Love as called boldly to do so by the Love of Christ. Lent reminds us that we are all tempted in life and that in Christ, we are made whole and forgiven.

I think sometimes we are quick to forget that God was made human in Jesus so that God may know what temptation exists on Earth so that through Jesus, God could be all-loving, all-knowing, and all-merciful. If Jesus had not been tempted on Earth, then perhaps God's love for us, while still unconditional, might not be grounded in an understanding of the temptation and suffering we humans face.

And so God made themselves incarnate in Jesus of Nazareth so that God may understand human suffering and so that God themselves may cultivate a love so great that nothing can separate us from God's love—no thought, no deed, no action.

In the Holy Gospel, according to Matthew chapter 4, we get a glimpse into how Jesus was tempted in the wilderness and how God's divine love helped Jesus during that temptation.

The Gospel says, "Then Jesus was led up by the Spirit into the wilderness to be tested by the devil. He fasted forty days and forty nights, and afterward he was famished."

Now, this chapter of the Gospel, as we know it, goes on to describe how Jesus was led into temptation in the wilderness and how Jesus stayed grounded, not into temptation. For queer people, this passage from Matthew can offer several layers of meaning:

Looking at this story as spiritual preparation and resilience, we see Jesus fasting and being tested, which can be seen as a metaphor for personal spiritual journeys, including those faced by queer individuals. It highlights the idea that periods of testing and challenge can lead to deeper spiritual growth and resilience. Just as Jesus faced temptation and emerged stronger, queer people might see their own struggles and challenges as opportunities for spiritual and personal development.

Take me, for example. I grew up in a traumatized church with traumatized people and traumatized text. God was always angry. God always felt far away and was always disappointed in my sins; God was always judging my mistakes. I could see no future where love was calling me to belong. And I didn't know at the time that there could be a future that fully names how there is no image of God without an image of self, and no self without love, and no love without community, no community without justice, and no justice without healing from traumatized text and traumatized legacies.

This is the work of our faith, the work of the Church, the work of the institution of religion, and people. Today, I know God is love and that love is always kind, delighting not in evil but rejoicing with the truth. I know that love always protects, trusts, hopes, and perseveres. I was bold enough at thirteen to speak out, to be kicked out, for beginning to try to find myself in the text as the queer, nonbinary, BIPOC Christian and to wander in the wilderness to find the loving God, the one who made me in Their image, the one who loved me before I could love myself.

Jesus's wilderness experience can also symbolize the journey toward living authentically. For queer people, embracing their true selves in the face of societal or internal challenges mirrors Jesus's commitment to his mission despite temptations. It's about staying true to one's identity and purpose even when faced with difficulties.

A friend once shared with me that they often felt like they were passed out in the wilderness and that every challenge presented to them felt like a temptation. They felt like every action they took was leading them into temptation. They were addicted to drugs and drank way too much; they were trying to find their place in the wilderness, and they had lost their way.

For queer people finding a place in the wilderness is not always easy. So much of the world tries to tell us to forsake our identity, and when that happens, queer people can lose track of their purpose. Yet, in Jesus, we might find a new wilderness as we find a way to face social and internal challenges and change how temptation affects us—the temptation to conform to a straight white cisgender heteronormative world. The message of passage for LGBTQ people is that in the wilderness, we might be able to find healing if we can survive long enough.

This passage in Matthew also holds a message for allies of trans, nonbinary, and LGBTQ people as well. The temptation is there for you to conform as well, for you to go along with the norm and to dim the light of trans, queer beloved children of God by not embracing your wilderness and by falling victim to your temptations of the mind.

To be committed to Jesus's mission and the love of God in such a way that works to counter these temptations, both for queer people and for allies, changes the traumatized text and narrative. The literal text and the text of turning one's life into a narrative of healing, love, justice, and liberation becomes the lifesaving work of building up a community of loving a people into their full potential, thus ensuring that we all not only survive, but that we are thriving and know our worth and our purpose.

Imagine a community where everyone is welcome, where people of all identities and backgrounds come together in love and acceptance. This is the vision of the beloved community we strive to create—a place where we can all feel seen, valued, and supported. Within such a community, we can find the strength to resist temptations, stay true to our authentic selves, and grow in our spiritual journeys.

In this beloved community, we can share our stories and experiences, learn from one another, and support each other in times of need. We can celebrate our joys and mourn our losses together, knowing that we are not alone. This sense of belonging and connection is essential for our well-being and spiritual growth.

Lent offers us a unique opportunity to reflect on our lives, examine how we have been tempted and succumbed to those temptations, and seek forgiveness and renewal. It is a time to reconnect with our values, realign ourselves with the divine love that calls us to be our best selves and commit to living in ways that reflect that love.

As we journey through Lent, remember that we are not alone. We are part of a larger community of faith that supports and sustains us and helps us grow in our spiritual journeys. Let us embrace this season as a time of reflection, repentance, and renewal, and commit to living lives that reflect the love and grace of God.

May we all find the strength and courage to face our temptations, stay true to our authentic selves, and grow in our spiritual journeys. May we find healing and wholeness in the wilderness and emerge from this season of Lent renewed and transformed, ready to embrace the fullness of life that God has created for us.

SECOND SUNDAY IN LENT

The Rev. Alene Campbell-Langdell, MDiv, MSW

Genesis 12:1–4a
Psalm 121
Romans 4:1–5, 13–17
John 3:1–17

"For God so loved the world . . ." It's one of the most well-known passages in all of scripture, and it reads like a simple equation: A + B = C. But do I truly know what A, B, or C means? For the Christians in Paul's day, it was the "world" part of that statement that was posing difficulties. The biological descendants of Abraham, those who count Abraham as their ancestor "according to the flesh" as Paul puts it, had been formed for centuries as a people with the understanding that God had chosen them in particular, through Abraham, to have a special relationship with God. Sarah Henrich puts the problem bluntly, "If God could simply cast aside all the covenant promises made to Abraham, David, and through the prophets in favor of a new people, it is God who is unreliable, indeed, unfaithful."[1] Or, as the New International Version translates verse 14 in Romans 4, "Faith means nothing and [God's] promise is worthless." And so, Paul is intent in today's reading from Romans on making clear that from the very beginning of the story, God had in mind every person and every nation. God's choice of Abraham and the nation of Israel was intended as a blessing to the nations, as an illustration of

[1] Sarah Henrich, "Commentary on Romans 4:1–5, 13–17." *Working Preacher*, (Luther Seminary, March 8, 2020). Available online at https://www.workingpreacher.org/commentaries/revised-common-lectionary/second-sunday-in-lent/commentary-on-romans-41-5-13-17-5.

what faith and trust in God could do. Paul concludes that God did not cast aside his promises to Abraham and his biological descendants by including Gentiles. Instead, it was a fulfillment of that promise, the ultimate sign that God is indeed faithful. Abraham was promised "in you all the families of the earth shall be blessed" (Gen. 12:3). Far from breaking that promise, the Gospel's expansion to the Gentiles was a sign for Paul that God's promise had begun to be fulfilled in a new way.

But what about the "love" part of that equation? "God so loved . . ." Talking about love can leave a bitter taste in the mouth in a world where love has been used as an excuse for condemnation and judgment. Before Abraham is given that promise of blessing for all the families of the earth, he is told that the "one who curses you I will curse" (Gen. 12:3). We humans talk about people as being "unlovable" or make claims that our words and actions intended to control others and strip them of their God-given identity or free will are somehow "loving" them. I wrestle in these scriptures with who gets cursed and who gets blessed. God, Paul says, is the one who "justifies the ungodly" (Rom. 4:5) or as the Good News Translation puts it in plain English, "God . . . declares the guilty to be innocent." Can I stop right here and admit that this pushes my buttons? I'm very happy for God to get rid of my failings and declare me innocent, and I get a bit uncomfortable with the idea that God might let those who curse me (or those who want to wipe my trans neighbor off the map) off the hook. But here's the thing, love isn't about pretense or falsehood. When Paul attempted to explain love to the Corinthians, he made a point of saying that "[Love] does not rejoice in wrongdoing, but rejoices in the truth" (1 Cor. 13:6). When the child comes running up to their mother covered in mud from head to toe, that mom is not going to say, "Why, child, you look so beautiful today!" Love tells the truth, "It looks like you got into some mud there." And then, love sets about cleaning up the mess.

"For *God* so loved the world . . ." Paul identifies God as the one who cleans up the mess. And God does this in very striking ways. "God," Paul says, "gives life to the dead and calls into existence the things that do not exist" (Rom. 4:17). John's Gospel sets Jesus's encounter with Nicodemus right after the Wedding at Cana and Jesus's prophetic announcement of his death and resurrection in the context of driving the money changers out of the temple. It is in this context that

Nicodemus tells Jesus, "We know that you are a teacher who has come from God; for no one can do *these signs* that you do apart from the presence of God" (John 3:2, emphasis added). What are the signs of God's presence that Nicodemus refers to? Creation of wine from water and a prophecy of life from the dead in the temple. On one level, Nicodemus recognizes these as signs from God, and Jesus affirms that Nicodemus has indeed glimpsed the kingdom of God. And yet Nicodemus, like the rest of us, struggles to make sense of it all. "How can these things be?" (v. 10). How could God continue to love the world in its messed-up state? How could God love me in particular with a whole world to care for? How could God create innocence where there is nothing but guilt? How can new life come from the dead?

Rather than answering these questions directly, Jesus speaks of water and wind. God isn't a puppet master, even a benevolent one, sitting outside of history manipulating the strings. Instead, Jesus says, a better analogy is water and wind. Sometimes God's work in the world is so big we can't fathom it like the ocean or a wind rushing across deserts and through canyons. We can see where it has been, but we don't know what will happen next. And sometimes God's presence is as gentle and welcome as a baby's first breath or a cold glass of water on a hot day. It is this fierce yet gentle presence that the psalmist seems to extol in Psalm 121. This is a psalm that comes easily to mind when caught with wonder at the beauty of a mountain range filling the horizon. There is a longing in this psalm. I want to believe in God's protection like I want to believe in my enemies being cursed. Mental health and trauma specialists tell us that before we can feel loved or learn new things, we first have to know that we are safe. We have to know that we have our basic needs met. And that is not yet true for my trans neighbor, for the queer kid growing up in a fundamentalist home, for the child living in Gaza, or for so many others.

Water and breath are the essence of life, flowing in and through each of us. Jesus tells Nicodemus that it's not enough to see the signs in the world (although that is a good place to start). At some point, we must enter in. We must allow the water and the wind of God's spirit to flow through us. We must follow Abraham and Jesus into the promise of God's blessing, a blessing that is given not for our consumption or to make us feel special, but for the blessing of all. Perhaps being born again, born of water and Spirit, is less about saying the right words or believing in eternal life, and more about being willing to allow God to love the world through us. Perhaps being born again is about joining the Spirit in Their work of creating a world where every queer kid can pray Psalm 121 without irony and every child (no matter who or what or where they are born) knows what it is to dwell in safety.

"For God so loved the world that God gave God's son, so that all who believe might have life instead of death, and healing instead of condemnation" (John 3:16–17, paraphrased).

THIRD SUNDAY IN LENT

The Rev. Naomi Gardom

Exodus 17:1–7
Psalm 95
Romans 5:1–11
John 4:5–42

I wonder how many disputes you have solved in your life with a game of "Scissors, Paper, Stone," or "Rock, Paper, Scissors"? It's a marvelously arbitrary way of resolving disagreements or competitions; moreover, it has a fundamental flaw in the underlying logic of the game. (Never let it be said that preachers avoid naming the important injustices in the world!) Scissors cut paper, sure. Rocks blunt scissors, naturally. But paper . . . wraps up the rock? What's the deal? Are rocks breathing creatures, in danger of strangulation? Or maybe rocks photosynthesize, and wrapping one in paper cuts off its access to light. It just doesn't work. A rock is a rock is a rock. Until, of course, Moses gives it a whack with a stick, and hey presto, it's a stream!

Rocks have a strange mutable quality in the Bible, it would appear. A rock is a rock, until it's a spring of lifegiving water in the wilderness. A rock is a rock, until it is Christ, the living cornerstone. A rock is a rock and remains a rock, but it could so easily be a loaf of bread eaten with the Devil. A rock is a rock, until it's St. Peter, an impulsive and unreliable foundation for the Church. A rock is a rock, until it gives birth. Deuteronomy 32:18 reprimands Israel for forgetting God, described as "the Rock that gave you birth" (as the New International Version translates it). This is far from the only gender-bending image of God in the Bible, but it is one of my favorites, because of how imaginative it is. It's an image of contrasts: the softness of a birthparent's body contrasted with the hardness of a rock; the unchangeability of stone affected by the inevitable changes of birthing, of nurturing and caring. And, when held in mind with our reading from Exodus, the rock in the wilderness seems to burst forth with the amniotic waters of birth.

This bursting forth is unrestricted and uncontrollable, but not overwhelming. This is not water from a tap. But neither is it the waters of the Red Sea that rolled across and drowned the Egyptians. This is not the terrifying impersonal force of nature, a crashing ocean wave or the crushing weight of water in an abyss. It's a personal response to their need, from a God who is holding their needs close as they travel through this perilous time of reinvention, of rebirth. It's a water source shaped in response to their need. Because the Israelites really need this water, that much is clear. Without reliable and plentiful water in their desert wanderings, they will all perish. It's the gift of a God who hears and responds to their need.

But their needs are more complex than that, in the way that every child's relationship with their parents is more complex than the mere fulfilment of physical needs. The waters that spring forth in the desert are the waters of Meribah, the waters of Strife. I would like to suggest that the Israelites, collectively, are behaving like children testing the boundaries of a parental relationship. They have been through some testing times, and in order to remain assured in their faith, they begin to act out. They're seeking reassurance that, despite these needs and complexities, God is still there and is still up to the task of caring for them.

And, as a good parent should, God responds to the emotional need as well as the physical need. God allows the pain of this moment to be acknowledged. This is a moment of strife, of tension and redefinition for the Israelite people. Their bond with God remains a secure one, but it has deepened in complexity. As well as a moment of birth, this is a moment of reaching toward maturity. It's a moment of recognition: recognition that God is endlessly seeking to be in relationship with them, not just provide for their material needs. It's a moment of self-differentiation, as the Israelites discover that this is a relationship from which they can walk away, if they want to.

As often happens with key moments in the journey from childhood to adulthood, this turning point becomes a story that is retold—in this case, in the words of Psalm 95. The majority of this psalm is a song of praise, about the joy of basking securely in the presence and love of God. It's a song of homecoming; but from verse 7, it's also a reminder that the waters of life are simultaneously the waters of strife. It's a reminder that love is costly, and relationships are hazardous.

It is always a complicated business, to compare God to a parental figure. On the one hand, it is one of the foundational, inescapable metaphors of Christian theology. It's so deeply embedded in our thinking about God that it barely even registers as a metaphor anymore. And yet, for so many queer people, comparing God to their parents results in an immense cognitive dissonance. When the love of parents has been unconditional, it's not a bad comparison to make, always admitting that all language about God is partial and flawed. Even the best of human parents has nothing on God. But for people who have found that the love of their parents is limited, or conditional upon the performance of heterosexuality or their assigned birth gender; for those who have survived abuse from their parents on the basis of their gender or sexuality; for those who have to exert all their powers of imagination to create a found family around themselves; for these people, being asked to relate to their loving God as father or even mother can be painful. It can be hard-as-rock impossible. It can feel like an endlessly rigged game of Scissors, Paper, Stone.

Instead of having just one story of birth, of a mum giving birth and bringing home a tiny baby from a hospital with dad, queer people often have many stories of birth and rebirth. The moment we decided to cut or grow our hair. The first time we realized that this intense friendship might in fact be a crush. Coming out. Coming out again. Coming out as something else. Trans people sometimes speak about the experience of the eggshell breaking: a realization that the world can be very different outside the restrictions to which they have grown accustomed. Paul, likewise, writes of a series of births in a reading from Romans: Affliction produces or gives birth to endurance, endurance gives birth to character, and character gives birth to hope. The defining story that he is telling, like the story of the Israelites in the wilderness, is one of ongoing discernment about who we are. It's a story that has space for reinvention and rebirth. It's a story that recognizes every human being's need for grace and help, as we work out who the hell we are, what defines us, what makes us, *us*.

This is the struggle that greets Jesus in the woman at the well, in John's fragile and powerful account of an encounter between two human beings. Notice that there are no witnesses to this meeting: The disciples have gone into the city to buy food. There is no audience. Neither party has to pretend to be anything other than what they are. And so begins this conversation over a drink of water. Already, in John's Gospel, Nicodemus has visited Jesus by night and been told of rebirth through water and the spirit. Already, we know about the new life that water can give.

But the water described by Jesus in his encounter with the woman at the well isn't for washing, but for drinking. Nicodemus was told to wash and be clean; this woman is told to drink, and drink deeply. It's an incredibly intimate and personal encounter, responding to her needs, encouraging her to take a moment to admit that there are things she might need herself. She is someone who is used to providing for others, and being self-sufficient in herself. She travels to the well alone to draw water for herself and her household. She is capable of historical and theological discussion about the differences between Jews and Samaritans. She is unafraid in the face of her encounter with this strange man. She is clearly a force to be reckoned with, a prophet in the making.

And yet, it would appear that what defines her, in her mind, is her sexual history and the judgment she has received for it. For when she leaves that encounter, her testimony to those around her is "Come and see a man who has told me everything I have ever done!" What exactly has Jesus told her? That she has had five husbands, and that she is now living with a man she is not married to. This cannot be the sum total of everything she has ever done, but clearly, this is what she feels defines her. Perhaps this has been a tactic of self-defense for this woman, naming herself in this way in the knowledge that others will be judging her and defining her by this part of her story.

But something about this intimate tête-à-tête with Jesus provides a turning point. This ancient well is pregnant with the possibility of a new identity for her. If we look again at the way the conversation is narrated in John's Gospel, we see that he takes us through layers of identity for these two people: First, they are a man and a woman, alone at a well. Then, they are defined by their ethnicity, a Jew and a Samaritan. Next, they are defined by a common ancestor, Jacob. Then, they have the discussion of the woman's sexual identity. Then, they are differentiated by their religious practices, by where they choose to worship. These are all profoundly important aspects of who these people are. This is an immensely rich encounter, in which they are both giving of themselves and being willing to name themselves and each other, over and over, in different ways, in order to deepen their understanding of who the other person is. Finally, with all these identities in the air around them, a new possibility wells up for the woman, like an irrepressible spring flowing from the rock that is Christ. She is empowered to name Jesus as the Messiah, the Christ. She is to become a prophet and a harvester in the fields of the Lord. She is newborn in this role and tentative at first, but clearly brings all that she has been—forthrightness, independence, intelligence—to this new identity, this new calling. Many in her city are so impressed by her testimony that they are compelled to seek out Jesus for themselves and so they, too, have their lives changed.

How we define ourselves and how we name ourselves change over time. For some of us, that involves a literal renaming, a chosen name superseding the one given at birth. Some take on new names and titles as new family roles or professions emerge for us. We may try on different labels for our gender or sexuality, finding that one fits for a time, and then, like hermit crabs, we take on another that fits better. Sometimes, one identity gives birth to another, as we move more fully into the people we're called to be, like the cascade of character building in our reading from Romans. We may need to remind ourselves over and again of the story that shaped us, like in Psalm 95. We may need to go through painful processes of self-differentiation, like the Israelites at the waters of Strife. But in all of these processes, there is one figure, sitting quietly by a well, waiting for us to notice him, so that he can invite us into a conversation—not to erase who we are, but to bring it to fruition. He is our rock. He is our water. He is the Messiah, the Christ. Amen.

FOURTH SUNDAY IN LENT

The Rev. Mollie Winninger

1 Samuel 16:1–13
Psalm 23
Ephesians 5:8–14
John 9:1–41

Can I Pray for You?

As it turns out, disabled people are incredibly good at sitting. We are connoisseurs of chairs, benches, wheelchairs, and rollators, knowing the best ways to bear a body. In fact, Keah Brown[1] has written an entire essay on the gifts of sitting. Disabled people are also gifted with emotional sitting—sitting in discomfort, waiting, slowing down. We are positively perched, and when life gets uncomfortable, disabled people know to sit down.

I was twenty-five years old when I was sitting in my own discomfort (physically and otherwise) and received the diagnosis that would affect the rest of my life and my identity. I sat on the crinkly, stale exam paper and stared at my first rheumatologist as she explained the implications of my disease we had been trying for months to name.

"You will be in pain for the rest of your life, Mollie. And it will likely get worse as you age. You will never not be in pain."

I wish I could remember what happened after that. I depersonalized from myself and my body, watching from the outside as an audience to myself. The rest of my life flashed before my eyes like

---

[1] Keah Brown, *The Pretty One: On Life, Pop Culture, Disability, and Other Reasons to Fall in Love with Me* (Atria, 2019).

a ticker tape of potential kodak moments. Some dreams died on the exam table that day.

We come from a tradition with myriad healing stories, and we assume that God wants to "heal" us from states that we deem are abnormal or uncomfortable. Surely God has not intended to call people that are diseased—we must pray the gay away and anoint the sick! Hate the sin but love the sinner. There is an underlying assumption that the sick must be doing something wrong, missing something, or are being tested by the Lord somehow. Being embodied in an atypical way makes other people uncomfortable. We can sit in the discomfort, but the ableds cannot.

There was a spiritual element associated with disease in the ancient Near East, and people were treated and shunned as outliers because of it. Leprosy was catching, and so was sin, so the community abandoned the sick and disabled. They lived at the outskirts of the community, touch starved, and often denied their basic needs or human comforts. It was considered merciful to conduct community in this manner, and most disabled folks shunned by family were forced to beg for alms, relying on community support or pity to meet basic needs. This treatment was at the forefront of institutionalization, where we stored away our sick and untreatable patients in villages, communes, asylums, and sanitariums.

Author and activist Alice Wong talks about disabled people not as outliers or contagious punishments, but as oracles.[2] We find this paradigm amongst ancient Greek cultures and the early church fathers. On the border of progression, they argued that disabled folks were deserving of care and charity. Engaging with the feeble members of the community was considered merciful. Disabled people deserved basic dignity that was not a seat at the table per se, but at least a meal.

If we look at some of the Greek used in the New Testament, we find the word for disease can be interpreted multiple ways. *Astheneo*[3] can mean disease as we conventionally view sickness today. But it also meant madness, weakness, lack of faith, and demon possession. These interpretations can radically change the text depending on translation choices. This informs the views of the wider community about disability, and the Jewish

---

[2] Alice Wong, *Year of the Tiger: An Activist's Life* (Vintage Books, 2022).

[3] Bill Mounce, "Ἀσθενέω," *Bill Mounce Greek Dictionary*, www.billmounce.com/greek-dictionary/astheneo.

community in particular treating disabled people not as oracles of God, but lessons from God in response to sin. Jesus rejected these notions in how he healed to restore outliers back into the community. It wasn't about the fixing of disease, but rather restoration and belonging. While Greek and Roman cultures were obsessed with how one was embodied, God was looking to make us visible and valued.

Looking into the text of John, we see the conflict between these views on disability. Jesus himself has to combat ideologies of sinfulness in a kind of divine pedagogical moment when his followers ask if the blind man had sinned or carried the sins of his family. Jesus reassures them that sin has nothing to do with it. Disability is neutral to Jesus. God has a history of working with atypical vessels to do the work, and disabled vessels are no different. It was how an outlier navigated their embodiment that mattered to God. Willingness, faithfulness, and openness were honored with important work in the world.[4] From men with stutters, those lowered through roofs by their beloved, the illness of Mary Magdalene, nothing could prevent a willing heart from accessing God.

You'll note Jesus doesn't ask to pray over the blind man, he doesn't insinuate he is a sinner but actually combats this notion. He takes something basic and banal and spreads mud over the man's eyes. Jesus loves using the ordinary. Disability itself is ordinary, natural. The man sees and goes on to tell the community what was done for him. Jesus restored him back to the community. The healing wasn't in the restoration of eyesight, but the restoration back into the wider Jewish community.

Most disabled people you meet will have some kind of story of healing or intervention from their community. I even heard of someone in the community who was prolifically exorcised until her parents gave into mental health care. I have been suggested everything from cannabis tampons, to yoga, to tumeric with all sincerity.

When I was young, I had a brain tumor that was causing intractable epilepsy with life-altering side effects. Other kids were out playing and participating, and I spent most afternoons with a paralyzed leg on the couch, learning how to take pills twice my size with applesauce. I could no longer attend school or Girl Scouts, and I went to bed every night praying for less

---

[4] Brian Brock and John Swinton, *Disability in the Christian Tradition: A Reader* (W.B. Eerdmans, 2012).

seizures and no SUDEP.[5] I wanted so badly to be the boy healed of epilepsy in Matthew.[6]

My photo was on the pastor's bathroom mirror, I was on the "prayer chain" for years, and before I was due for my life-saving surgery, the church community (and my mother) arranged a laying-on-of-hands. We gathered in one of the small chapels on a Saturday evening after church. I was surrounded by a circle of adults I both knew and didn't. The pastor anointed my head with oil and started a prayer that popcorned around those in attendance. When he ended the prayer, he asked the group if anyone had any visions. Not only were people I didn't know touching me, but they were having *visions*?

I remember one woman describing a vision she had where the tumor fell apart in the surgeon's hands as he was transferring the tumor into a container to be sent to pathology. (My mother loves to tell folks this actually happened.) The main recollection I have of this event was I was confused about what was happening, I couldn't have consented to what happened, and I was in tears by the end, completely overwhelmed.

I went on to have a successful surgery, having eight more seizures post-op and then experiencing them cease completely for the first time in years. I went from having eight to twelve debilitating complex-partial seizures per day to none at all. This was both a mercy and a goodness. I could now keep up with kids my own age and was no longer the weird girl who had seizures. I had earned back my belonging, I was being brought into the light. I was lowered through the roof by my friends.

That doesn't mean I made it out without consequences. Until I reached certain milestones as a nonactive epileptic, I lived with certain restrictions from how I managed eating, to what medications I could take. I had to be cleared to get a driver's license, I have blind spots in my eyes, and I will wear glasses for the rest of my life. I have complex anxiety disorders because of what I went through. I can't be around a strobe light (photosensitive epilepsy, which occurs in less than 5 percent of the epilepsy population),[7]and I can't do anything that jostles my head too much, as I have empty space in there. We'll never know the full extent of the damage, and there

---

[5] Sudden Unexpected Death in Epilepsy (SUDEP)

[6] Matthew 17:14–21

[7] https://epilepsysociety.org.uk/about-epilepsy/epileptic-seizures/seizure-triggers/photosensitive-epilepsy

are several health issues that are attributed to "it could have been a brain surgery thing."

My surgery carried hefty risks of blindness, worsening seizures, and even death on the table. The week after surgery I was able to read again. My hair at the back of my head is a different texture than the rest after surgery. When my mom washed my hair in the sink after surgery, she saw my scar and said, "No one will believe this actually happened to you."

I was used to strangers knowing everything about my health at that point because of safety concerns, or the nature of the grapevine at church, but I will never get over that thousands of people ended up learning my story and touting it as miraculous. They made the narrative their own, for their own purpose without asking me my thoughts. I was used as an example of someone who never complained during hardship, one with an exemplary attitude. "If Mollie could do it, you can too."

I enjoyed growing older and having more anonymity and control over who actually deserved my story. With maturity and work in therapy, I was okay with disagreeing with my parents about this season in my life being "miraculous."

I no longer believe in an actively intervening all-powerful God—if that was the case he gave me a pretty shoddy, incomplete miracle. However, I do see the God of the incarnation curled up on the operating table next to little me. A god that sat next to me during over 6,000 seizures. A God that wanted to understand what it was like to be me. Why become human if not to experience more than knowledge of human existence, but first-hand omni-empathy?

This isn't a commentary on parenting, nor evangelicals and their rituals. But it is a reminder that disabled people (including children) should be afforded dignity, and without doing so we dehumanize the oracles in our midst. A story must be told by the disabled person, or we are creating disability porn, inspiration porn to make ourselves feel better. The blind man told his story, and was believed. What we bring to light will prosper. Mercy and goodness will follow us all our days if we're looking for it.

Are we healing to restore, or just laying on our ego and our hands?

FIFTH SUNDAY IN LENT

Dr. Gabrielle M. W. Bychowski, PhD

Ezekiel 37:1–14
Psalm 130
Romans 8:6–11
John 11:1–45

Are There Trans Women in Heaven?

Symbolic Resurrections in John 11

As transgender teen, I saw two roads ahead of me: the short and the long. The short road was the one I was on, continuing to pretend I was a cisgender boy. It was so called because I could not see a future for that version of me. That life would end soon one way or another. At the time, I did not even feel very sad about it. It was a cold matter of fact. Even if I could stumble forward through the weeds of the graveyard without dying, I would nonetheless be like the undead: walking the earth without a living soul. The body stirred by the soul as asleep.

This is what comes to my mind when Jesus tells his followers of Lazarus being asleep (the same as being dead) in John 11. Jesus said:

> "Our friend Lazarus has fallen asleep, but I am going there to awaken him." The disciples said to him, "Lord, if he has fallen asleep, he will be all right." Jesus, however, had been speaking about his death, but they thought that he was referring merely to sleep. Then Jesus told them plainly, "Lazarus is dead." (John 11:11–14)

Going through the day-to-day journey of my pretransition life was like sleepwalking. It all amounted to the same thing, my body would live but my soul—my authentic self—would never be allowed to live and walk in the waking world.

The alternative to the short road to the land of endless sleep was the long road that led into the unknown, into mystery, into the waking world. I knew there would be loss and grief. After all, Lazarus really died so that he might later be raised. Something is sacrificed in the process. There are things worth mourning. Even Christ joins in the mourning upon the death of Lazarus. "When Jesus saw her weeping and the Jews who came with her also weeping," records the Gospel of John, "he was greatly disturbed in spirit and deeply moved" (John 11:33). I expected the long road of life to be far more painful than the cold embrace of death. Life as an out, transitioned trans woman would mean facing a lot of prejudice, ignorance, and misunderstanding. It would mean giving up the dream of who I had been in order to awaken into who I am. That was scary. That would be painful.

Between the choice of a numb death without transitioning and a painful life after transitioning, I chose life. This is what I remember when I read Jesus say to Martha, "Your [sibling] will rise again. . . . I am the resurrection and the life. Those who believe in me, even though they die, will live" (John 11:23–26). Each of us have a choice to live, one we may need to make every day. We all may have our own matters forcing such a decision. For me, this choice came in form of death or transition. If I was to experience suffering and death, I decided, I would rather not be my own executioner. If the world wanted me dead, it would have to do the dirty work itself. Instead of being an agent of my own death, I would be an agent of my own life.

Transition (like other resurrections) is a calling. Christ summons us to actively participate in our rebirth, like he calls to Lazarus, "Lazarus, come out!" (John 11:43). Each of us have tombs in which we find ourselves. For trans people, this tomb may be the false life of our assigned genders or an overly restrictive gender binary. Yet tombs take many forms, systems that point us in the direction of our own destruction. Some may feel capitalism does this. Others might see the government or police as our constant bullies. Our tombs may be smaller, tiny and personal enough to hold us like a closet or an inauthentic identity. Even if we cannot always liberate ourselves completely, we can take steps to saving our own lives.

Most of us will need help on the long difficult road of life. When Lazarus walks out of his tomb, John tells, "his hands and feet bound with strips of cloth and his face wrapped in a cloth" (John 11:44). On my own path, I needed legal help to change my name, medical help to receive hormones, reproductive help to freeze, store, and later use my genetic material. I needed my community of trans people to show me how to survive and thrive. Mentors helped me complete my degree and find work. Each step of the way, there were bindings around me that I could not break on my own. In a couple cases, I found myself in T4T relationships (romances between trans people) that helped teach me how to find love myself and others like me through the dysphoria and euphoria we both shared.

Embodied Resurrections in Ezekiel 37

Yet I would be remiss if I only considered the resurrection of the body and the eternal life of Christ ONLY as metaphoric. Growing up Catholic and adding witchcraft practices as an adult, I take seriously that we are embodied beings.

We hear in Ezekiel that he was brought by the Spirit to the valley of dry bones. Here he is taught to prophesy that these bones shall live again. And so the bones came back together, "bone to its bone," covered all in flesh, sinews, and skin. Then life is breathed back into them from the Spirit, from the mouth of the prophet and from the four winds. I wish to dwell on this language of "bone to its bone." Within the bone (מֶּצֶּע, Ezekiel 37:7), we find enclosed the marrow that contains meaning, strength, closure, substance, identity, and independence. Like returns to like. Soul returns to soul. The self returns to itself.

Socially, resurrection emerges from the orchestra of many bodies, many bones, resonating together. The prophecy does not produce a single standing body but a community of selves. Who am I without the trans community? Who am I without the language that comes to me through the mouths of other bodies? I do not exist without us.

Physically, resurrection speaks to the cybernetic self. We are constituted by all parts that give us form, substance, and context. Who am I without my special endocrine system in which the estrogen-producing organ exists outside my body and crosses into my bloodstream through a little teal pill. When flesh meets pharmaceutical, I become myself again. Likewise, what are my legs without the dress or skirt that transforms their shape and movement?

The self that is resurrected does not only exist within the marrow of one bone but across the network of collective pieces. Flesh is not bone, and yet by coming back together they constitute a return to a shared sense of self.

But this begs the question: What "self" do we say is resurrected into eternal life? What things are brought back together and what things are discarded, burned away in the purgatory of sacrifice and death? Too often, when such lists are made within Christian communities, the parts of me that I consider most crucial are among those marked for exclusion for the divine and the eternal. What if the parts others would consider too profane and mutable are inextricable from my whole being?

Within the house of God, are there any trans women? Are there any autistic women? Are there bodies that we called disabled, dysphoric, or divergent in this life that are glorified in heaven without being erased?

Spiritual Resurrections in Psalm 130

Several years ago, I was attending a panel on disability and theology. I was not enjoying myself. The respondents were all Thomists who took the opinion that while people with disability would enter heaven, nonetheless there would be no disabilities in heaven. The resurrection and the eternal life promised by Christ, they argued, meant that each person would be reborn with the ideal human forms imagined by Aristotle.

During the question-and-answer section of the panel, I could not hold back my frustration. "What about the saints who are imagined bearing the signs of their ailments or martyrdom? Does this not suggest that the divine image of the person remains enmeshed in the human conditions of their bodies?" After some murmuring, they retorted that such depictions of the saints involved artistic license. Even if a person claimed to have seen such a miraculous vision, these markings of disability would merely be added context to make the saint recognizable for the audience. The momentary disruption resolved, the three men nodded to one another in agreement.

"Sorry," I interjected again. "What about the Risen Christ? Are his wounds also merely empty signifiers? If so, what of Thomas penetrating the wounded body of Jesus? Or the many illuminated manuscripts with icons of Christ's wounds? Does this not suggest that wounds, ailments, or impairments persist in some form in the resurrected body?" My goal was not to stump the panel but to resist the impulse present in far too much Christian theology that disabilities are signs of sin, and the sinless life of heaven principally involves the erasure of disability.

Psalm 130 asks, "If you, O Lord, should mark iniquities, Lord, who could stand?" The answer provided by the text asserts that God returns us to life, ourselves, and community only if our iniquities are not considered. Read through the Christian lens of the resurrection, this has led to many sundry purgatories by which our disorders and dysphorias shall be burned away or left behind. Yet I worry about an eternity without those parts of me that others would call disabled or sinful, but I have found constitute the very marrow of my bones, the substance of that which I call myself.

As an educator, I am familiar with the tension that exists between doctors and patients, parents and children, pastors and parishioners: Are disabilities illnesses or identities? Do we pray for disorders to be cured or differences to be embraced? This theme is explored in one of my favorite winners of the Anisfield-Wolf Book Awards, *Far from the Tree* by Andrew Solomon. Interviewing minor and adult children with various diagnoses (such as dwarfism, deafness, down syndrome, autism, and gender dysphoria), the seeming contradiction between treating a disability as an identity and an illness leads to many ontological conundrums.

For example, an autistic child remembers his parents speculating once how his life would have been different if he didn't have autism. The conversation hurt him deeply. I am an autistic person, the child told the interviewer, there is no "me" that exists without autism. In his opinion, what his parents were imagining was how their life would be different if he never existed, and they had a neurotypical child instead.

This is how I felt when I was sitting on the panel on disability and theology. That is why it was important to me to argue that there could be disabilities (in some form) in heaven. Otherwise, what place could be called heaven without autistic people? Are there no deaf people in heaven?

As a queer person, I also reflected on similar conversations in our families. How many parents have prayed that their children would be cured of the "illness" or "sin" of homosexuality? But for me, a paradise without lesbians would be hell. A resurrection without my special gender in fact would simply be another word for death.

Put another way, are there trans women in heaven? Even if being born into eternity is the ultimate medical transition, where I would live forever in a form indistinguishable from cisgender women, this would mean that my immortal soul would be saved only by erasing all transgender traits. However compassionate the intention, this vision is not benign. It is not substantially different from the prayers of conversion therapists who teach gay men to pass as straight or trans people to suppress noncisgender behaviors.

That I would be a woman in heaven is certain in my mind, if I were to be there at all. Years ago, I embraced the idea that my ideal form would essentially be as a cisgender woman. Yet as time went on, hormone replacement therapy transformed my body and living my authentic life changed my mind. Perhaps I am happier as a trans woman than I would be as a cisgender woman. There is something special about my transgender life experience that I would not want to lose.

This sentiment was only deepened through romantic relationships with other trans women. I loved their transness as a part of them and would never wish any piece of it away. A couple of them were also autistic, and I found myself soothing them with the words, "I love your 'ism!" Thus, I felt all the more assured that like my love for these girlfriends, God too held me and my neurospicy trans womanhood as beloved. Not one hair should be harmed nor one hormone pill.

The fact that my bodies have changed through transition does not contradict this statement about essential belovedness. What is bound on earth shall be bound in heaven, says scripture. What dies a mortal body is raised a spiritual body. Transformation is an inherent part of the Resurrection and the Life, especially changes that make us more ourselves. Transgender transitions—medical, social, legal, and spiritual—play out the Paschal Mystery. Far from taking us further from God, I believe that trans-ness can bring us closer to the divine. May we all, trans and cis, binary and nonbinary, intersex and normate recognize the ways that the transformation of our stories, embodiments, and lives unbind us from the short road of death. May each transition be a foretaste of resurrection, may each moment of gender euphoria be a glimpse of the long road of heaven.

PALM SUNDAY AND HOLY WEEK

PALM SUNDAY

Dr. Peter Carlson

Liturgy of the Palms

Psalm 118:1–2, 19–29
Matthew 21:1–11

Liturgy of the Passion

Isaiah 50:4–9a
Psalm 31:9–16
Philippians 2:5–11
Matthew 26:14–27:66
or *Matthew 27:11–54*

This is a short sermon, because this is a long service.

I am learning to be more comfortable with the bipolarity of Palm Sunday, the liturgical whiplash between All Glory Laud and Honor to "crucify him!" And I think that's because, more and more, I recognize that the Gospels speak the Truth.

Not a literal truth, as in being able to assert that so-and-so actually did thus-and-so, but Capital T Truth, as in showing us, sometimes ruthlessly, who we are, as in revealing exactly how fucked up we can be, as in how much we need to acknowledge that fucked-up-ness before we can find redemption.

There's an old rabbinic story that says a person should carry two stones in their pocket. One should say "For my sake was the world created!" and the other, "I am but dust and ashes," and they should use each as necessary.

I'll be honest: Understanding that for my sake the world was created is difficult for me, told by a faith tradition with absolute and terrifying consistency that my very queer existence is an abomination. Too many queer kids, too many un- or underdocumented immigrants, too many women, too many poor people, have been assaulted by the message that who they are is sinful, and learning that G-d might indeed rejoice in their existence is so desperately important. Even so, I do see a tendency lately for folks (including, or especially, me) to spend all of their time with Stone Number One, and to forget that, even if our *identity* is not sinful, we still sin. I am still, as uncomfortable as it is for me to admit, dust and ashes.

Sin is a big word, and it's been abusively and heretically used on too many vulnerable people, including me. But if, as I believe, sin is a damaged relationship with the Divine, then I have sinned, and deeply. I have not, as the baptismal covenant (with which I pretend to assent) demands, sought or served Christ in all persons, loving my neighbor as myself. I have despised people rather than, as Ruby Sales reminds me, ask them where it hurts. I have acted as though I am the only one who is hurting, the only one who is feeling crucified, the only one who matters.

This Lent has been (or should have been) traditionally a time of looking deeply at ourselves and staring really honestly at the myriad ways in which we have failed our relationships, failed to consider others' experiences as fully as our own, failed actually to seek Christ in every human being. As hard as it can be, we need, as the the Anglian prayer books dating back to the 1549 edition remind us, to "acknowledge and bewail our manifold sins and wickedness, which we, from time to time, most grievously have committed, by thought, word, and deed" against G-d and our neighbors.[1]

We really, really want to believe that *we* are the ones who are living right, *we* are the Disney Princesses who deserve to be rescued, *we* are the ones who have been wronged, even though we are, too often, the ones screaming "Crucify him!" at the top of our longs.

We cannot be forgiven if we refuse to acknowledge the need for forgiveness.

We cannot repair relationships if we refuse to admit our role in breaking them.

We cannot resurrect if we do not die to our selfish ways.

I encourage you to admit your part in the Passion, but don't stop there. Keep moving into Holy Week. The only way forward is through.

---

[1] http://justus.anglican.org/resources/bcp/1549/Communion_1549.htm. The language I use is modernized.

MONDAY OF HOLY WEEK

Dr. Peter Carlson

Isaiah 42:1–9
Psalm 36:5–11
Hebrews 9:11–15
John 12:1–11

There is so much all-over-the-place-ness in the lessons for Monday in Holy Week. But maybe that's just residual from yesterday: If the Sunday of the Palms isn't the best example of all-over-the-place, I don't know what is.

Isaiah opens up the readings with the first Song of the Suffering Servant, who doesn't say anything or even apparently *do* anything, but who somehow will faithfully bring forth justice. The psalmist, speaking loftily of G-d's loving kindness, tells the bald lie that G-d will "save humans and animals alike." The author of the epistle to the Hebrews skates perilously close to substitutionary sacrificial atonement, suggesting that G-d demands blood—is, in fact, blood-thirsty—in order to be okay with being in relationship with us. And in the Gospel of John, Lazarus, who had been raised from the dead by Jesus, now finds his own life threatened by the Religious High Honchos, because of something over which he had no power to control.

If there's a depressing set of readings to start the most depressing week of the church year, these are they.

Of course, the entire point of Holy Week is to take us through the muck, because *through* really is the only way out. And the thing is, we're lucky, we folks who have been through previous Holy Weeks, because we know the ending—but that doesn't mean we don't still have to go through the muck once again.

The collect of the day sets out the message for the day in startling bluntness: that as Christians we are called to nothing less than walking the way of the cross, to recognize that the journey includes crucifixion. Indeed, we are reminded that our job is to be Christlike and, as the collect reminds us, Jesus the Christ did not experience joy before experiencing pain and did not enter into glory without being crucified. In an age when most people think of church as something that should make us feel comfy-loved by G-d, a Cosmic Teddy Bear, these are hard words indeed. And I freely admit that, as a usually-male-presenting whiteperson with a good job and a comfortable life in the United States, these words are like a smack upside the head. And it is in these moments that I look to my queer identity as a reminder that it teaches my other identities how to walk the way of the cross.

We queerfolx can teach you a lot about death. So can other oppressed peoples, whether they be people of color, people with disabilities, asylum seekers, un- or underdocumented people, or anyone forced to dwell in society's margins.

We can tell you about literal death—if you don't think transgender folx are still among the most vulnerable people in our society, do a quick online search to see how many of our trans siblings have been murdered this year, or to discover that the mortality rate "from external causes" for transfolx is significantly higher than that of cisfolx. But we can also tell you about the death of dreams of fitting in, the death of family relationships, the death of opportunities based on our identities.

Something important: I am not saying this to evoke pity (though I hope it might evoke a desire to pursue justice). I am saying this because this is one more arena in which queerfolx are a blessing to the Church: We can teach Jesus followers how to walk the way of the cross, because we've walked it. In fact, we can teach ourselves about this, too, because walking the way of the cross is something all of us need constantly to relearn, any time we begin to take comfort for granted.

Deutero-Isaiah is a powerful and even disturbing mix of hope and sorrow. The so-called "Songs of the Suffering Servant" do indeed provide rays of hope, but it is hope found at a terrible sacrificial price. This first song speaks of G-d calling "my servant, whom I uphold, my chosen, in whom my soul delights," who is anointed by G-d to bring forth justice to the nations. But like any prophet who dares to suggest that G-d's mercy and justice might be available to a far broader demographic than those of us who think we are specially "chosen," this servant will, inevitably, suffer. It remains one of the great unlearned lessons of Christianity that G-d is a tart, and will love anyone and everyone—we are always angry when we find that we are not G-d's One and Only.

The Suffering Servant, indeed, has a daunting task, when we find out exactly what G-d means by bringing forth justice: "to open the eyes that are blind, to bring out the prisoners from the dungeon, from the prison those who sit in darkness," all without crying, or lifting up a voice, or breaking a bruised reed, or quenching a dimly burning wick. A challenge, indeed.

The psalmist seems to be reminding the Suffering Servant about the love and faithfulness of G-d, and it's probably an important reminder, considering that the world does not deal kindly with those who work to bring justice to the nations. The rosiness of this section of Psalm 36 actually sits in stark contrast to the first four verses, which is a message to those who think they're too good for a relationship with G-d:

> Transgression speaks to the wicked deep in their hearts; there is no fear of God before their eyes.
> For they flatter themselves in their own eyes that their iniquity cannot be found out and hated.
> The words of their mouths are mischief and deceit; they have ceased to act wisely and do good.
> They plot mischief while on their beds; they are set on a way that is not good; they do not reject evil.

So, like the words of Isaiah, the passage of the psalm that we read in the lectionary today is a message of ultimate hope, even though we'll have to be dragged through the muck first.

I freely admit that I find the passage from the letter to the Hebrews to be deeply problematic, even though I know it is rooted in the ancient sacrificial atonement theology of Judaism and, for that matter, most ancient religious traditions. But I can come to terms with it when I link it back to the Suffering Servant songs, and to the prayer of the collect. In this light,

Jesus's blood is not a "payment" to appease a bloodthirsty G-d whose anger at not being worshipped well enough can only be satisfied by murder. Instead, the author of Hebrews is telling a simple statement of fact: If you seek to proclaim G-d's profligate love, if you offer yourself to G-d and G-d's will, which includes justice for the nations rather than for a select few, sacrifice will be the result, because those who think that they are part of an elite few selected to be recipients of G-d's mercy will do everything in their power to harm you. We humans find love too freely given to be abominable, and we still happily murder, or at least excommunicate, those who preach it.

Indeed, the gospel is a story of harassing those who love too much, or have experienced too richly G-d's lavish love. Mary's anointing of Jesus's feet with expensive perfume is, quite frankly, an outpouring of love that mirrors divine abundance, filling the house with a beautiful fragrance. Judas, of course, echoing the sentiment of the world, complains that the value of the perfume could have been given to the poor. To be honest, this strikes me as the equivalent of billionaires criticizing folks on food stamps for buying cookies for their families. How dare a parent want to provide a small moment of joy?

We also see that the religious whoop-di-doos were trying to murder Lazarus, because his resurrection from the dead was causing lots of people to follow Jesus instead of giving the whoop-di-doos the respect they thought was owing them. Poor Lazarus! Raised again from the dead, only to have his life threatened, not by illness, but by people who were convinced they had a chokehold on access to the Divine. Really, Jesus? You brought me back to life for this? Could you have just let me keep being dead? You're making me walk that path one more time?

Yes. You are being asked to walk that path one more time.

Because once again, it is Holy Week, and you are not allowed, as a Jesus follower, to skip over the hard bits to get at the pastel bunnies at Easter. I want to be clear: There is no inherent virtue in suffering; instead, it's just that suffering is what happens if you seek justice in the world, if you dare to live life out in the margins, hanging out with the poor and the imprisoned and the disabled, and the queers and the immigrants, and all those who can teach us about the death of the body, the death of dreams, the death, in fact, of our egos.

The message of Holy Week is *not* that you don't have to walk the way of the cross because Jesus walked it for you. The message of Holy Week is that, because Jesus walked the way of the cross, you have to walk it, too, if you really mean it when you say you'll follow Jesus.

Don't stop there, though. Because the other message of Holy Week is that those values are worth braving the cross. The foot of the proud and the hand of the wicked might, despite the psalmist's prayer, push us aside, but the hope of the Suffering Servant still lives in the margins, and we are confident that we shall someday, in some life, see the day when the former things have come to pass, and the new things are declared.

TUESDAY OF HOLY WEEK

The Rev. Melvin M. Soriano

Isaiah 49:1–7
Psalm 71:1–14
1 Corinthians 1:18–31
John 12:20–36

I've walked the Camino de Santiago six times to date. It's an ancient pilgrimage that ends at the Cathedral in Santiago de Compostela, Spain, where the relics of Saint James the Apostle are on display. *Camino* in Spanish means "The Way." Hundreds of thousands of people walk hundreds of miles every year on this pilgrimage. Most walk in the summer, under that hot Spanish sun, enduring blisters, bedbugs, and back aches. We stay in towns, the occasional city, and mostly remote villages, hoping that the line for the dormitory and restaurant restrooms won't be too long. Despite all the discomforts and the time needed to get away, I know I'll be walking the Camino again. I love the people I meet from all over the world, the stories that we share, the countless languages that I hear, the sheer audacity of what we are all doing together. And most of all, I enjoy the way I get to let go of all my pretenses, all the fake-me-isms, all the formality of working at a cathedral. I get to just be dirty, sweaty, tired, loving, laughing, listening me.

For many who head to the Camino, it's a hiking adventure. For others, it's a chance to get away and do something totally different. But for those who originally walked from their front doors throughout Europe 1,200 years ago, it's a religious journey, a journey of the spirit that means much to those of us who have walked it alone or with people they love or with those they befriend along the way. And for those who have never heard of the Camino de Santiago? It's insane. Walk five hundred miles with a backpack going from village to village? Nonsense!

It's probably not that different from those who see us walking with Jesus this Holy Week. We start this week with the earthly glorification of Jesus, and we end with his body in a tomb. And like his disciples, we hear Jesus describing things that did not make sense to them. The journey this week is laden with emotions and blisters, politics and tears. We look at the Holy Tuesday readings as though we are literally on that journey beside him, a journey marked by love, sacrifice, and a kind of divine foolishness that defies the wisdom of the world. A "holy foolishness" that opens our eyes to a vast landscape of joy and grace. And especially because this week is a journey of the soul, we should consider how we can find joy in the broken world with Christ, by being authentically ourselves, no matter who we are, including those of us who are queer, people of color, immigrants.

Holy foolishness is about embracing the paradoxical wisdom of God—a wisdom that often seems foolish to the world but is, in fact, the path to true freedom and joy. For those of us whose identities do not conform to the dominant norms—whether because of our sexuality, gender, race, or immigrant status—the call to holy foolishness is a call to reclaim our truth, find joy in our authenticity, and challenge the systems that seek to diminish us.

As a queer immigrant and person of color, my life has been a journey of navigating multiple identities in a world that often sees difference as a threat. But in God's eyes, our differences are not foolishness; they are a reflection of the infinite diversity and creativity of the Creator. So let's dive into the holy foolishness of God and discover the deep joy that comes from living authentically as who we are created to be.

The Wisdom and Foolishness of God

Our readings today each challenge us to reconsider what it means to be wise, powerful, and strong in the eyes of God.

In Isaiah, we hear the servant's voice, called by God from the womb, chosen to be a light to the nations. This calling might seem foolish to those who look for power and domination, but God delights in choosing the seemingly weak and insignificant to accomplish great things. As a person of color and an immigrant, as someone bullied as a child growing up in suburban Illinois, I resonate with this calling. Our society often views us as "less than," as outsiders who do not belong. But, God's ways are not our ways, and the servant's calling is a reminder that our true identity and purpose come from God alone, not from the labels or limitations imposed on us by others.

Paul's words in 1 Corinthians further highlight this theme as he speaks of the "foolishness of the cross." The cross, a symbol of shame and defeat, becomes the ultimate sign of God's wisdom and power. "God's foolishness is wiser than human wisdom," Paul writes, "and God's weakness is stronger than human strength." The cross shows us that true strength is found not in power over others, but in self-giving love. When we live each day being othered by others, we know what it means to be seen as foolish, to be dismissed or devalued by the world. But in the foolishness of the cross, we find our strength, our purpose, and our joy.

In the Gospel of John, Jesus speaks of his impending death, knowing that it will be seen as a failure by many. Yet, he embraces his destiny with joy, understanding that through his death and resurrection, new life will spring forth. Jesus's willingness to be "lifted up" on the cross is the ultimate act of holy foolishness, an act of love that defies the logic of the world. For those of us who live with a marginalized identity, perhaps even with multiple intersectionalities, Jesus's journey is a powerful reminder that the path to joy and liberation often involves not just acknowledging but embracing the very things that the world sees as foolish or weak.

As a queer person, as a person of color, and as an immigrant, I have often been taught that my identities are something to be hidden or are shameful. Sometimes those teachings are words, other times by the actions of those in authority or who have power. We have been labeled as "foolish" by those who do not understand us or who fear what is different. But in God's eyes, otherness—queerness, skin color, foreignness—none of these are foolishness; they are beautiful reflections of God's infinite creativity and love.

Holy foolishness invites us to embrace the joy of being authentically ourselves, even when the world around us doesn't understand. It calls us to live our truth boldly and without apology, knowing that in doing so, we are living into the fullness of who God created us to be. There is deep joy in this authenticity—a joy that comes from knowing we are loved and accepted by God just as we are.

When we embrace our queerness, our cultural heritage, and our immigrant identities as gifts, we discover the freedom to live with joy. No longer bound by the expectations or judgments of others, we are free to love, to express ourselves, and to find community with others who celebrate us for who we are. This joy is a powerful testimony to the goodness of God, who delights in us as we delight in our true selves.

As an immigrant, I have often found myself caught between cultures, languages, and expectations. It might not seem that way because I have been assimilated into the dominant culture. I am white-presenting. I've faced the challenge of navigating a world that can be both welcoming and hostile, often at the same time. But in the midst of these challenges, I have also found joy—joy in the richness of my Filipino heritage, joy in the resilience that comes from adapting and thriving in new environments, and joy in the knowledge that I am part of a larger story of migration and survival that spans generations. This joy, too, is a form of holy foolishness, for it defies the narrative that says immigrants are a burden or a threat. Instead, it proclaims that we are bearers of God's image, with stories and gifts that enrich our community and indeed the world.

The cross, while often seen as a symbol of suffering, is also a symbol of liberation and joy. For queer people, people of color, and immigrants, the cross can represent the journey from shame to pride, from hiding to being fully seen. Just as Jesus transformed the cross from a tool of oppression into a symbol of hope, we too can transform the narratives of our lives from ones of rejection to ones of joyful celebration.

When we live authentically, embracing rather than hiding our queerness, our cultural heritage, and our immigrant identities, we participate in the holy foolishness of the cross. We defy the voices that tell us we are not enough, that we are broken or sinful, that we do not belong. Instead, we declare with joy that we are fearfully and wonderfully made, that our identities are a reflection of the divine image within us.

This joy is not just personal—it is communal. When we come together as queer people of color, as immigrants, we create spaces of radical joy and celebration. We sing, we dance, we love, we support one another in living our truth. This communal joy heralds the kingdom of God, where all are welcomed and celebrated for who they are.

For those of us who have faced rejection, violence, or discrimination because of our identities, the joy we find in holy foolishness is also a form of resistance. It is a declaration that we will not be silenced, that we will not allow the world's definitions of worth to dictate our value. Instead, we will live fully and joyfully as the people God created us to be, knowing that our joy is a reflection of God's love and creativity. Wear that flaming red wig, that studded leather jacket, those rainbow socks. If they bring you joy, if they tell your story, wear it with joy!

The Church has often struggled to embrace the joy of queer people, people of color, and immigrants, seeing our identities as something to be tolerated rather than celebrated. But holy foolishness calls the Church to a new understanding—to see our joy as a gift that enriches the entire body of Christ. A Christlike love moves beyond mere inclusion to deep incorporation.

When we live authentically and joyfully in our otherness, we bear witness to the expansive love of God. Our joy challenges the Church to move beyond mere tolerance to full affirmation and inclusion. It invites the Church to see that the diversity of God's creation is a cause for celebration, not fear.

To be joyful in our otherness is sincerely prophetic. It speaks to a world that often seeks to diminish or erase us, declaring that we will not be silenced or shamed. Our joy is an act of resistance, a refusal to be anything less than who we are created to be. And in this joy, we find our strength, our community, our calling.

I know how challenging it can be to claim space in a community that has not always welcomed us. The Church is a prime example of how difficult it can be. But I also know the deep joy that comes from finding and creating spaces where all of who we are is celebrated. This joy is a powerful witness to the Church—a reminder that God's love knows no boundaries and that the kingdom of God is a place of radical inclusion and joy.

How do we live out this joy in our daily lives? How do we embody the holy foolishness of God's love in a world that may not always understand or accept us?

First, we must embrace our joy as a divine gift. This means celebrating our queerness, our cultural heritage, and our immigrant identities—not as something to be hidden or ashamed, but as beautiful and holy parts of who we are. It means finding joy in our relationships, in our communities, and in our connection to God.

Second, we must share our joy with others. Holy foolishness is not just about our individual experience; it's about creating spaces where others can also experience the joy of being fully themselves. This might mean advocating for full participation in our churches, supporting LGBTQ youth, or simply living openly and joyfully in our daily lives. In doing so, we help to build a world where all people are free to be who they are, without fear or shame.

Third, we must continue to challenge the systems and structures that erase us, and in doing so diminish our joy. Holy foolishness is not passive; it is actively, vibrantly, passionately transformative. It calls us to speak out against injustice, to stand in solidarity with those who are marginalized, and to work for a world where everyone's dignity is respected and celebrated. Our joy is a powerful force for change, and when we live in that joy, we help to bring about the kingdom of God here on earth.

As we move through this Holy Week, let us remember that the journey of Jesus—a journey marked by love, sacrifice, and holy foolishness—is also our journey, our Camino. We are called to live authentically, to embrace the joy that comes from being fully ourselves, and to share that joy with the world.

For those of us who are queer, people of color, and immigrants, this journey is both challenging and beautiful. It requires us to navigate a world that may not always understand or accept us, but it also offers us the opportunity to experience the deep joy that comes from living in the fullness of who we are created to be.

In the holy foolishness of the cross, we find our strength, our purpose, and our joy. Let us embrace that foolishness with open hearts, knowing that in doing so, we are living into the divine wisdom of God—a wisdom that calls us to love, to celebrate, and to find joy in the beautiful diversity of God's creation.

May the joy of being authentically yourself fill your heart today and always. Amen.

WEDNESDAY OF HOLY WEEK

Dr. Peter Carlson

Isaiah 50:4–9a
Psalm 70
Hebrews 12:1–3
John 13:21–32

I cannot deny that Holy Week pushes me to the limits of my faith—not because I don't believe Jesus was betrayed, and suffered, and died, but because we are apparently expected to pick up our own crosses and follow right along. And as a queer person who is hypersensitive to the sufferings and wrongs that marginalized peoples face in this world, that idea makes me supremely uncomfortable. I refuse to accept that the suffering of the oppressed at the hands of corrupt power systems confers any virtue whatsoever.

So what do we do with this, this invitation to crucifixion? How can we, who seek justice, nonetheless not complain when we come to the all-too-close attention of a violent world?

Liberation theologians of every stripe have wrestled with this conundrum, pushing back against colonialist and white supremacist assurances that the oppressed were racking up points in heaven, using the Beatitudes as bondage, arguing that the poor were going to get their pie in some future sky, whilst conveniently ignoring the fact that Jesus outrageously promised woes to the wealthy. But liberation theology does not, in my opinion, do a really great job of explaining these bits of the Christian scriptures that seem to glorify suffering. I think, ultimately, we can only consider the "worth" of suffering insofar as it is suffering that is inflicted because we have been willing to lay aside our privilege, willing to sacrifice that privilege for the cause of Divine Justice, for the establishment of the Reign of G-d.

The Suffering Servant of Deutero-Isaiah, commonly interpreted by Christians as a presaging of Jesus, though almost certainly written centuries earlier, toward the end of the Babylonian Exile, is an interesting case of biblical valorizing of suffering. Today's reading, the third of four Songs of the Suffering Servant, actually starts out in a way that thrills my heart, as a professor:

> The Name of G-d has given me
> the tongue of a teacher,
> that I may know how to sustain
> the weary with a word.
> Morning by morning he wakens—
> wakens my ear
> to listen as those who are taught.
> HaShem has opened my ear,
> and I was not rebellious,
> I did not turn backward.

So far, so lovely! I like to imagine that, at least on my better teaching days, I might sustain the weary with a word, and that I am open to being taught, and not rebellious. Yay, me. Am I not fabulous?

This beginning, though, with the implied nobility of the teaching profession, makes what follows even more jarring. Because you would think that G-d would reward teachers, right? But it turns out that the result of listening to G-d's words, and teaching them, is a perilous task indeed. "I gave my back to those who struck me, and my cheeks to those who pulled out the beard; I did not hide my face from insult and spitting."

There's a joke in here about what teachers have to put up with these anti-intellectual days, but it's not a very funny one. And it's not funny in the context of this passage either. It's a simple declaration of fact: If you are a servant of G-d, if you prophesy, if you preach the reign of G-d, *if you tell the truth*, the powerful will strike you and insult you and spit on you, because radical justice and equity is utterly antithetical to power. In fact, the Suffering Servant's claim that in spite of this abuse, "the Name of

G-d helps me; therefore I have not been disgraced" feels rather desperate, like someone trying to convince themselves of hope, in the teeth of overwhelming evidence to the contrary.

Indeed, the psalmist seems to be a little more realistic, though still believing in the power of G-d to save them. Who among us, even if we claim not to believe in Magic G-d, has not prayed a prayer like this? "HaShem, make haste to help me! Let those who take pleasure in my misfortune back off, and be ashamed of themselves!" And who among us has continued to suffer the taunts of those who take pleasure in our misfortune? Indeed, the faith of the psalmist is impressive, and a model for us, believing to the end that G-d is indeed both helper and deliverer, and praying (admittedly rather desperately) that They will not tarry. Tarrying, however, seems to be something G-d is all too willing to do, and the oppressed continue to suffer in a world that is in no hurry to change. And I continue to struggle with believing that there is virtue for the oppressed in this suffering.

The author of the epistle to the Hebrews (Shall we call her Priscilla? Why not?) opens this passage by reminding us, gorgeously, of the great cloud of witnesses that surrounds (and presumably supports) us, suggesting that they are there to help us run the race that is set before us. This, at least, is a cheery little athletic metaphor, and we like athletics, don't we? At least, we do until we remember that running a race means pushing your body to the limits of endurance. And what's the goal of this race? A gold medal? A silver cup? No such luck. The goal is Jesus Christ, "who endured the cross, disregarding its shame." Indeed, just in case we thought that enduring punishment and having to deal with shame wasn't in our own cards, we read, "Consider him who endured such hostility against himself from sinners, so that you may not grow weary or lose heart." The implication is clear: Being a Christian, if you are *truly* following Jesus, will cost you, and the only way we'll be able to endure to the end is by accepting the support of that cloud of witnesses, and keeping the eyes on the prize, Jesus—who went through the same thing.

Look, I get it. We are promised that it will all work out in the end. But we're also told to fight like hell for G-d's justice. And the reality is that fighting for justice—at least, fighting for justice for those whom our society thinks don't deserve justice—is a dangerous thing to do. It will lead us, like the suffering servant, to have our backs exposed to beatings. It will have us begging, like the psalmist, that G-d will hurry the hell up and save us.

It will have us trying desperately, whilst clutching our sides in pain, to run the race that has been set before us.

But again, and again, and again, I will repeat in the clamor of all these lessons that suffering does not confer virtue. It is not "the price we pay" to get heaven as a prize. And I cannot believe that G-d takes any pleasure in the suffering of the people forced to live on the edges of society. So how do we make sense of these passages without suggesting that those who are treated cruelly by the world shouldn't complain?

I return to my thought at the beginning: The suffering spoken of here is something that is experienced when those with privilege voluntarily step outside of the safety of their privilege and move into the margins to stand with the oppressed. James Cone famously suggested in his black liberation theology that G-d does this, and for that reason, G-d is black. And further, that we must all therefore become black with G-d.[1] Marcella Althaus-Reid, running with the idea that G-d is most concerned with the most marginalized, claimed that Christ is a teenaged girl being prostituted between two urinals in a men's room in Buenos Aires.[2] I would suggest that Christ is also the thousands upon thousands of people who died of AIDS, shunned by a nation that could not be bothered to care for them. Christ is the black transwoman, deadnamed because police couldn't be bothered to look beyond the legal ID when she was panic-murdered. Christ is the miner, coughing and hacking their way into an early grave with black lung disease. Christ is the child who became collateral damage in another internecine war that older white men started. Christ is the disabled person who cannot access services because the door isn't wide enough for a wheelchair. Christ is the classroom shot up because America will not admit its addiction to guns.

Christ is on the margins, *not* at the centers of power.

Look: Jesus didn't suffer cheerfully or even willingly. Jesus suffered because he allied himself with the outsiders and those on the edges of society and pushed back hard against the religious and political elites, flipping tables in the temple and instilling panic in kings. In fact, the Christian belief that Jesus is G-d is arguably the single finest example of stepping

---

[1] James H. Cone, *A Black Theology of Liberation*, fortieth anniversary edition (Orbis, 2010), np (chapter 4).

[2] Marcella Althaus-Reid, *From Feminist Theology to Indecent Theology* (SCM Press, 2004), 84.

outside of one's privilege to stand in alliance with the oppressed. And we are called to follow him, not only in Holy Week, but throughout our lives.

When we do that, as today's familiar Gospel story of Judas's actions makes abundantly clear, we *will* be betrayed. It's not a question of if, but when. There will be those who simply cannot abide the thought that we would risk reputation and even life to defend people who could never repay us. There will be those who thought the idea was cool, but who despise us because we're not responding to violence with violence. There will be others who simply become disillusioned, because the ideals are unattainable. And they will betray us, if we are Jesus followers.

But there is more: If we are honest, very often *we* are Judas. We are the betrayers of what we say we believe. We sell Jesus and all the marginalized for thirty pieces of silver, or a 401(k), or inexpensive clothing on Amazon, thinking nothing of the cost to those whose labor made it possible, upon whose broken backs our comfort rests.

And this is perhaps the hardest lesson of Holy Week: that we do not get to conveniently play the victim. We are called to recognize that, too often, we are the ones beating the suffering servant, the ones jeering at the psalmist, the ones mocking the runner, the ones betraying the cause.

It is only when I face my own participation in the systems of oppression that I can come to a place where I can step outside of my privilege, ally myself with the poor and oppressed and marginalized, and—quite literally—suffer the consequences.

MAUNDY THURSDAY

Dr. Peter Carlson

Exodus 12:1–4, (5–10), 11–14
Psalm 116:1–2, 12–19
1 Corinthians 11:23–26
John 13:1–17, 31b–35

In the twelfth chapter of Exodus, our Hebrew scriptures for today, we read of the first Passover—and fairly appropriately, since Holy Week so often arrives around the same time as the eight-day festival marking G-d's deliverance of the Israelites from slavery in Egypt. The story tends to be very familiar to Jews and Christians alike: G-d has sent Moses, who was living contentedly as a shepherd in Midian, to the king of Egypt to demand that he release the enslaved Israelites. The Pharaoh, who was probably not enamored of the smell of sheep, of course refused. G-d then, through Moses and his brother Aaron, started a contest with the gods of Egypt. By the time we get to our reading today, nine plagues have, well, *plagued* the land. The tenth plague is on the verge of descending upon Egypt, and it is a dread-filled one indeed, because G-d will, horrifically, strike down the first-born male in every family, including nonhuman animal families, across the entire nation. Setting aside for the moment the *unbelievably* problematic theology of a G-d that would wreak this kind of vengeance upon an entire people because of one man's (the Pharaoh's) obstinacy (and, for that matter, the theology of a G-d who would, and I quote, "harden Pharaoh's heart," giving him no real chance even to do the right thing), I am struck by the fact that this final, devastating plague is the only one where the Israelites themselves have to do something to avoid it. Throughout all the other plagues, we are told that the damage simply did not come near the Israelites—the land of Goshen, the slave quarters, as it were, of Egypt, was apparently immune, divinely spared from flies, frogs, boils, pestilence, and so on. But in Plague Number Ten, the Israelites no longer had the option of just sitting it out; in this one they had to take action to be spared from the horror.

But look at the action they were asked to take: *Make dinner!*

G-d, instructing G-d's people how to avoid death, tells them, not to go to church or synagogue and pray, but to make a meal. To eat together. To attend to their bodies, and to be in community with each other. "If a household is too small for a whole lamb, it shall join its closest neighbor. . . ." G-d knows that not everyone has enough—but c'mon over, folks; we've got plenty! In fact, to this day, the door is *still* traditionally kept open at the Passover seder, not just in case the prophet Elijah should return, as the hopes and dreams of the people celebrating the festival imagine, but as a sign: If people come to the door, friend or foe, they are to be welcomed in and given a place at table. There *must* be room for anyone at *any* table where we are celebrating freedom.

So, eat.

Nourish yourself and each other.

Be at table together.

This is a command of G-d, and a duty for G-d's people to follow.

This act of community, this welcome on your doorposts, will mark your household, and death will pass over your house; it will have no power here.

The psalm, a portion of Psalm 116, continues with the idea of responding to G-d's goodness by attending to our duties, as well as the notion of eating and drinking as part of that responsibility. Perhaps remembering the liberation from Egypt, the psalmist declares, "I love HaShem, because G-d has heard the voice of my supplication, and has inclined Their ear to me whenever I called upon Them." After echoing the beginning of Exodus, where we read that G-d heard the cry of the Israelites, the psalmist then echoes spiritually the literal eating and drinking that G-d commanded the Israelites to partake of, vowing to "lift up the cup of salvation and call upon the Name of G-d" and, reminiscent of the lamb slaughtered for the Passover, offering to G-d "a sacrifice of thanksgiving" as part of their vows to HaShem.

It really is no surprise that Jesus, a good and observant Jew, continues this very Jewish tradition of eating and drinking at Passover with his own community, with those ragtag folk he has been tramping around with, preaching the wild and radical inclusivity of G-d's kindom. Paul reminds us in the first letter to the Corinthians (11:23–26) that Jesus asked his followers to drink wine and eat bread in his name, continuing a practice begun in Egypt centuries previously. Paul writes that Jesus called it a new covenant, but it is important for us Christian to remember that in fact it is not new at all. It is an *ancient* covenant that G-d established in a foreign land, with oppressed peoples. And the seal of that covenant? Dinner. Eating and drinking.

The first Passover marked an end that was actually a new beginning; it was the end of the Israelites time in slavery, in a foreign land, as outsiders, and the beginning of a journey that would take them to freedom and self-determination and the ability to worship their G-d. In much the same way, we see an end that is not an end in the account from John's Gospel (13:1–17, 31b–35). We read that "Jesus knew that his hour had come to depart from this world." But that didn't stop him from celebrating Passover, of retelling, as Jews worldwide do every year, the story of freedom with his besties.

John's Gospel has always struck me as a kind of hyperspiritualized biography of Jesus—the least "fleshy" of the Gospels. But in the midst of all this spiritualization, the scene presented to us, on Maundy Thursday, is all about bodies—and perhaps the least regarded part of our bodies (aside from the appendix, which we only heed when it causes trouble): our feet.

The scene is familiar enough to Christians who observe Holy Week: Jesus washing the feet of his disciples. Jesus reminding them that true leadership is true servanthood. Jesus explaining this obviousness to his mind-numbingly dense disciples, who clearly need it all spelled out for them, because metaphor is obviously inexplicable, bless their hearts.

I'll be honest: I despise foot-washing ceremonies. Especially when it is my feet that are being washed. I freely admit, I feel an all-too-close connection to my namesake of the Gospels. These rituals are wildly invasive of my personal space and a nightmare for an introvert with body (and a horde of other self-esteem) issues. As a queer person who has been told over and over that my body is itself an abomination, I feel (quite naturally, I think) a certain amount of trepidation at putting any part of that body out there for others to touch, to wash. To condemn once more.

But this is the nature of G-d's covenant: It is not just a covenant with G-d, but with all G-d's people (look again at the Ten Commandments and tell me how many of them are about our interactions with G-d, and how many are about our interactions with each other). It is a covenant that demands not only that we wash each other's feet, but that we honor those who are willing to wash ours. It is a covenant that demands that we open our door at dinner, even if the person who walks through that door and eats with us is going to betray us later. It is a covenant that requires us to be uncomfortable, to be in community even with people we don't like, to hold each other's bodies in reverence, to love one another as G-d loves us: not with Hallmark-y, smarmy love, but with deep, fleshy, risky, betrayable love, right until the end.

In this covenant, though we will all most certainly die, death's grip will in fact pass over us, no longer wielding its authority.

It is the end that is not the end.

GOOD FRIDAY

Dr. Peter Carlson

Isaiah 52:13–53:12
Psalm 22
Hebrews 10:16–25
or *Hebrews 4:14–16; 5:7–9*
John 18:1–19:42

Who among us has not, in desperation, cried out the words at the beginning of Psalm 22, even if (or perhaps because) we do not believe in G-d? When the world is rolling over us, crushing the life out of us, isn't it perhaps natural to cry out to some greater being that we hope against hope exists and possibly even gives a fuck about us?

Isn't it also, if we are honest, natural to find that Greater Being wanting, whether that being is our parent, our professor, our pastor, or even our G-d?

Scholars who read Psalm 22 with an historical-critical eye have noted the almost bizarre turn in the final third of the song, where suddenly everything seems magically okay; indeed, verses 22–30 were almost certainly a later addition to the psalm, likely tacked on in the postexilic period, as a kind of Hollywood ending, when things were going pretty well back in Judea again. Of course, it is far easier in hindsight, after the nightmare has passed, to suggest that G-d saved us from it; but that still, if we are honest, begs the question: Where was G-d when we were actually wallowing in the shit? If G-d *really* gave a rat's ass about us, wouldn't G-d have stopped the shitstorm from happening in the first place? It's like ascribing to G-d the end of World War II: yippee, G-d. Except that doesn't really help the millions of people who were shoved into ovens while the war was still raging, does it?

Looking back at things that have "turned out okay" doesn't help when you are a trans kid living rough and hungry because your parents have kicked you out. And G-d's silence is devastating when that kid screams out, "My G-d, my G-d, why have you forsaken me? Why are so far away? Can't you hear my crying, is that it? G-d *damn* you, G-d! I'm crying out all day, and you don't answer! I'm homeless and sleeping behind a dumpster at night, and you apparently don't give a shit! Why should I believe you, or believe *in* you, if you can't take care of me when I'm most desperate?"

Shusaku Endo, in the novel *Silence,* wrestles with the unwillingness or the inability of G-d to solve the problem of the world's evil.[1] Following the journey of Father Sebastião Rodrigues, a Portuguese Jesuit priest who has been sent to Japan to investigate the possibility that his own mentor has committed apostasy during the persecutions of Christians in the seventeenth century, the reader is presented with the great conundrum: In the midst of G-d's silence, of G-d's refusal to act, is it better publicly to renounce one's faith if one can stop the torture of others, or ought one stand firm and refuse to apostatize, ensuring their continued torture and slow deaths? Underlying the entire book are the great questions: If I can stop evil when G-d won't, should I, even if it means denying Christ, like Peter in the Gospels? Or, more devastating, if G-d is able to stop evil and doesn't, can we blame G-d as either ineffective or a conniving bastard?

If G-d could stop queer-bashing and doesn't, is G-d useless?

If G-d could end poverty and doesn't, is G-d a failure?

If G-d could smash the patriarchy but women are still sexually assaulted, does G-d give a shit?

If G-d could cure cancer but can't be bothered actually to do it, is G-d actually the cancer?

G-d's silence about suffering—and, I freely admit, about my own suffering as a queer person at the hands of the Church—is probably the single greatest reason I have had, as a queer theologian, to rethink all of my early evangelical Christian ideas about G-d and abandon the theological "omnis"—the idea that G-d is "all" anything expect, possibly, all-loving. I simply will not believe in an omnipotent G-d who loves the created

[1] Shusaku Endo, *Silence*, translated by William Johnston (Taplinger Publishing, 1980).

universe and yet who appears so unwilling to help when everything is fucked beyond the fuckiest fuckery. I will not believe in an omniscient G-d who is unwilling to intervene if they know we're hurtling toward hell in our individual handbaskets and can't be bothered to send a clear signal that is comprehensible to all humanity. I will not believe in a perfectly just G-d who nonetheless allows billionaires to hoard more money than they can ever use, taking scenic space tours, whilst millions starve. A G-d that gives even the tiniest shit about justice ought to be able to do better than that, if They can.

But perhaps They can't. And maybe that's the point. Perhaps G-d is not actually omni-anything *except* love. Perhaps G-d is just that ongoing presence of love that, contrary to all expectation, is so marred in appearance, like the suffering servant in Isaiah; is so startling to the nations; is, even so, there with us, making sure we don't suffer alone, not in spite of the fact, but *because* of the fact that neither They nor we can stop suffering. Maybe Emmanuel, G-d With Us (not G-d Making Everything Okay), is exactly the point. Maybe—just maybe—on this Good (ha!) Friday, all we are to do is to recognize that sometimes the world really *is* fucked, that all too often evil *does* win, and the enemy *does* decimate us.

The author of the Epistle to the Hebrews writes that Miz Holy Spirit Thang will "put My laws in their hearts, and . . . write them on their minds." Lovely as that sounds, we see, in the second reading that is provided as a option for the day, what it actually means. If anyone had the laws of G-d in their heart, it must have been Jesus, right? But we read that "in the days of his flesh, Jesus offered up prayers and supplications, with loud cries and tears." Having the laws of G-d inscribed in your heart is clearly no protection from evil. In fact, it would appear to guarantee that you become the *target* of evil.

And that, of course, is the entire message of the Gospel reading from John for today: If you stand up against the Powers and Principalities, they will come after you with a vengeance and destroy you. Your besties *will* abandon you. You *will* be tortured and die, or, at best, left to suffer outside of the view of anyone who has the wherewithal to stop it.

The promise of Christianity is not that G-d will come in, like some theological Superman, to save the day. In fact, the promise of Christianity is not that G-d will, like some billionaire theological Batman, come in to execute lone justice against an evil Joker. No matter what people say after the fact, it wasn't G-d that relieved us from that last wave of torture; or even if it was, then G-d isn't going to stop the next one, so what's the theological point of it all?

This is the only promise of Christianity: that we're not alone as we journey this hellscape. That Love, as William Butler Yeats wrote, "has pitched his mansion / in the place of excrement."[2] Our faith is one that insists that G-d is Love, that Love gives a shit, and that Love is with us in the shit.

It's Good Friday, but literally nothing is good. Jesus has been murdered, powerless against the religious powerful elite and the political imperial forces. Today is not a day when we can pretend that we're sure of an Easter Day, because today is a place of excrement.

Weep.

Cry out.

Scream "My G-d, my G-d, where the *fucking hell* are you?"

And then look around.

And discover that G-d is right there, screaming exactly the same thing, with you.

---

[2] William Butler Yeats, "Crazy Jane Talks with the Bishop," from *The Collected Poems of W. B. Yeats*, edited by Richard Finneran (MacMillan, 1989), 122.

HOLY SATURDAY

The Rt. Rev. Deon K. Johnson

Job 14:1–14
or *Lamentations 3:1–9, 19–24*
Psalm 31:1–4, 15–16
1 Peter 4:1–8
Matthew 27:57–66

It is finished!

The Christmas angels had long gone. The shepherds, a fading memory, had since returned to their sheep and the Magi had settled back into a cozy life of star gazing. The baby of Bethlehem had shed his swaddling bands for a robe and walking shoes. The manger had been reclaimed for its original purpose. The glory of that night seemed the echo of memory—no angels, no shepherds, and certainly no sheep, just the women and his mother, Mary.

Mary had treasured so many things in her heart along the way. Mary who had watched her baby grow into a man, a man who lived and taught and shared the most dangerous combination in history: hope and love. Love had brought him to the cross and hope had pounded the nails. The hopes and fears of all the years were gathered up and nailed to a Roman instrument of death. Emmanuel—God with us—hanging on a cross.

It was on a Friday. Babies were hungry, merchants were trading, and gossip was passing. Ships set sail for destinations unknown, political leaders plotted. Life in the world went on pretty much as it had on any given day. It was just another Friday in Jerusalem.

A group of forlorn disciples hurriedly left the city. They had followed him. They had believed him; they had trusted him. They had hailed him as a teacher, master, and Rabbi. He was Messiah, the anointed one. The One on whom they had placed all their hopes and fears and longing. They had seen the miracles. The blind could see and the deaf could hear. He even raised the dead. But that was a memory now.

Even as they marched him through the streets, mocking him every step of the way, these followers turned disciples carried hope. Hope that this will be the time. Hope that even after the arrest, the beating, the mocking, the pain, the blood, the humiliation, he would call down lightning, summon thunder, shake the very foundations of the temple, and show the formidable power of God's Messiah. But it was not so.

It is finished!

Three words with solemn finality. Three words that took everything away from them. How could they have been so wrong? How could they leave everything behind for it to end like this? They felt betrayed, abandoned, deceived. And the world kept on going, paying little attention to a failed prophet. All of it was for nothing! The same crowd he had fed, the same crowd he had healed, the same crowd who had hailed him as their king, called for his death. He was in the tomb now. They had fled. Joseph, the some-time follower of Jesus, laid him in his tomb. This was the last act of love for the one who showed so much promise.

Jesus the failed prophet, Jesus the defeated messiah, Jesus the wannabe savior is dead.

Silence.

We know the silence of this day. We mark the silence, the uncertainty, and the waiting of this Holy Saturday wedged between the deep despair of Good Friday and the triumphant hope of Easter morning. But before we can move from the foot of the cross to the joy of the empty tomb, we must face the reality of the suspended silence of this Saturday. This silence is the breath between "it is finished" and "he is not here." A day suspended betwixt death and resurrection. And in this waiting, we find a space that many of us can relate to deeply—especially those in the LGBTQ community. We know what it means to live in a space that feels like the "in-between"—between acceptance and rejection, between love and fear, between hope and despair.

The sacred space of Holy Saturday is a time when it feels like the story is unfinished when we do not yet know how, when, or where resurrection will break through. It is a day that acknowledges the weight of grief, the pain of rejection, and the silence of seemingly unanswered prayers. But in this very space, this silence, God is at work.

We know what it means to live in between. We are familiar with the feeling of waiting in the long deafening silence. Many of us in our lives have made friends with the in-between space of waiting—waiting for full acceptance, waiting for the world to recognize your dignity and your worth, waiting for reconciliation between faith and identity, or waiting to hear from God when all you feel is silence.

John's Gospel reminds us that "in the beginning was the Word," and the "Word became flesh" and dwelt among us, dwelt with us. As we spend our time at the tomb, with its questions and uncertainties, as we enter this cloud of unknowing, we can be assured that here in the in-between place we find God's declaration of unfenced love. The occupied tomb of Jesus reminds us that even in the midst of death, even when hope unborn dies, that God is in the business of resurrection. The cross towers over the wrecks of lost hope and despair. In God's love, it is never, ever finished.

Yet even in the silence, even in the waiting, God is present. Holy Saturday teaches us that in those moments when nothing seems to be happening, God is preparing something greater than we can dare to imagine. Just as Christ lay in the tomb, transforming the world through love, so too are we being transformed in our waiting. God is not done with our story, and neither are we.

Here just past the foot of the cross and at the door of the sealed tomb is where human cruelty and divine love meet. Here is where Jesus, the anointed one, the Messiah, the son of Mary, leans into the darkness of human suffering and pain. Here in the in-between silence of Saturday is where we bring our hopes and fears of all the years, and cry out to the heavens for recognition. Here Jesus shows us the lengths to which God is willing to go to bring us into God's loving embrace.

The promise of resurrection does not come without the cross, without the suffering. Without the cross, the resurrection has no meaning. As LGBTQ followers of Jesus, we have borne the weight of rejection, misunderstanding, and pain. But our scars—like Christ's—are not the end of our story. The scars we bear are a testament to the awesome power of resurrection, to the power of love that overcomes death, despair, and denial. Like Jesus, we have experienced persecution, abandonment, and rejection. We know the crucifixion only too well. But let us not forget, even as we sit in the stillness of silence, that we are a part of the resurrection story. God sees us, God loves us, and God's love is working in and through us, even in this quiet moment. This in-between time is not wasted. It is a time of transformation and transition.

Jesus went through death to bring new life, through the cross to bring the empty tomb. The same is true for us. New life is coming. Acceptance is coming. Justice is coming. Love is already here, and it is making all things new. The waiting is painful, but resurrection is just beyond the horizon. God is at work in our lives, even in the moments of silence. Therefore, we can hold fast to the truth that God's love is for you, exactly as you are. The resurrection is for you.

God is not done. God is not done because we know that God's work of salvation is never done. We know that God's work of redemption of the world is never done. We know that God's work of loving humanity is never done. When things seem at the most dire, and most desolate, God is at work. Brutality does not get the last word. Injustice does not get the last word. Fear does not get the last word. Love will have the last word. Because in those three last words live the promise of more.

More says to us that God is not done with Jesus and not done with us. More reminds us that God is never done with longing and loving each and every one of us. May we find strength in the God who never abandons us in the tomb but leads us into the light of Easter morning. And may we hold on to the truth that we are beloved, holy, and fearfully and wonderfully made, created in God's image.

And so in the silence of this day, in the deafening finality of the sealed tomb, we hear a whisper, a murmur, a stirring.

Be still.

Listen.

It is *not* finished.

EASTER

EASTER DAY: PRINCIPAL SERVICE

Dr. Peter Carlson

Acts 10:34–43
or *Jeremiah 31:1–6*
Psalm 118:1–2, 14–24
Colossians 3:1–4
or *Acts 10:34–43*
John 20:1–18
or *Matthew 28:1–10*

In my experience, the lessons read at the principal celebration of Easter Day have been from the Acts of the Apostles and the Epistle to the Colossians, rather than starting with the prophet Jeremiah, and I freely admit that this gives me sad emoji vibes, because it's one of the passages where Jeremiah is actually, refreshingly, being hopeful, and not a gloomypoop, doomscrolling G-d's ominous social media shitposting. Jeremiah also, I think, sets the tone for the day, which is more than just the theme of renewal, though renewal is nothing to be scoffed at. In the very queer tradition of the Christian year, I am convinced that Easter is possibly the queerest celebration of all. And its queerness is not the proclamation of victory over death—heck, that's a theme in multiple religions. Rather, it is the insistence that divine love is outrageously profligate and is not limited to some elite group of holy-holies. Indeed, divine love is proffered first and foremost to those whom we would be least inclined to include on the guest list: everyday people, not high officials; ordinary folks from Colossae; Roman soldiers; and women in a graveyard, grieving bitterly.

Back to Jeremiah: The core of his message is basically a big ol' "you stupid shits brought this on yourself" which, granted, is not particularly thoughtful, given the Judaeans have been taken to Babylon as prisoners of war. When I'm experiencing Divine Wrath, the last thing I want is someone telling me how completely I deserved it. But, as they say, sometimes the truth hurts. And sometimes those of us who are convinced we saw it coming can hardly be blamed if we want to indulge in just a tiny bit of "I told you so," right?

But in this passage, coming near the center of the book, Jeremiah changes from lamentation to longing, to a vision of something better: to a resurrection, in fact. Having made clear that the Judaeans deserve nothing less than what they are experiencing—that, in fact, they deserve nothing less than the death of their national identity—he holds out, not Divine Wrath, but Divine Hope. This is a message, not to the country of Judea, not to a political entity, but to the *people*: the descendants of Jacob/Israel. The promise is not that the country will rise again and be a nation-state, but that human beings will dance to tambourines, and plant vineyards, and make merry. The descendants of Israel (and I'm going to keep pointing out that Israel is Jacob here, not the nation) will be given new life; in fact, they are described in sexual terms as being virgins again. This is nothing less than a surprising twist for a supposedly whorish people whom G-d had, apparently, left for dead!

The psalmist provides another example of Divine Surprise. I confess always to being quick to wonder why the lectionistas omit bits from the readings for any given day. Sometimes it's obvious: We don't, after all, like to think of our G-d as being spectacularly and capriciously violent, even though there are problematic passages in the scriptures that would attribute such omnipotent crankiness to Them. Other times, such as today, it's less clear. Indeed, the theme of G-d's expansive love for people rather than nation states is seen most clearly in verses 3–14: Immediately after Israel saying that G-d's love endures for ever, we read that the priestly house of Aaron proclaims the same, and then leaps to all those who are in awe of HaShem. The psalmist knows that there is trouble all around, but that trusting in humans, even if they are princes, is not the answer. It is in response to this that our passage picks up, "HaShem is my strength and my defense, Who has become my salvation." And this salvation is open to all who are righteous, not those of any particular nation, or religious sect. And though Christians have traditionally interpreted the stone that the builders rejected in verse 22 as referencing Jesus, it is important to remember that the psalmist had no such intent: Instead, the stone the builders rejected is the person who has maintained their faith in G-d rather than their faith in rulers. In this light, just as we are asked to follow Jesus to the cross, so we can anticipate becoming foundation stones for the City of G-d, for the resurrection promise, if we refuse to put our trust in human institutions.

In the reading from the Acts of the Apostles, the expansion of grace continues: We read of Peter proclaiming that G-d's grace is available to everyone, even non-Jews. It is important to remember that, though Peter particularly dotes in this passage on the idea of believing in Jesus for forgiveness of sins, Cornelius the centurion was specifically chosen by G-d to receive the Gospel message not to be forgiven, but because G-d "heard your prayer and remembered your gifts to the poor." Cornelius, then, has virtually no specific sins that need forgiveness. Indeed, what's actually going down in this passage is that Peter has not realized that the Gospel is available to Gentiles, as though the Jews had some terrific gift to offer everyone else; rather, Cornelius has already been *living* the Gospel, and Peter is simply acknowledging that fact. G-d's grace preceded Peter's preaching—which, when you think of Peter's doofusness throughout the Gospels, is actually not all that surprising after all.

In this light, we can read the passage from Colossians, not as a mission sermon from Paul, hoping to convert people to Jesus, but as the reminder to all those who are experiencing G-d's grace, whatever their circumstance. Just as Cornelius was already living the Gospel, and had already died to himself, by caring more about the poor than about his own status, so the Jesus followers in Colossae are reminded that they have in fact already died; but rather than being annihilated by death, their life is hidden with G-d. The verses that immediately follow the passage from today, warning them to avoid "sexual immorality, impurity, lust, evil desires, and greed," have often been used against queers (though prosperity theologians might do well to attend to that last marker of our "earthly nature"), but the passage is marking all of these things that separate us, leading up to the triumphant insanity of the statement that there is no separation in Christ, that "Christ is all, and is in all."

So, yeah: Christ is not just in the disciples. Christ is not just in the ordained. Christ is not just in whitepeople. Christ is not just in straightpeople.

Christ is not just in richpeople. Christ is all, and is in all. And that means that our sexual relations need to be framed in that light: not straight versus queer, but consensual and joyful versus nonconsensual and violent. It means we need to begin fighting injustice by actually believing, and in believing, acting, in such a way that we mark no difference between people from different nations, that the poor have every right to life and health that the rich claim to have, that women have been granted the same responsibility to preach the gospel as authoritatively as men have.

Indeed, this is the lesson that the disciples were so stupidly slow to learn in both of the Gospel narratives that can be read for this service. They differ in many details, except one: In both John and Matthew, it is the *women* who stick around, determined to do whatever they can to honor the life and death of the one they thought was going to change everything. It was the *women* who first understood, with both fear and outrageous hope, that death didn't win. It was the *women,* the outsiders, the Jesus followers who were even more marginal than the already marginal Jesus followers, who had already died to any dreams of authority and power. *They* were the ones given the authority and power first to preach the gospel message that, yes, death is the only guarantee of living a life that builds up the reign of G-d, but that death is actually common as mud, and ultimately has no power.

This message is one that, across the narrative arc of the Hebrew and Christian scriptures, is consistently understood only by those who have been abandoned to the edges of society by political powers, or who have been considered the least worthy by religious powers: the prisoners of war in Babylon; those who refuse to trust in political powers, like the psalmist; those whose job meant supporting political powers, like Cornelius, but who nonetheless remembered the poor and the destitute; those who had worldly power, but walked away from it.

This reminder is one that we Christians today need to hold before us all the time, as we move to and stand in the margins of society protecting or at least accompanying those who cannot protect themselves or who otherwise would encounter danger alone: *We have already died.* As Aslan says of King Caspian in *The Silver Chair,* "He has died. Most people have, you know. Even I have. There are very few who haven't."[1] This is not an

---

[1] C. S. Lewis, *The Silver Chair* © 1953, from *The Chronicles of Narnia* (HarperCollins, 2001), 662.

excuse to ignore the suffering of this world, but a reason to work to alleviate it: Too many of us fear taking a stance, we fear speaking out against the powers and principalities that work to destroy the most vulnerable, because we are afraid of dying.

I am asked all the time why I am so publicly queer in my job as a college professor, and my answer is always the same: It saves lives. I am asked, too, whether it does not sometimes make me afraid to be so publicly queer, to know that I will always be the target of haters, of the religious people who are convinced they own G-d. My answer is always the same for this too: Once I realized that the most they can do is kill me, and once I realized that I've had to die to myself so many times already and that I'm not afraid of dying again, I became fearless.

Become fearless. Stand with the persecuted, close enough so that you get hit by the same stones, the same bullets, the same laws, the same hatred, the same apathy. All you have to lose is your life. But everything you have to gain is your life.

SECOND SUNDAY OF EASTER

Dr. Peter Carlson

Acts 2:14a, 22–32
Psalm 16
1 Peter 1:3–9
John 20:19–31

I have to say that, like Mary Magdalene being turned into a slut by Pope Gregory, the disciple Thomas has been made the butt of all sorts of ridiculous scorn by the Church over the centuries. "Doubting Thomas" is the disciple who is seen as the one who couldn't believe in the resurrected Jesus until he had seen him; the implication, of course, is that all the other apostles were paragons of belief in that which is unseen.

Horseshit.

In all three Synoptic Gospels, the male disciples are staggering examples of unbelief, refusing to trust the testimony of a woman. And even in the Gospel of John, from which our account is taken today (20:19–31), the disciples who *do* believe are the ones who have actually seen Jesus. Let me phrase this bluntly and loudly for the back row: THEY ONLY BELIEVE BECAUSE THEY HAVE SEEN. In fact, it is the very physicality of the resurrected Christ that cements their belief: "He breathed on them," we are told. This is startlingly erotic, when you come to think of it: the breath of a lover, a sigh of intimacy, felt on our cheek, in our hair. Had Jesus brushed his teeth, or did his breath smell of coffee maybe? I cannot help but think that it was that breath that made them understand the reality, the bodifulness, of the resurrection; this was no mass delusion that had come upon them. "We have seen (and smelled!) HaShem!" they cried out to Thomas.

But dear, dear Thomas. He hadn't had their breathy, physical experience. Is it any wonder that Thomas said, "Yeah, yeah. Glad all y'all think that. But I wasn't there. I haven't felt the intimacy of his breath caressing my neck. I need his body, too. I need to be so close to him that I can feel the wounds, put my hand in the hole in his side. I need to be with him as you were with him."

Jesus's famous words, of course, have haunted our stories about Thomas ever since: "Blessed are those who have not seen and yet have come to believe." But Jesus could not possibly have been talking about the other (male) disciples at that point, because they didn't believe until they saw, either, the sanctimonious little shits.

Actually, if anyone is blessed because they believed without seeing, it's "the Jews" in the account in the Acts of the Apostles (2:14a, 22–32) to whom Peter was preaching today.

There have over the centuries been readings of this passage that reek of anti-Semitism and Jew-baiting (in addition to the entire Gospel of John, come to think of it: Notice that the disciples were hiding for fear of "the Jews"). I am convinced that these anti-Semitic interpretations come from interpreters who fail to understand the institutionalized power dynamics at work in first-century Judaism under the Roman Empire. In fact, I would suggest that people with privilege (whites, men, heterosexuals, the cis-gendered) can learn a great deal from this reading, because it is not talking about Judaism and Jews, but power. Peter, finally having gotten a spine, stands up before a crowd, and says, "You that are men, Israelites [it is amazing how the gendered term adds to the punch here—perhaps it has been left out because men don't want to take responsibility for the death of Jesus?], listen . . . Jesus the Nazarene, a man attested to you by G-d with deeds of power . . . you crucified and killed by the hands of those outside the law."

Peter is not blaming "the Jews" for the crucifixion, except insofar as the power structures of Second Temple Judaism made that crucifixion inevitable, because Jesus dared to challenge those very structures. This sounds to me a great deal like the prophetic language being spoken today, to the power structures that continue to crucify people who challenge them. Listen to Peter's words again, in a new light:

> You that are men, white straight men: Listen to what I have to say: Dr Martin Luther King Jr., a man attested to you by G-d with deeds

> of power, wonders, and signs that G-d did through him among you . . . this man, handed over to you according to the definite plan and foreknowledge of G-d, you crucified and killed by the hands of those outside the law.

Or substitute Harvey Milk. Or Ciara McElveen. Or Matthew Shepard. Or Latina Herring. Or substitute anyone who has suffered and died because systemic power structures were either threatened by their existence, or could not be bothered about them.

The tragedy of today's reading from the Acts is that it does not finish the job. Because after the reading finishes with the devastating, "Therefore let the entire house of Israel [let all the beneficiaries of the straight white male power structure] know with certainty that G-d has made [Christ] both ruler and Messiah, this Jesus whom you crucified."

But here's the key: Instead of recoiling, the way we (I) do so often, in all my white male fragility, the people listening to Peter recognized that he spoke truth about institutionalized violence and power, and they repented of their participation in that power. And "they devoted themselves to the apostles' teaching and fellowship, to the breaking of bread and the prayers."

And it gets even more astonishing: because that fellowship, that shared meal, and that praying? They resulted in a radical lifestyle change that dared to challenge Capital P Power. "All who believed were together and had all things in common; they would sell their possessions and goods and distribute the proceeds to all, as any had need." Is it anyone wonder that "day by day the Lord added to their number"?

If we end the reading with Peter blaming "the Jews" for all the fuckery that happened to Jesus, this reading has no meaning except meanness. But Peter wasn't blaming the Jews: He was blaming systemic power wielded by those who had no qualms whatsoever about using violence to maintain that power. And the people who heard him were convicted, not because they were the ones hammering nails into Jesus's hands, so that Thomas later could finger the holes, but because they recognized that they had bought into those very systems that were killing people.

I can only ask myself what institutionalized power is crucifying people today. What power structures are so desperate to keep health care out of reach that we will let people die in a land that claims to protect its citizens?

What institutions are driving a world in which having a roof over one's head is not considered a right, but a luxury? What systemic governmental structures are so desperate to maintain control that they would allow the children of Flint, Michigan, to suffer lead poisoning rather than rebuild the infrastructure so it could deliver clean water? What corporations are so concerned about maximizing profits that they are willing to dispense with clean air? How long will we provide equal rights for queers, but only if it is economically profitable for alcohol companies that encourage or at least wink at startling rates of alcoholism and addiction in queer communities? How long will we ignore the financial structures that do not provide equal access for people of color?

And how long are we going to let our own fragility, our own insistence that it is not ME doing this, that I am not the one responsible, how long will we let our desperate need to be innocent of these grave, corporate sins, keep us from daring to challenge the systems?

When will we spend time together in the temple, then go home and break bread together, knowing that there is enough for everyone if we refuse to be greedy? When will we find ourselves eating our shared food with glad and generous hearts?

Many Christians across the United States seem to have an idea that Christianity is under attack. They may in fact be right. But what they seem not to realize is that it is usually those very Christians who are on the front lines of that attack. They are killing their faith, because they have turned it into a religion that celebrates soteriological selfishness and greed. It is about ME getting into heaven, and it is, more often than not, about assuming that G-d's blessing is seen in how much shit I've been able to collect, and how deeply I've been able to nestle into the systemic power structures of this world.

There's a serious problem with that: Jesus didn't preach it, and neither did Peter.

Peter wasn't saying, "Stop being Jewish," or "Stop being white," or "Stop being male." His message was harder than that. He preached, "Stop the temple power structure. Stop white supremacy. Stop patriarchy."

Jesus preached this too: "Stop accepting the world's values. Stop thinking you have to participate in the world's power structures because 'that's how the world works.' Stop thinking you can't make a difference. You may not be able to see it yet, but some things have to be believed to be seen.

Look! My wounds are all around you. Finger me. Shove your fist in me. Then believe me. And even if your participation in racism, patriarchy, and heterosexism keep you from seeing? Believe me anyway."

As Peter wrote to the diaspora (1 Peter 1:3–9), "Even though you do not see him now, you believe in him and rejoice with an indescribable and glorious joy, for you are receiving the outcome of your faith, the salvation of your souls."

Blessed indeed are those, like the Jews in the Acts of the Apostles, who have not seen, and yet have believed and recognized that resurrection power is stronger than systemic violence.

And did something about it.

THIRD SUNDAY OF EASTER

Dr. Peter Carlson

Acts 2:14a, 36–41
Psalm 116:1–3, 10–17
1 Peter 1:17–23
Luke 24:13–35

I think it can be a challenge, in the "down days" following Easter, to keep up the excitement of the resurrection.

I mean, don't get me wrong: Jesus dying and coming back to life again is a zinger plot twist! But at that point, you kind of feel like the author of the story should just sort of wrap things up on the high note, and tidy everything away. But here we are, stuck with fifty days to get through after the emotional staggerment of Holy Week and Easter. There's a reason we tend to call the first Sunday after Easter, when all of the church workers, unpaid and paid, lay and ordained, are completely bulldozed, "Low Sunday."

But these low days, in their persistent flow toward the fiery downdraft of the Holy Spirit on Pentecost, are an invitation to be still, and to learn to attend to what is around us. Attending to things is something we're not very good at in these busy, digital days. Consumer culture wants us always to be looking to the next thing, distracted by the next sound bite, lusting after the next influencer's promotion. Indeed, they want us, not to attend to what they say and do and show us, but to *pay attention*, a result of their thinking in cold economic terms. But today, for this time together, I am going to ask us to stop, and breathe for a moment, and attend.

The reading from the second chapter of the Acts of the Apostles can feel a little disjointed, and no surprise, as it is, as it were, a sound bite from a much longer speech given by Peter after the in-spiring Holy Spiriting of Pentecost. Indeed, the *glossolalia*, or speaking in various languages, was so outrageous that some of the onlookers accused the Apostles of being stinko (to which Peter responded that they couldn't be schnockered, because it was only nine in the morning—to which I can only respond that he'd obviously never been to a gay brunch). The key, though, is that we are only getting the very end of the speech, in which Peter is quoting from the prophet Joel, proclaiming wonders in the heavens, and connecting it all to Jesus, "a man attested to you by G-d with deeds of power, wonders, and signs," and who was then murdered, and raised from the dead "because it was impossible for him to be held in its power." After quoting a portion of Psalms 16 and 110, Peter suggests to the audience that the psalmist David was, indeed, speaking of Jesus and, with a beautifully dramatic flourish, concludes with the opening of our lesson for today. It is that entire previous speech, not just verse 36, that cut the people to the heart. Peter's own witness to the resurrection and ascension of Jesus and to the descent of the Holy Spirit gave him the ability to speak so passionately that "about three thousand persons were added" to their number that day. The people, attending to Peter's words, heard, I am convinced, more than the words alone. Who among us has not been lifted up by words, eloquently spoken or written, to a place where we see new things and have knowledge that goes beyond mere logic?

Indeed, we are convinced that these people saw something powerful and new in their lives, because the first thing they did (in the verses that immediately follow our reading) was to "sell their possessions and goods and distribute the proceeds to all, as any had need." I will freely admit that, if this is what contact with a truly Spirit-infused person will do to me, I'm not sure I want to attend to their words. I am a very timid gay, and I like my stuff.

Psalm 116 is a poem of salvation from disaster, and praise to G-d for that salvation. The psalmist was in fear for their life: "The snares of death encompassed me; the pangs of Sheol laid hold on me; I suffered distress and anguish." Many of us may have been in a situation like this. For those who live as members of marginalized communities, the snares of death may seem to entangle more than is fair. But the psalmist was saved by G-d, and—this is key—instead of just saying "thanks," and getting on with things, the psalmist stops, taking time to attend to the miracle, and to consider most appropriate response. "What shall I return to HaShem for all Their bounty to me? I will lift up the cup of salvation and call upon the Name of HaShem." There is something marvelous in this psalm about the willingness to stop and sit and, as it were, raise a glass to G-d, and call upon G-d's holy Name.

The author of the First Epistle of Peter, whomsoever it might actually be, is also calling Jesus followers to attend to what is actually going on. Writing to Christians dispersed throughout Asia Minor, Peter (let's just call him that) is encouraging them not to be disheartened by the persecutions that are taking place, and to persevere in their faith and holy living. He writes, "If you invoke as a Holy Parent the one who judges all people impartially according to their deeds, live in reverent fear during the time of your exile." (I am, by the way, inclined to think that "exile" in this reading actually means our life here on earth, as opposed to the "home" of eternal life in heaven.) The reason they are able to invoke G-d as a loving parent is because, as we read a few verses before, "although you have not seen him, you love him; and even though you do not see him now, you believe in him and are filled with an inexpressible and glorious joy, for you are receiving the outcome of your faith, the salvation of your souls" (1 Peter 1:8). These are people who attended to the message of Jesus as witnessed by the apostles, and who, even though they'd never met him, heard truth in the words, and believed in that truth. And while they might have been getting anxious that Jesus had not yet returned, Peter is encouraging them to persist, to continue attending, "by your obedience to the truth so that you have genuine mutual love, love one another deeply from the heart." And because of that sustained attention, Peter reminds them, "You have been born anew."

Arguably the most beautiful scriptural story of attending to things is our reading from the Gospel of Luke today; it's probably familiar to many of you. We are told that two of the disciples of Jesus (apparently not two of the eleven apostles) were walking along the road toward a town called Emmaus and talking excitedly about nothing less than the news that Jesus was missing from the tomb and had risen from the dead. A hot topic indeed! In fact, I can't really imagine them talking about anything else, can you? And while they're ambling on, we're told, "Jesus himself came near and went with them, *but their eyes were kept from recognizing him.*"

I really think this is important. How many of us have been so excited about something, or have been so occupied by certain thoughts or events, that you couldn't even see what was right in front of you? I admit to letting this happen on a regular basis. My heart is overwhelmed with cares, or I'm so focused on getting to my next class, or I'm busy working on writing a sermon, and I stop attending to the moment, to the present, to what and who is, truly, present. This is obviously what's going on here. Jesus, playing it cool, asks, "So what're all y'all talking about?" And they say, "Dude, seriously? You haven't heard about the wild stuff going down lately?" And Jesus (I imagine him inwardly smiling) says, "What stuff?"

And I love this response that Cleopas, one of the guys, gives:

> The things about Jesus of Nazareth, who was a prophet mighty in deed and word before G-d and all the people, and how our chief priests and leaders handed him over to be condemned to death and crucified him. But we had hoped that he was the one to redeem Israel. [*insert sad emoji*] Yes, and besides all this, it is now the third day since these things took place. Moreover, some women of our group astounded us. They were at the tomb early this morning, and when they did not find his body there, they came back and told us that they had indeed seen a vision of angels who said that he was alive. [*insert disbelieving emoji*] Some of those who were with us went to the tomb and found it just as the women had said; but they did not see him. [*insert OMG emoji!*]

Jesus, then, unpacks for the two people (who, remember, still do not recognize him) the entire prophetic history, leading up to Jesus himself, and showing them most definitely that Jesus is, in fact, the Messianic hope. By this time, of course, they're getting close to their destination, and Jesus makes as if to keep walking, but they (clearly impressed with his ability to interpret the Law and the Prophets), ask him to hang out and have something to eat with them.

And all this leads to the kicker: "When he was at the table with them, he took bread, blessed and broke it, and gave it to them. Then their eyes were opened, and they recognized him; and he vanished from their sight."

Then their eyes were opened. Not while Jesus was expounding scripture, not while he was walking along with them all that time, but when they stopped, and slowed down, and attended to their bodies with a meal. It was in the simple act of sitting down together and breaking bread, that they saw Jesus—that they saw, in fact, the Divine, present in their lives.

I have sometimes joked that having a PhD is not a sign of intelligence, but of persistence and sustained attention. Even so, I cannot deny that slowing down and giving attention to things is difficult for me, and our technology has not made it easier. We no longer meet potential romantic interests at a shared meal—we have potentially appropriate mates preselected according to some obscure metric. Even something as primal as cruising for sex is now on apps like Grindr, where you can just swipe someone off your screen with the flick of a finger, and the art of small talk is irrelevant. Probably those moments when I have been most fully attentive have been, like the psalmist, when "the snares of death entangled" my queer body. During the AIDS pandemic, I lived from moment to moment, seemingly offering deep attention to every moment. Why do I not bring that attentiveness into my life now, when AIDS is no longer the threat it used to be? Perhaps like Peter's audience in the Acts of the Apostles, I need to listen carefully and, when I hear the truth, live into it with my fullest, fabulous self, sharing everything I have with those in need.

And like the persecuted audience of Peter's Epistle, we queerfolx need to learn to turn our backs on the forces that seek to harm us, and instead attend to living holy lives, in the moment. And we all of us need to learn to attend to our bodies, because very often it is when we are eating with others that we will most fully know that they too are an incarnation of Christ resurrected, burning our hearts within us.

FOURTH SUNDAY OF EASTER

Dr. Peter Carlson

Acts 2:42–47
Psalm 23
1 Peter 2:19–25
John 10:1–10

"Good Shepherd" is pretty much a contradiction in terms. Just sayin'. But that's a point I'll get to later.

The readings for Christ the Good Shepherd Sunday are a mish-mash of wonkiness, if you're trying to get an answer to the age-old question, "How shall we then live?" (Although the Israelites Ezekiel was referring to were asking the question quite literally.) How SHALL we live? What will mark us in the world as Christians? With what attitude ought we face the insanity of this world? What on EARTH are the lessons offering me as I struggle through the weight of grading, writing a book review, prepping a paper for presentation, and trying to get my tenure packet together?

Or, if I'm not going to be completely and totally selfish, what are they offering me in a world that shuns refugees, that murders people of color and trans folk, that assumes women are lying about having been raped, and that blames the poor and the sick for their lack of access to health care?

Actually, quite a bit, though perhaps at first it might seem that we are getting a mixed message.

The shepherd-y bits of the readings are only in the psalm (good ol' Psalm 23), and the Gospel. The first reading, from the Acts of the Apostles, is the Commie Pinko reading, where no one owns anything, where they all hold property in common, and distribute the proceeds of their efforts to everyone, regardless of name, rank, or serial number. "And day by day the Lord added to their number those who were being saved."

There are some important things to note here: Many were saved by Peter's preaching apparently, but more are saved because of the actions of the community. This ought to be a massive alert to mainline Christian churches who wonder why their numbers are shrinking. The assumption is that, if you walk the walk, people will recognize it, and join you. (That's not necessarily true, of course, but it's probably helpful to remember that the Roman Empire was in no way interested in the well-being of its most desperate people. Strangely, that sounds very much like the attitude of recent movements in our national government. If so, this passage might very well function as a warning cry to the churches.) The key, it seems to me, is that this community of early believers was radically countercultural, refusing to buy (literally) into the prevailing economic and class viewpoints. What is remarkable is that these people go to church, but then they GO HOME to break the bread. They eat their food not only with glad hearts but with generous ones, and they have the goodwill of the people (if not of the government).

I love the liturgy of the church—but I often wonder if it is entirely the wrong way to be worshipping together. Should we, like the early community of Jesus followers, be going to church (temple) to atone for our fractured relationship with G-d, literally to at-one with G-d again, and then go home to break bread together there? When did church become an "I'm Okay-You're Okay" place so we could go home and ignore the plight of those who do not have our benefits? When did church become a place to affirm our goodness, rather than a place to bring our brokenness to G-d for healing?

Don't get me wrong: I spent years assuming that my brokenness was beyond repair. I needed to hear that I was known and loved by G-d. False guilt is lethal and can lead to despair. But there's a danger in helping people get rid of their false guilt too: The danger is that we throw our real guilt out the window at the same time. We assume that because G-d created us in G-d's image, male and female and nonbinary, gay and straight and bi and asexual, dis- or differently abled or temporarily able-bodied, we too often assume that G-d's image in us means we have nothing to confess.

Sin is a Thing, folks. Just because queer folk and people of color and nonmales and non-Americans are made in the image of G-d doesn't mean that we are not fully capable of separating ourselves from G-d, of fracturing our relationship with the Divine.

We *need* church to be a place that welcomes us, not because we are whole, but because we are fractured. Church needs to be a place where we can confess that and know that G-d is willing to work in and around our fracturedness, and give us light that can shine out through the cracks. But then we need to take the affirmation received and bring our fractured lives back into the world, where we see everyone as just as fractured, just as loved, and we break bread together, and we share everything we have with everyone we know and everyone we don't know. We need to confess our willingness to have health care available only to a deserving few, to blame the poor for their own poverty, and not really to care that people are dying because we won't open our borders to refugees. Until we confess that, and change our lives, and go back to our homes and open the doors, and welcome the strangers to our tables, we will only be able to eat our food with greedy and suspicious hearts. And that is *not* what the early church modeled for us.

FIFTH SUNDAY OF EASTER

The Rev. Melissa Campbell-Langdell

Acts 7:55–60
Psalm 31:1–5, 15–16
1 Peter 2:2–10
John 14:1–14

Jesus said, "Do not let your hearts be troubled. Believe in God, believe also in me."

"And they'll know we are Christians by our love, by our love."

In our current world, we hear many statements about love. One statement that I heard recently struck me as kind of sad, and another was a challenge to me. A friend referred to the song "They Will Know We Are Christians by Our Love"[1] and said that it sometimes makes them cringe because many folks do not feel love from the Christians in the public square. And I had to agree. Many who identify as Christian support legislation that feels outright hateful to many in various communities, whether they be people of color, LGBTQ folx, or other communities. We queer folk just don't feel the love when our families feel under attack and our very identity feels under siege.

To balance this, I think of another quotation of varying attribution that has made its way around social media platforms:

> Hate has talked so loudly for so long.
> Greed has talked so loudly for so long.

[1] "They'll Know We Are Christians" (also known as "They'll Know We Are Christians By Our Love" or "We Are One in the Spirit"), written by Fr. Peter Scholtes, 1960s (exact date of composition unknown).

Liars have talked so loudly for so long.
Love has got to stop whispering.

Wow, that hit me because I serve in a loving, inclusive multicultural and intercultural church and I like to think that we are speaking in a normal voice. But what if we are whispering? I have realized recently that I want to be louder about love and helping others. Even if by personality I am not the loudest or brashest preacher.

I realized I don't want to be on the sidelines. I want to be a part of love in action.

I don't know if you have noticed this about the image of Stephen, the first martyr and also one of the first deacons, being stoned. But there is a point at which he sees God's glory and those who are set on killing him have to cover their ears in order to move forward. They have to prevent themselves from hearing about God and God's glory and God's love, because it might interfere with the hateful action in which they are participating.

How about us? Are we on the sidelines when the Stephens of the world are being injured or killed? Do we close our eyes or ears when our transgender siblings get misgendered or when laws in other states change because they "don't affect us"? Thinking back to Stephen, can we imagine not just those who stoned him, but also Saul, standing on the sidelines, perhaps having encouraged this act? What if hearing about Stephen's vision of glory convicted Saul, Saul who would become Paul, one of the most ardent teachers and promoters of the Christian faith? He stood on the sidelines then, but his glimpse of Stephen's communion with God and his forgiveness of the crowd, had to have moved him.

It had to have moved him, even though his conversion happened later. Because I will tell you, one of the most moving parts of visiting the Holy Land for me was visiting the underground grotto underneath St. Stephen's Orthodox Church just outside the old city of Jerusalem. Stephen was probably driven out, and here was stoned. But that underground place shines somehow in its darkness. All along the walls there are murals of Stephen's life and death, and the most amazing to me, is an image of Jesus's face in the sky. I imagined Stephen, fixing his eyes on Jesus, and just commending himself to God. His faith moved me to tears, in that underground grotto filled with candles of the faithful.

Who are the Stephens in our world? Perhaps you have felt like Stephen, under attack just for living and loving the way you love. Because we know Stephen loved Jesus, and that caused a ruckus. Perhaps you have someone else in mind. Thomas asks Jesus to show him the way to the Father, but we know that the way is through Jesus. And the way is through showing love. Showing love to one another and to those whom God has given us. Showing love to those who are feeling victimized and under attack. To our queer selves but also to our queer siblings. That is how we do greater works. Not because we are better than Jesus, or can do more impressive things. But because if all of us Christians can work together for love, we will be an unstoppable force.

How do we do this? I suggest that first, we do not close our ears. We might be tempted, in the overwhelm of the news cycle, to close our ears. And of course, for our sanity sometimes we need a break from the news. But what we do read about, we must pray on. And we must act, in whatever small way we can. Sometimes just through prayer, but sometimes by doing one small act of love and mercy. But it all starts with simply not stopping our ears so we can let the other's experience enter in. So, we can hear about God's grace, even when it is not what we expect to hear about. I can't tell you how many times people have preached to me about abundance when I have expected to hear about scarcity. God is bigger than our imaginations. We must repeat that to ourselves and keep our ears and hearts open. As queer folk, we are used to hearing a negative point of view regarding the scripture and God's love for us, but many of us are interpreting the scriptures anew in a way that shows just how much God loves and affirms us, and how we should be affirmed in Christian community. Do we have ears to hear this message of our own loving acceptance and to preach that message of loving acceptance to others?

Second, we must act out that same love. What if just one person had stopped a person throwing rocks at Stephen? What if we happen to see someone being verbally or otherwise assaulted and can say, "No, that's not right." What if we don't call someone out but call them into their best selves. "Hey friend, I can see you are angry. But (so-and-so) doesn't deserve those words. How can I help you?" What if we pray for those in need as we pass them on the freeway or read about them in the paper or online? What if we are part of the solution? What if we find ways to publicly advocate for our queer siblings who are experiencing some form of oppression, whether it is marching, advocating for policy, writing our lawmakers, or taking any other concrete step to be a part of a different approach? Every step we take to be a part of the solution, to be the visible voice of love, is powerful. And you never know when a Saul is watching who will be an even bigger part of spreading the Good News.

Now, I will be honest. This is tiring stuff. Speaking of showing up like this in her book *See No Stranger: A Memoir and Manifesto of Revolutionary Love,* Valarie Kaur recognizes this fact and then reminds us: "The good news is that you don't need to feel empathy all the time. *Love is not a rush of feeling. Love is sweet labor.* What matters is the work your hands do. So, breathe and rest and, when you are ready, see if you can wonder about the world just a little, just enough to show up to the labor one more day. Let wonder surprise you" (emphasis added).[2]

This made me think of an image my wife, Alene, who is also an Episcopal priest, shared with me of a choir sustaining one long note. She said, "It is not that the members of the choir have stopped breathing while making this note, but they take turns breathing and singing to maintain the unified sound." We are like that choir, singing and breathing our notes of love.

We are not alone. There are many of us Christians who love, and love deeply. There are many queer Christians who love and love deeply, as well as many more queer folks who need to hear that message of love. Who need to hear that we as a Church honor the dignity of every human being. Let us, like the psalmist, fix our eyes on God. Let us fix our eyes on God and not stop up our ears. Let us show up and not just wonder about the world. But to paraphrase St. Teresa of Avila, let us be Christ's hands and feet in the world and remember that Love has got to stop whispering. Amen.

---

[2] Valarie Kaur, *See No Stranger: A Memori and Manifesto of Revolutionary Love* (One World, 2020), 59–60.

SIXTH SUNDAY OF EASTER

Dr. Peter Carlson

Acts 17:22–31
Psalm 66:7–18
1 Peter 3:13–22
John 14:15–21

Literally everything you know is a lie.

Literally everything you care about is irrelevant.

Literally everything.

The lessons for this Sunday are so easy to read in a thrill of resurrection joy—in the mood of giggly happiness that comes from having been so gloomy during Lent and so clinically depressed during Holy Week. Even so many weeks on, we can still smell the lilies and can still hear the trumpets, and the taste of "Alleluia!" denied us over the preceding weeks, is still sweet on our tongues. Easter is a heady, mountaintop ecstasy, and it's no great wonder that we want to stay there, like a spiritually desperate sojourner, longing for more than mundacity, stumbling into an Asbury Revival to get a jolt of spiritual defibrillation.

But you can't live on a mountaintop. For one thing, mountaintops almost never have a grocery store. More important, that's not where our neighbors, who need us, and who we need, live. Eventually, we have to scramble back down into a not-ecstatic life, and find the Divine there.

Paul, in the Acts of the Apostles, gives us some suggestions about where we should look: not "in shrines made by human hands" and certainly not in "gold, or silver, or stone," but in our own selves and in those around us because "in G-d we live and move and have our being."

The implications are profound, aren't they? We look for divinity, not in the things most humans think are worthy of praise, but in humans themselves, and in the things that we don't value. G-d does not sit in grand halls or beautiful basilicas, but lurks in the alleys, in the back streets, in the trackless forests, and in craggy cliffs of existence. G-d is untamed and wild and is found in the untamed wildness of our lives, where we are called to repent—to regret again—the fact that we have believed we can put G-d in a box and to keep Them safe, taking Them out when we need a spiritual, teddy-bear hug.

The psalmist knows that this is where G-d hangs out. Though we are caught in a snare, though we carry heavy burdens, though enemies ride over our heads and we go through fire and water, we can find refreshment. We must never imagine that suffering confers virtue; but we must never forget that we can find the Divine even in the midst of suffering—this is what folx who use the twelve steps often refer to as Hitting Bottom. Or what Madeleine L'Engle was talking about when she got furious with people who, when things go well, would say, "Surely G-d was with me," as though ease and worldly success were signs of G-d's presence. L'Engle insisted, referencing W. B. Yeats's poem, "Crazy Jane Talks with the Bishop," that our G-d is the G-d who is with us in the places of excrement.[1] And the psalmist insists on this as well. If our G-d is not present at the bottom of the pit, or in the shithouse, then that G-d is not a god with whom I want to be in relationship.

Scholars have suggested that the First Epistle of Peter was written during the Domitian persecutions—whether this is accurate or not, faith lived in a shithouse was clearly on the author's mind. (Actual persecution, incidentally. Literally being killed. As opposed to the claims of some modern-day Christians who think that being called—accurately—bigoted and hateful constitutes persecution.) In this passage, the author, rather ironically, I think, asks, "Who will harm you if you are eager to do what is good? "You can imagine the audience thinking to themselves, "Um. DOMITIAN, MAYBE?" And the author, knowing that, says, even so, we ought not to be intimidated. Suffer for what is right. Say what you believe,

---

[1] L'Engle wrestles with this concept in *Two-Part Invention: The Story of a Marriage* (Farrar, Straus, & Giroux, 1988). For the poem, please see William Butler Yeats, "Crazy Jane Talks with the Bishop," from *The Collected Poems of W. B. Yeats*, edited by Richard Finneran (MacMillan, 1989), 122.

but with gentleness and reverence. Imitate Jesus, who suffered for the unrighteous—not so we wouldn't have to suffer, but so we could see HOW to suffer, for something worthwhile.

It is not by accident that Peter talks about baptism in the context of suffering, by the way. Baptism, that cheery little ritual in which we sprinkle (or, if you were in my church, attempt to drown) an infant (or, if you were in my church, a person supposedly old enough to make their own choices, peer pressure of course having nothing to do with it) with water.

Baptism, in the prophetic work of John the Baptizer, was a call to repentance—regretting again—a promise of turning away from the glittering gods of gold-and-silver and turning toward our unglittering, powerless neighbors, lying battered alongside the road. Baptism for early Christians was a promise that they would continue turning away from earthly power, even when that power was strong enough, as the psalmist knew, to snare us, and drag our bodies through fire and water. Baptism WAS repentance, and a guarantee of suffering at the hands of worldly authorities, of people who value gold and silver more than human life and dignity. Suffering, of course, is part of everyone's life in some way or another, but the author of Peter is reminding us that, since we're going to suffer, we should suffer for the right reasons: for that divinity in the alleys, in the back streets, in the trackless forests and craggy cliffs of existence.

And the resurrected but still enfleshed Jesus, in the Gospel of John, is nailing (ahem) the message home. We are to keep Jesus's commandments. Remember those? Love G-d with heart, soul, and mind, and love our neighbors as ourselves. And remember: Our neighbor is the asshole we really don't want to love, because they are not Productive Members of Society, and they have been mauled by the world, and ignored by all the people in power—especially by the churchy people in power.

This is so hard, especially when WE are the people being mauled by the world, and the churchy people, all too often, don't want to have anything to do with us. A student of mine once said, "Queers can tell you a lot about death." Oh, yes we can. So can nonwhite folx. And womyn. And people on the borders of this country seeking asylum. And all of those on the borders of society everywhere. We are the neighbors that churchy people in power are too often unwilling to stop and help, with every tithe and coffee hour and budget and church campus that is available to them.

Don't get me wrong: I'm not writing this from a place of virtue. I am an always-white, often-cis, male who has access to education, housing, and (usually) health care. I have so much in common with the centers of power, and I admit that, all too often, I don't even reflect on the authority that those centers hand to me, unquestioningly.

And therefore, it is because of my privilege, not in spite of it, that I lean so heavily into my queerness and "rub it in people's faces" (as the accusation goes). I deliberately acknowledge my privilege and walk out to stand at the margins, with those who do not have the privilege of standing anywhere else. And I admit that this isn't always easy, and I am quite honestly often afraid.

But then I remember that Jesus promised the Paraclete—the Helper; the Advocate; the Called-In-Alongside—which the world cannot understand. The One Who Will Be With Me For Ever Even In The Shit Places; Miz Holy Spirit Thang. And Gurl, She is totes gonna help me, first to repent—to regret again—my unthinking relationship with privilege, and then to keep the Commandments of Love.

Because when I keep the commandments, I see G-d. I see G-d in the people on the edges—the edgy folx—and when I see G-d in people, I am with them. And when I am with them, I am in Jesus, who taught us to see them. And when I am in Jesus, I am in G-d, and G-d and Jesus are in me, and fuck the world's silver and gold, because even though I am no longer on a mountaintop, I am drowning in a baptism of Spirit—Holy Breath—and as I drown, I suddenly discover that She is actually the Wild Air in which I can finally breathe free.

ASCENSION DAY

Dr. Peter Carlson

Acts 1:1–11
Psalm 47
or *Psalm 93*
Ephesians 1:15–23
Luke 24:44–53

You know, I've been baptized with the Holy Spirit.

I mean, I've been baptized by water too, but that didn't really do anything for me, possibly because it took place in a branch of Christianity that didn't place a lot of emphasis on sacramental living, so what I chiefly remember was my junior high school pal's chest being visible through the wet whiteness of his baptismal robe, like some kind of holy wet T-shirt contest, which was disconcerting, because I was so obviously supposed to be thinking about Jesus, I guess (though I'll admit that I also thought, based on some of the pictures that I'd seen, that Jesus was pretty hot too). It didn't help that I was a scrawny kid, and I constantly compared my own skinny body to the comparative brawn of my baptism buddies. So, yeah. My baptism in water was filled, not with the inspiration of the Spirit, or with actual repentance, but with convictions of my own bodily inadequacy, my pal's hotness, and all the time wondering if lightning would strike me dead because I wasn't thinking about Holy Things, but glistening pectoral muscles.

But my baptism in the Holy Spirit was what I was going to tell you about. Many people tend to think of baptism in the Spirit in terms of evangelical Pentecostal Christian fervor: an arms-in-the-air, rolling-in-the-aisles, speaking-in-tongues, snake-handling extremity of Christianity.

My baptism in the Spirit, on the other hand, was when Miz Holy Spirit captured my big ol' 'mo soul, took me gently by the hand, and taught me that appreciating the beauty of a male body, even though I identified as male, could in fact be a Holy Thing. I mention this because I now wonder if the Hot Jesus of my baptism in water needed to ascend right out of sight before the Holy Spirit could show up and teach me these things.

At the beginning of the book of Acts, which is generally considered to be a continuation of the Gospel of Luke by the same author, we are given a quick reminder that Jesus rose again after being put to death, and we meet up with Jesus talking to his disciples, saying, "John baptized with water, but you will be baptized with the Holy Spirit not many days from now." The disciples, dim to the end, get excited: "Is this when you're gonna bomb the ever-living shit out of Rome and make Israel a powerful kingdom?" Jesus (I imagine him shaking his head in frustration) avoids an answer by saying that times and periods cannot be known to us. Instead, he tells them, "You will receive power when the Holy Spirit has come upon you, and you will be my witnesses in Jerusalem, in all Judea and Samaria, and to the ends of the earth." And then *poof*! Up he ascends, leaving them gawking at the sky until two strange men in white tell them to get out of their heads and get busy.

At the end of Luke, we see a similar scene, in which Jesus gives a hint of the power that they will receive. It is power to proclaim "repentance and forgiveness of sins . . . to all nations, beginning from Jerusalem." He goes on, in words that are echoed at the beginning of Acts: "You are witnesses of these things." The power from on high, then, is the power to be a witness.

I'll be honest: I can understand the disciples' hopes for a worldly Messiah. In fact, it was probably only natural. Look at either of the psalms appointed for today: They sound suspiciously like victory poems, in which G-d has made the Israelites the winners. Psalm 47 trumpets, "G-d subdued peoples under us and nations under our feet!" G-d indeed may, as the psalm continues, be ruler over all the nations, and as in Psalm 93, G-d may be the firm ruler over all nature, but underneath G-d, we're Nation Number One!

This sounds disturbingly like many Christians today, doesn't it? Even so, I get where the disciples are coming from, and they must have shivered with anticipation when Jesus promised them power in the Holy Spirit. But we should note, again, that Jesus actually never promises worldly, military power; it is the power to be a witness, and specifically to be a witness to the audacity of repentance, forgiveness, and resurrection.

The letter to the Ephesians has something to say about that power. Paul (or, more likely, pseudo-Paul) prays that the Jesus followers in Ephesus will receive "a spirit of wisdom and revelation" as they come to know G-d, "so that, with the eyes of your heart enlightened, you may perceive what is the hope to which G-d has called you, the riches of G-d's glorious inheritance [and] the immeasurable greatness of G-d's power." This wisdom is not worldly wisdom found in education or even in worldly experience (remember that Paul has claimed that G-d's wisdom appears foolish). These riches are not the worldly riches—lottery winnings or even sensible retirement plans. This power certainly is not worldly military power, nor the power of political machinations. Rather, it is power "far above all rule and authority and power and dominion." The author of Ephesians is telling us that the power we receive is to be Christ's body—the ecclesia, the community gathering. It's possible that this power might be wildly subversive, but it's not really what we (or the disciples) immediately think of when we hear the word. This is a queer kind of power.

Of course, the whole Feast of the Ascension is really quite queer , when you think about it. But then, what isn't queer about Divine Incarnation or, for that matter, Divine Aspiration? The task of encasing divine expansiveness into a body—or, conversely, of expanding a physical flesh-sack to the point where it can embody the Divine—is such a weird doctrine (though by no means exclusive to Christianity). It is so strange, in fact, that we Christians tend to ignore it, or even forget it. I know, I know, we celebrate Baby Jesus and Crucified Jesus, but admit it: We romanticize them. We hardly ever focus on the real, live, fleshy, living-in-a-body-day-to-day Jesus, do we? I would argue that, particularly in the United States (due, I am convinced, to an outsized Puritan influence in our national history), we are stunningly bodyphobic and have consequently as a society created so many countless proscriptions for bodies (and especially for bodies that are not white, straight, and male) that we ultimately refuse to believe that the Divine might actually traverse our digestive tracts and inhabit our erotic charges as much as the Divine traverses the heavens above. This is why it is so important—and so powerful—to proclaim, however insane it may sound and however often I am not able to believe it rationally, the Nicene Creed's statements about Jesus: He became incarnate through the

Virgin Mary, and was made human. He suffered. He died. He rose again from the dead. He ascended into heaven.

He also ate. He slept. He walked. He stubbed his toes. He peed. He pooped.

Jesus did all this *in his body*. And his *body* ascended into heaven.

This then, in fact, is a promise for us, isn't it? And it isn't just the promise, so central to our faith, that though our bodies will die, death doesn't bat last. It is the absurd, outrageous promise of our own holy embodiedness; it is the promise of our own enfleshed ascension, that our bodies themselves are holy, and worthy of salvation. And that is one wild-ass promise, isn't it?

Look, I'll freely admit that I don't care if you (or I) believe in a literal ascension or a metaphorical one. With C. S. Lewis, I stand by the claim that myth is truer than fact—that the literalness of a story is simply not anywhere *near* its most important point.[1] Stories are *always* more than stories. Nothing is *ever* "just" a myth. My faith of resurrection and ascension does not and cannot rely on observable evidence or quantifiable data, but on the absolute conviction that nothing as ordinary as death can wipe an extraordinary me out. Indeed, the fact that the core of Christianity has, however haltingly or even inappropriately, survived the death and ascension of Jesus (or, perhaps even more shockingly, survived Christianity's acquiescence to worldly imperial power) is evidence enough of the truth (*not*, I say again, the factual history) of our stories. What Jesus said and did, in his body, mattered, we say, and so we try, however ineffectively, to follow Jesus's lead in our very own, precious bodies.

---

[1] See C. S. Lewis, "Myth Became Fact," pages 63-67 in *God in the Dock* (Eerdmans, 1970).

SEVENTH SUNDAY OF EASTER

Dr. Peter Carlson

Acts 1:6–14
Psalm 68:1–10, 33–36
1 Peter 4:12–14; 5:6–11
John 17:1–11

This Sunday follows this past Thursday's Feast of the Ascension, and we are handed a bit of a recap in the readings of Jesus being taken up into heaven—a scene that is often depicted, to my delight, in medieval manuscripts, usually with the disciples gawping up at a cloud, from the bottom of which we see Jesus's feet dangling (always accurately depicted with the holes of the crucifixion). In many ways, then, this seventh Sunday in the Easter season is actually a kind of letdown. All the drama of Jesus's life is over, he's zipped up to heaven, and Miz Holy Spirit Flaming Tongues hasn't showed up yet.

But that's so much of life, actually, isn't it? Those queer, in-between periods where we're not quite one thing or another, where we've finished one project but haven't begun the next, when we are required to figure out that hardest lesson of all: how just to *be*.

The reading from the Acts of the Apostles, a slightly longer version of what we read on Ascension Day last Thursday, gives a sense of this in-between time, when action has been spent or not yet spurred, and it seems that all that's left is prayer. The scene for today begins with the apostles asking Jesus if now, after they've witnessed the astonishment of Jesus's resurrection, if *now* is when the Roman Empire's ass will finally get kicked, and when Israel will once again become a nation, a political power in its own right? In fact, they're asking when the psalm for today, Psalm 68, will come true: When will the "enemies be scattered"? And Jesus (I imagine him sighing) essentially tells his followers to stop worrying about dates and times and when G-d will see fit to do what. Instead, he says, get your butts back to Jerusalem and wait for the Holy Spirit.

And so, flying heavenward, feet poking out beneath the cloud, Jesus goes away, leaving the disciples to stare, jaws agape, until "suddenly two men in white robes" show up saying, in essence, "Close your mouths folks, and go back to Jerusalem. There's nothing more to see here." We have no idea who these people are, but they are helpful to advance the narrative, and get the disciples back to the city, which wasn't far (a "sabbath day's journey" was the amount you could walk on Shabbat without breaking the rules that prohibit work). They went to the room where they were staying, and, stuck in hurry-up-and-wait mode, devoted themselves to prayer "together with certain women," which is frustratingly consistent with the accounts of the crucifixion and resurrection, in which women were the ones who stuck with Jesus to the end, and women were the ones who witnessed the empty tomb. I am reminded of "Naked Pastor," David Hayward's cartoon that shows Peter at the head of a group of men, talking to some women, and saying, "So ladies, thanks for being the first to witness and report the resurrection and we'll take it from here." Apparently, the men took it into the Acts of the Apostles too, and we should be grateful that the women in the upper room even got a mention.

But that prayer. Prayer is an interesting thing, and I admit that I have trouble with it, because too often prayer is associated with a kind of Magic Jesus appeal in which, if I pray "without ceasing" and "with the faith of a mustard seed," I will get whatever I want. I don't know about you, but in my own experience of praying desperately to G-d to make the gay go away, I learned that prayer doesn't work that way. (And yes, I was praying without ceasing, and with huge faith, convinced that G-d could do this—and Magic Jesus teaching, along with the fact that I kept waking up gay actually did a lot of spiritual harm.) So prayer, I am convinced, is not about getting shit or fixing shit; it is about relationships. I pray for my students when I get to my office in the morning. It does not make them good students, or me a good teacher, but it reminds me that we have a holy relationship that I need to honor. I wonder what sacred relationships the disciples "together with certain women" were keeping in mind as they prayed together in Jerusalem? I like to imagine that it was, quite simply, their relationship with G-d that they had experienced in their companionship with Jesus.

The First Epistle of Peter is, in fact, a kind of prayer for Christians suffering persecution under the oppression of the Roman Empire: It is a prayer reminding them that they are indeed G-d's holy people. In chapter two, the author writes, "Once you were not a people, but now you are G-d's people." And in the passage we heard today, we are reminded that the Roman Empire was not an easy place to be a Jesus follower. Whether this book was actually written by the Apostle Peter or not, there is no doubt that by this time, Christians (and Jews, we should remember) had undergone periods of stunningly harsh treatment by Rome. We need only recall that Nero, in the 60s CE (only thirty or so years after Jesus's crucifixion), delighted in extreme cruelty and public spectacles of violence against monotheists, perhaps quite literally a "fiery ordeal." The relational prayer of this epistle must have been necessary, with Jesus followers probably wondering if G-d had, perhaps, abandoned them. And Peter reminds them that, when you are in relationship with G-d, and you are doing the right thing, then you are in fact following Jesus—and look what happened to him. Peter, in effect, is saying what I have always said about Christianity: If you do what Jesus did, you'll end up like Jesus. The hope that Peter is reminding the Jesus followers of, however, is the reminder that we *are* in relationship with G-d, and that, just as with Jesus, death doesn't win, that we will indeed share in "G-d's eternal glory in Christ."

Chapter 17 of John's Gospel is another prayer in the face of persecution. This is Jesus's own prayer, just before his arrest, trial, and crucifixion. The Gospel of John is the mystical Gospel, as I think of it, with far less of the practical biographical information about Jesus and far more spiritualized meaning wafting about. This makes it a beautiful read, but a difficult one, because metaphor is hard to pin down, and Jesus's prayer here is arguably as mystic as the rest of the book. Jesus begins by praying for himself: "Glorify your Child so that the Child may glorify you," he implores, "to give eternal life." And get this: "And this is eternal life, that they may know you, the only true G-d, and Jesus Christ whom you have sent." John frames eternal life with a relationship. To know G-d, to have G-d know us; that's eternal life.

Jesus follows his prayer for himself by praying for the disciples, who have witnessed that relationship, "so that they may be one, as we are one."

And Jesus finishes this prayer (in the section following our reading for today) by praying for all believers. The progress from self to all, it seems to me, is actually the entire narrative arc of the Hebrew and Christian scriptures: What began, in Abraham, as a covenant with a single person turns out to be eternally expansive until, through prayer, we realize that G-d is in relationship with all of us.

The disciples had been promised power in the Spirit. The scattered Christians who are the audience of First Peter needed the Spirit's power to withstand the violence being committed upon them by the empire. But it is important, again, to remember that this power does not look like what we think of as power. The Holy Spirit? When She comes, Jesus promised the disciples they'd receive power. Not the power to kick Roman ass, but the power to "be my witnesses in Jerusalem, in all Judea and Samaria, and to the ends of the earth."

In Deutero-Isaiah, we can find another divine call for humans to be G-d's witness, and I wonder if Jesus is making a specific reference back to that prophet here. G-d, in the book of Isaiah, needs to be justified before the world, and says, "You are my witnesses . . . and my servant whom I have chosen, so that you may know and believe in me and understand that I am he." Elie Wiesel tells of a Talmudic riff on this, which suggests that G-d is saying, "I need you as my witnesses, so that I can be G-d," and further, that "if you are not my witnesses, then I am not G-d."[1] To be a witness to the Divine, then, is for us and the Divine to be in relationship with each other. And that is power indeed: to bring the Divine into existence by witnessing to the deep relationship between human and divine—a relationship modeled in the enfleshed Christ.

So, think about this: The kind of power the apostles will be given is the power to witness to, to make real, G-d. It is, in fact, the power of prayer: the power to enflesh G-d in our lives and to stand up against imperial powers that seek to harm the defenseless.

In this in-between time, this not-one-thing-or-the-other moment, let us take time to pray for that power, because I am convinced that if we pray G-d into being, into relationship, without ceasing and with the even the tiniest bit of faith, Miz Holy Spirit Thang will descend on us, flaming queen that She is. And the world? The world will be powerless to stop us.

---

[1] Public Broadcasting Service, *Elie Wiesel: First Person Singular* (Films Media Group, 2002).

PENTECOST, AND THE SEASON FOLLOWING

DAY OF PENTECOST

Dr. Peter Carlson

Acts 2:1–21 or *Numbers 11:24–30*
Psalm 104:25–35, 37
1 Corinthians 12:3b–13 or *Acts 2:1–21*
John 20:19–23 or *John 7:37–39*

Of queer days, a day when flaming tongues dance on our heads has got to be among the queerest.

Queer theologians remind me regularly that queerness is nothing new in the Church or its history, and that the Church calendar itself and the lectionary attending it are both really quite queer. And so, of all the queerness in the queer lectionary representing all the queer feasts and holy days of a very queer religion, it is absolutely plain to me that Pentecost, the day on which the Holy Spirit makes flaming queens of the disciples, offers up some of the queerest queerness that two thousand years of religion has worked desperately to unqueer.

The queerness begins in the collect for the day, in which we make a delicious request that G-d "shed abroad" the gifts of the mischievous Holy Spirit, which perhaps inevitably as a cat dad draws my brain to the reality that a cat's hair ends up in every blessed nook and cranny in the house. (This observation is based on experience.) But the implication of all this Spirit-shedding metaphor is actually wonderfully theologically sound; the reality is that you can't escape Miz Holy Spirit Thang's fur-shedding if She chooses you, and no earthly lint roller is gonna clean it off your sexy-ass, worldly outfit. You might as well just roll with it. Or roll in it. And, like a cat's clichéd tendency to shed on the one person who actually hates cats, Miz Holy Spirit's gifts tend to descend upon some of the most unexpected people.

The Spirit-y unexpectedness first appears today in the book of Numbers. It's important to include the Hebrew Bible in the readings for the Feast of Pentecost if for no other reason than that Christians have tended, in their supersessionist[1] approach to literally everything, taken over ownership of Shavuot, the Jewish holy day, just because something important in our own calendar happened on that day in history. The reading from Numbers tells a story of the Israelites being messed up by G-d's Spirit just after they had resumed their journey after a break at Sinai (where they'd received the commands of G-d about how to stay in relationship with Them). Let's be real: This had to have been a hard journey, and it is not surprising to me that the people were complaining, wishing for something heartier in their diets than manna. (I have tried to imagine living on communion wafers, and I am less than thrilled with the idea.) G-d's response is not just to send the food, but to order the Israelites, "Consecrate yourselves, and then I'll make sure you have meat." So Moses gathers seventy elders in the Tent of the Meeting, and G-d takes some of the Spirit that had been given to Moses on Sinai and spreads it around (sheds it around?) and the elders prophesy, because *that is what you do when the Spirit is upon you.*

Prophecy, remember, is quite simply telling the truth in the face of power, which explains why prophets are usually treated so very badly. But the prophecy isn't really the key here; what is most intriguing in this story is that a couple of the folks who had been chosen didn't make it to the tent, and there they were, out there prophesying out in the camp, and other prophecy-fulfilled folks were offended by that (as though the place where prophecy was most needed wasn't among the people). This is a classic theme across scripture: Hey! How come *they* get to join in! They're not special, like me!

Gurl. The Spirit, She is whippin' around. Quitcherbitchin.

The unexpected continues as the psalmist sings a creature chronicle. At first, it might seem that this is one of the wonderful praisy-praisy-yay-G-d psalms, bubbling over with awe and joy. But it's helpful to realize that the

---

[1] Supersessionism (sometimes also called "replacement theology") is the teaching among some branches of Christianity that Christians have replaced Jews as "G-d's chosen people," replacing the Mosaic Covenant.

psalmist is identifying not just the pretty-pretties in creation, but *all* creatures, as the words go, great and small, delightful and dangerous. This is not just birdies and butterflies, but the bloody awful Leviathan—the great sea monster! When G-d's Spirit is sent forth, the psalm warns us, they are created. It really can't be made much clearer than this: The Spirit of G-d is not something to be messed with lightly.

Paul reminds the Jesus followers in Corinth that there are multitudes of gifts that the Spirit can dump on us, and that they are all activated by the same G-d. This passage seems to me to speak directly to those who would claim authority to people who want to limit G-d's activity to the goody-goodies, or the spiritual elites, as the religious leaders in Palestine tried to do in the face of Jesus's radically egalitarian message. Paul is trying to get the Corinthians to stop assuming that some people have special access to G-d's Spirit, that some people have, as it were, been breathed on by G-d, while others are just, if you will, blowing hot air. This is actually a theme established at the beginning of his letter, where Paul is reminding the Corinthians that it doesn't matter one shitty little bit who was baptized by whom—we're all trying to do the good work, just like the prophesiers who weren't in the tent in Numbers and who were in the camp, who were being, as it were, campy.

Jesus, in the Gospel of John, has a touching moment with his followers before returning to heaven. He appears, magically passing through a locked door, and says the comforting words, "Peace be with you." Beautiful. And then: "As the Father has sent me, so I send you." When he had said this, he breathed on them and said to them, "*Receive the Holy Spirit.* If you forgive the sins of any, they are forgiven them; if you retain the sins of any, they are retained."

So first of all, I love that Jesus's body matters here: *He breathed on them. Spirit* does, after all, come from the same etymological root as *breath.* The Incarnation, the enfleshment of Jesus, is at work, even after his resurrection, even in his Spirit. Jesus is sending his followers out with his breath here, and seemingly giving them some impressive power to forgive or not. (And before we go all Apostolic succession on this and assume that they received the ability to prevent people from receiving salvation, I'd like to suggest that this is simply a statement of fact: If we do not forgive, we retain the sin; if we forgive, we let it go.) But I want to backtrack to the "sending"; the word *apostle,* after all, means one who is sent. Jesus is sending the apostles out of a locked room into a world that is quite frankly dangerous—they have, after all, just witnessed what happened to Jesus for preaching a radical Gospel of Divine Ultra-Welcome. And he is sending them with the words "Peace be with you." Those words in this context can seem darkly ironic, if not actually misleading and cruel, when we think about what happened to the apostles. I cannot help but remember, as I read this passage, the poem by William Alexander Percy, "His Peace," which was put to music as the hymn "They Cast Their Nets in Galilee." The poem was included in Percy's book, *Enzio's Kingdom and Other Poems*, published in 1924. I can only assume that the horrors of the so-called "War to End All Wars" was still very much in Percy's mind as he wrote the poem, and perhaps especially the desperate truth of the final stanza:

> The peace of God, it is no peace;
> But strife closed in the sod.[2]

I doubt the apostles—those unlikely sent ones—really knew what they were getting in for when Jesus breathed the Spirit on them; but they certainly found out, perhaps to their surprise.

Luke, traditionally identified as the author of the Acts of the Apostles, is also shocking us with Spirited Surprises, even if the story has become so familiar to us as to have lost its punch. By the time this story is happening, Shavuot/Pentecost had been established not just as a harvest festival but as one of the three great Jewish pilgrimage festivals, when a multitude of Jews from all over the Roman Empire would make their way to Jerusalem to offer sacrifices in the temple—hence, the presence of Jews who spoke so many different languages in the story.

We're told that the apostles (the eleven remaining after Judas met a bad end) were self-isolating in some house, when the Holy Spirit whipped through like a storm, and they "were filled with the Holy Spirit and began to speak in other languages, as the Spirit gave them ability." The following hilarious and awkward list of places and languages that the various Jews could recognize is really only there, I'm convinced, to trip up the poor person who's been assigned to read the lesson, and to impress us with the apostles' unexpected linguistic agility. And the humor continues, when

---

[2] William Alexander Percy, *Enzio's Kingdom and Other Poems* (Yale University Press, 1924).

the public assumes they're dealing with some rip snorting sots who'd been hitting the wineskins too early in the morning. (Seriously, though: the fact that Peter claims they can't be drunk because it's only nine in the morning just shows that he's not really a committed drinker.) But before that, they all say something telling: "Are these not Galileans?" Surely uneducated rubes from that area can't be fluent in multiple languages! And Peter, for once eloquent, reminds them of the prophet (because the Holy Spirit and prophecy, remember) Joel, who proclaimed:

> In the last days it will be, God declares,
> that I will pour out my Spirit upon all flesh,
>   and your sons and your daughters shall prophesy,
> and your young men shall see visions,
>   and your old men shall dream dreams.
> Even upon my slaves, both men and women,
>   in those days I will pour out my Spirit;
>   and they shall prophesy.

I really want to be clear here: This is as universalist a spirit-shedding as can possibly be described. All genders are included; all ages are included; even the least powerful economic classes are included. In fact, the only people who seem to be unmentioned in the Pouring Out of the Spirit are the wealthy and the politically connected.

And really, this is the way it is with Miz Holy Spirit Thang. She blows where She will, and it is *always* the unexpected, the unattractive, the unwelcome, the unconnected who shall prophesy, who shall speak truth to power. Those in the centers of power are terrified of the truth, because it speaks of a Power that is greater than their sad, earthly dreams. This means that those in power will also use every ounce of their own earthly power to crush the prophets—and this is the danger of Pentecost, of the Spirit's whirlwind: It is dangerous. The peace of G-d, it is no peace . . .

So, be careful about praying too lightly or naively for the inspiration of the Holy Spirit. Because Miz Holy Spirit Thang, She's gonna fuck things up, and then the world is gonna try to crush you. But if you're not afraid of dying, you can be fearless. And then? She's gonna use the outcasts and unacceptables to blow away the world's values, unruly windstorm that She is.

TRINITY SUNDAY, THE SUNDAY AFTER PENTECOST

Dr. Peter Carlson

Genesis 1:1–2:4a
Psalm 8
or *Canticle 13 (or Canticle 2)*
2 Corinthians 13:11–13
Matthew 28:16–20

I can still remember my professor in a PhD class on medieval Spain talking about our Gospel for today (Matthew 28:16–20), which is sometimes called "The Great Commission." In it, Jesus tells the disciples to go throughout the earth and "baptize in the name of the Father, and the Son, and the Holy Spirit." My professor added, "but he didn't tell anyone what the hell he meant."

Hence the ongoing state of Trinitarian theology/heterodoxy.

I have a running challenge in my Religion 100 classes: If a student can explain the Trinity in a way that is logically coherent *and* that has not been described as heresy, I will give them an A.

Amidst all of the heresies used to describe this fantastic (as in fantasy—yes, I'm using it that way) concept of Christian theology, my favorite tends to be Sabellianism, or modalism: the three persons of G-d as the three aspects, or modes, of the one G-d. We turn to modalism when we use ice/water/steam or creator/redeemer/sustainer to describe the Trinity. So modalism: logical; biblically defensible; comfy; heretical.

I'm down with that.

But most pastors (yes, I'm looking at you, pastor-friends) try to avoid the whole heresy thing by explaining the Trinity as through relationship/

relationality and that our creation *imago dei*, in the image of G-d, means that we are to replicate that relational nature. Kallistos Ware, an Eastern Orthodox bishop, described it in a way that I find attractive:

> Each social grouping—family, parish, diocese, church council, school, office, factory, nation—has as its vocation to be transformed by grace into a living icon of [the Holy Trinity], to affect a reconciling harmony between diversity and unity, human freedom and mutual solidarity, after the pattern of the Trinity.[1]

I want to follow this through, though, to its conclusion, because I see two important and very queer suggestions that arise out of it. One is that the Trinity models polyamory. The other is that it models multiple and sometimes conflicting desires, methods, and intents.

Okay, I'll wrestle with the polyamory first.[2] But really, you can already see it, can't you, even though it makes you squirm? I remember, during the great debates (I'm writing about this as though these arguments are past, ha ha) about "same-sex marriage," people using the argument that, if we allowed same-sex marriage, the next step would be plural marriage. (Okay, other people said that the next step would be marriage to goats, but that's a theological conundrum for another day.)

And perhaps weirdly, I remember thinking: "Oh. Like the relationship between the three persons of the Trinity?"

The Trinity is a holy three-way, a throuple. It models personhood AND relationality in three different directions. And at least since the medieval period, it has been used to describe marriage (in fact, John Mirk, author of the handbook *Instructions for Parish Priests*, provides us with a delectable genderfuck by describing the Second Person of the Trinity as the wife in a marriage). So the Trinity, as a way of modeling healthy relationships, gives us divine decadence—polyamory.

But I'm frankly more intrigued with the second problem: the idea that the Trinity suggests that G-d might be modeling something less than fixity

---

[1] Kallistos of Diokleia, "The Human Person as an Icon of the Trinity," *Sobornost* 8 (1986): 17–18.

[2] This concept is not original to me, and has been toyed with by queer theologians for years. Indeed, you could argue that the idea is lurking in the early church writings about perichoresis—the interpenetration of the Trinity.

of purpose. Just as when we talk about people "becoming one" when they get married, we know that that *oneness* does not mean they will always agree, so the relational model of the Trinity suggests, G-d does not always agree with G-dself. One of the great dangers in thinking about G-d (aside from the fact that we think we can even think about G-d "correctly" or that our thinking about G-d, if correct today, will necessarily be correct tomorrow) is that we assume constancy and permanence about the Divine. "G-d is working his purpose out . . ." "Jesus Christ, the same yesterday, today, and tomorrow." "The Changelessness of G-d." These are standard assumptions about the Divine in Christian theology.

But another word for this constancy and permanence might be *inflexibility*.

It is amazing to me how many people want to insist on certain aspects of G-d, even when those particular aspects don't seem to be present, at least in the biblical account (which Christians tend to rate pretty highly). We talk about G-d's permanence and changelessness, even as the Hebrew scriptures tell us of a G-d who is on occasion whimsical, and sometimes even able to be swayed by humans. In the account of Noah and the flood, we are presented with a G-d who determines to destroy absolutely everything because humans are so sucky (I'm reminded of Anne Lamott's concept of the shitty first draft). And *then*, casting a glance over the world, G-d discovers Noah, who is righteous. G-d in this account is totally just (G-d saves Noah, because Noah deserves it), but let's be honest: G-d is not very nice.

The Trinity takes this divine changefulness even further: It suggest that the one G-d, in three persons, often has different and even conflicting methods, and even different and conflicting goals.

Wait? How can G-d have multiple and conflicting goals?

Well, the biblical accounts certainly suggest it. You even see it in the first creation account in Genesis, our Hebrew Bible reading for the day (Genesis 1:1–2:4). You've probably read it yourself: It's the seven-day, G-d poofs things into being version (as opposed to the one-day, G-d messes with clay and ribs version of Genesis 2–3). In the beginning, G-d was creating. That's what G-d does. G-d creates. A world here, a universe there, a poem everywhere.

The Spirit of G-d (the *Ruach Elohim*, the breath of G-d) gets excited about this creativity, and moves upon the deep, the *tehowm* (could this be related to Tiamat, the Babylonian goddess of watery chaos?), bringing to the chaos, to the void, a kind of order, a presence.

But the Word of G-d demanded a role, and began to speak things into being with words, with indefinite definition, of fluid (watery? deep-y? *tehowm-y*?) identity.

And yet medieval theologians (and modern ones) say that G-d is sufficient unto G-dself. If so, then why did G-d need to create? And even if we accept that need (which would imply that G-d is *not* sufficient unto G-dself), then why is the whole thing so confusing? Why is G-d at one moment panting heavily on the chaos and the next moment babbling things into being? Can't G-d pick a method? Why must G-d eventually rely on words, which are, after all, only symbols? For that matter, why does G-d (who was not human until G-d became human) have breath? (This is the ultimate heavy breathing creepy phone call, isn't it? If someone phoned me with this kind of breathing, I'd totally hang up.)

But the disagreement of/within the Trinity has other, even more disconcerting biblical justification: G-d "the Father" seems, in Pauline theology, determined to subject us all to justice, for which we must necessarily be banished to eternal punishment. G-d "the Son" seems, however, to have an entirely different goal: "I, when I am lifted up from the earth, will draw all people to myself." G-d the Spirit, in the meantime, seems to be the peacemaker, coming to comfort those of us who have received these desperately conflicting messages, saying, "There, there, my poppet. It will be okay."

And Jesus, in Gethsemane, makes a very clear distinction between his own will ("Let this cup pass me by") and that of the Father ("not my will, but yours be done"). How is this the same man who said, "I and the Father are one"?

Paul's admonition to the Corinthians, which makes up the itsy-bitsy reading from the Epistles today is so cute (particularly when we consider what most of our religious communities are like): Put things in order, listen to my appeal, agree with one another, live in peace; and the God of love and peace will be with you. Greet one another with a holy kiss. All the saints greet you.

But you know what the cutest bit is? What is so cute is that he follows it with the blessing of the fucked-up Trinity—that unity of G-d that has different methods, different goals, and sometimes even bitchy indecision:

"The grace of the anointed one, Jesus Christ, the love of G-d, and the communion of the Holy Spirit be with all of you."

So it seems to me that the relational doctrine of the Trinity is pretty damned queer. It's polyamorous, it's indecisive, it's shifty, it's multifarious (or at least multiplicitous). But then, perhaps that's the point. I, too, am a bundle of contradictions, of motivations, of emotions, of desires. What is interesting to me in all of that is that I am, arguably, at my best when I take into consideration, when I honor, all of those different me-forms as I live my life. I am certainly NOT at my best when my emotions are purest, because the purest emotions I tend to have are those of anger and hatred. I am much more complex when I am trying to do the right thing, and I think that complexity and even contradiction is ultimately for the good, even though it is messy, and difficult, and—yeah—hella queer.

So maybe that's the point. We *are* created *imago dei*, in the image of G-d, right down to our messy and conflicted and ultra-queer relationships with ourselves.

G-d in three persons, blessed Trinity.
Me in three (or more) persons, blessed Identity.
Us in multiple, polyamorous relationships, blessed Humanity.
G-d and us and a Big Holy Mess. Blessed be We.

PROPER 1, THE SUNDAY CLOSEST TO MAY 11

Dr. Pace Warfield

Deuteronomy 30:15–20
or *Sirach 15:15–20*
Psalm 119:1–8
1 Corinthians 3:1–9
Matthew 5:21–37

I remember when the text message came in. It was a hot Monday morning. I was living in my studio apartment that had no air conditioning aside from a small window unit my friend helped me purchase. It was too hot for coffee, too hot to even really want to get out of bed, so I lay in bed thinking of what I could do to escape the heat. I had checked my messages as always and saw a string of deleted messages from my husband that he had sent all before 9 a.m. I texted a "question mark" emoji, confused as to all the deleted messages. And then, after twenty minutes or so, the text: "At this point, I give up. Game over. Marriage over, Pace."

Deep sighs.

While not all divorces are this way, of course, many can be amicable or even happy, for most who have been divorced, myself included, divorce is a shitty, heartbreaking process. My husband and I had been married for seven years, lived on both the East and West Coasts, raised two dogs, shared a life together. Then COVID-19 hit, and I couldn't find a sustainable source of income as a trans, fat, disabled person. Financial stress upon financial stress. Our dear friend told us he was moving from DC to the Twin Cities and, having been unable to find a job for going on three years during the pandemic and with the costs of living in DC insurmountable, my husband and I agreed that I would go with our friend in hopes that the cheaper costs of living and change in setting would help, while he would stay in the DC region at his current job until he could find a better one in the area. I got my small studio apartment, found a job relatively quickly, and began life out in Minneapolis. But the cracks in our relationship from financial stresses of COVID, plus underlying hurt and communication issues, formed. The long distance made it hard. Almost every phone call would turn into a fight. And then, after many nights of crying myself to sleep, the text. It had been a long time coming, and yet, it also caught me off guard. I won't share more of our story or the path we both walked on, unintentionally or not, that brought us to that text. After all, it is as much his story as mine and I am not sure I could tell my own side of things even now, over a year after the divorce was finalized, over two years since that text, over nine years since we married, almost fifteen years since we first met.

But I can say something about the heartbreak that still lingers. The tears that clear trails down the side of my face at every unexpected photo to show up in social media memories. I can say something about love and about heartbreak, and about the queerness therein. I can speak to how the loss of my husband to divorce is not quite the same as a loss to death, because even though we have not spoken since well before the divorce was finalized, he is still out there, somewhere. It's not like the loss of my brother, who died at the age of eighteen from a drug overdose. In the case of my brother, any future with him is gone, the grief of possibility and loss forever closed. But there is a queerness to the loss of divorce, the way that my ex-husband is still alive yet estranged. It is almost as if our relationship is a ghost that haunts, that lingers, that refuses to fully leave.

This is the backdrop I have in mind when I approach the words Jesus says about divorce today. Jesus is near the beginning of his ministry. He had spoken throughout much of Galilee and then climbs a small mountain (which gives this oration its name, the Sermon on the Mount), and sits down. His disciples followed, and the text tells us that crowds began to surround Jesus anywhere he appeared. He first preaches the Beatitudes and then compares his followers to salt and light, warning them not to lose saltiness or hide their light. He mentions that he is there to fulfill the Law and the Prophets, not abolish them, and says that one's righteousness must exceed that of the scribes and Pharisees, the most righteous people his listeners could likely imagine, if they have a hope of entering the kingdom of heaven. And then, to the part we hear in today's Gospel story.

Jesus goes through several of the Ten Commandments, redefining each for his followers. Not only committing murder is sinful, but holding anger in your heart at and insulting others is sinful. Forgive one another before making an offer to God. Pay your debts. Don't swear by heaven, but let your yes be a yes and your no be a no.

And then Jesus speaks about divorce, lust, and adultery. Jesus's words strike harsh against my ears: "I say to you that anyone who divorces his wife, except on the ground of sexual immorality, causes her to commit adultery, and whoever marries a divorced woman commits adultery" (Matt. 5:32). The sting of divorce is bad enough, but to be accused of either forcing my spouse to commit adultery or committing adultery myself because our marriage failed? What the hell, Jesus? My heart is already broken, bleeding out, and this passage throws salt into the wound.

But when we take a step back to look at the context of this passage among the others chosen in the lectionary for the day, and when we also apply a historical context, it begins to make a little more sense. Deuteronomy chapter 30 is a continuation of explanations around the covenant that God made with Israel. God has already promised the Israelites safety and a land to call their own. God has already freed the Israelites from captivity in Egypt. And God promises ongoing prosperity if Israel continues to show kindness to each other and the stranger and worship God alone. If Israel, as a people, turn away from kindness toward bitterness and turn away from the God who brought them safety and a land of prosperity, the consequence is death and curses. So Moses says to Israel, "Choose life so that you and your descendants may live, longing the Lord your God" (Deuteronomy 30:19b–20a). The psalm continues this theme, that good things come to those "who walk in the law of the Lord" and seek God with their heart (Psalm 119:1–2, paraphrase).

Then we get to Paul's first letter to the Corinthians, in which he calls the church of Corinth infants not ready for the fullness of a spiritual life, since they continue to have "jealousy and quarreling among" them, fighting over who their spiritual leader is, and failing to understand that God is so much bigger than their arguments. Paul reminds the church of Corinth that God is ultimately responsible for the church's growth, not him or

Apollos or anyone else, and thus they should stop their quarreling so that they may be ready for a more spiritually full life.

To me, the theme of these passages is clear: God wants and calls us toward unity and kindness to our neighbors, especially the least among us. God provided us with growth and life. And yet, we, as humans, whether the ancient Israelites or the church of Corinth, or we as church today, continually fail. In that context, Jesus's call for forgiveness makes much more sense. Forgive one another, reconcile with each other, work toward wholeness and unity, don't dwell in division or hatred.

Jesus's harsh words against divorce, then, also make sense, particularly in historical context. Women had very few legal protections under the Roman occupation of Judea. Their wealth, protection, and legal standing were tied to their father if they were a child and to their spouse if they were an adult. Widows and divorced women sometimes had the legal protection of their own male children, provided they had male children who were old enough and willing to provide those protections.

It seems as if Jesus is trying to provide some legal protection for these women. Don't divorce your wife except in cases of sexual immorality so that she may continue to have legal protections and safety. If you do divorce her, you are causing her harm and violating her safety. It is interesting to me that Jesus is speaking to the husbands, not the wives, in this situation, which seems to drive the point home that this is a message to those with legal standing to provide better protection and safety to those without.

And yet, I still am troubled by this passage. It still does not sit right within me. I have worked in domestic violence shelters and the message that one needs to forgive the perpetrator of their harm has done so much damage. The message that divorce is a moral failing and inherently sinful, no matter the cause, also has done great damage. Many of the clients I have worked with have felt pressured by their churches, their community, family, pastors, and spouses to forgive sexual violence, infidelity, physical violence, or emotional violence. I see the heartbreak and pain that goes into the ending of relationships in almost every instance, even ones that are overall a decision made amicably and mutually. The words Jesus offered to his listeners two thousand years ago were meant to keep people safe within a broken system, a system that undervalued women and genders other than men, and a system that did not account for physical, sexual, or emotional violence. It is not enough for me to say that in the original context, these words were meant to help and provide safety when the political, religious, and cultural systems were broken and without addressing that this advice can do so much harm.

To queer this text is to hold it accountable for the ways it has failed to live up to the protections and care for neighbor and stranger that it was meant to inspire. It is to recognize the complexity of relationships and the work, communication, joys, and heartbreaks that go into all relationships. To queer this text is to yes, say let us always work toward forgiveness, but also let us leave room and space for those who are still hurting and let us commit to holding ourselves and each other accountable to the harm we do to one another.

We do not live in a morally clear world where there is always a right decision and a wrong decision. Sometimes, we have to choose between two or more bad decisions or painful decisions. Sometimes, to do what is best for ourselves and one another, we have to end relationships. Sometimes, to keep ourselves safe and to work through the harm we have been dealt, we need more time to forgive and sometimes the hurt is so deep that forgiveness is not even possible. What do we do in those situations?

There is a trust implicit in all the texts for today: Trust in God's forgiveness and err on the side of kindness. Yes, just as the church of Corinth, we will continually make mistakes. We will continue to harm one another. But we know that God continues to patiently wait alongside us, calling us to a different future. And it means trusting that in those queer in-between spaces, spaces between joy and heartbreak, hurt and healing, love and grief, God dwells with us and will not abandon us.

PROPER 2, THE SUNDAY CLOSEST TO MAY 18

Dr. Peter Carlson

Leviticus 19:1–2, 9–18
Psalm 119:33–40
1 Corinthians 3:10–11, 16–23
Matthew 5:38–48

"Give me understanding," the psalmist cries, "and I shall keep your law." I freely admit that I often feel this way, particularly as I look at the outrageous commands that I claim to take seriously as a Christian. "Help me understand, G-d" I cry. "Your ways are so utterly contrary to everything I have learned in life, contrary to everything the world is telling me I should be concerned with and striving for. But if I could just understand, G-d, I'm absolutely sure I'd be able to follow your law exquisitely."

Every semester, on the first day of classes, I like to explain to my students that it is important for them to know what biases their professor brings into the classroom—not biases in the negative sense, but in the reality sense: We all lean (which is, after all, what *bias* means) in certain directions. And so I tell them that they should know that, as their religion professor, I identify as a Christian, but I am a shitty one.

This probably surprises no one who knows me. I struggle all the time with what it means to be a Jesus follower, with the fact that I am asked to love those who hate me (and whom I, if I am honest, relish hating), to do good to those who harm me, to sell everything I have and give the money to the poor, to pick up that goddam cross, and actually follow Jesus.

So, yeah. Shitty Christian here.

Maybe it's a good thing that Proper 2 isn't heard very often; it only appears when Easter shows up ultra-early in the calendar year. I say this, because the lessons today are ultimately a list of reasons why the tradition we Christians claim to follow is actually ridiculous, if not downright impossible. There is deep irony, in fact, in the request of today's collect, which asks that G-d will keep us from all things that will hurt us, whilst simultaneously accomplishing those things that belong to G-d's purpose—as though doing those things that will accomplish G-d's purpose isn't exactly what will actually end up getting us hurt, and sometimes very badly, by the world.

The portion of the Levitical code we read for today should give us a hint of this, beginning with G-d's commandment, "You shall be holy because I am holy. I am The Name." I can understand wanting to read this as a cause-and-effect thing, but I really do think it's a command: "You wanna be holy? You wanna be in relationship with me? Then be holy, for My sake." And The Name goes on to explain exactly what being holy means. Our reading omits, perhaps understandably, a few verses where G-d is laying out some pretty strict rules about sacrifices, and being cut off from the people if you still have leftovers from your sacrifice on the third day. But we pick up again in verse 9, where we find that being holy means that you leave a portion of your harvest, of your profits, for the poor and the immigrants. You do not, in today's capitalist language, "maximize your profits," and you certainly don't build a wall to keep immigrants out. Indeed, if you do these practical, capitalist things, Torah makes clear, it will make you literally unholy.

Moreover, you don't deal falsely with each other, and you don't lie to each other, and you absolutely don't *dare* to bring the Name of G-d into the conversation if you're planning to cheat, because G-d is totally going to get you for that. (This, incidentally, is the real issue behind using G-d's name in vain in the Exodus version of the commandments—it's not anger-cussing.) And more: You pay your employees *immediately*, and you make sure the disabled have access to everything (refusing to make your buildings accessible because it's not financially convenient is another way of maximizing your profits, isn't it?). You ensure that justice is available to everyone, not just those who can afford fancy lawyers. You must not profit from another's blood (take that, military industrial complex!). You shall love your neighbor as much as you love yourself. The Name is The Name.

As I read through these, I was trying to imagine a business administration degree program that teaches these as foundational business principles. My guess is that it would not do well.

Of course, it is tempting—oh, how tempting!—to dismiss these details of the Levitical code as irrelevant for Christians. I mean, after all, how many of us eat shrimp, right? It would be easier to do this if Leviticus 19 were not the second iteration of the (in)famous Ten Commandments that so many folks seem to think belong posted in our courthouses and public school rooms. Indeed, given how absurd some of the commandments we are hearing today are, it's kind of shocking to think that people would *want* to post them anywhere in public. It almost makes one wonder if, in fact, they've ever read them.

But even if we Christians might seek, in a supersessionist mindset, to pretend that the Levitical code has naught to do with us, that Christ has, shall we say, freed us from the law (I'm looking at you, Saint Paul), we are brought face-to-face in the Gospel of Matthew with a new Moses, and a new Mount Sinai, reminding us that the Law is with us still.

It seems absolutely certain that the author of Matthew (whatever their actual name was) was writing to a Jewish Christian audience, because they include so many references to Jewish tradition, scripture, and practice throughout, and no self-respecting, even nominally practicing Jew could possibly have missed them. The Sermon on the Mount is one such reference. In this part of Matthew's story, Jesus climbs a mountain, and talks about the Law, the Torah. And while Jesus is represented throughout the entire Gospel of Matthew as a new Moses, the connection here is so explicit as to be unmistakable. Jesus, the new Moses, climbing a new Mount Sinai, to receive from G-d a New Covenant, and a New Law.

Except that it's not new. And this is the part that really sucks eggs: It's the same Law, only *it's even harder*. Really, Jesus? *Really?* Having just finished dropping the bombast of the Beatitudes, in which Everyone Who We Don't Think Is Blessed Is Blessed (and I really want people who sport "God Bless America" bumper stickers to read these, so they can know what G-d's blessings actually look like and for whom they are reserved), Jesus goes on to explain what the Law actually means, using a series of "You have heard that it was said . . . But I say" bombshells on the crowd: You have heard it said that justice looks like taking an eye from the person who poked out your eye. But I say don't resist evildoers. If someone punches you on the right jaw, turn and offer them the left. If someone steals something from you, give them more of your shit. If someone puts you in a forced march, go even further.

I'm sorry, Jesus, but what the ever-living fuck? The Levitical code seeks to ensure that everyone has access to justice, and here you are telling me that I'm not allowed to seek justice? Screw that.

"Give to everyone who begs from you and do not refuse anyone who wants to borrow from you."

Okay, I'll freely admit that I'd love Citibank and Wells Fargo to pay attention to this, but surely it doesn't mean *me*? Can I at least draw up a repayment contract at a reasonable rate of interest, Jesus?

"Love your enemies and pray for those who persecute you, so that you may be children of your heavenly Parent."

Oh, sweet Jesus. I'm not you. When I get beaten up, while my attackers are yelling "FAGGOT!" I don't have a lot of energy left over to pray for them, much less love them. Frankly, Jesus, I don't want to live in a world where victims of sexual assault are asked to pray for their attackers, or where the poor trying to get sustenance-level food are asked to love the politicians who don't think they've "earned" it, or where my transgender siblings cannot access health care because paranoid legislatures need an "ick" factor to stay in power.

You can tell me all day long to be perfect, as our heavenly Parent is perfect, Jesus, but this is a place where I'm going to just admit that I'm a shitty Christian and tell you to kiss my imperfect ass.

But Paul, in his letter to the Corinthians, has a reminder for us. His reminder is that we are right in our response to all this do-good-to-assholes messaging: It *is* insane. It doesn't make any sense at all. It's outrageous and foolish and will probably get us killed. In fact, verse 19 is cutting right to the chase for me: "The wisdom of this world is foolishness with G-d." And presumably, the reverse is also true, that the wisdom of HaShem is foolishness to the world.

Being queer in a straight-run world seems foolish indeed, particularly if, as some folks claim, it is a "lifestyle choice." I remember a comedian long ago, when it was even more dangerous to be gay than it is now, asking rhetorically, "We're 'converting' people? Really? What are the selling points? Hi! We're here! We're queer! People won't let us rent from them or teach their kids and often want to kill us! Join us!" When I came out in my final year of college, my parents' very real concern was for my literal safety. And we can certainly see many ways in which the world (or at least this part of the world) has gotten safer for queers, all it takes is the most cursory look around to realize that there are still plenty of people who hate me enough to wish me, if not dead, at least not in their neighborhood. And there are probably even more who might claim to love me but who still vote for politicians who have made it a goal to harm me.

I can't love these people, Jesus. I just can't. I don't have the capacity to love people whose fear of my queer family drives them to do hateful and horrible things. I simply don't have that kind of a heart. I long for your commandments, O G-d, but I do not have the wisdom that will enable me to keep your law. I'm a shitty Christian.

But I *am* a Christian. And so I struggle. I acknowledge the outrageousness of thinking that what Jesus says is right, even though the world has shown me over and over again that if I actually follow Jesus, I will end up like Jesus, crucified by imperial forces. And I remind myself, particularly at this beginning of so-called "Ordinary Time" that follows so close on the Easter season, that I can fight for justice so that the world comes a little closer to being safe for my Queerly Beloveds, and maybe even have enough energy left over to pray for those who persecute me.

PROPER 3, THE SUNDAY CLOSEST TO MAY 25

The Rev. Jeremy S. Whitner, MDiv

Isaiah 49:8–16b
Psalm 131
1 Corinthians 4:1–5
Mathew 6:24–34

Hooking Up with Jesus: Growing in Relationship with the Triune God Through Trust

In today's scripture lessons, we have four readings that guide us to focus on trusting in God and not fretting about the small things that occur in everyday life. I know these lessons are challenging in a world where current events are distressing and there is so much division. It isn't healthy or safe, and we have legitimate concerns for our safety. However, we can view trusting in God as a relationship that encourages us to reach for the stars in everything we do. When we look into these lessons, we learn that as we trust God along the journey, we do not need to worry, but as we follow God, God will provide all. That's today's theme: "Trust in God."

In our first reading from the book of Isaiah, we have the words from "second Isaiah." This is from the time right before the King of Babylon, Cyrus, allowed the people of Israel to return to the land. The words of the

Lord paint an image of liberation and restoration of the land. In verses 8 and 9, Isaiah gives voice to God saying:

> Thus says the Lord:
> "In a time of favor I have answered you,
> on a day of salvation I have helped you;
> I have kept you and given you
> as a covenant to the people,
> to establish the land,
> to apportion the desolate heritages;
> saying to the prisoners, 'Come out,'
> to those who are in darkness, 'Show yourselves.'
> They shall feed along the ways,
> on all the bare heights shall be their pasture."

The author says this restoration shall not have thirst or hunger. We must remember that in the mind of the Jewish people of the day, *salvation* and *peace* are not just metaphysical words, they are very physical terms. Their bodies were taken care of. The word for "salvation" or "redemption" is the imagery of the "cloud" leading the people of Israel out of Egypt, or "shading them out of Egypt." Again, the theme of trust in God is clear.

Our psalm is a Song of Ascent. It was a psalm sung as people journeyed from their hometowns to Jerusalem to celebrate Holy Days at the temple. They would ascend the hill of Jerusalem, hence the term *Songs of Ascent*. It is also titled *A Song of Quiet Trust* in most of our bibles. It is only a short 3 verses, whereas most psalms have upward of 30 verses, which is why we break them up in our lectionary and as sung responses. Most psalms contain two parts: a "supplication" (or a call out to God) and an "ask." This psalm doesn't include that second portion. It is *all* supplication, no ask. It is a simple psalm that is a supplication to God but builds on a deep sense of trust. In verses one and two, it says, "O Lord, my heart is not lifted up, my eyes are not raised too high; I do not occupy myself with things too great and too marvelous for me. But I have calmed and quieted my soul, like a weaned child with its mother; my soul is like the weaned child that is with me." This deep trust uses the imagery of a child with its mother. One of the first places we learn of God is from our parents. Not only our parents of blood but also our relatives and families that we choose. Not all of our parents love us unconditionally. Some LGBTQ folks learn unconditional love in other places. It could be a drag house or some other type of familial dynamic. It could be the drag mother who may help the young person experience putting on makeup for the first time. Or mentors on how to perform in front of a crowd for the first time. We have all seen this depicted on television shows like *Pose* and films like *Paris is Burning*. We see a young person on the streets, maybe in a dangerous situation, taken in by a person and given things they need to survive. They are then also given the power to be themselves and flourish. The young people eventually learn to put on their makeup by themselves and walk in whatever category they are suited for and want to in most cases—winning all the trophies of which they have been deprived. Verse 3 ends this psalm by saying "O Israel, hope in the Lord from this time on and for evermore." The author implores the listeners and the people of Israel to place their trust in the Lord. This is from where their and our hope comes. Our hope comes from God who liberated Israel and continues to liberate us and care for us to this day.

In Paul's first letter to the Corinthians, he is telling them that he trusts in God no matter the outcome of what may occur. He tells them we are "stewards of God's mystery." He tells them to put their trust in God and God will judge them accordingly. He says he doesn't know of anything he has personally done wrong, so the courts do not scare him. He says he will stand before God who is the judge. He ends with verse 5, saying, "Therefore do not pronounce judgment before the time, before the Lord comes, who will bring to light the things now hidden in darkness and will disclose the purposes of the heart. Then each one will receive commendation from God." For Paul, God alone can judge any situation, and any person. We are not meant to be judging ourselves and others in situations. I admit that flies in the face of so much of the theology of churches that I was raised with. People in a lot of those churches love to judge; it's almost an Olympic sport. They judge people for their clothes, for what they eat or don't eat. The list can go on and on. The letter goes back to our Gospel today and says that we shouldn't worry but trust in God in all we do. In the end, God will judge and that's where we place our trust. The letter indicates that real trust involves avoiding judgment. It also circles back to a similar theme as our psalm: There is no need to ask since God is so great and is doing so much.

In our Gospel reading today, we have a section on what people recognize as the Sermon on the Mount. People typically think the Sermon is only chapter 5 in Matthew, but it is actually chapters 5 through 7. This particular section is repeated in Luke, as well. We can safely assume it was something both Gospel writers took from the source or *Quelle* (also known as Q). We don't have a full copy of this source document, but it is safe to say it was a collection of sayings that was gathered by the early church. In this section, Jesus tells us not to worry. True discipleship and following God's words and Jesus's words are the very root of discipleship. We are building on the trust that flows from God. Jesus tells us that God provides for the plants and other animals, so why wouldn't God also provide for us? Worry is something hazardous to our health. Worry is something like a plaque. It's a waste of good imagination. Instead, use every bit of your imagination to picture all the good things. Worry causes us to picture every worst-case scenario. What happens if the sun explodes? What happens with a certain political outcome? What happens if you lose an employment opportunity? Now for some of us, living in our modest means, most of the world survives on way less. Yes, we struggle sometimes, but a lot of us have shelter, and we have food in the cabinet. In this lesson, Jesus implores his disciples to not worry about the clothes we wear, or where we are going to get our next meal. The Gospel tells us that we pray to God for our daily bread and then trust God to provide it. God is imploring us to use our energy for something bigger by putting our trust in him and reaching for the stars. Say yes to trust and "no" to worry and judgment.

Trusting in God and the work of discipleship is like forming a romantic relationship. We are in a sense hooking up with the Trinity. One can look at it as dancing and hooking up in all sorts of ways with Jesus, the Creator, and the Holy Spirit. It starts with going on a first date, and nurturing the relationship as it grows. Queering this trust in God is, in a sense, the very queering of discipleship. When we put our faith in God, we don't worry and we don't judge. Trust starts on that first date and builds as you build in a relationship. No matter how you love, relationships grow from that same starting point. A person trusts the other person enough to submit to something they may not have full control over, in everyday life or sexually. The person trusts enough to be vulnerable with someone else. We build trust in ourselves to the point of saying yes. Over time, you eventually get to the point where it becomes natural to get in the car with your partner and God and go on a seven-day road trip across the continent. You may also do something you wouldn't typically do because your partner suggests it. It is being open to trying new things, including all the firsts that come with time. Trusting in God is the same way. It is building a relationship in that discipleship where love is the key. It is being open to intimate acts and saying yes to the craziest things that may be proposed.

It may also look like the dynamics of joining a drag house (*Haus O'Gawd?*) or other houses of nonblood relatives. You may want to experience the culture and life of walking the runways of life, of winning categories. You do that by learning to first trust your Drag Mother or Mz. Holy Spirit. Experimenting with the gifts that the Holy Spirit gives, then going out into the world to win the trophies and categories.

Enjoying life and trusting in God is about savoring all the moments of life and not worrying and overthinking the moments that may occur. Saying yes to the liberation and hope of God, like we would on a "say yes" night (if you will), or fully engaging in a relationship with God like so many of our ancestors did. The list goes from Abraham who said yes and left his homeland of Ur to journey to follow God. It includes Mary when she said yes to the conception of Jesus through the Holy Spirit. Our yeses are not always clean or easy; there is always the messiness of life involved. May we say yes to God and allow our romance to grow. Life can be one big "yes" night to God if we allow our trust and faith to grow in God. So may it be!

VISITATION OF MARY TO ELIZABETH, MAY 31

Dr. Gabrielle M. W. Bychowski, PhD

1 Samuel 2:1–10
Psalm 113
Romans 12:9–16b
Luke 1:39–57

A Dysphoric *Kulning*: Queer Calls and Responses to Women's Ministry

The Song of Elsa

"Ah-ah, ah-ah!" The echoing refrain throughout the second *Frozen* film derives from a practice developed by Scandinavian shepherds, called a *kulning*. Each shepherd creates a unique variation of a kulning to sing for their sheep. This is especially helpful when two herds get mixed together. The two shepherds can stand on separate sides and by singing their song, the corresponding sheep split off towards their caretaker. *Frozen 2* imitates the musical style of these *kulnings* but deploys them towards a person, rather than livestock.

Early in the film, a Spirit calls to Elsa with a mysterious *kulning* that no one else can hear but her. At first, through the song "Into the Unknown" Elsa rejects the Call to Adventure with the Spirit. She sings in response that she can hear but refuses to listen. She cites a thousand precious things about her current life that this Call would disrupt. Yes, our hero rejects the Call. In part, this might be because she misunderstands it and what it wants from her. "What do you want?" She pleads. "'cause you've been keeping me awake." This scene of repeatedly being awoken by a mysterious voice is like the prophet Samuel's experience when he is likewise awoken by the Spirit. (1 Samuel 3). Samuel wakes up his mentor multiple times, thinking it was he who was calling the young boy. Finally, Samuel is told that the voice may be that of the Spirit and that if the Spirit calls again, he should answer, "Speak, your servant is listening."

Yet in another sense, Elsa does understand what the Spirit asks of her but fears what it could mean. Returning to her thousand reasons to maintain the status quo, Elsa agonizes over the thought of losing her beloveds and the current relationships she shares with them. Also, Elsa adds, she has had one adventure already! (See: the first *Frozen* film.) Why challenge her hard-won peace with another adventure, when the very etymology of *adventure* comes from the French words for "a veering" away from the expected path. Elsa does not want any more life lessons because they tend to involve even more life changes. Elsa does not want a sequel film! What else might she learn about herself and her world? What else might she lose? What lurks in the unknown of her world? The Call of the Spirit, the call to Prophecy and Ministry requires letting go of a more conventional life, a more normative life.

The turning point for Elsa comes when she considers that the voice may be a resonant Spirit that vibes with what makes her so special. She asks the voice if they are someone who might, in fact, be a little like herself, and she acknowledges, finally, that she is not where she should be, and that some small part of her soul actually is longing to go "into the unknown." Elsa is the Queen of Arendelle and by the end of her hero's journey, she will surrender her throne to become a Spiritual leader living in the woods among the indigenous peoples of Norway. And this change of heart comes through admitting that there may be something strange, alien, queer about the Spirit that resonates with the way that Elsa is different, non-normative, queer. After all, a *kulning* is a song that connects shepherd and sheep, singer and audience in a special relationship of coidentification and interdependence. Queer lives may be non-normative but that does not mean they are not communal, familial, or even domestic.

Personally, I remember watching the first *Frozen* film with my stepkids. We were down in Silver Springs, Maryland, as I was completing my PhD in Literature. The film as a whole did not speak to me, except for the one portion that seemed to be everywhere that Christmas: the song "Let It

Go." This musical number changed the course of the whole franchise. For years, Disney had been trying to adapt the Hans Christian Anderson story, the Ice Queen, with little success. In these early drafts, the Ice Queen (later named Elsa) was the villain. A cursory listen to "Let It Go" reveals how the song could have originally been imagined as a Villain's song, standing in the lineage of other queer-coded Disney villains like Scar's "Be Prepared" and Ursula's "Poor Unfortunate Souls." Like these other antagonists, Elsa is declaring that she will no longer play nice, she won't follow the rules anymore, she is turning her back on society. All of these things are usually enough to tell audiences, oh this is the bad guy. But in the twenty-first century, a song like Elsa's resonated strongly with coming-out songs from the LGBTQ community. This raised the question, is Elsa really a villain? What if she is misunderstood like so many other queer women who reject social norms to live more authentic lives? This all did not occur to me in my first listen, but by the hundredth time my kids had me play the song in the car, I was hooked. When *Frozen 2* finally came around, I was more into the franchise than the kids and taught the sequel in my college seminar, Queer Christianity.

The Song of Mary

In my classrooms, I pair the Song of Elsa with the Song of Mary, the Magnificat (Luke 1:39-56). In both cases, women are hearing the Call of the Spirit and respond to it through music. "My soul magnifies the Lord, / and my spirit rejoices in God," Mary sings. "Surely, from now on all generations will call me blessed." In this opening, Mary rejects the notion that women should be demure, small, and humble. Mary declares that her Calling is a blessed vocation. Yet she recognizes that her song does not originate in her, but is an echo of the divine Spirit. Her song and soul magnify the musical of the spheres, the *kulning* of God.

As women called by the Spirit, Mary and Elsa both know that their songs will result in the fall of Kingdoms. For Elsa, she is the one who steps down from her throne. For Mary, the threat of spiritual revolution is aimed much wider than one monarch or one nation. "[God] has scattered the proud in the thoughts of their hearts," declares Mary. "He has brought down the powerful from their thrones, / and lifted up the lowly; / he has filled the hungry with good things, / and sent the rich away empty." The God of Mary is not a God of the Status Quo. Who we are as individuals or as a nation is not fixed. This is a God of change, growth, and deepening self-discovery. Specifically, the Spirit speaking through Mary is the prophetic call to break down existing hierarchies. This broad language cuts widely, suggesting that hierarchal binaries of class, race, gender, and sexual will be deconstructed as those on the margins are risen up to stand on level ground with their oppressors.

The threat and warning that Mary's song embodies may sound like a dangerous dissonant revolution song to some. But those who already live the dysphoria of an unjust and unequitable world resonate differently to this call and response.

As a woman, I vibrate with the longing to see the marginalized and subjugated lifted up as the multiheaded institutions of the patriarchy fall. As a trans person, I also wish for all our lives to be filled with good things so that we too might embody our own versions of the true, good, and beautiful. As a neurospicy individual, I pray with Mary that the diverse range of bodies, neurologies, and spectrums of experience be called Blessed.

Embodying some or all of those forms of specialness, Elsa's song brings about a change in the hierarchy of her Queendom, the end to colonial practices, and a spiritual transformation in the lives of those marked by the rainbow light of the north and the songs of their foremothers.

The Song of Hannah

As we put Elsa's song into the context of Scripture, it is not enough to consider only Mary as a Spiritual Foremother. The Disruptive and Dysphoric Call for Women to Prophesize is not a modern or Christian innovation within ministry. These build on traditions developed with Judaism. In the chapter before Samuel hears the Spirit calling to him in the middle of the night, Hannah professes a prayer that likewise calls for a Spirit of Revolution that would disrupt the status quo of normative society (1 Samuel 2). "My heart exults in the Lord; / my strength is exalted in my God," Hannah prays, in language Mary would later echo. Again, Hannah does not create her song whole cloth. She too is responding to a *kulning* of sorts issued by the Spirit.

Hannah too sings the revolution into being. "The bows of the mighty are broken, / but the feeble gird on strength. / Those who were full have hired themselves out for bread, / but those who were hungry are fat with spoil . . . The Lord makes poor and makes rich; / he brings low; he also exalts. / He raises up the poor from the dust; / he lifts the needy from the ash heap / to make them sit with princes / and inherit a seat of honor."

Elsa, Mary, and Hannah are three women called by a queer spirit, magnifying and echoing the song of social Revolution. Without needing to be explicitly LGBTQ, each women envisions a queering of the world, a turn away from the status quo. All three prophetic women anticipate the fall of a Kingdom and the rising of the downtrodden.

The Song of Our Foremothers

In the case of Elsa, however, the *kulning* of queer women may be more explicit as her final song evidences. As Elsa sings "Show Yourself," she arrives at the end of her pilgrimage north to a frozen fortress called Ahtohallan. As she enters the yonic opening of the ice cave, descending into a cavern reminiscent of a vagina, Elsa proclaims her state of excitement. She is trembling. However, the Queen of Ice and Snow acknowledges, this trembling is not because of the cold. Elsa thus suggests a form of arousal that might edge on the sexually erotic or the spiritually ecstatic.

Frozen 2 plays with a resonance between the Spiritual and the Sapphic. Elsa sings that this feeling she has is rooted in something familiar and yet something she cannot fully grasp. This familiarity of the Spirit flirts with the Transcendence of God, a beyond that cannot be quite grasped. At the same time, it honors a divine imminence, a Goddess who is the Womb of All Creation. She senses the Spirit as a friend, a lover, a kin who has been connected to her from the very beginning. Although Elsa arrives at a totally new place and new experience, she somehow feels like this arrival is a returning home. Augustine of Hippo imagines God as the place where his restless heart can finally find rest. Yet Elsa adds a specifically sapphic dimension to this image.

Delving deeper into the ice-Womb of Ahtohallan, Elsa reflects that she too (in body and spirit) is like this vaginal cavern of ice. As she sings, Elsa admits that she too is like a frozen castle, keeping deep mysteries hidden inside herself. Then turning on the feminine voice echoing throughout the body of caves, Elsa begins pleading like a desperate lover following after her beloved. Elsa is dying to meet the speaker of the Voice. She has taken the first step to expose herself and now it is the other's turn to unmask. She insists that neither Elsa nor the Spirit need to hide any longer, their mysteries resonating with a shared queerness.

Begging for the Spirit to end her great adventure, Elsa repeats the name of the song, "Show Yourself!" She desperately asks the voice if she is the one for which her heart yearns. She wants to know if she is the home she has been desiring. "Open your door," pleads Elsa, echoing a refrain from the first *Frozen* film where all doors had felt locked to her. She asks that her beloved not make her wait a moment longer for this great climax. Time is both accelerating and collapsing into the no-time of joy, an immediacy that can be said to participate both in spiritual and the sexual experiences. Elsa feels like she is on the brink of an orgasmic ecstasy, a queer revelation that she is not alone. More and more, Elsa seems convinced that the Spirit is like her, and it is time that they come out to one another. They are opening their doors to one another, opening their bodies, sharing inner most secrets. Whether or not this encounter is read as explicitly sexual, the sapphic intimacy here is undeniable. There is deep longing and resonance between a like and like who are both unlike the wider normative world.

Elsa contemplates how she has always felt different as she comes closer to the inner room of Ahtohallan. Elsa was not born to follow the normal (or normative) rules of life. This confession of queerness applies both to her role as spiritual leader and as a person with non-normative sexuality. Multiple groups coidentify with Elsa in the LGBTQ community. Lesbians and other sapphic women connect with Elsa's seeming aversion to partnering with men. Asexual and aromantic people also feel kinship with Elsa's history of not yet partnering with anyone outside of friends or family. Normal scripts for life or for Disney Princess movies do not apply for Elsa or the *Frozen* franchise.

The final revelation of Ahtohallan is that the person Elsa is called by the Spirit to embrace is not another woman but a version of herself as minister. While the film does not discount a call to the vocation of wife to another woman—in fact *Frozen 2* seems to suggest a potential female romantic partner for Elsa in the person of Honeymaren—the special queer calling that this episode promises is one of spiritual leader. Elsa is called to step into her power. She is called to grow into this new version of herself. Who has Elsa been yearning for this whole time? Her authentic self.

The Spirit of Ahtohallan makes these revelations in the voice of Elsa's mother. This is the synthesis that began back when Elsa heard the first *kulning*: By stepping into the role of queer woman minister, she has come to embody both parts of the call and response. In doing so, she embodied an echo of all the foremothers who came before her: Iduna (Elsa's mother), the indigenous Northuldra People and the colonizing people of Arendelle, yet also her spiritual foremothers Mary and Hannah.

Each of us today—especially those blessed to be queer, trans, ace/aro, women and femmes representing many cultures, embodiments, and neurodivergences—hear our own kulnings. Whatever vocation the Spirit sings to you, may you likewise find your own ways to respond. In time, may you too step into your power, grow yourself into something new, raise up the low and bring down harmful institutions, and follow the path set by our foremothers. May you hear their songs, resonate with them, and in time come to sing your own call and response, "Ah-ah, ah-ah!"

PROPER 4, THE SUNDAY CLOSEST TO JUNE 1

Dr. Peter Carlson

Track 1	or	Track 2
Genesis 6:9–22; 7:24; 8:14–19		*Deuteronomy 11:18–21, 26–28*
Psalm 46		*Psalm 31:1–5, 19–24*
Romans 1:16–17; 3:22b–28, (29–31)		*Romans 1:16–17; 3:22b–28, (29–31)*
Matthew 7:21–29		*Matthew 7:21–29*

There are times when the naïveté of the collects drives me absolutely bananas. Today, the person presiding at the service has to bring themself to speak of G-d's "never-failing providence" that "sets in order all things both in heaven and earth." I'll be honest. It is supremely difficult to look around the world today and believe that all things are set in order, or that Divine Providence is in any way at work. Call me a doubter, I don't care. The evidence is with me.

Perhaps ironically, however, in the midst of my doubts, both tracks in the Hebrew Bible are referring to Divine Providence. This idea that G-d orders everything for the good and is in final control is a concept that is hard to reconcile with theodicy—the question of the role of evil in the world and G-d's part in it. In track 1, we hear the classic story of Noah, and in track 2, we get the final promise of G-d to the Israelites about entering the so-called Promised Land. In one story, we have humans behaving badly and being punished; in the other, we have the warning that, if humans behave badly, they'll be punished—but if they behave well, they'll get goodies.

Indeed, it seems in the story of Noah that G-d G-dself had days when They believed that all things in heaven and earth were very much *not* set in order, and it made Them really cranky. The reading hops and skips about, but interestingly omitted is the bit just before the reading, which is stunningly important theologically: HaShem saw that the wickedness of humans was great in the earth and that every inclination of the thoughts of their hearts was only evil continually. And HaShem was sorry that They had made humans on the earth, and it grieved Them to Their heart. So HaShem said, "I will blot out from the earth the human beings I have created—people together with animals and creeping things and birds of the air, for I am sorry that I have made them."

I really want us to sit with that for a moment. This is G-d deciding to wipe out everything on the planet because humans are fucked up. Rational? Absolutely not. Loving? *So* not loving. Setting all things in order? Not asswipe likely. Rather, just wiping it all out.

And only then, after G-d has made up Their mind to erasing the entire Etch-A-Sketch picture, do They see that "Noah was a righteous man." G-d apparently, took another gander at earthland, saw Noah being good, and thought, "Shit. Missed him at the first glance. Hmph. I guess I can't wipe out a righteous person, can I? That wouldn't be quite cricket. So hey; I'll save him, and just wipe out everyone and almost everything the hell else. That'll be totes fair." And so, we get the old familiar story that now shows up in nurseries around the world: Noah and the ark. And I don't know about you, but I grew up being told how merciful and gracious G-d was, to save Noah, and to keep the various breeding animal species alive, and all the while Child Me was wondering what kind of nasty-ass divinity would create humans who, because of original sin, were unable to do good, and then bloody *murder* them for not being able to do good. In my childish understanding, that didn't look merciful to me. It still doesn't, even to my adult understanding. Let's be honest: G-d's destruction of the earth doesn't sound like never-failing providence; it sounds like an out-of-control divinity with major anger issues whose actions seem more like the arbitrary and freakish fates of the Greek pantheon than any kind of omnipotent and omnibenevolent monotheistic Daddygod.

I'm fascinated that the lectionistas put Psalm 46 with the story of Noah. I mean, I get that G-d as "refuge and strength," "a very present help in trouble," "though the waters rage and foam" is probably meant as symbolism for the ark, but again: The only humans who made it out alive in that story are Noah, his three sons, and his nameless wife and daughters-in-law. Clearly G-d was not a very present help in trouble for anyone else. And in verse 10, where we are told that G-d makes war to cease in all the world? Please. The merest glance at the daily newspapers tells us otherwise. Why won't G-d make wars to cease in the Middle East, at least, if They can't manage all the world? We are left, in track 1, with the intimation that, if Providence is indeed in control, then Providence probably needs some pretty extensive therapy.

The reading from the Deuteronomic Code in track 2 is literally headed, in the New Revised Standard Version, "Rewards for Obedience," which frankly makes me think of humanity as dogs who rely on treats for heeling properly and not peeing on the Persian carpet. The passage for today is the source of some Jewish traditions that persist to this day: the tefillin, or the small black leather boxes that contain scrolls of Torah verses that are strapped onto the arms and the forehead during prayers, and the mezuzot, which are also scrolls with Torah verses, attached in a small case on the doorpost of the house. Of the words of G-d, the Israelites are told "you shall bind them as a sign on your hand and fix them as an emblem on your forehead. . . . Write them on the doorposts of your house." And the reason is clear: "So that your days and the days of your children may be multiplied in the land that HaShem swore to your ancestors to give them." The reading goes on to describe the stark choice before G-d's people: It is nothing less than the choice between blessing and curse.

Of course, the lectionary skips the disconcerting, militaristic, colonialist stuff in between the two bits of Deuteronomy assigned for today. The stuff about Israel "dispossessing nations larger and mightier than you," which has unfortunately been utilized out of context as a modern justification for Israeli expansion into Palestinian territory and the destruction of Palestinian lives.

But what the lectionary also doesn't include today is exactly that essential context: It doesn't include what has come just before, which is the definition of what keeping the law means. At the end of chapter 10, we see the summary of the entire Deuteronomic Code: "to fear HaShem your G-d, to walk in all G-d's ways, to love G-d, to serve HaShem your G-d with all your heart and soul. . . . You shall also love the stranger, for you were strangers in the land of Egypt." This is definitely a context that tempers the "You shall beat the shit out of other nations" bit, isn't it? Even so, it's a problem. And the psalm (one of those lovely, confused, bipolar psalms) continues this thinking: "G-d! I'm dying here! I seek refuge in You! I'm the Good Dog, G-d! You saved me! But my bones are wasting away! But no, really, you're great! But *I'm dying here, G-d*!" It ends on a high note, but not after pleading to smack down my enemies because, no really, I'm the faithful one, and why can't you see that, G-d?

So Noah's ass is saved because Noah was good. And the Israelites will get to dwell in the land and pound the shit out of their neighbors if they're good. And here is a really problematic conundrum in both the Hebrew Bible readings: If the only value in obeying the law is to get out of being shafted by Providence, then are we, in fact, any better than dogs?

Even Paul is struggling with this in the letter to the Jesus followers in Rome: the reading starts with the letter's thesis statement in chapter 1: The Gospel is for everyone and reveals G-d's righteousness through faith. This book, of course, is Martin Luther's calling card and his response to the medieval Roman Catholic Church's practice of selling indulgences—a kind of "get out of purgatory free" card. But then the reading jumps to Paul's explanation of what righteousness through faith actually means, in chapter 3. The key for Paul is that it is faith, not works, that reveal G-d's righteousness (not our own, mind you—our righteousness is diddlyshit) to both Jews and Gentiles alike: regardless, he notes, of the details of the "work" of circumcision (which was commanded in the Deuteronomic Code).

So Paul, it seems, is giving us a different kind of indulgence, a different kind of "get out of jail free" card: Just have faith! Have faith that, even though we're all sinners, we "are now justified by G-d's grace as a gift, through the redemption that is in Christ Jesus, whom G-d put forward as a sacrifice of atonement by his blood."

And here is where the Good Doggy theory begins to get even more creepy. Paul suggests that we are all, in fact, Bad Dogs, but that our Owner has sent their own Child to be mauled by us, so that we could be saved, and become Good Dogs, because we have faith in the Owner.

I'm going to go out on a limb here and suggest that this theology perpetuates the idea that Daddy G-d either needs a lot of therapy, or that we're in a consensual S&M relationship with G-d and actually *relish* being beaten by a G-d who relishes beating. Paul's Gospel is radical, let's not doubt that, by breaking down barriers to G-d's grace for the non-Jews. But Paul's rationalization for that grace is still bound in first-century thinking that divinities demand blood in order to be appeased. And I will freely admit that I find bloodthirsty gods unworthy of my adoration or gratitude.

Jesus, in the Gospel of Matthew, has some things to say about Cranky Master G-d *and* the idea of faith being all you need. Just before our passage today is the warning against false prophets; a warning that I always read with trepidation because, as a queer theologian, I am told regularly that I am a ravenous wolf in sheep's clothing, determined to make everyone's kids queer. But verse 21 is arguably just as daunting: "Not everyone who says to me, 'Lord, Lord,' will enter the reign of heaven, but only the one who does the will of my Parent in heaven." Many of us will, Jesus says, argue "But I had faith! I prophesied in your name! I did bucketloads of mighty works in your name!" And Jesus will look blankly at us, and say, "Who are you?"

And here's the key: Jesus reminds us that we have to *act* on his words (though how casting out demons in Jesus's name isn't acting on his words is a question I still ask of him). It is our *actions*, our *works* (are you listening, Paul?) that are like building a house on a solid foundation. And of course Paul even acknowledges this at the end of our reading in Romans (something Luther kind of blips over): "Do we then overthrow the law through this faith? By no means! On the contrary, we uphold the law." On Christ the solid rock we *build*.

As someone who feels as though their sand-house has been washed away over and over again, these words set my heart a-trembling. I am not a masochist (despite the argument that everyone who pursues a PhD must have a streak of self-punishment in themselves). I do not like being whipped or chained, even by G-d. I am constantly struggling with what it means for me, as a big ol' homo Christian, to think that I might have either faith or works enough to appease G-d, to avoid G-d's wrath, to be a Good Dog.

All I can pray is that I'm building my doghouse on a firm foundation.

PROPER 5, THE SUNDAY CLOSEST TO JUNE 8

Dr. Peter Carlson

Track 1	or	Track 2
Genesis 12:1–9		*Hosea 5:15–6:6*
Psalm 33:1–12		*Psalm 50:7–15*
Romans 4:13–25		*Romans 4:13–25*
Matthew 9:9–13, 18–26		*Matthew 9:9–13, 18–26*

The two tracks available for Proper 5 in the lectionary go in two really different directions, offering two really different experiences of a relationship with the Divine. From Genesis, we have the outrageous story of Abram agreeing to follow an obscure G-d to an unknown land that "I will show you." From Hosea, we have a diatribe delivered to the northern kingdom of Israel, which the prophet has compared to an unfaithful wife.

Obedience, disobedience. Faithfulness and unfaithfulness. Good boys and tramps. And where are we to find any common ground, any thread to tie the stories together? Obviously, both tracks share the Epistle and Gospel readings, so perhaps that's the location of the common thread: Paul's letter to the church in Rome, and stories from the Gospel of Matthew.

So, back to Abram. This story is usually presented as a remarkable testimony of trust in G-d, with Abram blindly going to G-d knows where, following G-d's guidance, whatever that may have looked like. Of course, we know from the previous chapter in Genesis that Abram's father, Terah, had begun a journey to Canaan from Ur (way over at the mouth of the Euphrates River), but the family stopped and settled in

Haran, about halfway round the Fertile Crescent, which is where G-d apparently discovered Abram, ripe for the Chosen People Plucking.

The queerness of this story lies in its very randomness. In the prehistorical stories of Genesis 1–11 (particularly in what has been called the Yahwist elements), G-d is presented as changeable, cranky, and even destructive, but rarely irrational. In the flood story, for example, G-d decides to destroy the world, because it is "only evil always" (a remarkable phrase, when you think about it), and then decides to save Noah, because G-d realizes that Noah is, in fact, righteous. The famous Tower of Babel is destroyed because of the sin of pride. The key is that G-d might be nasty and vengeful, but G-d at least gives a reason for Their actions. But there is no reason given for the choice of Abram as a potential source for some kind of "Chosen People." Perhaps Abram had demonstrated some kind of righteousness, like Noah, but we're not told about it. It seems to me just as likely that G-d found someone who would believe voices from nowhere telling him to go somewhere and decided to take advantage of it.

The way this really comes across to me, though, is that Abram was having a midlife crisis and desperately needed a change to feel relevant. This may sound odd to say about a man in his nineties, but remember, Terah lived to be two hundred five years old, so Abram was, according to those calculations, quite literally at midlife. And he was clearly needing to shake things up. And, Corvettes not being available at that period of time, he chose to move. I have always wondered how that conversation might have gone with Sarai: "Honey, we're moving!" "Oh! To where?" "I have no idea."

If wives hadn't been property in that culture, I'm willing to bet Sarai would have beaten Abram with a stick for that. Even so, I'm betting that she had some words for him that didn't get recorded in the biblical record.

So Abram took Sarai, and all his property (including all "the people they had acquired in Haran," which does, and should, sound really creepy to us), and dragged them along with him, following a Voice, in a desperate midlife crisis search to be relevant and maybe to feel young again.

G-d leads them to Canaan, to a place the writers call the House of G-d (Beit El), and says, "This is the land I'm gonna give you. Pay no attention to the fact that there are other people here who might actually have a claim to the land more legitimate than you. But also not yet." And Abram stacks some stones there to make an altar, and then moves on, ultimately to Egypt (a foreshadowing of the story of Joseph and the entire book of Exodus).

Such faith! Such a willingness to follow G-d into the unknown!

Or, on the other hand, such a desperate person, listening to voices that come to him in the night, telling him to give up everything (except his wives and his stuff and his slaves, of course) and go somewhere to steal land from people who already live there!

You might almost think that the Pilgrims got their ideas about land ownership in the New World from this very story.

And then there's Hosea. Good old, cuckolded, grumpy Hosea. Warning the eighth-century BCE northern Israelites of the doom on their doorstep that they brought on themselves, because, like Hosea's own wife, they're sexually profligate tramps who won't stay faithful to G-d. (It is notable that, as in the Genesis story, we don't hear from the women; I do wonder what Gomer, Hosea's wife, might have had to say about the situation. Perhaps Hosea was abusive? Or didn't pay any attention to her because he was so focused on his job as a prophet? Of maybe he was just really bad in bed?)

G-d's message in this passage is like Hosea's own thinking: "Why are you so unfaithful, Israel? Why are you such an easy lay, Judah? Your love isn't real; it's like the morning dew—full of promise that disappears almost immediately. What am I supposed to do with you, when you're basically begging for me to divorce you? I'm going off on my own until you figure out that you're screwed without me!"

It's really pretty petulant. But as I suggested earlier, this is kind of an opposing story to the story of Abram: Abram was faithful; Israel is unfaithful. Abram followed the voices in his head; Israel followed the lusts of her heart. (Again, I'm going to point out the underlying gendered message here: Women are apparently not only silent, they are inherently unfaithful.)

Even the psalms repeat the comparison. By connecting the story of Abram with Psalm 33, which begins "Rejoice in HaShem, you righteous," we are being guided with really obvious hints to equate righteousness with Abram. The part of Psalm 50 that is attached to the reading from Hosea, on the other hand, is the voice of a G-d disgusted with fake righteousness, who won't accept sacrifices from the Israelites: "I will testify against you," this G-d says, disgusted with the people.

So, seeing these two disparate lessons set before us, what are we to make of the passage from Romans? Paul's reading of the Abraham story is far more orthodox than my own: Faith! Abraham was the perfect example of faith! Abraham believed that his shriveled old sperm could still swim, and that Sarah's shriveled old womb was still a legitimate swimming pool! Isn't Abraham amazing! What faith! Obviously Paul wasn't putting Abraham's age in context, seeing that he was, in fact, only middle-aged, given the life spans being described in the passage immediately preceding the Abram story.

Of course, Paul is using the Abraham story rhetorically: He wants to make a point, and the point is the entire thesis of the book of Romans: that Gentiles have access to the promises of Christ as much as Jews do, and that following Jesus is not exclusively a bizarre Jewish sect. So Paul finds it absolutely necessary to minimize the role of Torah, of the Law, and to put another form of reconciliation with the Divine in its place: faith.

And here is where the story from Hosea comes into play: If receiving the chosenness of G-d is the result of faith, then it is obvious that unfaithfulness results in unchosenness, right?

The problem with all of this, in my reading, is that both Hebrew Bible readings are being utilized outside of their larger context. Paul himself fails to mention the spectacular lack of faith demonstrated by Abraham later, when he tries to pass Sarah off as his sister *not once but twice*, and almost gets killed for it. On the other hand, throughout the book of Hosea, there is always hope being held out for repentance and a return to G-d. In neither case do we see examples, either positive or negative, of perfect faith. Why didn't G-d shaft Abraham for not having faith? Why did G-d shaft northern Israel? Paul draws a direct connection between our faith and our justification, but it's a complicated relationship.

I'll be honest with you: I have trouble with the way Paul's words have been interpreted. "Just have faith!" we're told in Protestantland. "Believe on the Lord Jesus Christ and you shall be saved!" was the verse screamed at me throughout my evangelical childhood.

There are three problems that I have with this: First, very few people were willing to explain what "being saved" actually meant (and I have come to the conclusion that salvation looks very different for every person, and is as individual as our very lived experience); very few people were willing to explain precisely what it meant to "believe in Jesus"—did it mean simply to accept that he was G-d? or that he was killed? or that his blood from his death did a kind of magic sin-wiping-out thing? Or . . . ?; and, finally, too many people equated faith with belief.

And it is this last problem that I think is the worst. Because having faith is not just some random believing, and the assumption that believing is enough. We have to *keep* faith, not just *have* it. I am not, I am convinced, called merely to *believe* that Jesus was real, or that he was G-d, or that he was murdered by an empire that found his preaching to be a threat. I am called to *keep faith* with that Jesus, which means that I am called to follow him, like Matthew the tax collector, or to come to him expecting miracles, like the synagogue leader or the hemorrhaging woman. Yes, belief is important, but if it does not lead to action, then belief is like Israel in the psalm: making all the right sacrifices, but without actually giving a shit about G-d or G-d's people, interested only in looking good for the community, in being perceived as holy, rather than actually doing the hard work of taking holiness on oneself.

And look who actually has faith! Paul's paean to Abraham aside, it's essential to know that Abraham fucked up royally, that he lied, that he treated Hagar like shit, and that he lived as problematic a life as any of us. And despite Hosea's (personal, and therein understandable) comparison of Israel to an unfaithful woman, Jesus, in the same Gospel we heard read today, makes clear that prostitutes will enter the reign of heaven before religious authorities. Gentiles, Paul is determined to proclaim, have as much potential to have righteousness reckoned unto them as Jews. And Jesus himself recognizes those who are willing to keep faith with him: not only certain of the religious authorities, but the socially ostracized tax collectors, and the ritually (though not spiritually) unclean hemorrhaging women.

Such a shitshow of examples!

I said earlier that it is the randomness of the Abram story that makes it queer.

And indeed, it is queer randomness that I see coursing through every lesson in the lectionary for today, in both track 1 and track 2. G-d wants us to keep faith, yes. But G-d is reminding us, over and over again, that the people who are, in fact, keeping faith are to our eyes completely random, utterly ineffectual, and totally outside all of the appropriate social groups. And it is the so-called "Chosen" who are very often completely unwilling to keep faith.

So, look carefully. And keep the faith.

PROPER 6, THE SUNDAY CLOSEST TO JUNE 15

The Rev. Dr. Jay Emerson Johnson

Track 1	or	Track 2
Genesis 18:1–15; 21:1–7		*Exodus 19:2–8a*
Psalm 116:1, 10–17		*Psalm 100*
Romans 5:1–8		*Romans 5:1–8*
Matthew 9:35–10:8 (9–23)		*Matthew 9:35–10:8 (9–23)*

Today's churches, like so many of today's nonprofit organizations, love mission statements. There are some good reasons for such love, not least the need to stay focused on the work at hand, assess the effectiveness of programmatic initiatives, and adjust organizational structure when needed.

The sometimes-arduous process of wordsmithing catchy language to infuse a religious institution with fresh energy (the old joke about a zebra being a horse designed by a committee comes to mind) can easily obscure a rather peculiar insight: The Church does not actually have a mission at all; *God* has a mission and calls the Church to participate in it.

Biblical texts (not to mention many centuries of theological traditions) offer a treasure trove of images for our shared discernment about divine mission. The Book of Common Prayer distills a great deal of that material in short, catechetical phrases, like this one: "The Church pursues its mission as it . . . promotes justice, peace, and love" (p. 855).

Most Christians, I'm guessing, would much prefer that distillation (even as challenging as it is) rather than the portion from Matthew's account of the Gospel assigned for this day, where Jesus sends out his disciples to proclaim the good news of the kingdom. "Cure the sick," he says, "raise the dead, cleanse lepers, cast out demons."

That's quite a mission statement! I wonder how many of us show up for worship on a Sunday morning expecting to be equipped for that kind of work in a world that isn't even quite sure about religion anymore.

Meanwhile, Sarah laughed.

Sometimes, participating in whatever we think God might be up to in the world feels a bit, well, ludicrous, like we've walked on stage in some theater of the absurd.

And so, as the classic story from Genesis on this day reminds us, Sarah laughed. She laughed quietly, but she laughed nonetheless when God said she would bear a child.

Most postmenopausal women understand this quite readily, especially if you're ninety years old and you're told you would soon give birth—that's pretty laughable.

By the way, even though the lectionary doesn't include this part of the story, Abraham also laughed about this procreative way to join in God's mission. In the chapter from Genesis before the one assigned for today we read that the one-hundred-year-old Abraham actually fell on his face laughing when God told him he would have a child.

These are wonderful moments of what we could call "sacred laughter" in what Matthew's Jesus calls the "kingdom of God." To see better why this might matter, and quite urgently, we need to notice something else about this Gospel passage that is no laughing matter and that is directly related to God's ongoing mission of a world remade.

As Matthew's Jesus sends out his disciples, he tells them that if any town will not receive them, "it will be more tolerable for the land of Sodom and Gomorrah on the day of judgement than for that town."

I'm quite sure the lectionary compilers had no awareness at all that this particular Proper would always show up not just in the "ordinary time" after Pentecost but also during LGBTQ Pride Month. Even decades after the Stonewall Riots of 1968, which many consider a milestone moment in the "Gay Liberation Movement," it's vital to understand this: Most, if not all LGBTQ-identified persons of faith, feel their stomachs churn whenever they hear the words "Sodom and Gomorrah."

Even in churches with well-publicized and explicit statements of welcome for all people, including LGBTQ people, hearing religious language that evokes the notion of "sodomy" is unnerving.

Hearing this text with queer ears, as it were, might actually tease out fresh insights. Such hearing begins by noting rather simply that it is at least unsettling for LGBTQ people to be in a religious space where they are reminded of that story in Genesis when God destroyed ancient cities with a storm of fire and brimstone, of burning sulfur. Countless preachers (and not a few politicians) have used that story as a religious weapon, terrorizing and traumatizing gay and lesbian people everywhere. Every year, a horrifying number of LGBTQ teenagers take their own lives because of those religious images—*one* would be too many.

Connecting the fate of Sodom with particular sexual acts even made its way into modern legal terminology. Still today the concept of "sodomy" is used in sixty-five countries to criminalize lesbian and gay relationships; in eleven of those countries, the penalty is death. In the United States, sodomy laws were still on the books in some states and even enforced as recently as 2003 when the US Supreme Court finally overturned them.

These religious and legal entanglements are so seamlessly woven into our cultural idioms that many of us scarcely think twice or even notice when they show up in jokes or in sitcoms or casually tossed into political speeches.

Back in 1966, John Huston directed a film called *The Bible: In the Beginning*, a Hollywood epic depicting the first twenty-two chapters of Genesis. The film won several awards, including for best director and even an Academy Award nomination for best musical score.

The segment in that film about Sodom and Gomorrah portrays every single resident of those ancient twin cities as limp-wristed, effeminate, lisping gay men—those stereotypes are emblazoned on our shared cultural memory, even though nothing about them bears any resemblance whatsoever to the biblical story; that scene in the film deals more directly with the misogyny of modern Western society than it does with the scene from Genesis!

Fresh (if not also uncomfortable) insights can emerge from this biblical text when we disentangle gender performance from sexual attraction, which actually do not align in any neat and tidy way, certainly not in the way they apparently did in Huston's cinematic imagination. These complexities deepen when noting more carefully that the biblical story of Sodom and Gomorrah's destruction is *not* about gay men at all and it's not even about sex! Rape is *not* sexual intimacy, even though it is often framed that way in patriarchal cultures; rape is a violent act of physical domination, usually for the sake of securing or maintaining power and control over another human being.

Biblical writers clarify these social dynamics in some rather startling ways, especially when they make reference to that ancient story in Genesis—as Matthew did in today's passage. When biblical writers cite Sodom's destruction, they do so with reference to a grotesque violation of hospitality, persistent patterns of injustice, and physical violence.

The ancient Hebrew prophet Ezekiel could not be clearer in that regard: "This was the guilt of . . . Sodom," he wrote; its residents lived with "hubris, excess of food, and prosperous ease, but did not aid the poor and needy" (16:49).

Interpreting *sodomy* as the behavior of a small sexual minority is far easier and more comfortable than to suppose this ancient story is really about economics and a community's collective failure to live hospitably and with justice. That kind of social analysis should make nearly all of us squirm a bit in our pews as likely candidates for the moniker sodomite!

This kind of framing of these biblical texts is one of the gifts LGBTQ people can offer to the wider church, in this case, helping us read in more lively and contemporary ways why Matthew's Jesus cites Sodom and Gomorrah as he sends his disciples out as emissaries of God's kingdom, to do the work of hospitality, and healing, and justice-making. Rather than suppressing or just ignoring that awkward (to put it mildly) evocation of Sodom and Gomorrah, in other words, facing sodomy directly could help us interpret what Jesus means by "curing the sick, and raising the dead, and cleansing lepers, and casting out demons."

How about this: God is calling the Church to soothe the hearts of those who are made sick from their social exclusion or from gendered bias; or to notice just how toxic racial hatred can be as it kills the human spirit; or to rescue those shunted to the margins and treated like lepers just because of whom they love or how they understand their own gender or what family means to them; participating in God's mission of reconciling love might mean naming and rebuking the demonic spirits of division and animosity that make our bodily and cultural differences sources of our social fragmentation.

Could this retrieval of "sodomy" provide a source of Gospel healing? That's a bit peculiar, to be sure, but it might qualify as the "hope that does not disappoint us," to quote from Paul in his letter to the Romans, also assigned for today. But saying so without any irony from a church pulpit during LGBTQ Pride Month presents a rather herculean challenge.

The church has certainly disappointed more than a few people quite frequently, and whether any of us can hear the Gospel without also thinking "church" continues to present one of the thorniest obstacles to whatever we think God might be up to in a world of pain.

Most of the time, quite honestly, I would really rather not be lectured by Paul from his letter to the Romans during Pride Month. The first chapter of that letter is usually paired with the story about Sodom in Genesis as a kind of religious "one-two punch" in the gut for lesbian and gay people.

Here again, though, taking even gut-wrenching experiences as a source of insight, Paul might become something like a spiritual companion to those of us who just can't seem to quit struggling with a religious tradition that won't let us go. Why not take that struggle as the "sufferings" Paul writes about? We know, he says, that suffering produces endurance, and endurance produces character, and character produces hope . . . and hope does not disappoint us (5:3–5).

I cannot imagine Paul himself would ever say that a life of faith never brings with it any disappointments. He writes about some of them in his own letters and his own life was never without significant hardship. The daisy-chain of suffering, endurance, and character he writes about here seems mostly about how hope itself is recalibrated. *What* we hope for is what matters to Paul, not just hope in general.

God's love has been poured into our hearts, he writes, and this is surely the source of our hopefulness that will never disappoint us.

And don't forget—Sarah laughed.

And Abraham fell on his face laughing.

I would certainly call this "sacred laughter"—perhaps not at first in this story, when they laughed because of the absurdity of God's promise, but over time they laughed because of God's astonishing grace, the grace that always exceeds our most reasonable expectations.

It is at least worth noting that this sacred laughter occurs in the very same chapter of Genesis as the story of Sodom and Gomorrah's destruction.

Beyond what even the Church has been able to tell its own queer members, God's promise of grace will not fail to extend to all.

We know and touch this grace ourselves whenever we laugh in the midst of our tears, trusting God's grace to transform what we cannot bear into something we cannot imagine—a hope that will not disappoint because its goals is recalibrated with love.

I love that Sarah and Abraham's child was given the name "Isaac," which means "laughter." The road we travel may indeed seem "barren" and even laden with tears, and yet—as Paul tried to name for the Christians in Rome—that road yields a hope that will not disappoint.

How wonderfully peculiar if queer people can remind the Church about its own life and calling: curing the sick, and cleansing lepers, and casting out demons.

That's a calling, both simply and profoundly, to live with an amazing grace and laughing hearts.

Queerly enough, that might be the only mission statement any Christian community would ever need.

PROPER 7, THE SUNDAY CLOSEST TO JUNE 22

The Rev. Alene Campbell-Langdell, MDiv, MSW

Track 1	or	Track 2
Genesis 21:8–21		*Jeremiah 20:7–13*
Psalm 86:1–10, 16–17		*Psalm 69:8–11, (12-17), 18–20*
Romans 6:1b–11		*Romans 6:1b–11*
Matthew 10:24–39		*Matthew 10:24–39*

Destroyed That We Might Be Free

This proper actually falls during Pride Month, so perhaps it's not too surprising to read them through rainbow-colored glasses starting with Jeremiah, who sounds a bit here like a drag queen in full dramatic flair, "Within me there is something like a burning fire shut up in my bones; I am weary with holding it in, and I cannot" (20:9). The gay community often talks about someone being "flaming," a humorous way of recognizing that sometimes there's just no way of hiding who you really are. Then, there are the words of Psalm 69, "I have become a stranger to my kindred, an alien to my mother's children. . . . When I humbled my soul with fasting, they insulted me for doing so" (69:8, 10). Instead of sackcloth and ashes, the LGBTQ community has too often used oversized sweatshirts and fasted from connecting with others all in a desperate bid to hide the truth of our identity. "I am weary" with trying to fit in and pass. For too many young people today, there is the stark realization that no matter how hard they try, they have become a stranger and a reproach to their families, kicked out of their homes simply because of their inability to continue to hide who they are.

It is hard to find good news in this regard from Romans 6. This passage comes to us weighted with centuries of commentary and culture beginning with the Stoics connecting bodily emotion and desire with sin. Too many LGBTQ Christians hear this from the perspective of "praying the gay away." If this passage is to be heard as good news, real credence has to be given to Paul's words about newness and freedom. The Rev. Bill Countryman speaks to this in his book *Love Songs and Reproaches*, "Jesus was never more of a problem than for us who knew God best, who read the scriptures and taught the rest to know their sins. . . . Grace can only come as a surprise. And when grace comes, it confuses all our accounts. All that time spent with the double-entry columns of our merits and our sins—all swept away."[1] Grace does away with sin not in some do-gooder, pious, look-like-a-fifties-TV-show way. Grace does away with sin as separation from God. Grace wipes out the accounts and draws us back in.

In much the same way, if the reading from Matthew today or the story of Hagar and Ishmael in Genesis is to be seen as good news for the queer community, it has to come from the realization that our plight is recognized. God sees Ishmael cast out of his home. And why is he cast out? Because he might get too close and "rub off" on the golden child? There are real problems with this story from a theological perspective, starting with God's reassurance to Abraham not to worry about the boy. Yet, as a social worker I have seen this reality. Sometimes the abuse and dysfunction in the family is such that the only way for the child to survive is removal from the home. In Matthew, Jesus acknowledges that the Good News of freedom might result in families turned against one another rather than living in perfect harmony. God's grace is not dependent on picture-perfect families and drama-free lives. Thank God!

Because the truth is that Jeremiah's lament, "I am weary with holding it in, and I cannot," rings true for anyone who has found themselves caught between living authentically or following societal demands. Every single one of the readings for this week contains hints and outright warnings that a life spent following God will not be easy. Barbara Brown Taylor says

---

[1] L. William Countryman, *Lovesongs and Reproaches: Passionate Conversations with God* (Morehouse Publishing, 2010), 63–64.

it this way, "What the Bible tells us over and over again—what our lives tell us—is that the only reward for doing God's work is doing God's work. Period. Furthermore, if we do it really well, we are likely to get ourselves killed. . . . That is what success looks like in the upside-down kingdom of God, and so far as I know, no one has ever liked it."[2]

And yet, at the same time, we are drawn in. We are still here, now, in this church. Even as we cry out with Jeremiah, "O Lord, you have enticed me, and I was enticed; you have overpowered me, and you have prevailed" (Jer. 20:7). What is it that has enticed us? Barbara Brown Taylor suggests several false enticements for believers: the lure of being effective, the hope of being respected and obeyed, or the desire to be protected and rescued from all ill that might come our way.[3] The ending of Psalm 86 is surely one that many of us have prayed in one way or another over the years, "Show me a sign of your favor, so that those who hate me may see it and be put to shame" (v. 17). Yet, there is an alternative list embedded in our readings today: We are enticed by the idea of freedom (Rom. 6:7). We long to live life without fear (Matt. 10:26). We want the promise that there will ultimately be justice in the world (Jer. 20:11), and that God's love and compassion is stronger than our sense of alienation. We yearn to know, in the midst of a world filled with death, division, and destruction, that our lives have meaning.

There is a story in the Sufi tradition about a woman who lived in the fourteenth century. Mahmouda was born with what many in her village in Anatolia and even her family deemed a disability. The left side of her body, both arm and leg, were shriveled and weak, leaving her unable to walk and considered "unmarriageable"—perhaps the greatest tragedy according to her family.

One day, Mahmouda went with her family to visit her uncle who was a potter. As she watched her uncle work, she suddenly realized that he had curled his body into a shape that looked familiar. His left leg was curled under his chair out of the way. His left hand stabilized the clay, allowing the right hand to do the work of molding and shaping the clay.

In that moment, Mahmouda realized that her body, as it was, had a purpose. For the next thirty years, Mahmouda contentedly made pots—ordinary pots for ordinary things. Then one day she saw a Sufi dancer praying in their own ecstatic, whirling meditative dance. At first Mahmouda

---

[2] Barbara Brown Taylor, *Bread of Angels* (Cowley Publications, 1997), 27.

[3] Taylor, *Bread of Angels*, 25–26.

grieved that she would never be able to pray in that joyful way—with uplifted hand calling God down into the life of the earth. And then Mahmouda looked at the pot spinning under her hand and realized that she was already praying in that way.

From that moment on, something changed. People began to come from miles around to buy her pots. There was a beauty in them that drew people to them. Some time later, Mahmouda left this life and went to face God. In the midst of sobs and tears, Mahmouda tried to confess what she felt to be her faults and mistakes in life. But the Divine One didn't let her finish. "Mahmouda! You have done so much more than I even imagined you could do!" Mahmouda exclaimed, "But, but you're God! You're the All-knowing. How could you not know everything I would do?" With that, God looked around, beckoned to her to come closer, leaned over, and whispered into her ear, "I'll tell you a secret, Mahmouda. I made the stars and the planets to obey me. And I made the angels and all the bright spirits to adore me. But you, Mahmouda—I made you to surprise me."[4]

This is the surprise of grace: "Do not be afraid; you are of more value than many sparrows" (Matt. 10:31). This is the promise to all who seek to live authentically as God created us, "Those who find their life will lose it, and those who lose their life for my sake will find it" (Matt. 10:39). Flame on, Jeremiah!

---

[4] This story is paraphrased from the Rev. M.R. Ritley's excellent version in the book *Gifted by Otherness: Gay and Lesbian Christians in the Church* by Bill Countryman and M. R. Ritley (Morehouse Publishing, 2001).

PROPER 8, THE SUNDAY CLOSEST TO JUNE 29

Dr. Peter Carlson

Track 1	or	Track 2
Genesis 22:1–14		*Jeremiah 28:5–9*
Psalm 13		*Psalm 89:1–4, 15–18*
Romans 6:12–23		*Romans 6:12–23*
Matthew 10:40–42		*Matthew 10:40–42*

I have a tendency to organize my sermonic thoughts from Hebrew Bible to psalm to Epistle to Gospel, but the lessons for Proper 8 seem to be calling me into the other direction: to start with the brevity of the Gospel passage, and to use it as the context in which to read the other lessons.

Indeed, this passage from Matthew is three little verses that sound quite sweet, really: Jesus talking to his disciples and reassuring them that "whoever welcomes you welcomes me, and whoever welcomes me welcomes the one who sent me." It all feels so lovely and glam, until we remember the context in which we find it. Jesus has just gathered his disciples to clarify their job description: Don't talk to Gentiles or Samaritans; proclaim that the reign of G-d is near; cure the sick; raise the dead; take no money (are you listening, prosperity theologians?); wish peace upon people who treat you well; wish ick on those who won't listen to you. It's kind of disturbing, as a Gentile, to listen to these words; they are harsh and foreboding, and not very Jesus Loves Me. But remember, Jesus has yet to learn his lesson from the Canaanite woman in chapter 15, so he's still being kind of exclusive and harsh. Cut him some slack, okay?

But what really matters for today's lessons is what follows: He is sending the disciples "out like sheep into the midst of wolves" (Matt. 10:16) and letting them know that they have literally no right to be naïve about the situation. And Jesus tells them what the real danger is: not physical death, but the destruction of their souls. And physical death is a distinct possibility, for Jesus comes not to bring peace but a sword, and whoever seeks to find their life will lose it, but those who willingly lose their life will find it.

So the end of chapter 10 in the book of Matthew is not three verses of sweetness and light, but three verses summing up a frankly terrifying message: If you follow Jesus—if you *really* follow Jesus—the world is going to be against you, and will almost certainly try to kill you.

In this light, welcoming Jesus is dangerous, and being a disciple of Jesus means that if you ask people to welcome you, you are, in fact, asking them to do something that is potentially fatal. If we welcome prophets in the name of a prophet, we will receive the prophet's reward. But look how the prophets are treated, because prophets speak truth to power—very, very powerful power. The reward of the righteous is being asked to give up everything you have. And it is in this ominous light that we need to go back and read the lessons from the Hebrew Bible and the Epistles.

I have, in various religion classes that I've taught, covered the story of Abraham's attempted sacrifice of Isaac, and inevitably I find it necessary to cut to the chase with students who, all too often, have been taught that questioning G-d or questioning the scriptural record is the ultimate blasphemy. I ask them the Really Big Question: What kind of fucked up G-d would ask a devotee to do something like this? And then I follow it with the Next Really Big Question: What kind of a fucked up father would agree?

There's a story from a feminist theologian who suggested that G-d didn't ask Sarah to sacrifice her son, because Sarah would have told G-d to fuck off. And I admit to siding with this particular version, because I'm a firm believer that any G-d who would ask me to kill another person to prove my love to Them is a narcissistic shithead. I mean, think about it: At the *very* least, Isaac probably needed a ton of expensive therapy to deal with this event, on top of the fact that his parents were literally counting on him to establish an entire race of Chosen People. Unpack *that*, psychologists!

In my evangelical childhood, this terrifying story was actually taught in Sunday school (which is frankly just creepy), and of course was always presented in light of the "Daddy knows best" theology that implies we should never question Providence (even though Abraham himself questioned G-d with regard to the destruction of Sodom and Gomorrah). I reject this theology entirely, if for no other reason than that G-d apparently made me curious and feisty and questioning, and I'm not going to offend G-d by not using those gifts. But seriously: If people want to take this story literally (but not the bits about power and wealth being satanic), then they have to deal with the fact that the G-d represented is arbitrary, nasty, and woefully insecure in Their own relationships with Their followers.

I can only read this mythically, remembering that the truth of myth lies not in its literal factuality, but in its revelation of a community's worldview and understanding of what matters most. And this myth tells us the difficult truth of what it means to learn what matters most, and follow it. It means that, in doing the right thing, everything else goes down in front of you, including what you used to think was of primary importance. It means that you are willing to trample over your own reputation, and even give up your own life to do the right thing—to give one of those little ones a cup of cold water in the name of Jesus, to take up the cross, to care more about justice and the reign of G-d even more than one's family.

The angst of trying to do the right thing, even though it seems to be costing us everything, is reflected in Psalm 13, which is assigned to be read with the Abraham story. "How long will you forget me, G-d? How long shall I have perplexity in my mind, and grief in my heart, day after day?" And even in the midst of the agony is the self-reminder: "But I trusted in your steadfast love." Even here is an echo of Jesus's later reminder that those who lose their lives for the cause of G-d will find their lives.

The passage from Jeremiah in track 2 also seems to make more sense in the light of the warnings in Matthew. Remember Jesus's statement about the prophet's reward? The reading is actually a kind of Prophetic Cage Fighting Smackdown between Jeremiah and Hananiah. Jeremiah, a truly gloomy gus, is getting snarky with Hananiah, who is telling the people what they want to hear, rather than what is true: that the Babylonian Empire is actually going to go belly up, and everything will be hunky dory, and we'll all be rich. Jeremiah responds, sarcastically: "Oh!" he exclaims. "Your mouth to G-d's ears, dude!" But then he cuts to the chase, willing to say the shitty things that no one wants to hear: that the Babylonians were as powerful as ever, and the country was going down, and that King Zedekiah (who imprisoned Jeremiah) would end up having his eyes gouged out after watching his sons be murdered, ultimately dying in Babylon. His sarcasm reaches its peak when he scoffs, "As for the prophet who prophesies peace, when the word of that prophet comes true, then it will be known that HaShem has truly sent the prophet." Remember, in the Gospel of Matthew, just before the passage for today, Jesus has said that his words will not bring peace, but a sword. And the fact of the matter is that Jeremiah paid an extraordinary price for speaking the truth. He was ridiculed, imprisoned, beaten, and had his life threatened. The prophet's reward, indeed.

Even Paul's ramblings about sin in the sixth chapter of Romans need to be encountered in the light of welcoming Christ, of welcoming the righteous, of welcoming the little ones: We are to present ourselves to G-d as "instruments of righteousness" rather than as instruments of sin. It is tempting to read Paul's obsession with Greek body/spirit dualism as a focus on the body as sinful; but I would suggest paying attention to the issue of righteousness, which is the gift of grace, that frees us from sin. It is this righteousness that once again connects us back to Jesus's words in Matthew: "the reward of righteousness." Paul must be all too aware of how dangerous it is to follow righteousness—he would, after all, end up being imprisoned several times, and ultimately beheaded in Rome for treading that path. But he turns the danger on its head, just as Jesus turned the idea of trying to cling to life on its head, and proclaims that the path of righteousness is enslavement to G-d, and the result of that enslavement is eternal life.

I admit that there are times when, as a queer theologian, I am tempted to tone down my preaching, to be a Hananiah, telling people what they want to hear, what will make them comfortable, rather than telling the truth. But I have been called to a mountain where I am asked to sacrifice what is most dear to me; I am called to preach the hard news of empires that care nothing for justice toward those outside the centers of imperial power; I am called to turn from sin to righteousness; I am called to give a cup of cold water to the suffering little ones, in the name of Jesus. Sometimes I even do these things, though not nearly often enough.

But maybe, if we practice righteousness, if we practice empire-bashing, if we practice giving up what the world tells us should matter . . .

Maybe we will gain our reward, which will be incomprehensible to others, but will, in fact, be reward enough.

PROPER 9, THE SUNDAY CLOSEST TO JULY 6

Dr. Peter Carlson

Track 1
Genesis 24:34–38, 42–49, 58–67
Psalm 45:11–18
or *Song of Solomon 2:8–13*
Romans 7:15–25a
Matthew 11:16–19, 25–30

or

Track 2
Zechariah 9:9–12
Psalm 145:8–15
Romans 7:15–25a
Matthew 11:16–19, 25–30

How do we know?

How do we know who is speaking the truth? How do we know the voice of a false prophet? How do we know we are following G-d, rather than just following our own desires? How do we know what is good? How do we know what is evil?

How do we know?

The lessons today from both track 1 and track 2 seem to shimmer with the theme of recognition: of being able to recognize a person or an event or a time or a motivation as "right" or as "good." Abraham's servant strives to recognize a potential spouse for Abraham's kid. Zechariah warns that recognizing a victorious monarch might be a challenge. Paul acknowledges that recognizing even his own actions is really difficult. And Jesus suggests that recognizing the return of Elijah—something hoped for at every Passover seder—might be harder than we think it ought to be.

As a teacher of religion in a university, I spend most of my class time directly or indirectly trying to help my students figure out what, in fact, is real, and how we can recognize truth or falsehood. It's a challenging task, to say the least. We live in an age of so-called Artificial Intelligence that seeks to deceive us, despite its claims to tell the truth, and we don't know, sadly, how to distinguish between what is artificial and what is real. We are seduced by beautiful images, even if the dancers are bent in physically impossible ways, and have six toes on their feet.

This isn't new, of course. We've been altering reality to fit in our comfort zones or to manipulate others from time out of mind. If you watch the documentary *Killing Us Softly*, you realize that advertising has manipulated photographs of models to present women with an unachievable standard of beauty, guaranteeing that the audience will never be satisfied with their bodies, and will keep spending money on an impossible goal. Further back, we can discover other alterations of reality: the so-called Donation of Constantine, which the Vatican used to claim lands and political power in the twelfth century was a forgery, created at least six centuries after Constantine died. Forgery and falsehood is even present in the biblical account; take, for example, Jacob conning his father out of his brother Esau's inheritance, by wearing an animal skin so as to appear as hirsute as his elder brother.

How do we know?

Abraham's servant, sent to find a bride for Isaac, comes up with a plan: "I'll just stand here by the well, until a woman comes by. Then I'll ask her for a drink, and if she offers one to my camels, too, I'll know it's the woman G-d wants." I'll be honest—this sounds supremely silly to me—but I'll also be honest—I've a feeling that most of us have done some kind of similar judgment call. "I'll flip a coin, and if it's heads I'll do thus and so." Or, "I'll apply to these schools, and whichever one accepts me, I'll assume that's G-d's will." So perhaps we shouldn't get too judgy on Abraham's servant.

We're told in the story, though, that this actually turned out to be a good plan. Creepy as the negotiations for marriage may seem to us (He put a ring on her *nose*? For what? To lead her like a donkey? Oy *veh*!), we can note that Rebekah was at least given the opportunity to consent or not, and she seems to have agreed. And the story goes on to demonstrate that this was a happy match indeed: Rebekah sees Isaac from a distance and is clearly enchanted; Isaac meets Rebekah, and loves her and is "comforted" (draw your own conclusions as to what that specifically means, on the night of a marriage). Cue the soaring music and the happy ending.

Whether this story happened exactly as it is related in scripture is ultimately immaterial. It is a story meant to show G-d's providential guidance and care for those who trust in G-d, as this servant clearly did. And again, it's really easy, when things work out, to give credit to G-d (or, perhaps slightly more self-congratulatorily, to our faith in G-d). How good of G-d to show me the way! How clever of me in my faithfulness to come up with a great test, so G-d could show me that way! Yay, G-d and me! I have seen the truth!

And so we sing psalms of a royal marriage (Psalm 45) or erotic poetry from the Song of Songs, and can rest, or have sex, comfortably, knowing that our relationship is divinely sanctioned!

Sometimes, though, the truth is harder to spot. The second half of the book of Zechariah has something to say about this. This second half is generally considered to have been written much later than chapters 1–8 and consists of oracles that proclaim the messianic salvation of G-d's people. King Cyrus of Persia has allowed the Judaeans to return home and rebuild the temple, and things are looking hopeful. But Zechariah suggests that salvation might not look like what the people are expecting it to look like: "Lo, your ruler comes to you; triumphant and victorious is that ruler, humble and riding on a donkey, on a colt, the foal of a donkey." Wait! Triumphant and victorious rulers ride war horses, right? Not donkeys, or baby animals. This is weird. And Zechariah explains what will be accomplished from the back of that foal: The ruler "will cut off the chariot from Ephraim and the war horse from Jerusalem; and the battle-bow shall be cut off, and [the ruler] shall command peace to the nations." This isn't victory by outgunning or outbombing the enemy, but by cutting off the bow, and detatching horses from their chariots. Nations who claim to follow the G-d of Abraham might want to take note of this before stocking up on enough weaponry to destroy the world several times over.

The key, in this second half of Zechariah, is that we're not able to recognize rulers who are truly worthy, or who will bring peace, because we're always looking for worldly strength, for the ruler who will stare others down and taunt them, for the hawkish manly man (even if you are woman-identified, you'll have to prove that you're willing to bomb the shit out of others). Zechariah is reminding us that humility is what we should seek, and a willingness to de-escalate and disarm. It is hard to recognize real leadership, and too often our own history has shown that we are utterly deceived by the people we thought would lead us well, not only in our nations, but in our congregations.

Psalm 145, a psalm of general praise to G-d, continues this theme: G-d is not the one who smashes everyone to bits in a fit of pique, but the one who "is gracious and merciful, slow to anger and abounding in steadfast love." This is the G-d who does not play favorites: "HaShem is good to *all*, and G-d's compassion is over *all* G-d has made." It is an ongoing theme in my theology that *all* is a really big word—big enough to make me really uncomfortable. But G-d consistently shows up, it seems to me, and to Zechariah, in really unexpected ways.

Paul's wonderful passage from Romans shows that even he wrestled with recognizing the good: "I do not understand my own actions. For I do not do what I want, but I do the very thing I hate." He writes about something that I'll guess is familiar to all of us: We are pretty sure we know what we should do, but we do something different anyway. Paul struggles with the fact that good and evil are constantly at war within him, even though he represents that struggle in what I see as a creepy, mind/body dualism (Paul obviously has *lots* of body issues that are magnified by his attempts to explain the Gospel of Jesus in a world steeped in Greek dualist philosophy).

But body negativity aside, Paul acknowledges that "when I want to do what is good, evil lies close at hand." Indeed, there are often lots of reasons for this conflict in our souls: Sometimes we convince ourselves that a certain choice is actually good for us; sometimes it can be as simple as knowing that as a diabetic, I really shouldn't have cake, but there are times when I'm simply going to say, "I want cake, dammit, and to hell with the elevated blood glucose"; and other times it may be more dramatic. We may know what is right, but out of laziness or even legitimate fear, we choose instead what is easy. How many of us have avoided speaking up when someone in our group says something racist, or homophobic, or ableist, or sexist, or merely mean? How many of us have thought, "Oh, homelessness is bad," but have done nothing to support the unhoused person we encounter living rough? We've all done it. We've all experienced the inner conflict. We've all struggled, like Paul did, not just to recognize what is true and right, but to follow it.

In our passage from Matthew, Jesus is also talking about how to recognize the good, to recognize what is right. Just before this passage, John the

Baptizer, who is languishing in prison, has sent a message to Jesus asking, "Are you the one? Because it's really hard to tell, Jesus. I need a sign." And Jesus's response is "Look around. Free health care is being handed out. The poor are getting good news. People who were dead are coming back to life." I often find this to be a bit of a dodge, I'll confess, because I look around and do *not* see these things happening. And Jesus goes on to talk to the crowds about how hard it is to see the signs of the reign of G-d, because they're acting like a bunch of irrational children: "John the Baptizer came, and was an ascetic. He fasted, and he abstained from drink, and you said, 'Ick! He must be possessed by a demon. He's not from G-d.' And then I come along, and I eat and drink, and you complain 'Gross! A glutton and drunk, who hangs out with the shittypeople. He's not from G-d.'"

In the verses omitted from this section, Jesus reminds the people of cities that in the Hebrew Bible had been represented as cursed by G-d: Tyre and Sidon and Sodom. Their curse is that they didn't recognize the signs of G-d's power and presence—a powerful bit of punctuation to follow Jesus's claim that the people are refusing to recognize John or Jesus himself.

It is always in the unexpected, though, that we find G-d. As Jesus goes on to say, the wise and the intelligent aren't the ones who will recognize acts of divine power. It is the foolish and infantile. The power of G-d is found in the contradiction that taking on a yoke, like oxen plowing a field, will actually give rest. The great irony of the Gospel of Jesus is that it once again demands that we set aside all our expectations and be ready to take up a burden in order to find rest. It is the reminder that if I keep looking for G-d in certain things, but not in others, G-d will be far too easy for me (for us?) to miss. I want works of wonder and power, when maybe what I should be looking for is some unprepossessing person riding on a scraggy donkey, or a woman kind enough to draw water for my camels.

PROPER 10, THE SUNDAY CLOSEST TO JULY 13

Dr. Peter Carlson

Track 1	or	Track 2
Genesis 25:19–34		*Isaiah 55:10–13*
Psalm 119:105–112		*Psalm 65:(1–8), 9–14*
Romans 8:1–11		*Romans 8:1–11*
Matthew 13:1–9, 18–23		*Matthew 13:1–9, 18–23*

I have often said to my students, when we get to talking about what matters to us most in the world, "Show me your bank account, and I'll tell you what actually matters to you." And of course, as always, I am talking to myself more than I am talking to my students.

It's true, you know. In a political and capitalist world, our bank accounts reveal more about what we really love than any words we could write on paper, or any sermons we could preach. However much you may protest at my saying it, the truth is it takes remarkable faith and courage to love people over things—especially if those people are not people we have been told are okay to love. It strikes me that the lessons for Proper 10 all reflect on attending to those things that matter the most, rather than the things that we are told should matter. There is a word that shows up quite a bit in the Hebrew scriptures: *shemah!* Listen! Attend!

I do not, by the way, care to use the phrase "pay attention," because it strikes me as too rooted in a capitalist understanding of society: It promotes the idea that attention costs money, and if we're rich enough, we can pay it. I prefer the simple verbs: *Attend. Listen. Heed.* And our lessons today are all asking us to attend to those things that in fact are truly important.

Look at the track 1 story of Esau and Jacob, for starters. Esau is the elder, and Jacob is the younger. By all rights, Esau inherits his father's estate. And what an heir! Esau is a hunter, a man of the field! He's a red-headed, hairy stud. A man's man, b'gosh and b'golly! His masculinity practically flexes its muscles off the page as you read the text. If you're going to draw a biblically accurate picture of him, you'd have to learn how to draw not just rippling muscles, but a gloriously large codpiece, at which Isaac is clearly pointing in pride: "That's my son, dammit!"

And then there's Jacob. Second of the twins to emerge from the womb, he's a "quiet man, living in the tents." Rebekah loved him, while Isaac loved the older brother. Jacob is a momma's boy, obviously sensitive, depicted as more than a bit effeminate. A potential fag, even. But the prophecy given to Rebekah before their birth alerts her to the fact that, though nations will arise from both, the younger is actually the one who will have power over the older; the sissy shall surpass the butch; the cooking pot shall overpower the codpiece.

The story skips from their birth past their childhood to when the twins had grown up. Esau was out being a manly man, probably planting, or reaping, or merely sportsing in the fields, and came home, understandably hungry. Jacob had been in the tents, doing girly girl things, like cooking, and Esau demanded food (the gendered shit going on here is screaming from the page, isn't it?). Jacob recognizes an opportunity and grabs it. (This, incidentally, is the way in which queerpeople have to operate in a world that does not love them: being savvy, and seizing those opportunities that become available to us, because society isn't going to help us.) "Sell me your birthright," Jacob says to his starving brother. And Esau, who I'm imagining is almost swooning in hunger now that he can smell Jacob's haute cuisine, agrees. Jacob demurely feeds his brother, probably smiling quietly to himself at the deal he's been able to cut because he stayed at home, learning how to do things like feed himself.

What is intriguing to me in this story is that it is Esau, who is clearly given the short end of the stick, who is blamed for the situation. Look again at the last sentence of our reading for today: "Thus Esau despised his birthright." This is hard stuff. I mean, look back a few sentences, to where Esau says, "I am about to die; of what use is a birthright to me?" This makes perfect sense, doesn't it? Why would I keep an inheritance if I'm not going to be alive to enjoy it? Take it, you greedy bastard, and let me live. But Esau is condemned in Genesis. And the condemnation seems to me to be rooted in a theology that is reminding us not only that G-d is supposedly in control of everything (a theology that the writers of Genesis are really wanting to make sure we understand), but that there are some things that are more important than life. The rejection of Esau's birthright is a rejection, perhaps, of his family, and even of the G-d of his grandfather Abraham. It seems that the story is trying to tell us that it is better to die with honor than to live having rejected all that matters. Attend, in other words, to what matters.

The section of Psalm 119 assigned to track 1 can be read in that same light. It begins with one of the most famous couplets in the Psalms: "Your word is a lamp to my feet / and a light to my path." G-d's word is designed to give us light to see what we should value most. Indeed, as we read later, "The wicked have laid a snare for me, but I do not stray from your precepts." Esau, it would seem, was blinded by his hunger and strayed from the path. He forgot, indeed, to attend to G-d's decrees that are, as the psalmist declares, our true inheritance.

Track 2 offers us chapter 55 from the book of Isaiah; it is the final chapter in Deutero-Isaiah—what many scholars consider was written by the second of three different authors. Whether this is so or not, Deutero-Isaiah (chapters 40–55) has a basic theme: The chapters are sometimes called the Book of Consolation and were likely written to comfort those Judaeans who had been taken away as prisoners of war to Babylon. Just before the verses in today's reading, the author has promised a coming future of free food and drink, and is asking, plaintively, "Why do you spend your money for that which is not bread, and your labor for that which does not satisfy?" Attend! the prophet is saying. Seek G-d, not the stuff that empires tell you matters! And where do we meet G-d? That's what is revealed in this passage today: G-d is in the earth that gives us sustenance; and in the words of G-d; G-d is in the mountains and hills, bursting into song, and the trees clapping their hands; G-d is in the cypress that grows up instead of thorns, and the myrtle tree that comes up instead of briers. G-d is in the hope that G-d will not, in fact, cut you off. *That's* where G-d is. Not in stuff. Attend! This majesty continues in the psalm appointed in track 2. G-d will, we are assured, forgive our sins, even though they are greater than we are, but more: It is G-d who shows Their signs through the marvels of nature, of the earth in its course. The psalmist is, in fact, attending to G-d!

Paul, too, is trying to get us to attend to what matters most. It is always perilously easy for me to hate on Paul, because he's a misogynous ass, and he obviously has some really severe body issues. But this means that I always must remind myself that Paul's mission was to make an obscure Jewish sect comprehensible to people steeped in a Greek, dualist philosophical worldview, and that as an elderly gay man, I've got a shed-load of body issues myself. Those reminders help me to be a tiny bit more forgiving as I read the Pauline Epistles. And really, Paul is in this passage saying nothing less than what following Christ promises: that we will die, but that dying isn't ultimately what matters, and that what matters will not die.

It's a lot to absorb, because it sounds too much like Paul is simply saying that bodies are icky grody, and that we should just pay attention to our spirits, which are wispy but really pretty and eternal. As a queer theologian, however, I hold as one of my central beliefs that our bodies are holy texts, and that G-d thought bodies were cool enough to want one. Over and over, I find myself screaming at Paul, "The incarnation is the absolute central point of Christian belief, you dingdong! Stop dissing bodies!" Honestly, I want to get Paul into therapy about that, because he started a fuckton of shame for all of us who feel any kind of enfleshed desire—which is all of us.

So I think the key to reading Paul (especially when he gets on to his yucko-flesh theme) is to understand that he is fully expecting to die at the hands of the Roman Empire (and in fact he did), and therefore needs to find meaning in something greater than our mere physical life. And this I can get on board with. Fleshly desires are not in and of themselves horrible; in fact, they are often the ways in which Jesus becomes most recognizable as G-d's Child. I often say, only slightly jokingly, that I am a Christian because our two highest sacraments are dinner and a bath. I relish being kind and generous to my body. And I think Paul did too. But Paul perhaps was thinking of Esau, who placed his bodily desires above something that was more important: his heritage. And I know too well that attending to bodily desires when other more important things require attention first is problematic: that problem is the root of addiction, after all. And Paul is trying to remind the Jesus followers in Rome that, in a world that was literally trying to kill them, there are more important things than staying alive. And so I'm going to be brash and presumptuous and rewrite verse 9:

"But you are not only in the flesh; you are in the Spirit, since the Spirit of G-d dwells in you." Paul tells us that the body is dead because of sin; but the reality is that, at some point, my body will be dead because of biology. The real issue, and I genuinely think Paul is trying to say this, but in a dualist kind of way, is whether I think anything as ordinary as biological death is actually what matters. Attend to the soul, Paul warns us. We ignore it at our body's peril.

And of course, Jesus is *always* telling us what we should be attending. This passage concludes the third narrative and discourse in the Gospel of Matthew, in which opposition to Jesus's ministry results in accusations that his miracles are satanic. He then proceeds to tell a number of stories, parables, about the reign of heaven. The parable of the sower is one of them, in which Jesus describes the reign of heaven as a sower who plants seed, which falls on various kinds of ground. Some is eaten by birds, some is in rocky soil and can't really grow, other seeds land among thorns, but some land on good soil and result in bountiful crops. The bit that is skipped in the reading is the part where Jesus's disciples are begging him to explain the parable (and where we can be tempted to feel so virtuous that we think we get it), and before Jesus explains, he notes that he uses stories and parables, rather than speaking directly, because that way only certain people will be able to understand, to attend to them.

And then he explains: When anyone hears the word and doesn't understand it, it's because the evil one has snatched it away, like the birds eat seeds; when someone gets it, but doesn't keep on the difficult path of the Good News, that's like the seed sown on rocky ground; the thorns represent distraction from the Good News by "the cares of the world and the lure of wealth"; and then there's the one who hears the Word, and follows it, and perseveres to the end.

And yay us who understand, right? Huzzah, because we've been given the secret of heaven. We can look around us and point at those who never understood. Idiots. We can see those who started out really strong but who couldn't last and copped out when the going got tough. And we can certainly identify those who have been distracted by the lure of wealth, right?

But I'm convinced that if those are our responses, then we are, along with those Jesus talked about in verses 10–17, listening but not understanding, and looking but not perceiving. Because the parables are *never*,

I am certain, talking about someone else. They are *always* talking about us. They are always pointing a finger at me. And if I listen, if I attend carefully, then I realize that I am *all* that seed. That I am, in the very next parable Jesus tells, both the wheat *and* the weeds. I have looked on, and will continue to look on, without comprehension, clueless to the injustices going on around me. Other times, I will recognize a way in which the reign of heaven can be realized and will be marvelously excited to help realize G-d's reign of justice, but lose interest or energy, or find out that the work involves getting into trouble with the law or society, and my zeal fades. Often, if I am honest, I get too caught up in my own well-being, working, not toward G-d's reign, but toward a solid retirement package, or a new car. But occasionally, the word of the Good News takes root, and I hear and understand it, and it stays strong in me, and I dedicate myself toward the realization of G-d's realm.

It's not me and someone else. It's all me. I am all that seed.

And the only way I can respond to that realization is to attend.

PROPER 11, THE SUNDAY CLOSEST TO JULY 20

Dr. Peter Carlson

Track 1	or	Track 2
Genesis 28:10–19a		*Wisdom of Solomon 12:13, 16–19*
Psalm 139:1–11, 22–23		or *Isaiah 44:6–8*
Romans 8:12–25		*Psalm 86:11–17*
Matthew 13:24–30, 36–43		*Romans 8:12–25*
		Matthew 13:24–30, 36–43

I spend a lot of time in my classes talking about knowing. What do we know? *How* do we know? How do we know we know what we think we know?

This is the field called epistemology: from the Greek *episteme*, knowledge (as opposed to *doxa*, opinion, from which we get the word *doctrine*—we'd do well to note that doctrine is opinion). The suffix, -ology, is something we usually translate as "the study of," but I prefer, since it comes from the Greek word *logos*, to say "the words or ideas about." So epistemology is the ideas about knowing.

Epistemology is an important thing to talk about with my students in this day and age, when we have government officials using phrases like "alternative facts," and students assuming that everything is "just that person's opinion." A day and age in which science is suspect, and I am untrustworthy, even when speaking in my field of study, not in spite of the fact that I have a PhD, but because of it.

I bring this up because it strikes me that today's lessons all have to do with knowing; indeed, the collect describes G-d as "the fountain of all wisdom" who knows better than we do what is good for us. This Knowing Stuff is probably most evident in the psalm (139:1–11, 22–23): "HaShem, you have searched me and known me. You know when I sit down and when I rise up; you discern my thoughts from far away. . . . Even before a word is on my tongue, O HaShem, you know it completely. . . . If I ascend to heaven, you are there; if I make my bed in Sheol, you are there."

Okay, ick.

This is creepy. It's a peeping-tom, trench-coat-wearing G-d who's gonna flash you with judgment, because of all the photographic evidence of everything you've fucked up in your entire life. There is a study that shows that if someone else is present in a public restroom, the likelihood of a person washing their hands increases by 23 percent.[1] For too many Christians, G-d is the other person in the restroom, who will know if we didn't wash.

But I think that the divine image in the psalm is something much less disturbing and, in fact, infinitely more hopeful. It's not that G-d knows everything about us and is going to thrash us in judgment for being pathetic and fail-ful; it's that G-d knows the worst about us and wants the best for us even so. Even at our worst, G-d only wants us to improve.

We see a classic case of that in the reading from the Hebrew Bible (Genesis 28:10–19a). Jacob (okay, I have a confession to get out of the way: Jacob irritates me, because he's a nasty piece of shit) has run away from his brother—understandably, because he stole his brother's blessing (a classic case of assuming that G-d doesn't have enough blessing for all of us). He lies down to sleep, using a stone for a pillow, which is perhaps the reason he has odd, sedimentary dreams: a ladder "reaching to heaven [with] angels of G-d . . . ascending and descending." Whereat G-d G-dself appears and confirms with Jacob the covenant that was originally given to Abraham: land, descendants, and nationhood. Jacob then woke, and said, "Surely HaShem is in this place—and [here's the key] I did not know it!"

Ya think, dinglebutt?

Of *course* you didn't know it! You didn't believe that G-d would have enough blessing for you, so you stole your brother's! You weren't seeking

---

[1] Rob Jordan, "Stanford Research: Watching the Hand Washers," Stanford, April 14, 2014, https://engineering.stanford.edu/news/stanford-research-watching-hand-washers.

G-d, because you were running away from your brother! You clearly don't know ANYTHING about G-d, you selfish snotrocket!

But the cool thing is that G-d knew Jacob. Knew Jacob at Jacob's worst. And only longed for Jacob to be better—to be a better Jacob. To be, in fact, the best Jacob that Jacob could be. And Jacob began to be better. There would be plenty of moments when he was still a shit. But he began to realize that G-d could be present, even though he, Jacob, might not know it.

The reading from Matthew's Gospel, too, is about knowing (Matthew 13:24–30, 36–43). But it's not, as too many people have suggested, about knowing Who's In and Who's Out. That's a tired theology that assumes that G-d only has so much grace to go around. No, this reading is about knowing ourselves, just as Jacob needed to know himself. Matthew is talking, almost certainly, to a Jewish Christian audience—an audience that has seen horrific persecution under Nero in the 60s CE, the destruction of the temple in Jerusalem in 70 CE, the diaspora under the ongoing brutality of the Roman Empire, and themselves unloved by both the Romans and by their fellow Jews. They must be wondering why G-d would allow injustice to flourish quite like, well, weeds. They must be wondering who, after all, is In, and who is Out.

So what they get from Matthew is a story. It's a story that many Christians are familiar with: a landowner who plants "good seed in his field," but who apparently has "an enemy" who plants weeds in the same field. The landowner's servants ask if they should rip out the weeds, but the landowner, knowing that they'd rip out the good wheat, too, said no. When the wheat is ready for harvest, we'll get everything, and separate out the good from the bad then.

The disciples (of course) don't get it. Jesus explains patiently: The good seed are the children of the Kindom of G-d; the bad seed are the children of the "evil one, and the enemy who sowed them is the devil." This phrasing is problematic, because it gets back to the Who's In Who's Out thing, doesn't it? But listen to what happens at the "end of the age": "The Son of Man will send his angels, and they will collect out of his kindom all causes of sin and all evildoers, and they will throw them into the furnace of fire, where there will be weeping and gnashing of teeth."

The key here, I think, is the phrase "they will collect out of his kindom all causes of sin." If I am honest, if I look at myself as honestly and (let's face it) ruthlessly as the G-d that the psalmist prays to looks at me, then I can only admit that within me are so many causes of sin, so many various evildoers that drive me to be unloving and against G-d.

This is not about Me vs. Them; it is about Me vs. Me. At the end of the age, or at the end of any age, at the end of the day, angels will help me know myself as only G-d knows me, and will cast those parts of me that do evil, that are hate-ridden, that are, well, *weedy*, into the furnace.

And there *will* be gnashing of teeth. It is so hard to give up our precious, selfish lives. I mean, for G-d's sake, I remember how hard it was just to give up cigarettes! Do I really think that giving up the most selfish parts of my being will not be filled with lament? But if we do this, if we (at the end of an age—would that be today?) thresh out the good from the bad, the selfish from the loving, "*then* the righteous [us!] will shine like the sun! . . . Let anyone with ears listen!"

Knowing takes a different route in the Epistle for today, as Paul writes to the Christians in Rome (Romans 8:12–25). Paul speaks of life in Christ as a life of adoption, in which G-d takes us as G-d's own children. It is so easy to romanticize this account, to present G-d as the Ultimate Perfect Parent who saves us from our Beastly Biological Parents (who are apparently deadbeats, drug addicts, dastards).

But adoption is far more complicated than that. My husband, who is adopted, does not regret being taken in by his adoptive parents at all. But that doesn't mean that he doesn't wonder who his biological parents are. There is both a practical reason for this (think medical history) and an emotional one. However much you might love your adoptive parents, it is not unnatural to wonder how much of your biological parents live on in you, or to wonder what your life might have been like if you had been raised by them (or one of them).

Adoption, even by G-d, is not necessarily all sweetness and light. And for those of us who had pretty darned wonderful biological parents, by whom we were raised, the notion of G-d as an adoptive parent might seem at best superfluous and at worst creepily intervening and threatening. This part of Paul's letter, which suggests that we, who are recipients of the first fruits (yes, I love that queer, homo-y phrase) of the Spirit, "groan inwardly while we wait for adoption, the redemption of our bodies." We are hoping to be family. We are hoping, Paul says, for the redemption of our bodies, for salvation. But we hope for what we have not seen.

Okay, so let any dyke, transperson, homo, or queerling tell you what we hope for: We, more than most straight people I've met, are hoping absolutely and resolutely for the redemption of our bodies. We are hoping for the day when we are free—free to enjoy our bodies fully, relishing them for the joy that G-d intended them to provide. We are hoping for the day when our bodies are not subjects of public commentary, or restroom investigation. We are hoping for the day when our bodies will no longer be the subject of someone else's self-righteous judgment. We have not seen it. We do not know it.

Yet.

But we hope, as Paul writes, for the unseen. We long for that day, when—glory!—we can look at our bodies and say, "Surely HaShem is in this place!"

Surely *then* we will be one with the Fountain of All Wisdom and will no longer need to ask for anything, because we will have discovered that it was ours all along.

PROPER 12, THE SUNDAY CLOSEST TO JULY 27

Dr. Peter Carlson

Track 1	or	Track 2
Genesis 29:15–28		*1 Kings 3:5–12*
Psalm 105:1–11, 45b		*Psalm 119:129–136*
or *Psalm 128*		*Romans 8:26–39*
Romans 8:26–39		*Matthew 13:31–33, 44–52*
Matthew 13:31–33, 44–52		

"Have you understood all this?" Jesus asked. "Yes," they answered. "No," said I.

We have heard the so-called kingdom parables in Matthew 13 so many times that I sometimes wonder if their absurdity has been lost on us. Because they are absurd, aren't they? Jesus is talking directly to his disciples at this point, after speaking to a large crowd earlier. And what talk! The reign of heaven (Matthew doesn't use the phrase "kingdom of G-d" as Mark and Luke do, presumably to avoid saying the name of G-d in a text written for a Jewish audience) is like a mustard seed that grows into a mustard plant. The reign of heaven is like yeast, that makes bread dough rise. The reign of heaven is like a hidden treasure that you buy a field to get. The reign of heaven is like a fabulous pearl that you sell everything you have in order to purchase. The reign of heaven is like a net full of fish, with gnashing teeth, or something.

First of all, we need to acknowledge that these parables are very queer stories; they're metaphors, providing brief if vivid images, and unlike, say, the parable of the Good Samaritan, they don't have a lot of narrative arc.

And like all queerness and imagery and metaphor, if you try to push them too far, they become unsustainable, like the implication of virginity symbolized by a white wedding dress. Treating imagery and metaphor literally is like trying to grip Jell-O; first of all, you can't, and second of all, you'll end up with a mess. But these particular queer stories that Jesus tells his disciples seem to be challenging even as metaphor or simile. Let's start with that tiny mustard seed, for instance. There's been a lot of reflection on how this parable should be interpreted. Some scholars have suggested that the plant is black mustard, which can indeed grow to about nine feet high. Even so, this is hardly "the greatest of shrubs," and it's not a plant in which birds would likely nest. I freely admit that if I'd heard this come out of Jesus's mouth, I'd be all, "Huh?"

It's tempting to tie this story to Jesus's comment about having faith the size of a grain of mustard in chapter 17 of Matthew, but today Jesus doesn't say that faith is like a mustard seed; he says that the reign of heaven is like a mustard seed. Which becomes quite shrubby. And which, if birds really do try to nest in it, they probably won't do too well. This is a good thing, Jesus?

Or yeast. The reign of heaven is like yeast that helps bread dough to rise. You put a little bit in with the flour, and all the dough rises! So the reign of heaven is fluffy-puffy? If that's the case, then why do so many churches use unleavened bread (which I grant you is a reference to the Passover) for communion? Wouldn't we want the reign of heaven in the body of Christ? Or am I pushing the metaphor too far? But sugar does the same thing, right? You add a little, and the whole recipe is sweetened! Why isn't the reign of heaven like sugar?

Or treasure. Ah, now this one makes more sense. The reign of heaven is like a treasure buried in a field. And you find it, and so you go and sell literally everything you have to buy the field, and con the original field owner out of what had been rightfully theirs. I'm going to suggest that this not only sounds a little deceitful, but saying that the reign of heaven is like money also doesn't sit very well with Jesus, a few chapters back, saying you can't worship G-d and money.

A pearl? A thing of beauty? That could work. But again, we have this idea that the reign of heaven is about stuff—stuff for which you will sell everything you have, so that you can . . . *buy it*? The reign of heaven is for sale? And with both the treasure and the pearl, we have to wonder if, like so many stories of lottery winners, the thing we thought we wanted turned out to be very sour grapes indeed.

And finally, a fishing expedition. The reign of heaven, like a trawler, drags all sorts of fish up, good and bad, and then the bad gets thrown out (and the good apparently gets eaten?). This sounds comparable to the wheat and tares parable that Jesus told the disciples just prior to today's reading, and it is helpful to remember that I am not the good fish whilst someone else is the bad fish, but that we are all good and bad and that, presumably, in the reign of heaven, the bad parts of us will be discarded so that only the good remains.

But really, Jesus? "Have you understood all this?" you asked your disciples. And the disciples, like my students when I ask "Does that make sense?" nod, clearly not really having thought about "all this" too deeply. And then Jesus finishes off with another bit of nonsense: "Therefore every scribe who has been trained for the reign of heaven is like the master of a household who brings out of their treasure what is new and what is old."

So, wait, Jesus. What does that even mean? Are you saying again that the reign of heaven is like treasure? Or that it's made up of new stuff and old stuff? Or that it's something precious brought out of hiding? Or . . . ?

The reason I call these stories queer is because they are elusive and hard to pin down definitively. The word *queer* itself is the same way: It can function as a noun, a verb, an adjective, and defining it is tricky, because it tends to be wildly contextual. Of course, I'm convinced that this elusiveness and indefinite quality is something that could be said of all scripture, particularly as we try to understand an ancient text in a modern context.

How, for example, do we read the story of Jacob working seven years for a wife, only to have the woman's father replace her with her older sister? We not only have a story in which women are being used like bargaining chips and property, but in which they are being used deceitfully. How must Leah have felt, knowing that, despite her beautiful eyes, she wasn't loved by her spouse? Laban was a nasty piece of work, yes—but Jacob was obviously so stupid that he banged Leah without even recognizing it was the wrong bride. What do we make of this story? That men are either unscrupulous or stupid? That buying a wife is a perfectly acceptable practice? That having pretty eyes isn't enough to make someone love you?

Or is it something deliciously tawdry and sensual, such as what might come to mind when the second psalm given as an option to pair with this story declares, "You shall eat the fruit of your labor"? Can we draw a sexual reference to Jacob eating out his new bride? Twice? (Because, remember, he bought two wives with his labor to eat.) The point I'm trying to make here is that this is a biblical story that does not become any easier to untangle for spiritual edification even when we try to read it in its cultural and historical contexts.

In track 2, we have a reading from 1 Kings, where Solomon, who has risen to the throne after the death of his father, David, is in Gideon, gathering all the leaders of the land to consolidate his power. In a famous dream, G-d offers Solomon anything he wants. I was told growing up how Solomon was so good that he didn't ask to be rich, but asked for wisdom instead. As an adult, I think this is really the only practical request for the new king of a nation that's had serious problems since its first king, Saul, went bonkerdoodles, and its second king, David, always lifted up as the paragon of kingship, literally had a man killed so David could fuck the man's wife, and whose son Absalom rose up in rebellion against him. But we'll credit it to Solomon's virtue, sure. Even so, we need to remember that literally in the very next passage of the first book of Kings, Solomon's "wisdom" leads him to suggest to two women who both claim to be mother of a baby that they actually *chop the baby in half*. With wisdom like this, who needs stupidity? Do we ask G-d for wisdom? If so, is this what we're going to get? What are we supposed to take from this?

Paul seems to be spouting nonsense, too, let's be honest. This passage from the book of Romans has been used by theologians to argue for predestination: the doctrine that G-d foresees everything and, if you take that idea to its logical conclusion as John Calvin did in the sixteenth century, that G-d has ordained that some of us should be born for the express purpose of going to hell. But Paul's writing here seems really confused, like he's not quite sure how to say what he wants to say. "We don't know how to ask for the right thing, folks, so the Spirit is willing to help us. But hey! We know that all things work together for good for those who love G-d, right? That must mean that G-d's, like, totally in control, right? And that G-d, like, predestined everything, right? I mean, if G-d is for us, who is against us, right? I mean, who will bring any charge against G-d's elect?"

"What could possibly go wrong?" the man who would be beheaded for Jesus asked.

But in all this confusion, Paul lands on the hard paradox of the Christian faith: "For I am convinced that neither death, nor life, nor angels, nor rulers, nor things present, nor things to come, nor powers, nor height, nor depth, nor anything else in all creation, will be able to separate us from the love of G-d in Christ Jesus who is our Sovereign."

Love can't stop a sword from cutting Paul's head off. Love can't keep Laban from stuffing his elder daughter into a tent to get banged by Jacob. Love can't keep Jacob from being so senseless with lust that he can't tell Leah isn't the woman he bargained for. Love can't keep Solomon from offering to chop a baby in two. Love can't even make sense of the various reign of heaven parables, no matter how many times the disciples have said they got it.

But love *can* give all these queer stories some perspective. Because at the root of our faith is the idea that there are lots of things going on that defy explanation, that we can't really understand with logic or reason, but that those things can still offer us something, when encountered through the lens of love.

Because, after all, I've been the person who has thought he found a pearl of great price, only to find out it was Woolworth's costume jewelry. I've been the person who tried to plant a tree for birds to nest in, but only came up with a shrub. I've been the person who worked to achieve something I thought I was in love with, only to find that what I got was something else. And I've been the person who asked for wisdom but found that I still had to rely on my gut instincts, because wisdom didn't really have any firm answers.

I've learned that queer stories, that metaphors, don't have firm answers or interpretations, but that in telling them—in telling all the stories of the scriptural narrative, for that matter—all of us, who are all scribes who have been trained for the reign of heaven, have occasional flashes of insight, some new, some old, that we can bring out of our treasury and share with those around us.

PROPER 13, THE SUNDAY CLOSEST TO AUGUST 3

Dr. Peter Carlson

Track 1	or	Track 2
Genesis 32:22–31		*Isaiah 55:1–5*
Psalm 17:1–7, 16		*Psalm 145:8–9, 15–22*
Romans 9:1–5		*Romans 9:1–5*
Matthew 14:13–21		*Matthew 14:13–21*

What must we do to be vindicated, as Christians? Especially those of us who are queer Christians? We inhabit an awkward, often uncomfortable, crossover space in the Venn diagram of Christians and Queerpeople. The Christians in their circle all too often play G-d and tell us we are not welcome or even salvageable; queerfolk, perhaps understandably, often sneer from their circle at the very idea of G-d, and tell us that we are like a lover staying in an abusive relationship. A touchy position indeed, and one that if I'm honest, I'm actually fairly regularly tempted to abandon. (I mean, I'm tempted to abandon my faith. I tried abandoning my sexuality for Jesus, but that didn't work.)

What I have discovered over the years in which I have not abandoned my faith, is that being both a queer lover and a Jesus lover means that I spend a lot of time wrestling, like Jacob, and the fact of the matter is that, like Jacob, I've gotten some wounds in the process. But that's what vindication costs.

I know I say this all the time, but I really don't like Jacob. He's a shitty person, who steals his elder brother Esau's birthright, who with his mother literally tricks his blind father into bestowing Esau's blessing on him, who in a dastardly move cheats his brothers-in-law out of their inheritance from his father-in-law's flocks (granted the father-in-law was a sneak, too, and swapped wives after Jacob had bought one of his daughters), and who is an all-around conniving, unpleasant git. And because of this, he is also the prime example of G-d choosing to work with the Person Least Expected.

One thing I've gotta say for Jacob, though: He's tenacious. Our story today begins with him having left his father-in-law's land to return to his father Isaac's land in Canaan. By this time, incidentally, he has two wives, two "maids" (sure, we'll call them that), and eleven children (welcome to biblical models of plural marriage, by the way); he has sent them across the stream at Jabbok with all their belongings. Back on the other side of the stream, we are told rather casually that "a man wrestled with him until daybreak," as though this is something that everyone does, given the chance. Jacob refused to let go and demanded a blessing, even when the man eventually put Jacob's hip out of joint with a thwack. And what a blessing. It's a name change. "You shall no longer be called Jacob, but Israel, for you have striven with G-d and with humans and have prevailed." I always tell my students that, if someone's name is changed, that's a sign that something really huge has just happened. So Jacob becomes Israel, and Israel is tenacious, and usually gets what he wants, even if he ends up limping the rest of his life.

Psalm 17 is a kind of wrestling with G-d, too, demanding that G-d speak up for the poet, whose prayer "comes from lips free of deceit." It's hard for me not to read this with more than a little bit of petulance, probably because I have over the past year felt, like the psalmist, to have experienced injustices, made worse because one doesn't know if they are rooted in homophobia, or just unjust first-world cussedness. I confess that I have behaved probably more than a little self-righteously in the process (though, c'mon: Who among us has not been indignant at the way we've been treated sometimes?), very much saying things to G-d in line with the psalmist's "Let my vindication come from you; let your eyes be fixed on justice (paraphrased)!" It seems too often that I have been wrestling with G-d (or at least with humans who have power to affect my work), and that I am shouting, with Jacob, "Bless me, dammit!" or with the psalmist, "I have avoided the ways of the violent, . . . [so] incline your ear to me and hear my words!" I'm not sure I've been blessed, or vindicated, but I certainly feel the complaint.

Paul, too, is hoping to be vindicated. We can never forget the fact that Paul's primary goal in the Epistle to the Romans is to argue that the Law has basically become irrelevant, while still upholding the importance of the Covenant that G-d made with Abraham and his descendants. Having in the first several chapters of the letter established his core doctrine of justification by faith (which is spiritual) rather than by following the details of the Law (which is bodily), he finishes triumphantly in chapter 8 looking forward to that spiritual future: "In all these things we are more than victorious through him who loved us. For I am convinced that neither death, nor life, nor angels, nor rulers, nor things present, nor things to come, nor powers, nor height, nor depth, nor anything else in all creation will be able to separate us from the love of G-d in Christ Jesus our Lord."

Glory!

But then, we're given a total buzzkill at the beginning of chapter 9: "I have great sorrow and unceasing anguish in my heart. For I could wish that I myself were accursed and cut off from Christ for the sake of my own brothers and sisters, my own flesh and blood." Paul here is talking of course about the Jewish people, of which he is one. And he's trying to justify, after eight chapters of saying that the Law doesn't justify us and why Gentiles can be Christians too, why Judaism still matters.

I actually love this reading, because Paul is feeling something that is really noble: He says he would be willing to cut himself off in order to save them—an act that reminds me of the village of Eyam in Derbyshire, England, that chose in 1665 to cut itself off entirely so as to prevent the spread of the bubonic plague that was killing its people. But our passage doesn't begin really to address the theology that he is advancing in this chapter, which is that not all people technically descended from Abraham are going to be inheritors of the promise (in fact, he makes a reference to the bizarre fact that G-d chose Jacob and not Esau, the elder son, touching back on the track 1 Hebrew Bible reading for today). Paul, too, is wrestling, in this case with what seems to be an unfair act on the part of the Divine, wishing he could assure all the Jews that they would inherit the blessings of the covenant.

The Hebrew Bible reading from track 2, and the passage from Matthew, in a slightly different take on the issue, appear to be signs of how divine vindication might manifest. Isaiah chapter 55, the final chapter in a group sometimes called the Book of Consolation, was probably written during the Babylonian Exile, so the vindication of G-d's people is not technically at hand, but these consoling poetic lines were designed to give the Judeans hope, and the strength to hold on, to persevere in their wrestling match. It is a glorious vision of plenty: "Everyone who thirsts, come to the waters; and you that have no money, come, buy and eat! Come, buy wine and milk without money and without price. . . . eat what is good, and delight yourselves in rich food!" And the promise goes on, assuring the exiles that they shall live, and that G-d will, indeed, glorify them. This, then, is what G-d's vindication will look like.

Or will it? Maybe it will be something a bit less flashy and as a result of shared humanity. We read in Matthew the old familiar story of the feeding of the five thousand (besides the women and children, of course). Jesus, dogged by people who are seeking healing, learning, or maybe just a chance to believe that someone gives a rat's ass about them, is trying to get away to rest, but they still follow him. And we are told that, when he sees them, "he had compassion for them and cured their sick." And time went on, and healing went on, and Jesus's disciples began to get edgy, and to suggest that he should send the people away so they could get food. And Jesus responds, "You feed them." And they were, like, "Wait wut? Jesus. Dude. We've only got five loaves of bread and two fish. Ain't gonna happen." But of course, it does, and there's more than enough to go around.

Vindication doesn't, in this story, come with fireworks or in sumptuous banquet halls. It comes in a field, with people sitting around, and in the willingness to put oneself out for others, and to share what we have. The Sisters of Perpetual Indulgence are an order of queer and trans nuns, who believe that everyone has a right to express their unique joy and beauty. According to their mission on their web page, "Since our first appearance in San Francisco on Easter Sunday, 1979, the Sisters have devoted ourselves to community service, ministry, and outreach to those on the edges, and to promoting human rights, respect for diversity and spiritual enlightenment. We use humor and irreverent wit to expose the forces of bigotry, complacency and guilt that chain the human spirit."[1]

The Sisters of Perpetual Indulgence have been called everything nasty, including blasphemous. But they're the ones who were on the streets of San Francisco and Los Angeles in the 1980s and '90s, chatting up the sex

---

[1] www.thesisters.org.

workers, making sure they were having protected sex, or getting their meds when they contracted HIV. It was the Sisters who were wrestling with G-d then, and they have not given up. In fact, the Sisters did and to this day do demand a blessing from G-d. Like Paul, they have been willing to be cut off, getting derided, mocked, and even assaulted, for the sake of the least of their fellow queers. They are the ones who have shown us what the world might look like, if we dream big, where people whose lives are lived in the margins can "eat what is good, and delight in rich food." They are a group who, I swear, can magically feed thousands with five loaves, two fishes, and a feisty dose of irreverence and trash talk.

They have showed us what holy, queer vindication looks like. And I'm convinced G-d has blessed them and has blessed us through them. Their wrestling has paid off, and they are blessed and beautiful and outrageous, even if they're limping a little bit in their habits.

PROPER 14, THE SUNDAY CLOSEST TO AUGUST 10

Dr. Pamela Lightsey

Track 1	or	Track 2
Genesis 37:1–4, 12–28		*1 Kings 19:9–18*
Psalm 105:1–6, 16–22, 45b		*Psalm 85:8–13*
Romans 10:5–15		*Romans 10:5–15*
Matthew 14:22–33		*Matthew 14:22–33*

When the Lord Passes By

Albert Einstein is reported to have said, "It is strange to be known so universally, and yet to be so lonely."[1] Each of us has had moments of loneliness. It seems to feel worse when you're in a room full of people or during the holiday season. There's nothing like knowing you should feel connected or knowing you should feel the spirit of the times, but you're just not there. Thinking about loneliness, I think of the kind of loneliness that queer folks can feel being around their family who love them but whom they know don't quite understand them. Imagine, if you can, the loneliness of our elder LGBTQ folks before coming out became more commonplace or the loneliness of LGBTQ folks who even now live in areas where it's not safe to come out. The loneliness of being in a dangerous place, a dangerous environment, a dangerous time, and believing you bear that weight all by yourself.

---

[1] Quoted in Robert J. Morgan, *Nelson's Complete Book of Stories, Illustrations, and Quotes: The Ultimate Contemporary Resource for Speakers* (Thomas Nelson Publishers, 2000), 715.

Elijah, the prophet, had every reason to feel—true or not—that he was alone. Here was a man who had the boldness to speak out against the idolatry of Israel. Elijah had the audacity to confront King Ahab, who'd married the Phoenician princess, Jezebel. It was that marriage that led to the nation's worship of Baal.

I want to be clear because I realize how the name "Jezebel" has often been invoked against women to suggest that a woman is sexually promiscuous, deceptive, or a danger to others. There ought to be a way to look at this text and hold the characters in the text to task without resorting to *ad hominem* attacks. Jezebel *and* Ahab and the nation of Israel worship Baal. This was a national sin. The nation turned from the Lord, the God of Abraham, Isaac, and Jacob, and began to worship lesser gods and idols. The king gave his ear to the prophets of Baal rather than the prophets of the Lord. So treacherous was Ahab that it is written, "Ahab son of Omri did evil in the sight of the Lord more than all who were before him." (1 Kings 16:30). So, it was not Jezebel alone. But we have a way, don't we, of scapegoating others for our weaknesses and for our bigotry?

For decades, there were leaders and parishioners within the United Methodist Church who used LGBTQ folks as scapegoats to keep the denomination from being the truly inclusive entity that it now has a chance of becoming. "It's the gays who are hurting the church! We've got to stop the gays! The gays are going to destroy OUR church! The gays are a danger to our children!" That was their stance. Yet there we remained. Loving God, serving our communities, and trying to practice biblical obedience. We did that even as we remained scapegoats to hide their greedy desire for power and control of the denomination.

So, no, let us not use this passage to harken back to a time when Jezebel is made a scapegoat for our bigotry. Instead, let's hold in our minds the picture of national sin. A nation that does not care for the poor. A nation that does not tend to orphans or hungry children. A nation that spends more money filling its coffers with weapons than building housing for the homeless. This is the national environment that God is calling us, just as God called Elijah, to speak against. And that, my friends, can be a dangerous and lonely task. It'll get you in trouble. Good trouble. But trouble, nevertheless.

Elijah's commitment to God led to violence—the slaughter of the prophets of Baal. It included harsh prophesies about the future of the nation. When I sit with this, it provokes me to ask questions about the effect of such violence on the prophet of God. The prophet, God's messenger, slaughtered the prophets of Baal. And what is more, God gives instructions for the slaughter of others! This kind of violence is hard for me to imagine being commanded by God. Yet, time and again, the Hebrew Bible describes this God who is queer in nature. A God of love and a God of war.

Now, I have a better sense of Elijah. He's had to speak truth to power. His hands are bloodied by war. His lips have uttered a dark future for the nation. He's on the run from the rulers of the nation who seek vengeance on him because of his obedience to God. Sitting in the cave on the mount of Horeb, hungry, tired, and lonely, the Lord begins a conversation with him by asking what seems like such a simple question. "What are you doing here, Elijah?" In fact, the Lord asks him the same question twice! "What are you doing here, Elijah?"

What are you doing in this cave? What are you doing in this closet? Why are you in this place?

Pssst. God already knows the answer. It seems to me that God is giving the prophet an opportunity to deal with his own feelings by saying the things that are in his heart out loud. Speaking out loud helps our thought process. It's clarifying. Speaking out loud can also help us encourage ourselves. That's why I love the saying attributed to activist Maggie Kuhn, "Speak your mind, even if your voice shakes."[2] Here sits Elijah in the cave, and it's almost as if the Lord is encouraging Elijah to speak his mind. "What are you doing here, Elijah?"

And after Elijah is able to begin to purge himself of the trauma he has experienced, God asks him the same question again . . . for Elijah's benefit. There are some things that we experience in life that just won't go right away. The sense that you are alone in the struggles of life may take time to resolve. What I like about this passage is that Elijah is given the time—repeatedly—to process what is in his heart *and* the Lord waits patiently. The Lord will wait on you. Wait on you to speak your mind. And the Lord will wait with you. Wait with you to heal. And in the midst of it all, the Lord will ask you to stand outside your comfort zone to be

[2] The origin of the quotation is uncertain, but the attribution can be found in several places, including on the National Women's Hall of Fame website: https://www.womenofthehall.org/inductee/maggie-kuhn/.

able to discern the true presence of the Lord. *Come out of the cave and wait for me to pass by, Elijah.*

When you are going through something, it's easy to shut yourself off from the rest of the world. Now, I'm not saying that Elijah had no right to be in hiding, but what happened to the faith that he carried into battle with the prophets of Baal? He slaughtered an entire company of prophets. Prophet, come out of the cave and wait on the Lord!

You may be lonely, and you may be afraid, but you cannot do the work of the Lord hiding out. Yes, take some time for self-care. Yes, take some time for healing. Yes, take some time to process how you truly feel about the work. But prophet . . . people of God, at some point, you've got to pick yourself up, dust yourself off, and step back outside into the world. Step out of the cave and see the sky. Step out of the cave, feel the winds, and experience the storms of life. Step out of the cave and feel the ground shaking under your feet; experience the rocks cracking from the mountains. For after all of that has been seen, heard, and felt, still, you must wait for the presence of the Lord.

In the presence of the Lord, you and your family shall eat and rejoice (Deut. 12:7). In the presence of the Lord, "there is fullness of joy" (Ps. 16:11).

The Lord invited the prophet to stand outside the cave, outside his loneliness, and outside his fear. Just as the Lord invites queer folks and freedom fighters for justice to stand outside our closets, outside our fears, and outside our loneliness, to feel the world as it is, not as we imagine or desire it to be. Stand outside in the earthquake and wait for the presence of God.

The late transactivist Miss Marsha P. Johnson learned early on to live in the presence of God. Though her life was often filled with trials and storms, one thing was true of Ms. Johnson: She had a deep and abiding relationship with God. She could have been brought low on the night of the Stonewall Riots, but she took courage and stood up to injustice. In 1973, when members of the LGB community told her that she could not march in the Pride Parade because the presence of our trans siblings wasn't a good look for the community, she and Sylvia Rivera showed up anyway. She showed up for us because God showed up as a loving presence in her life from the time she was a teenager.[3]

---

[3] Jim McDermott, SJ, "Remembering Transgender Icon Marsha P. Johnson, a Saint of Welcome," *Outreach*, August 9, 2022, https://outreach.faith/2022/08/remembering-transgender-icon-marsha-p-johnson-a-saint-of-welcome/.

When the Lord passed by, Elijah heard God and wrapped his face in his mantle. He heard God as "a sound of sheer silence." The Lord passed by in silence and yet Elijah heard God. Many of us strain to hear God in the loud and charismatic voices of our day. But God passed by after the noise. Many of us hope to see God in the fire and the windstorms of life, only to make it through all of that and hear God in the silent whispers of life. Elijah heard and witnessed a lot of drama on Mount Hebron, but what made Elijah cover his face in sheer awe was the presence of God in the sheer silence of the moment. When the Lord passes by, it may not be as we imagined or as we demanded. (Remember? God's thoughts are not our thoughts; neither are God's ways our ways [Isa. 55:8].)

What shall we do with ourselves in our loneliness, fear, and despair? Sometimes, well, most times, the best that we can do is wait for the Lord to pass by. While we're waiting, face ourselves and make our confessions to the Lord. Then, hear God proclaim, "You are not alone. There are many more who have not been overtaken by the bigotry, the anger, the greed, and the sins of this world." Be encouraged. God has many followers. Our collective work of justice-making will prevail. God will not leave us nor forsake us. You are not alone.

PROPER 15, THE SUNDAY CLOSEST TO AUGUST 17

Dr. Peter Carlson

Track 1	or	Track 2
Genesis 45:1–15		*Isaiah 56:1, 6–8*
Psalm 133		*Psalm 67*
Romans 11:1–2a, 29–32		*Romans 11:1–2a, 29–32*
Matthew 15:(10–20), 21–28		*Matthew 15:(10–20), 21–28*

Surprise!

That seems to be the theme for these lectionary readings, in both tracks: Divine Surprise. (It sounds like a dessert from the 1950s.)

I'll be really up front with you here: I do not like surprises. My ideal life is one that is planned, well in advance if possible, and that proceeds according to plan. If I *must* have surprises, I would like to schedule them in my calendar, thank you. Say, for Tuesdays at 2 p.m., and lasting no longer than half an hour.

You may have heard, however, the old saw: "Life is what happens when you're making other plans." Today I'd like to amend that to "G-d is what happens when you're making other plans."

In year A, track 1, which follows the events of Genesis and Exodus relatively continuously, we hear the ultimate "Surprise!" moment in the whole Joseph story, where his brothers, having long before sold him into slavery, are shocked to discover that, far from being dead or forgotten (or even still enslaved), Joseph has in fact become prime minister in the very country to which the brothers had to run to escape famine. It's not really shocking that Joseph plays a pretty nasty trick on them, since they treated him really shittily when he was young (though there is a practical lesson in that story: Never tell your siblings that your dad loves you best or that you have dreams about the older sibs bowing their unmanly, limp wheat sheaves down to you, even if it's true; they won't take it well). Indeed, the pairing of this story by the lectionistas with Psalm 133 is a stroke of wry genius: siblings living together in unity? Sure, except when they sell you as chattel into slavery, soak your pretty drag queen coat in blood, and tell dad that you're dead. Can you say "irony"?

But the revelation of Joseph's identity—having become the powerful one to whom the brothers are, in fact, limply and helplessly bowing down and begging for food—is meant to be read as the ultimate surprise. And the credit for the surprise, according to Joseph, goes to—you guessed it—G-d! He comforts his brothers (who, let's be honest, were still probably in shock), "do not be distressed, or angry with yourselves, because you sold me here; for G-d sent me before you to preserve life. . . . G-d sent me before you to preserve for you a remnant on earth, and to keep alive for you many survivors. So it was not you who sent me here, but G-d; he has made me a father to Pharaoh, and lord of all his house and ruler over all the land of Egypt."

G-d had a handle on things the whole time, and all that pain and suffering? G-d made us go through it so that all y'all wouldn't starve to death! Cool!

In track 2, Trito-Isaiah has a surprise, too, if not quite as narratively dramatic as the Joseph story's surprise. In this last section of the book of Isaiah, we are reading oracles likely intended for the Judaeans who have returned from exile in Babylon, and are rebuilding the temple after a long period where none of their familiar markers as Jews, none of the promises made to Abraham, were available to them: Abraham's descendants were decimated first by Assyria and then by Babylon; the land they had been promised was taken from them; and their nationhood was meaningless. They had, in Babylon, to learn how to be Jewish without any of the things that they thought made them Jews. And now they were back, and getting those things back. But the oracles of Trito-Isaiah are warning them against the very complacency that was the cause of their exile in the first place: not keeping the Sabbath; idolatry; corrupt rulers; self-interested worship; not caring for the hungry and the afflicted. And here is the Divine Surprise: non-Israelites are among the favored of G-d! In fact, in the verses that are skipped over in this reading (*always* read those verses!) we find that not only foreigners will receive G-d's endorsement, but to the eunuchs—those who are non-traditionally gendered—"I will give, in my house and within my walls, a monument and a name better than sons and daughters; I will give them an everlasting name that shall not be cut off." In a culture that is hypercon-cerned with descendants, the idea that someone unable to breed might have more favor with G-d than the those who pop babies out regularly? That's got to be disconcerting. In fact, this oracle is insisting that the outcasts will get first dibs on G-d's favor, and those who thought they were doing everything right, but who were in fact pursuing their own interests rather than G-d's justice on the Sabbath, will get the sloppy seconds. And the psalm for this reading reminds us that G-d will judge with equity, not equality. That *all* nations and *all* people will know G-d's saving health.

Surprise!

Now, if this sounds unfair—the idea that G-d, having "chosen" the descendants of Abraham to be G-d's people, then tells them to piss off because they're behaving like selfish brats, and then chooses a bunch of foreigners to receive G-d's blessing—that's because it probably is. G-d's interest, at least in this passage, is not fairness; it is equity; it is justice. And let's be honest: Justice often appears unfair to those of us born to privilege, who find out that G-d is going to tilt the scales against us, and in favor of the outcasts and the outsiders.

Paul is also wrestling with the "who's in and who's out" question. His ultimate theme in the book of Romans is not who is doing what with their sexybits, but the fact that Gentiles have full entry into G-d's reign of justice, too. And he's all over that theme in this passage, but turning it around: Are you asking (he says) if my insistence that non-Jews can be Jesus followers means that Jews can't? And his answer is, "Of course Jews can be Jesus followers!" His rationale is a kind of weird read for me, I'll admit. Paul says, in essence, "Just as you Gentiles were disobedient to G-d and have thus received G-d's mercy, so the Jews are currently disobedi-ent (for not recognizing Jesus as the anointed one), so they can receive mercy." This is that really problematic *felix culpa*—blessed guilt—theology that tries to paint the original sin of Adam and Eve as a good thing, because it paved the way for Jesus to come and save our asses. And we're back to Joseph, aren't we, saying that his brothers treating him like shit was actually a yay.

I have a confession: I don't believe that everything happens for a reason, and when people say that to me when I'm going through a really bad time, it takes all my moral strength not to deck them. I believe fully that evil exists, that chance is whimsically real, and that sometimes we're impaled upon it. Shit, as they say, happens.

But here's the other thing I believe: I believe that we humans can make meaning out of the meaningless. I believe that we can use our pain to create beautiful things. I believe that *everything* (and that's a big word, my friends) can be baptized, can be redeemed.

I cannot believe that it is G-d's will that a family would sell their sibling into slavery. I cannot believe that G-d somehow willed or foreordained our disobedience, just to give us the joy of being accepted into the reign of Christ. But I believe G-d can redeem evil actions and make goodness and art from them. I do not believe that G-d wills cancer, or war. I believe that G-d is with us in the places of excrement, and makes them more bearable, and sometimes even makes them beautiful, not in spite of the excrement, but right there in it. Because I believe in a G-d who is in relationship with us, even when we are not particularly wanting to be in relationship with Them, and I believe that relationships change those who are in them—even G-d.

So I believe in a G-d Who is changing as we change; and Who grows with us; and Who is in a constant state of becoming. I believe in a G-d Who still needs to learn new things and is delighted to learn them. And that brings us to the Gospel, which has the biggest Divine Surprise of them all: the surprise that the divine Themself can be surprised.

I want to insist on including the "optional" bits of the Gospel lesson, if for no other reason than the fact that, as a queer person, I don't want to skip over the hard bits, even if they are bits that may seem to speak against me as a queer person. And in this optional part (verses 10–20), Jesus appears to come down hard on sexual immorality, which lots of folks think is queer people having sex with the "wrong" gender. But aside from the fact that I have a very different view of what constitutes sexual immorality, I'd like to acknowledge the bigger point that Jesus is making: It is what comes from the heart and out of our mouths that defiles us, not what we put into our mouths. Jesus gets pretty gastroenterologically graphic here: "Don't you understand that what you put in your mouth goes into your stomach and you ultimately shit it out? That shit (as it were) isn't the problem!

It's the evil that comes from your heart that defiles you. Stop quibbling about the nitpickies of the Law! Start worrying about how you're treating others!" (Echoes of Isaiah, in case you didn't catch that . . .)

But then, of course, to the nonoptional bit: the story of the Canaanite woman's faith. This story is familiar to many Christians, but it still strikes me how often we skip over the obvious to try to find some vaguer, more comfortable truth: Jesus has to learn a hard lesson, and he learns it from a foreigner, who is a woman, who is a *nasty, loud* woman, and who is pushy to boot. First of all, the (male, probably) disciples get all icky-wicky-poo-poo about this annoying wretch, who is screaming "my daughter is tormented by a demon!" Literally the disciples ask Jesus to send her away, because "she keeps shouting after us." "Jesus," they are whimpering, "she's not behaving like a biblical woman! Make her stop!" And weirdly, Jesus seems to concur: "I was sent only to the lost sheep of the house of Israel. They're the ones who are 'in.'"

Nevertheless, she persisted.

And Jesus keeps up his exclusivist bullshit, comparing her to a dog: "It's not fair to take the children's food and throw it to the dogs." And the unnamed, feisty, persistent, loud Canaanite woman proceeds to throw serious shade: "Yeah, but even dogs get crumbs from the master's table."

And, finally, the light dawns, and Jesus gets it. Maybe he *isn't* just sent for the "Chosen People." Or, put another way, maybe he finally figured out that chosenness is a helluva lot more expansive than even he thought it was. It is the nasty woman, the pushy, brazen, foreign, unbiblical woman who *demands* G-d's grace, who *insists* that it is hers (or her daughter's) to claim.

That's a shocker, isn't it? Every time we think we know who's in and who's out (and G-d? If you need any suggestions about that, I have some thoughts), we get the news that we're thinking, as it were, inside the box—the box we've created to keep G-d under control.

But G-d isn't controllable. And the foreigners, the outcasts, the undocumented immigrants, the women, the disabled, the queers, the poor . . . they're all demanding that G-d throw some crumbs their way. And G-d. shockingly, is inviting them to the table.

Surprise!

PROPER 16, THE SUNDAY CLOSEST TO AUGUST 24

Dr. Peter Carlson

Track 1	or	Track 2
Exodus 1:8–2:10		*Isaiah 51:1–6*
Psalm 124		*Psalm 138*
Romans 12:1–8		*Romans 12:1–8*
Matthew 16:13–20		*Matthew 16:13–20*

I have had the honor of doing work at various points and in various capacities at the University of Oxford. And when I am there, my spiritual community is found at the University Church of St. Mary the Virgin. And I often find myself reminded of the minor differences between worship in the Episcopal Church and in the Church of England. One year, I was in Oxford for Proper 16, and I realized that the collect used in England is different from the one in the Episcopal Church's Revised Common Lectionary. I mention this because the collect so often sets the tone, as it were, for how I listen to the lessons of the day, and that Sunday in Oxford was no exception. It started with the lovely reminder that the Divine is always being more willing to be in relationship with us than we with Them, but the phrase that even more deeply moved me in this hearing was "pour down upon us the abundance of your mercy."

Abundance is a recurring theme for me, I admit it. This is because it is so difficult for me to think in terms of abundance whilst living in the fishbowl of capitalism, the foundational principle of which is to implant in all of us the fear of scarcity. It's not just capitalism, of course; we humans are ultimately sketchy and selfish creatures, which is probably why we think capitalism is so cool. Our sin of selfishness, not just our economics, is deeply rooted in our utter conviction of the inevitability of scarcity.

But the abundance of mercy suggests something quite different, doesn't it? If we are (un)naturally programmed, as it were, to fear that there is not enough, then a message of abundance is wild-ass, radical, good news indeed. It suggests not singularity and individuality, but plurality and multiplicity, and—well—hope. Hope because I do in fact matter, but also because it is not all about me, and even more, because it is not all *on* me. There is enough for all of us: enough grace, enough food, enough water. Everything we need is available abundantly, if only we do not try to possess it all for ourselves.

Ideas about multiplicity have been humming in my heart over the past several years, almost certainly primarily because I am queer, and teach queer theory and theology, and have been influenced by postmodernism, and liberation and queer theologians, all of whom have struggled with the church handing down a single teaching that is orthodox—literally "correct teaching." A church refusing to accept the theologies of those whose relationships with the Divine have been experienced on the margins of society, outside of the centers of power. This church (lower-case *c* intentional) is utterly obsessed with one-ness, with unity, which isn't in itself a horrible thing; but historically the church has equated unity with homogeneity, with everyone ascribing to the same, rather bland (if we're honest) teachings that uphold existing power structures and do nothing to cast down the mighty from their thrones. Multiplicity, on the other hand, suggests that experience (and theology, which is, after all, the words and ideas about our experiences with the Divine), cannot be reduced to a simple binary of human/divine, or orthodox/heterodox, or even good/bad. Multiplicity refracts divine light into varieties of wavelengths, with at least one that each pair of eyes can see, and can proclaim as Good News.

The comforting words of Deutero-Isaiah are an assurance, likely given to the Judeans in exile, that G-d's deliverance is imminent, and that G-d's salvation will be forever. The prophet offers a reminder of how G-d's mercy has appeared in the past, by raising up the story of the matriarch and patriarch of the people: "Look to Abraham your father and to Sarah who bore you; for he was but one when I called him, but I blessed him and made him many." I know the intention of this sentence is to reflect on the miracle of Abraham and Sarah having descendants when they were old farts, supposedly beyond childbearing years, but a flight of fancy (of heterodoxy?) took me to a vision of Abraham being "but one"—being utterly single-minded and having only one way of encountering and understanding the Divine—and being expanded, refracted, open to diversity and plurality and multiplicity in the divine relationship. This is a reminder to me of what it means to be in covenant with G-d. How often, how regularly, do I need to be "made many" by G-d, opened up to whole worlds of divine experience different from my own? How often do I need to have my precious individuality and correctness challenged, so that I might, in my being made many, be made one with others? Indeed, I am reminded in the psalm of those others that G-d desires me to be one with: "Though HaShem be high, They care for the lowly." Who or what is too lowly to be in communion with, to be in divine community? When I cut myself off from those in the margins of society, from the nonhuman elements of creation, from that which I think is not good enough, I make myself singular. And if I am singular, alone, then I have lopped myself off from G-d.

Paul, too, is on his rather regular but marvelous theme of plurality: one body, many members. It strikes me how often we are willing to recite this passage quite piously, yet at the same time are also completely willing to declare who, in fact, is or is not a "real" member of the body, who is worthy of divine communion. How often do we need to be reminded how eager we are to preach a damnable doctrine of the scarcity of G-d's love, rather than of Their abundance? The overarching message of the Hebrew and Christian scriptures, in my reading, is the mind-boggling expansiveness of G-d's relationship with creation. Paul in this passage is reminding that *wildly* heterogeneous group of Jesus followers in Rome that their differences are not what make them separate, but what make them helpful. "We have gifts," Paul exhorts "that differ according to the grace given to us." Again, this is a pretty thing we repeat regularly, but we tend to avoid the actual impact of Paul's (bodily) metaphor here. How often do I look at others and refuse to see the gifts that they offer the community? How often do I assume that certain bodies aren't helpful or beloved? How often do I revert to the belief that uniformity and singularity and so-called orthodoxy are the same thing as community?

How often does the church despise bodies that are not "appropriate" because the church refuses to believe that grace has been given to those bodies too? Queer bodies, women's bodies, disabled bodies, bodies of different races and ethnicities . . . For fuck's sake, even Jesus had to learn, just last week, that Canaanite women with daughters in distress were as much a part of G-d's Kindom as Jewish men!

The Gospel for today—the famous passage in which Jesus names Peter as the rock on which the ecclesia will be built—is also rooted in plurality. As Will Lamb, vicar of University Church Oxford, has made clear, Peter is not actually saying anything new.[1] In fact, he is rather stupidly reiterating what *all* the disciples said when Jesus saved Peter's ass after the walking-on-water debacle in Matthew 14: "You are the Child of G-d!" So it's important to remember that G-d did not suddenly and miraculously reveal this pearl of wisdom to Peter alone and individually; Peter, and all the Jesus followers, experienced it, and they experienced it as a *community*. Peter was simply naming once again what they all, each in their individual experiences, knew and had previously named. And the *ecclesia*—usually translated "church"—is quite literally a Greek word that means a meeting of the people. Even in this passage, we see that Church cannot exist without community, without multiplicity, without plurality, without abundance.

Incidentally, this whole passage is based upon a hilarious joke: hilarious not just because the name "Peter" derives from *petra*, the Greek word for rock, but because Peter, of all the disciples, is the one *constantly* with a foot in his mouth, clueless, and saying the wrong thing. We really need to remember that Jesus's "praise" of Peter here scans best when read a bit snarkily: "Whoa. Dude. It's not like we don't know you're the impetuous dickwad of the group! Obvs G-d in heaven revealed that one to you, because we all know you wouldn't have come up with it on your own!" Indeed, the abundance of G-d's mercy is shown here too: Even *Peter*, the babbling, sincere, all-too-eager dinglebutt, has a place in the meeting of the people.

I, too, am Peter. I recognize that too often I live *really* problematically into my name. I talk too much and awkwardly because I am afraid simply

[1] This observation was made in a sermon delivered at the University Church of St. Mary the Virgin in Oxford, on August 27, 2023.

to *be*, naturally and honestly, with others. I am so convinced that the lenses I use to view the world and the church are the correct ones, that I override (for example) the women who actually have experienced the good news of the resurrection. I imagine that I am the rock on which the church will be built because I am so fucking special, when sometimes, if I'm honest, I realize I'm just a rock blocking the path.

In my better moments, though, I hear G-d encouraging me to laugh at my foibles, and maybe even through my example welcoming others into the laughter, to treat their own individual foibles a little more gently, and to see each other's gifts, and hear each other's wildly heterodox and glorious experiences of the Divine. And when we do that, I am convinced that we will discover that the multiplicity of identities, the plurality of experiences, the abundance of mercy, has made us, not just into some rando meeting of the people, but into a body.

Into Church.

PROPER 17, THE SUNDAY CLOSEST TO AUGUST 31

Dr. Peter Carlson

Track 1	or	Track 2
Exodus 3:1–15		*Jeremiah 15:15–21*
Psalm 105:1–6, 23–26, 45c		*Psalm 26:1–8*
Romans 12:9–21		*Romans 12:9–21*
Matthew 16:21–28		*Matthew 16:21–28*

I'm just going to state up front that I'm focusing on track 2 today.

In the collect from the Episcopal Prayer Book, we hear the following:

> HaShem of all power and might, the author and giver of all good things: Graft in our hearts the love of your Name; increase in us all true religion; nourish us with all goodness; and bring forth in us the fruit of good works; through Jesus Christ HaShem, who lives and reigns with you and the Holy Spirit, one G-d for ever and ever. Amen.

Turning and turning and turning some more. It seems as though we are constantly being asked to turn to G-d in the lessons today. And that gives us a little insight into the human condition, doesn't it? We are so drawn by the world, so enchanted by it, believing that it can save us, believing that if we can just get *enough* of it, we'll be fine. And that, if we *don't* have what we think is enough, we are not blessed.

G-d has other ideas, though. We are to turn away from the world's vision of goodness. Jeremiah (who I tend to see as the Eeyore of prophets:

perpetually gloomy and morose) reminds G-d that he "did not sit in the company of merrymakers, nor did [he] rejoice." He was trying to do the right thing, he claimed, but still asks, "Why is my pain unceasing, my wound incurable, refusing to be healed?" In fact, he has the utter gall to say to G-d, "You are to me like a deceitful brook, like waters that fail."

Who among us hasn't, if we're honest, said something similar, convinced we've been let down by G-d? In those dark days when I read teaching evaluations that are utterly scathing, condemning me for daring to be actually gay in the classroom, I've felt like G-d failed me. I'd gone forward, righteously, utterly believing I was doing the right thing, being a public homofag Christian, trying to be, openly, everything G-d had made me to be, and then that.

I want you to know that on your account, G-d, I suffer insult. You should know that I feel as though you've abandoned your promise to me. Your waters have failed, and I have nothing to sustain me.

Some goddamned god *you* are.

The psalmist (26:1–8) seems to be in the same place—because when we are in this self-righteous, self-pitying (and how those two emotive states go together!), we assume that G-d is not being just towards us. "Give judgment for me, HaShem! for I have lived with integrity! Test me! Try me! Look how faithful *I've* been, when everybody else has abandoned you! I'm the one sticking with you G-d! Look at me! Me! Me! I've been so good! Why is my life shit, G-d? *I'm innocent, and all I did was try to follow you.*"

Usually, when I'm in this poisonous, self-pitying space, however, G-d sends me a reminder, just as G-d sent to Jeremiah: It's not about me. In my certainty that my own well-being is what matters most, I have turned away from G-d. I am, in fact, not very innocent at all. But there is still the promise: "If you turn back, I will take you back, and you shall stand before me. If you utter what is precious, and not what is worthless, you shall serve as my mouth."

The promise from HaShem does not say that I won't be reviled—in fact, it pretty much guarantees the opposite. But "I will make you to this people a fortified wall of bronze; they will fight against you, but they shall not prevail over you." The shit will still be flung, but we will be Teflon, says HaShem. But it can't happen if I don't turn, turn, turn. Turn back. Even the psalmist finally gets it, resignedly saying, "I love the house in which you dwell and the place where your glory abides."

I do, you know. I do love the house in which the Holy Name dwells. But too often that house (Oh, crap! It's me!) is filled with my own ego, my own sorrows, my own greedy need.

T. E. Brown, in the nineteenth century, wrote an amazing poem, called "Indwelling":

> If thou could'st empty all thyself of self,
> Like to a shell dishabited,
> Then might He find thee on the ocean shelf,
> And say, "This is not dead,"
> And fill thee with Himself instead.
> But thou are all replete with very thou
> And hast such shrewd activity,
> That when He comes He says, "This is enow
> Unto itself—'twere better let it be,
> It is so small and full, there is no room for me."[1]

And this is what Jeremiah and the psalmist (and I) suffered far too often: not the railings of G-d's enemies, but the assumption that we ourselves deserve more than we have. I am replete with very me, and my activity is shrewd indeed, so busy that there is no time or space for G-d.

I write this, of course, from a place of privilege. I know that I will have another meal today, and that I will have a bed to sleep in and a roof over my head tonight. I know that, even if I am anxious, I will have a job tomorrow, and that, even if I should lose my job, I have skills to get another, that my white skin and advanced degrees will certainly get me an interview. I know that my privilege protects me from the sheer physical desperation of millions of people around the planet. So many people do not have what they need to survive, because I participate in an economy that is predicated on their oppression. We are drawn, enchanted by the world, but we forget to care for nature, and we take more than we need from her, killing her and millions of others with her, in our greed. Our willingness to hasten global warming because we feel we deserve to burn fossil fuels, however much damage that continues to do to the planet, is all the evidence we need.

---

[1] Thomas Edward Brown, *Old John and Other Poems* (MacMillan & Co., 1893), 151.

And we are offended that we don't have all we want and claim that it is because we think we are doing G-d's will. It seems that every few weeks, the country witnesses the devastation of yet another "once-in-a-lifetime" storm or fire event. During one hurricane, Joel Osteen, prosperity gospel theologian extraordinaire, refused to open his mega church to the victims of the storm, until he was shamed into it by tens of thousands on the internet. I do not wish Joel Osteen ill—truly I don't. But I do have a feeling he was a little Jeremiah-ish, thinking about how G-d had abandoned him in his mega-mansion, how, because of the devastation, church might not be able to happen that week and how much money in offering plate revenue might be lost, and all the while, G-d was saying, "If you turn back, I will take you back. . . . If you utter what is precious, and not what is worthless, you shall serve as my mouth."

Paul understood this and recognized this kind of self-pity and self-righteousness among the Christians in Rome. That seems to be why he had to remind them to let love be genuine. Rejoice in hope, Paul wrote. Be patient in suffering, persevere in prayer. But he goes on, as if to cut off the argument that hope, patience, and prayer are simply spiritual-ooh-ooh things, and enough. Indeed, for Paul, rejoicing in hope, being patient in suffering, and persevering in prayer seem to lead directly to contributing to the needs of the saints, and extending hospitality to strangers.

Here's truth: Paul gives us a completely fucked up, not-sensible, unworldly, checklist of things that Christians *do* (which is particularly important in this letter to the Church in Rome, which has been used to stress justification by faith to the point of not bothering to *do* anything). It's worth mentioning them all:

Contribute to the needs of the saints (notice we do not get to choose who the saints are).

Extend hospitality to strangers.

Bless those who persecute you; bless and do not curse them.

Rejoice with those who rejoice (easy!).

Weep with those who weep (less easy . . .).

Live in harmony with one another (hard).

Do not be haughty, but associate with the lowly (oh, golly).

Do not claim to be wiser than you are (ouch).

Do not repay anyone evil for evil (but justice!?).

Take thought for what is noble in the sight of all (but all isn't me . . .).

Live peaceably with all, so far as it depends on you (oh, so *now* it's me).

Never avenge yourselves (shit).

If your enemies are hungry, feed them; if they are thirsty, give them something to drink.

Do not be overcome by evil, but overcome evil with good.

Oh, for crap sake.

Turn, Paul says. Turn away from everything you want and do what G-d wants. It's completely insane, and the world will probably end up killing you for it. Notice that nowhere does Paul say, "Do all this, and G-d will make you rich. Do all this, and G-d will make sure your material goods are tons and tons."

No. Paul is saying "All those material goods? Give them away. And give them first to the people you don't like, and who hurt you. The result is *not* that G-d will replace all the material goods for you. The result is that you will not have all those material goods anymore, and that you will have done the right thing." Irritatingly, I've discovered that when I do the right thing, hoping to heap burning coals on the heads of my enemies, my enemies seem to be just fine with burning coals, and I'm just stuck with less stuff.

This does not sound like salvation to my world-bound ears.

Of course, that's the point. Christianity is utterly impractical. Christianity is not about "making it." Christianity is not even, dare I say, about *my* salvation, about *my* personal relationship with Jesus. Christianity, like justice rolling down like waters, like the Ten Commandments, like the Sermon on the Mount, *is not about me.*

It's about all of us.

Jesus makes it stunningly clear in the gospel of Matthew today. He's trying to explain to his disciples what happens when you do the right thing, when you make it not about you, but about everyone: You get killed; you get crushed; you get destroyed by governmental systems that are designed to protect the powerful at the expense of the weak; you languish in a school-to-prison pipeline because of the color of your skin; you are murdered by someone who found you sexy until they found you are trans; you drown in the waters of a hurricane because churches don't open their doors.

The world is not kind to lovers of peace and justice.

And poor, naïve Peter simply couldn't believe it. Peter may have seen how badly empires treat the poor and disenfranchised, the weak, the other, but he couldn't believe that would happen to Jesus—surely not Jesus! Shouldn't G-d, after all, be able to overthrow even the greatest empire?

Apparently not.

Turn. Turn from the empire's rules. Turn from the world's values, which assume that *stuff* is what matters the most, or even that *life* is what matters the most. Turn away. There are things more important than being alive, such as saving the lives of others. Turn, Peter, from human things, and set your mind on divine things. If you want to save your life, give it up. If you try to hang on to it, though, look closely: You don't even *have* a life. You just have stuff. Crap. Litter. What will it profit you (Prosperity theologians? Me?) if you gain the whole world but forfeit your life?

The world is a sparkly bauble, tempting us to get more and more.

The Earth, on the other hand, is a glorious miracle, ready to sustain us all, if only we stop trying to own it.

Turn. Turn from the world. Turn toward G-d. Turn toward each other. Turn toward the Earth. That is our only salvation. Not even death matters more than that.

PROPER 18, THE SUNDAY CLOSEST TO SEPTEMBER 7

Dr. Peter Carlson

Track 1	or	Track 2
Exodus 12:1–14		*Ezekiel 33:7–11*
Psalm 149		*Psalm 119:33–40*
Romans 13:8–14		*Romans 13:8–14*
Matthew 18:15–20		*Matthew 18:15–20*

Probably the single biggest question that Christian theologians have asked over the centuries is "What must we do to be saved?" And of course, this question begs another question, which is "What is salvation?" I grew up being told that what I was being saved from was hellfire and damnation, with no one willing, apparently, to ask what kind of a deity would create the impossible situation of original sin, and then damn everyone born originally sinful to an eternity of pain and suffering. Even as a young person, though I was terrified of dying and burning (after all, a faggot is a bundle of kindling, meant to be burnt, right?), I was really troubled by this theology of a loving G-d whose love seemed so vicious.

Whenever I chat with my students about soteriology, the branch of theology that asks about salvation, I want for them to consider what they think a person is being saved *from*, and what they are being saved *to*. For the Christians of my childhood, it was some fantastic uber-wealthy, uber-comfy life lived in fancy-pants mansions on streets of gold. But as I got older, I learned that salvation can look very different and more profound: It is sobriety for an alcoholic; it is escape from an abusive relationship; it is having basic shelter, or a meal for the poor; it is health care for the sick; it is a body that is consistent with gender identity for a trans person; it is the freedom to hold a partner's hand in the mall for the lesbian or gay man; it is access for the disabled. I don't need a mansion, or glittery streets to be saved. I need a world that cares about the least powerful, about those who do not have access to justice or equity. And I will argue to my dying day that the Gospels and all of Jesus's teachings are consistent with that.

If that indeed is salvation (at least as I understand it), then the lessons today seem to me to be pointing us toward what we must do to achieve it. Paul's famous answer to the jailer in Acts 16 might seem to sum it up: "Believe on the Ruler Jesus Christ, and you shall be saved." We used to sing, in my evangelical days, a cheerful, upbeat ditty that repeated this verse (King James Version, of course) ad nauseam until the theme infused itself into our brains permanently (the tune still pops unbidden into my head from time to time). But again, my childhood self complicated the issue: What does it mean to believe on Christ? Does it simply mean that I have to believe Jesus existed? Does it mean that I believe he was G-d incarnate? Is that really *all*? Just . . . *believe*?

Paul, of course, throughout the letter to the Romans (from which we hear a reading today) is reminding us that faith, not works, justifies us. And of course Martin Luther especially picked up this theme. It is essential to remember, by the way, that Luther was utterly obsessed with his own sinfulness and fear of hell—so I feel a strong connection to him in that light. But Luther, of course, has to figure out, as Paul did, how to respond to those who would ask the obvious: If faith is all that matters, then, as Luther asked rhetorically in *On Christian Liberty*, "If faith does everything, and by itself suffices for justification, why then are good works commanded? Are we then to take our ease and do no works, content with faith?"[1] Of course Luther (and Paul) have no recourse but to say, "Of course not!" but Paul at least is less than effective at explaining why works might actually matter if works don't matter. Luther imagines that good works come from *being* saved by faith—hence the works we do for others are good. He argues that, if we are not justified by faith, then

[1] Martin Luther, *Concerning Christian Liberty* in *First Principles of the Reformation, or The Ninety-Five Theses and the Three Primary Works of Dr. Martin Luther*, translated by Henry Wace and C. A. Buchheim (John Murray, 1883), 118.

even if we do good works for others, they are not good, because we're really just doing them for ourselves.

And Paul himself tries to respond to this same issue in today's reading from Romans: "Love one another. . . . Love does no wrong to a neighbor; therefore, love is the fulfilling of the law." Paul is, in fact, pointing out that faith alone does not justify, but that we must follow the law by loving one another. And here's the thing for me: Even if Paul and Luther can explain the importance of works as a result of justification with G-d, rather than as a step toward justification with G-d, they are both in the stunningly awkward position of very nearly making works meaningless. And all of the lessons today are about works, those things that we are to *do*, if we want to be saved.

Many of us have heard the story of Moses and Aaron, and the plagues sent to subdue the Pharoah of Egypt. And we are familiar with this final plague, in which G-d murders the eldest male of every family, human and nonhuman animals alike. And setting aside for the moment what kind of G-d would inflict that kind of punishment on the Egyptians, who had no control over what their king did (like the question of hell), we can notice that, in the first nine plagues, the Israelites did not have to do anything to avoid them. The locusts never went to Goshen, which was the Israelite housing development. Goshen's cattle were spared from disease. The Israelites didn't get boils, or frogs, or gnats.

But in the tenth and final plague, things change. Now, the Israelites have to take action, literally in order to survive, to be saved. They are commanded, with staggering detail, to prepare a meal, and even told how to eat it with "loins girded, your sandals on your feet, and your staff in your hand; and you shall eat it hurriedly. It is the passover of HaShem." They need to be ready, in other words, to run. Of course, this story provides the origins of the Passover feast today: the annual retelling of G-d's ultimate act of liberative salvation. In this story, *salvation* is an active verb; it is a miracle, yes, but one in which we must take part, refusing to be among those who sit, passively, waiting for the Divine to do it all.

I have to admit, on the other hand, that Psalm 149, to be read with the story from Exodus in track 1, seems to suggest a kind of passivity in salvation: G-d "adorns the poor with victory" and the faithful are tantalizingly being "joyful on their beds" (which, let's be honest, sounds like a really healthy way to approach both sex and sleep). But keep reading:

It is the faithful who wield the two-edged sword to wreak justice, by putting unjust rulers and nobility in chains. The faithful do, after all, have to do something in order that salvation might be effected.

In track 2, the Prophet Ezekiel is being given an assignment: that of being a sentinel, or lookout, for G-d. The book of Ezekiel relates six visions of the prophet, organized around three main themes: prophecies against Judah; prophecies against foreign nations; and prophecies of hope and salvation. Our reading today is from chapter 33, which begins the final section. We see, as I mentioned, Ezekiel being assigned the job of sentinel, but it is important to note what happens just before this reading in the opening verses of the chapter: G-d is explaining what a sentinel does, and why the job matters. "If I'm about to punish people," G-d explains, "and the sentinel sees the punishment coming, and warns the people, it's on the people to repent and stop the punishment." So far, so good. "But if the sentinel sees the punishment coming, and doesn't warn the people," G-d continues, "then the guilt is entirely on the sentinel." Daunting responsibility, eh?

But G-d, having laid this responsibility on Ezekiel's shoulders, goes on to explain what is about to happen. The remnant of Israel in Babylon are understandably groaning in their exile, and understand that it took place because of their sins (this is standard providential history, incidentally, in which G-d is never to blame for Bad Things but makes them happen because we deserve it). But they are asking the ultimate question of despair: "How can we then live?" And G-d asks Ezekiel to tell them, "I have no pleasure in the death of the wicked but that the wicked turn from their ways and live; turn back, turn back from your evil ways, for why will you die, O house of Israel?" In other words, the prisoners of war in Babylon are being told that they are acting like the person who keeps doing the same thing and is shocked that nothing changes. And G-d is letting them know that their salvation is actually on them; G-d is perfectly willing to save them, but they need to get off their wicked little asses and start doing the right thing. My twelve-step friends will understand this. It's great that you want to be free from addiction, but ultimately you have to get off your sofa or your barstool and go to a meeting. G-d may, as the portion of Psalm 119 assigned to track 2 implores, give me understanding, but it's up to me to keep G-d's law and keep it with all my heart.

Jesus is also talking about how to bring about salvation. He is talking to his disciples at this point in the Gospel of Matthew, and it seems to me that he is impressing upon them the fact that salvation is not individual, but communal; that, as my friend Ed Bacon who was for many years rector of All Saints Episcopal Church in Pasadena would say, we are not the human race, but the human family. Jesus is telling his disciples how to deal with the inevitable hurts and harms that we do to each other in community: "If a sibling harms you, try to settle the issue one-on-one. If that doesn't settle it, do justice by asking witnesses to attest to your harm. And if that doesn't work, bring it to the entire community. If they are unwilling to be reconciled, then it's on them." Matthew, who is writing to Jewish Christians, uses the phrase "let them be to you as a Gentile and a tax-collector," which of course is deeply ironic, since Jesus literally hung out with tax collectors. But the point is, some people can't bear to be part of the community.

That doesn't mean, though, that we treat them like shit. And this is important. Because at this point we circle back to Paul, don't we? We must love our neighbors as we love ourselves.

This summary of the law can be hard to put into practice. For some people, it can be hard because we love ourselves too much, and in our narcissistic self-referentiality can't bear to think of lavishing any of our precious love on others. For others—and this is a challenge that I have noticed among all my marginal, queerly beloved siblings—the difficulty is that we have never learned, truly, how to love ourselves.

And I blame the church for that. Too often Christians have dragged us queerfolk aside, either metaphorically or literally, telling us that *we* are the ones who have harmed *them* by our existence. We are told that we are trying to "convert" young folks to gaydom or lesbianity, or transishness, and that we are "corrupting" the church by our very presence and by our unconscionable longing for community. How, in a community that claims to speak for G-d, can we find any way to love ourselves?

No one should be surprised that we have left the church in droves, creating our own communities—in drag shows, or gay and lesbian dives, or sex clubs—where we might, finally, learn to love ourselves and ultimately to love others. It is not surprising, after all, that we have taken action, so that HaShem, who loves us, could liberate us from the Egypt of White, Ableist Heteropatriarchy, assuring us that we are not only loveable, but overflowing with love to offer to others.

FEAST OF THE HOLY CROSS, SEPTEMBER 14

The Rev. Phoenix Bell-Shelton Biggs

Numbers 21:4b-9
Psalm 98:1–5
1 Corinthians 1:18–24
John 3:13–17

Liberation Through the Cross—A Queer Black Perspective

We are at the crossroads of suffering and liberation, witnessing a truth that has carried generations of the oppressed. It is the truth that, through the cross, God declares solidarity with the marginalized. This is the heart of James Cone's *The Cross and the Lynching Tree*: The idea that both the cross and the lynching tree are symbols of terror transformed into emblems of divine love and justice.[1]

We begin our journey with the Israelites in the wilderness. From there, we travel through the psalms of deliverance, wrestle with the paradox of the cross as both foolishness and power and finally arrive at the liberating love of God made manifest in Christ. Each move we make brings us deeper into the mystery of a love that redeems even the darkest suffering. Together, let us ask: What does it mean to live

[1] James Cone, *The Cross and the Lynching Tree* (Orbis Books, 2011).

in the tension between crucifixion and resurrection? Let us open our hearts in prayer:

> God of the lynched and the crucified, breathe your Spirit into this moment. Let your truth rise in us. Teach us to see your face in the oppressed and proclaim your love as a liberation force. Amen.

Our first stop is in the wilderness. The Israelites, wandering and weary, cry out in anguish. Poisonous serpents bring death, yet God offers salvation through an unexpected symbol—a bronze serpent lifted high on a pole. The very image of their suffering becomes a source of healing.

This wilderness story parallels the wilderness many of us know intimately. Just as the Israelites had to confront the thing that brought them pain to find healing, so must we face our suffering and the systems that perpetuate it. The bronze serpent points us to the cross, where death transforms itself.

Here is the tie that carries us forward: The cross is our wilderness serpent and like it, it confronts us with the brutal truth. But it does not stop there. It offers healing through solidarity. God's presence in the suffering is the lifeblood of liberation. This is where Cone's prophetic work begins—in the naming that divine love is found not in palaces of power but in the bodies of those whose hate systems have been crucified.

We turn to Psalm 98 from the wilderness, which calls us to sing of joy for God's marvelous works. But what does it mean to sing when the wounds of oppression are still fresh? It means to reclaim our voices.

The connection between the wilderness serpent and the psalm is this: Where the wilderness teaches us to confront our pain, the psalm teaches us to celebrate our survival. James Cone reminds us that joy is a revolutionary act. When Black, queer, and trans bodies dance in defiance of white supremacy and patriarchy, we declare that the forces of death do not win.

Joy becomes the bridge between our suffering and our liberation. We do not ignore the serpents that bite us, but we also refuse to let them steal our song. The psalms remind us that the story of liberation is alive in us—every breath we take, every boundary we break, is a testimony to God's marvelous deeds.

But joy, like the cross, is a paradox. Paul reminds us that while the cross appears as foolishness to those who are perishing, for us, it is the very power of God. It is at this point that we step into the next chapter of our journey. Just as the Israelites had to gaze upon a symbol of death to find life, the cross confronts us with a seemingly absurd truth: Real power is found not in domination but in suffering love.

Cone's work connects this truth to America's history of racial terror. The lynching tree is a symbol of crucifixion in our time. Just as the cross was used to break the body of Jesus, lynching was used to break the bodies of Black men, women, and children.

But the foolishness of God turns the tools of terror into instruments of salvation. Divine power does not reside in empire, but in the lynched Christ, in every person who has ever been told they are disposable.

Here, joy meets justice. The celebration of survival in the Psalms empowers us to confront the systems that crucify. Joy is not escapism—it is resistance. The cross calls us to look unflinchingly at suffering, name it, and declare with our whole being that God is on the side of those who suffer.

From this place of paradox, we arrive at the most profound truth of all: love. John 3:16, so often misused, proclaims a God who so loved the world. This love is not sentimental; it is revolutionary. Cone teaches us that the cross reveals a love that enters suffering, confronts injustice, and demands liberation. It is the love that holds lynched bodies in its arms and refuses to rest until justice rolls down like waters. This is where all the threads intertwine: The wilderness serpent calls us to face suffering head-on. The psalms invite us to sing the songs of joy. The cross shows us that true power is found in love that suffers alongside and sets free.

Beloveds, as we hold these truths, I invite you to reflect on your wilderness journeys. What serpents have bitten you? What crosses have you carried? Where have you been told that your very existence is too much?

My journey has been one of learning to love myself as a sacred, queer, Black body. Sometimes, I believed the lies of a theology that sought to crucify my identity. But God's love broke through. That same love calls us now—to personal healing and communal action.

The tie between personal and communal liberation is this: The God of the cross does not leave anyone behind. To be saved is to be called into the work of salvation for others. We must confront lynching trees in our world—systems of white supremacy, antitrans violence, and every force that seeks to crucify the vulnerable. And we must proclaim joy as an act of defiant, liberating love.

Beloveds, oh Beloveds, the cross is not just a symbol of suffering—it is a living testament to love's triumph over death. As we leave this space, we carry the sacred paradox of the cross within our hearts. We see the suffering through the lens of God's limitless love. We sing songs of liberation. Build sanctuaries of radical welcome.

Now Beloved, go in peace, empowered by the Spirit of the lynched Christ. Rise with the courage of resurrection. Let the power of love transform the world.

PROPER 19, THE SUNDAY CLOSEST TO SEPTEMBER 14

Dr. Peter Carlson

Track 1
Exodus 14:19–31
Psalm 114
or *Exodus 15:1b–11, 20–21*
Romans 14:1–12
Matthew 18:21–35

or

Track 2
Genesis 50:15–21
Psalm 103:(1–7), 8–13
Romans 14:1–12
Matthew 18:21–35

The foundation of my theology is that the Gospel is ultimately Good News for those on the margins, and that if the Gospel is to be meaningful to us, we must each find our own marginal identities and enter into them fully. And as a queer theologian, it is perhaps inevitable that I am interested in justice and am particularly interested in gender justice. But *justice* is a word (like *religion* or *salvation* for that matter) that we often use without taking much care to define with any precision. And I'm pretty sure that justice, like salvation, looks different to different people depending on what particular marginal space we occupy. And because those on the margins will be different groups at different periods in history, justice will, if you will, be dressed differently depending on the geographical or historical context.

The lessons today seem to me to be demonstrating what justice looks like in various times and places, and I'll admit to finding that it looks chilling sometimes.

As much as I love the idea that G-d's primary goal is to liberate G-d's people from slavery (either literal or metaphorical), I cannot help but cringe fiercely when I read the book of Exodus. And the passage in the readings for today is particularly cringeworthy, if you think about it. The final plague, the death of the firstborn male children, has swept over Egypt, and the Pharaoh has told Moses and the Israelites "Get out. Now." And so they gather their crap and pile it up in carts, and start moving out of Egypt. Pharaoh, of course, has a change of heart, and sends his armies after them, and we come to this terrific scene at the edge of the Red Sea, where the Israelites are stuck between the water and the chariots of Pharaoh and, understandably enough, scream at Moses: "What?! Was it because there aren't any cemeteries in Egypt that you brought us to die here? Why didn't you leave us there? It was a shitty life, but at least we were alive!"

G-d, of course (who tends to show up as fire and smoke in this and other stories), has a few tricks up Their sleeve. Moses is ordered to hold out his arms with his staff, and the Red Sea miraculously parts, with a great wind, and the Israelites can cross over on dry land. Pharaoh sends the chariots on after them, and of course G-d drowns them, and the Israelites are able to escape (into the wilderness for forty years, granted, but still . . .).

Liberation! Freedom! Justice!

But what of justice for the Egyptian soldiers, who were just obeying orders? What of justice for the Egyptian citizens who all lost their eldest child, because their Pharaoh was a stubborn asshole? And for that matter, what of justice for the Pharaoh himself, whose heart, we are told, *was hardened by G-d G-dself*? If we read this story closely, it seems as though G-d is, indeed, interested in the liberation of G-d's people, but is totally willing, in the process, to be a total asshole toward anyone else.

Is this justice?

Both Psalm 114 and the Song of Miriam, which are provided as options for the response to the Hebrew Bible reading in track 1, are gloating in a selfish and disturbing kind of way: "Haha! I win! G-d loves me more than G-d loves you! Neener, sucker! You're dead! Haha!" Justice, in this case, appears to be that I got free, but at the expense of a whole host of innocent lives; and I'm not sure I can cope with that, however much I might understand that it was a worldview common enough in the ancient world, and common enough even today.

Justice takes a different turn in track 2, the story of Joseph being reunited with his brothers in Egypt (where, incidentally, their descendants would end up being slaves, leading to the story in track 1). Just as a reminder:

Joseph was a younger sibling who had prophetic dreams that showed his brothers bowing down to him and was stupid enough to tell his brothers about those dreams. They then, perhaps naturally, sold him into slavery, poured animal blood on the dreamy gay coat that Dad had given Joseph, and went and told Dad that Joseph had been killed by animals. Joseph then ended up down in Egypt where, due to his ability to interpret dreams, basically saved the collective ass of the Egyptians who were threatened by famine. The brothers, trying to escape the famine up in Canaan, come down to Egypt, only to have a completely unexpected reunion with their kid brother who they had treated so poorly, and who now holds their survival in his hands.

Awkward!

But Joseph was, if not just, then merciful, and sent them back to get their father, Jacob, and their families, and all of them came down to Egypt, and settled in the land of Goshen. Eventually Jacob (who, remember, was renamed Israel) died, and his twelve sons (and his fifty-eight other kids, we assume, who are *briefly* mentioned elsewhere) mourned him, and in the lesson today Joseph reiterated his promise of mercy, and his conviction that it was G-d who had, in fact, been in charge the entire time. Justice, in this case, would presumably have been to cut off the brothers who treated Joseph so badly, but G-d, through Joseph, had other plans: notably, the continuation of the twelve tribes of Israel. It is interesting to me that Joseph is only able to extend mercy because things turned out okay for him, which begs the question: Can (or should) those for whom things have *not* turned out well extend mercy? Perhaps another way of putting this question is, "Does extending mercy to an evildoer mean that they should not be held responsible for their actions?" That is, for me, a better question. Joseph's brothers do seem, in this story, to have taken responsibility, or at least put up a good show of penitence. But what also strikes me is that Joseph is, in the end, not really concerned about them; he sees in their behavior a bigger story unrolling, and it is in light of that larger story that he ultimately offers mercy rather than eye-for-an-eye justice. We read in Psalm 103 that G-d "works vindication and justice for all who are oppressed," yes, but almost in the same breath also that "HaShem is merciful and gracious, slow to anger and abounding in steadfast love." Perhaps this is a reminder to us that, as we seek justice, we also need to consider the narrative arc of the larger story, rather than only our own vengeance.

Paul, in his letter to the Jesus followers in Rome, is also referring to a kind of merciful justice: the kind needed to form any sort of community. Throughout this Epistle, Paul has been harping on the fact that it is faith, not works, that justifies us before G-d. But even Paul is not so facile as to presume that works do not matter, as we saw in last week's lesson. At the very least, our actions, our works, matter, because they reflect our faith in G-d's justification of us. And Paul in this passage recognizes that we certainly each reflect our faith in different kinds of works. Some of us might be called to keep kosher, he is suggesting. Others may feel the need to be circumcised. Some of us, to bring it forward to today, might fast during Lent in order to focus on their relationship with G-d, whilst others feel no need to do so, instead performing a fearless moral inventory, as step 4 of the Twelve Steps encourages. Still others might see no need to do any of these things. We do not have the right, Paul is arguing, to judge others, or to claim that G-d's merciful justice is not available to them. Indeed, Paul reminds us, whether we live or die, we live and die to G-d, not for ourselves. As we saw in the story of Joseph, justice is not about us; it is about a much bigger story.

How do we connect to that bigger story, then? I think that is what Peter is actually asking Jesus at the start of our lesson from the Gospel of Matthew today, when he asks, "How many times do I need to forgive a sibling who has wronged me? Seven?" And Jesus, as we all rather regretfully know, answers, "Dude. Way more than that." But then Jesus goes on to explain the relationship between divine mercy and divine justice.

"There was a ruler," Jesus says, "who was settling their accounts at month's-end. And this ruler noted that there was a lowly worker who owed a shedload of money, and hadn't paid it back." This, of course, is something that we can't possibly imagine in the modern day (*cough, cough*—international banks—*cough*). The lowly worker, of course, begged for mercy, and the ruler (unlike international banks) had mercy, and forgave the debt, much to the lowly worker's relief.

So far so good. G-d's mercy at work!

But the story doesn't end there. We see the lowly worker, newly released from debt, coming across a friend who owed them a small amount, and bullying the friend, threatening to start a legal action against them if they don't cough up. When the ruler hears about it, the ruler is understandably furious, because the lowly worker couldn't extend the same mercy they'd been shown to the person who owed them money. And so the ruler handed the lowly worker over to be tortured.

Okay, wow. Yeah, justice. But really? On the other hand, is that unfair? Because the lowly worker had gotten their own debts forgiven and couldn't be bothered to pay it forward.

Do you see why I'm conflicted about biblical justice? Sometimes it just seems way too harsh, and G-d's role appears to be Omnipotent Jerkwad. Other times, it seems like people don't get what they deserve when they should. And in all of this, I'm convinced that I am still called, because of my faith in the Incarnate G-d, to seek out justice for those whose entire lives are spent on the margins, with justice unavailable to them. And I for one believe that the international banking system controlling all of our lives is *not* G-d, just to be clear, so I will fight their usurious practices in any way I can, in the name of justice. But the lessons today tell me that I have to be careful, that I am not, in fact, the final arbiter of justice, and that there may indeed be a bigger story, the plot of which I have not been told, and that, with Paul, I need to be very hesitant before I judge my neighbors as they work out how best to live their lives.

PROPER 20, THE SUNDAY CLOSEST TO SEPTEMBER 21

River Cook Needham, MA ThM

Track 1	or	Track 2
Exodus 16:2–15		*Jonah 3:10–4:11*
Psalm 105:1–6, 37–45		*Psalm 145:1–8*
Philippians 1:21–30		*Philippians 1:21–30*
Matthew 20:1–16		*Matthew 20:1–16*

Toward the end of the *Doctor Who* episode titled "Blink," the time-traveling Doctor appears on video answering questions and says that instead of time being a natural progression from cause to effect, "it's more like a big ball of wibbly-wobbly, timey-wimey . . . stuff."[1] Our texts today show the ways that different possibilities could play out, and offer us regular reminders about the nature of God: that God is not unchanging. That time can be a big ball of stuff, of possibilities and potentialities.

I hear again the queerness of life and death calling. Where to live is useful and to die is gain. The timey-wimeyness of hearing these texts fresh today, and in their ancient contexts, with ripples continually echoing out, continuously changing. We as humans are surrounded by change. As with everything in the household of earth and starry heaven, objects, events, and even living things are held in our hands for just a moment, and then we must release them.[2] And in the holding and in the letting go, we are changed, and the things held are changed.

---

[1] Steven Moffat, writer, Hettie Macdonald, director, "Blink," *Doctor Who*, (BBC One, Season 3, episode 10, 2007).

[2] This sentence is adapted from a phrase I heard by the Rev. Catharine Clarenbach (https://thewayoftheriver.com/).

In the past, in my personal life, I talked about living a Jonah 4 lifestyle. This particularly came true when I was dealing with one of the anger stages of recovery from trauma. When I realized what was taken from me when I was born and reared in a home where my personhood did not matter. When I was expected to live even when there was no external reason. When I was angry enough to die. So far, this response to unknowable depths of anger has not resulted in my death, but instead has taught me that it is not always my role to be gracious and merciful. The cause of Jonah's anger is the gracious mercy of God. The cause of Jonah's anger is God's complete disregard for his desires and wants. The desire to see his suffering and the ancestral suffering of the people of Israel and Judah at the hands of the Ninevites taken seriously. Anger at God's refusal to annihilate Nineveh and the Ninevites, even as they had sought the annihilation of Jonah's people. Here, God shows that She is committed to second, third, and more chances. That She is, in the words of the psalmist "gracious and merciful, slow to anger and abounding in steadfast love." And Jonah gets to be angry at God, even if God does not think Jonah makes much sense. God, much like my family of origin, takes my feelings and reframes them as wrong, invalid, and unworthy. Often, when emotions are invalidated, particularly as a child, the response is that as an adult, the child becomes suicidal.

For queer people, particularly bisexual and transgender people, having our sexual orientations and gender identities rejected as invalid and unworthy has led to astronomical suicide rates. In our capitalist political-economic system, there is a specific way that people are expected to treat suicidal people, that preserves them for the cause of capitalism, called suicide prevention. That, if someone is suicidal, the solution is to put them into what many people believe is a carceral mental health unit. There, many freedoms are taken away, and feelings are further invalidated, since suicidality is viewed as an emotion or mindset that will pass, and life is viewed as the ultimate good.

Recently, in my job as a church administrator, I was forced to confront the ableism in churches in a direct way. An infrastructural accessibility accommodation had become nonfunctional, and the congregation responsible for its upkeep was nervous about spending the money needed for this infrastructure. My needs as a disabled person were cast aside and invalidated for the comfort of the abled many. I was an inconvenience and an unwanted if not unnecessary expense.

Soon, I had images of the great disability activists that came before me: the Capitol Crawl of 1990, when people crawled up the steps to the Capitol advocating for the passage of the Americans with Disabilities Act. My queer and trans ancestors who held die-ins at the FDA demanding a gracious, merciful, and desperately needed response to the HIV/AIDS pandemic. I thought of my descendants; perhaps not mine by blood, but those who will come after me, to whom I owe a responsibility to prepare the world. Will they not need this accessibility?

I was back to living a Jonah 4 lifestyle. Did I need to get trapped in the lift, unable to get in or out, for the congregation to see that this basic infrastructural accessibility tool was, in fact, necessary? Was there a need for a public action, so that they could see the entire community of disabled people they were excluding from their congregation? Would the congregation even care?

In the Christian Testament, we see how Paul wrestles with living in service to the gospel, and facing the judgment and reward of the afterlife. And in Paul's wrestling in his writing to the church at Phillipi, he leaves instructions for how to be in community together—guidance for safeguarding their reputation and preparing for the future, whatever becomings it might contain. For Paul, this leads to a conclusion that living a life in service to the gospel, no matter how good the afterlife looks, is the beneficial choice.

In the book *Undoing Suicidism: A Trans, Queer, Crip Approach to Rethinking (Assisted) Suicide*, the author describes suicidism as the system of oppression that takes away agency, rights, and decision-making capability from suicidal people. Instead of compulsory suicide prevention, the book offers suicidist futures, where people are allowed to have honest conversations about death, dying, and life and living. Much as Paul does in this letter, life and death are considered as options and alternatives, and space is held for true and honest discernment. Although it would certainly be helpful for people to live, enforced living, as in suicide prevention, is also coerced subjugation to capitalism, and the other parts of the kyriarchy.

For Paul, the line between life and death is wibbly-wobbly. It's bending, because living is good, but dying is better. Joy is present, and so is soul-crushing oppression. Paul wrote this letter from jail/prison, yet would have needed this letter to get good news to his intended audience. Paul writes his discernment about death in this way to show his audience the dual citizenship of God's kindom and the Roman Empire. By resisting the social pressures of Roman imperial society, the church in Phillipi can more fully live into the principles of the kindom of God.

This lesson is all the more true today, where the powers that be, like racism, late-stage capitalism, patriarchy, fatmisia, queer antagonism, and scarcity mindsets all stand opposed to the generosity and hospitality of the kindom of God. Resisting these powers that be, this kyriarchy, is not easy. Saying and knowing that there are enough resources to meet all our needs, if allocated justly, stands in stark contrast to the US-ian society where pulling ourselves up by the bootstraps and hoarding wealth is prioritized. Celebrating the many ways that love and companionship are experienced while knowing that any individual's sexual orientation or relationship style is no threat to anyone else can be dangerous. The wibbly-wobbly, timey-wimey truth is that even as we are two thousand years after Paul wrote this letter, the principles remain, that as citizens of Heaven, of the reign of God, we will have to resist and die to the pressures that our society puts upon all of us.

The Gospel, then, ties up all these stories into a bow, where Jesus gives us a parable about a generous landowner. A landowner who, like God in the Jonah story, is kind and compassionate, not denying anyone, even those who only worked one hour, a full day's wages. We see here that even amidst the precarity and destitution of day laborers, the landowner takes care of people and seeks out their well-being.

The villains in the Gospel, if they can be called that, also fall into a Jonah 4 lifestyle. These workers, hired first thing in the morning, negotiated for a *denarius* for a day's wage and expected more when those who came at the end of the day also got a *denarius*. They got angry, maybe had visions of direct actions against the landowner, and grumbled about it. Just like Jonah grumbles at God about being angry enough to die. Their emotions and experiences were treated as less-than and invalidated, and they resisted the perceived slight of wages/the generosity of the landowner.

The landowner, like God, remains gracious and merciful and shows us a better way—a way that honors all the workers and shows a responsibility for the well-resourced to provide for those more precariously resourced. Some commentators say this is a story about those with abundant resources caring for those without. Others might say this is a story about the full inclusion of Gentiles in the early Christian community. These and many other interpretations offer insights into the possibilities of this text. However, in our timey-wimey, wibbly-wobbly world, this passage speaks to me about the importance of economic justice: That no matter how long one is able or willing to work, they should have the resources needed to meet their needs. That collecting wealth is only useful in as much as the wealth is redistributed to those that need it and not hoarded. That even the day laborer is worthy of a living wage—the fast-food worker, the cashier, the stocker, the essential worker—they are all worthy of a living wage.

To return to our story from earlier—where a pastor and congregation were debating the worth of fixing a lift—a necessary accessibility infrastructure for disabled people to participate in the life of the church. Soon after I had the flashback to the crawl and die-ins, I realized that both as a staff member, and as a theologically trained person, I needed to advocate for money to be spent and resources invested so that the lift, the tool, the infrastructure I require to access my workspace, and others require to participate in the life of the church, would be available. So that disabled people could be full and welcome members of this congregation. So that the church's sign that says "all are welcome" might mean something to disabled people.

When all was said and done, I was angry that my access needs were not essential, and that an overeager, ableist, budget-conscious pastor attempted to cut them. Throughout our stories, we see that humans do not and cannot live into our ideals of who God is, could be, or should be. Humans do not have the capacity to be a deity.

Yet, God, who is gracious and merciful, takes on this role willingly. In the wibbly-wobbly, timey-wimey ball of existence, God is who we can look to as the caregiver of the universe. As the generous landowner, She can make sure that the anxieties and fears of the money-stressed, ableist pastor are heard even while ensuring the disabled church worker can get to their workplace and earn a living wage. In Jonah, God can listen to Jonah's anger, and even answer his anger, while also choosing not to do a calamity against the Ninevites.

This is the powerful thing about God—She can hold the complexities and contradictions of our human conditions. She can hold suicidal ideation and capitalism's forced living. She listens to the desire to die, no matter its underlying causes, and holds space for healing, and for growth, without calling in the carceral mental health system. Indeed, God is gracious and merciful, slow to anger and abounding in kindness.

PROPER 21, THE SUNDAY CLOSEST TO SEPTEMBER 28

Dr. Peter Carlson

Track 1	or	Track 2
Exodus 17:1–7		*Ezekiel 18:1–4, 25–32*
Psalm 78:1–4, 12–16		*Psalm 25:1–8*
Philippians 2:1–13		*Philippians 2:1–13*
Matthew 21:23–32		*Matthew 21:23–32*

"How queer everything is to-day!" said Alice, "And yesterday things went on just as usual. I wonder if I've been changed in the night?" We are handed so many in-between-nesses and things-are-not-what-they-seems in the readings today, aren't we? It's like the tea party in *Alice's Adventures in Wonderland*[1], where everyone is mad. We read about children who say one thing and then do (or don't do) another. We have a kind of trans G-d trying to pass as human. We have people living in the wilderness of exile, and people wandering in the wilderness of Sin. How queer, indeed, everything is today.

The reading from Matthew's Gospel is one that always fascinates me, quite frankly. This is the chapter in which things start getting really heated up and quickly. Jesus has just entered Jerusalem in a kind of triumph, cast out the moneychangers from the temple, brought the sick in to be healed, and damned a fig tree in a fit of pique. It is perhaps not entirely unnatural that the religious authorities might want to know by whose authority Jesus was, in fact, doing these things. Jesus responds with a kind of trick question,

---

[1] Lewis Carroll, *Alice's Adventures in Wonderland* (Blackie & Son Ltd, ca, 1920), 16.

asking by whose authority John the Baptizer was preaching. They knew it was a trap, and so they responded, "We dunno." And Jesus basically said, "Well then, neener. If you won't answer me, I won't answer you," which I'll be honest has always felt a little bit third-grade-y to me. But then he starts telling stories, parables, that are edgier than the ones he'd told earlier, about the reign of heaven: There are two children, and the parent asks each of them in turn to go work in the family fields. One says no, and the other says yes; but the one who says no eventually goes and does the work, but the one who says yes slacks off. And Jesus asks, which one did the will of the parent? The answer is obvious, of course, but the takeaway is a kicker: "Tax collectors and sex workers are getting into the realm of G-d before you, suckers!" Just like the one who said no is the one who did yes, and the one who said yes is the one who did no, G-d's reign is topsy-turvy and *in* and *out* don't mean what we think they mean, and it's a really uncomfortable space and, O G-d! how do we know what to do, because I don't know where or what I am! I'm neither fish nor fowl nor good red herring, and I'm confused, G-d.

Are you saying I should go be a sex worker?

We'll leave that for the moment, perhaps.

Paul, in his letter to the believers in Philippi, is trying to encourage individual and corporate responsibility. Though the chronology of the epistle seems to be a little confused, in this section he has made clear that he is writing from prison in Rome. And in this passage, he is appealing to the Philippians, not so much to agree with each other on every doctrinal point, but "to be of one mind" and to "do nothing from selfish ambition or empty conceit." And the mind that we are to be one in is the mind of Christ. Paul then pens an exquisite hymn that is familiar to many of us: that Christ Jesus,

> who, though he was in the form of G-d,
> . . .
> emptied himself,
> . . . being born in human likeness.

This hymn describes a G-d who was willing to enter the ultimate liminal, or in-between space: Christ, as it were, in ultimate dysphoric experience of G-d trying to be human, in a sense knowing that G-dness, if you will, isn't enough. Indeed, the fleshy incarnation of G-d is the ultimate proof that G-d is *not* completely self-sufficient, that healthy relationships work in more than one direction, that G-d in fact needs us as much as we need G-d. G-d could have stayed completely, well, *goddy*, but knew that, if They wanted to be in genuine relationship with us, Their created joys, then They would have to become a bizarre, liminal, uncomfortable both/and.

And following the example of this emptying, this *kenosis* of selflessness is, Paul is suggesting, what will ultimately fulfill us most extravagantly. It makes no sense. Emptiness is fulfillment; death is not death, but life; obedience is freedom; here is not there. Everything is in-between, elsewhere and elsewhen, nowhere and everywhere, liminal, terrifying, leading with one mind toward a cross in a world that demands we be located, in one place and time, decisive and firm, confident of past and future alike.

I wonder if Paul's hand was shaking when he wrote about his experiences in prison?

The Judaeans in the book of Ezekiel, including Ezekiel himself, were also in a kind of prison, and so Ezekiel, too, is reflecting on the complexity of humanity in awkward place-times. The Babylonian Exile was a time in which the Judaeans had been dragged off to Babylon essentially as prisoners of war, and had to figure out how to be Jewish without any of the markers that had previously *identified* them as Jewish: Ten of the twelve tribes of ancient Israel had been decimated when the Assyrians overran the northern kingdom of Israel in the late eighth century BCE, so the promise of myriad descendants of Abraham had been hacked to bits. The southern kingdom of Judah was destroyed by the Babylonians; and even the temple had been leveled. They no longer had anything familiar to identify them as Jewish, as G-d's chosen people. It is perhaps only natural that they would worry, if not full-on complain, about that. And you'd think G-d would cut them some slack, because they were prisoners of war. But G-d has other ideas: namely, getting them to take a little responsibility for their fate.

Through Ezekiel, G-d is taking a moment in this passage to explain that it is not the sins of the parents that concern G-d, but the sins of the people whom G-d is dealing with at that very moment. Perhaps we need to be reminded of this, though, even today. How often do we blame parents for their children's failures? When kids misbehave in school, or if they "turn out wrong," we assume a failure in parenting. Hell, my own parents even assumed they failed for a time when they first learned I was gay. (As an aside on this subject, though, I will always hesitate to suggest that a three-year-old throwing a tantrum in a restaurant is a failure of parenting, because I'm convinced three-year-olds are wise beyond their years, and that they tantrum tactically.) But G-d at this point seems to be telling the Judaeans that passing the buck of blame here is not going to work. "G-d is so unfair!" they whine. But G-d responds with the remarkably rough-shod, "No, *you're* unfair; when the righteous turn away from their righteousness and commit iniquity, they shall die for it. Start accepting responsibility for your shittiness."

But *die*? Well! That suggests, doesn't it, a G-d who seems to be demanding perfection from creatures who are genetically incapable of being perfect, and then murdering them (or casting them into hell) for that genetic imperfection. Now, I get it. The point here is not that G-d is unmerciful or particularly cruel; the passage ends, after all, with a plea from G-d that the people repent and turn from their wickedness, so that they can, in fact, live. The point that G-d is making, if somewhat hyperbolically, is rather that we need to take responsibility for our own wickedness and stop blaming everyone else. And I truly and genuinely agree. But again, I'd suggest that the context—being held in a foreign land as a prisoner of war—might tempt even the best of us to find a scapegoat and complain.

Speaking of complaining. I remember when I was getting my MA at Claremont School of Theology, and taking Hebrew Bible with a marvelous Jewish scholar, and we were studying the book of Exodus. It was probably while we were wrestling, if not with this exact passage, then with one close to it, that a student whose cultural sensitivity had perhaps not developed as fully as we might hope, piped up, "So this is why Jews have such a reputation for complaining, right?" Awkward as the moment was, it opened up for me an opportunity to reflect on one of the ongoing streams of antisemitism that run rampant in the world even today.

But what always strikes me as I read this particular book of Torah is that quite frankly the Israelites had good reason to complain, and I feel like the later authors who are relating the story, in trying so hard to make G-d look like the hero, end up making the Israelites look like ungrateful shits for being really scared at facing the unknown, and being miserable about being stuck in the wilderness. I feel a significant sympathy for people who have been jerked out of a familiar way of life, however problematic, and have not yet been settled into anything else. It's a profoundly uncomfortable situation, and I'd be frankly concerned about anyone who *didn't* complain under those circumstances.

Transition times and places are really terrifying. What has been is no longer, and what will be hasn't arrived. We're not in one room or another. Instead, we're in a liminal, in-between place. And I'll be honest, that's what being queer has felt like across my entire life.

This is just an observation; I'm not angling for pity. I was born into a world in which I, as a gay person, was quite literally illegal. I watched with astonishment (if in fearful silence, because of my conservative Christian surroundings) as the gay liberation movement gained a voice, and people who refused to be ashamed of either their identities or their bodies refused to pretend they were anything other than themselves. I certainly never dreamed that someday I might actually be able to share in the culturally (and financially) beneficial institution of marriage, or, even more mind-boggling, that I might be able to teach a course called Queer Theology as an openly queer person at an institution associated with Christianity, whilst married to a marvelous man who happens to be Jewish.

Astonishing as this progress has been, over the course of my own lifetime, I am also fully aware that equality has not yet been achieved, that the stream of justice is not yet overflowing. Physical and spiritual violence against queers is real. There are still so many people who insist that I am no better than an animal, or that it is not possible for Jesus to love me, or that my marriage is not real, or that it is real evil. There are people even today who literally are trying to turn back the clock on the rights that queer people (and poor people, and people of color, and the disabled, and . . .) have achieved, to make us illegal once again. In other words, I am, as a queer person, still living very much in a liminal, in-between time-space. I may have escaped Egypt, but I am still, if you will, wandering in a wilderness, afraid, thirsty, hungry, and often wondering if G-d even gives a rat's ass. It is often difficult, in this world, to hang on to the vision of a Promised Land of freedom and opportunity.

So, bitch on, you Israelites. Complain that you're thirsty. And if G-d is really that grudging about performing a miracle, and then calling the water of that miracle Meribah, the Waters of Strife, then maybe it's your god you need to reevaluate, and who needs to calm down a little. The G-d of this story is a G-d who is needy and clingy, like some men I've dated. The portions of Psalm 78 that are included for today are all about the miracle bits, but omit the G-d-complaining-about-people-complaining bits, and that makes me sad, because I want to remember that complaining is an integral part of the work of leaving the past behind, and I don't really give a shit if that bothers G-d.

The thing is, in every one of those liminal place-times, I rediscover what I think is one of the true glories of being human: We are blessed and cursed with the ability to hold multiple and conflicting feelings in our hearts at exactly the same moment, not canceling each other out, but coexisting, all in full possession of our soul simultaneously. We can shout with joy at having escaped Egypt at the same time that we can be weeping with miserable thirst. We can be profoundly grateful for a bath, even if we are bathing in the Waters of Strife. This is not sin; it is humanity.

Indeed, I'm thinking that liminal time-places are best understood not so much as between one thing and another or between one period and another, but as something entirely different: as queer. Queer life is not on a binary, linear spectrum, but is a scattershot of stars, flaming balls of gas blazing in seemingly random patterns across multiple dimensions of space-time. And queers who are living their blazing lives are reminders of Jesus's promise that we all have wandered through the looking glass of Wonderland and that, if we start looking closely, things won't really make sense the way we've been told they should, and that waters of strife might quench my thirst anyway; that having to live away from home might not mean giving up my relationships that I started back home; that I might be free while I sit in prison; that being empty might be fulfilling; that my no might be a yes; and that the sexually profligate might get a privileged seat at G-d's dinner table.

And all that is left is to embrace this very queer universe, and trust in a very queer grace, that emptied itself, all over us.

PROPER 22, THE SUNDAY CLOSEST TO OCTOBER 5

Dr. Peter Carlson

Track 1	or	Track 2
Exodus 20:1–4, 7–9, 12–20		*Isaiah 5:1–7*
Psalm 19		*Psalm 80:7–14*
Philippians 3:4b–14		*Philippians 3:4b–14*
Matthew 21:33–46		*Matthew 21:33–46*

When I am teaching introductory classes in religion at California Lutheran University, we always do some work identifying the various holy texts in lots of different religious traditions, and of course the Tanakh comes up—the Hebrew sacred texts of Torah, Nevi'im, and Ketuvim. When we talk about Torah, which literally translates as "Law," I like to spend time considering the difference between our modern, primarily Western, attitude toward law and the ancient Israelite understanding of it. Today we tend to think of law primarily as a rather odious obligation that somebody else has enacted, and the breaking of which demands a fine or punishment. This thinking is certainly present in the Hebrew Bible, of course; but in Judaism, Torah is understood first and foremost as a gift, which is not something we tend today to associate with the law at all. Indeed, the Hebrew word for the 613 commandments in Torah is *mitzvoth* or *blessings*. The story of the ancient Israelites at Sinai, then, is not a story of some sterile business contract; instead, it is more like a road map, if you will, to guide us on the journey of staying in relationship with the Divine, of living fully into the covenant, that sacred agreement between the Israelites and their G-d. And so Torah, Law, is a gift indeed, and one that we see in the various readings today has been sorely underappreciated, and even badly misused.

In our reading from Exodus, of course, we hear the old familiar Big Ten Commandments—the basic dos and don'ts of the Israelites' relationship with G-d. And it is important to note that, aside from having no other gods before G-d and not making idols, none of these commandments are, in fact, directly about G-d; instead, they are about how we are to live with each other. "But," you might say, "what about using G-d's name in vain? Isn't that about G-d?" Well, I am convinced this *is* about our communal life: The misuse of the holy Name of G-d is when we make a vow in G-d's name and then treat that vow frivolously. It is a tradition in some Muslim cultures to recite the Al-Fatiha, the first surah or chapter of the Qur'an, before a business deal, not only as a request to G-d to be present in the dealings, but also as a reminder that G-d is keeping an eye on us and is going to make sure we keep our word. The commandment about the misuse of G-d's Name is making the same point. Even so, the larger point that I want us to understand here is that G-d is explaining to the Israelites in these commandments—and in all 613 mitzvoth—that being in a good relationship with G-d means being in a good relationship with our fellow humans, and even with the earth itself (something we would do well to remember as we read the plethora of vineyard-metaphor-stories in the other readings).

Psalm 19 reflects this communal totality in all of nature: We might at first not make a connection between verses 1–6, a paean to nature (which, incidentally, reflects a cosmology of the period with the sun having a "pavilion" where it rests at night), and verses 7 onward, which are an ode, as it were, to the beauty of the Law of G-d. "The law of HaShem is perfect, and reviving the soul," we sing. But it's important to remember: This is actually no shift at all. In fact, the law a few verses on is described in terms of nature as "sweeter than the honeycomb." The community of nature and the community of the Law are utterly intertwined, and well we should remember it, and what it means: When we abuse nature (which in other mitzvoth demands a sabbath as much as we human animals do and as much as G-d did in the act of creation), we are in fact breaking G-d's law, and refusing to be in relationship with G-d, and we will suffer the consequences of that broken relationship.

The hymn from proto-Isaiah continues to reflect this connection in all of creation and the breaking of divine relationship, although metaphorically and even erotically: In this hymn, the people of the northern kingdom of Israel are described as the vineyard of the Beloved (G-d's), that has been planted and tended and cared for (the erotic symbolism of a man "planting seed" in a woman's "field" has long been extant, and cannot be missed here). But the vines that grew up only yielded "wild grapes"—the seeded spouse-vineyards were, we can gather, unfaithful to the Beloved. Indeed, we are told exactly how they were unfaithful: G-d "expected justice, but saw bloodshed; righteousness, but heard a cry." They did not, in other words, live faithfully in community with each other. And so, the prophet continues, northern Israel has been destroyed. G-d declared, "I will remove its hedge, and it shall be devoured; I will break down its wall, and it shall be trampled down. I will make it a waste; it shall not be pruned or hoed, and it shall be overgrown with briers and thorns." The removal of the hedge, it becomes clear, was the opening for the Assyrian Empire to attack and ultimately destroy the northern kingdom, which we are told was due entirely to Israel's own failure to live righteously with each other and, inevitably, with G-d. And isn't the section of Psalm 80 in today's readings perhaps our natural response to natural or human-made (or divinely made?) disaster? To beg G-d to replant the vineyard, to plow our fields again, to make us fertile again? But it was too late for northern Israel: Their unwillingness to follow the mitzvoth resulted in their own destruction.

St. Paul is trying, in all of his railing against the Law, to get us to an understanding of Law that is closer to the idea of mitzvoth—blessings—rather than some cosmic naughty/nice checklist, like Santa's. I freely admit that I resent how Paul's (and, let's be honest, Martin Luther's) words have been interpreted, as though works are somehow unimportant, because Grace. (Don't get me wrong: Grace is an essential element of any relationship, and especially with our relationships with G-d, but it doesn't magically cancel out the need to do the right thing, and neither Pauly nor Marty have suggested that.) In this passage from Philippians, Paul is reciting his Jewish, Chosen-People credentials: his ancestry as a member of the tribe of Benjamin, his correctly and circumcisionally snipped private bits, his rigid adherence to the Law as a Pharisee. He is, in other words, a functionally perfect Jew. But Paul discovered, as we sometimes realize in our own lives, that doing everything according to the letter of the law doesn't mean you're obeying the spirit of the law, or even doing the right thing. I know, for instance, that there are lots of pedagogical best practices in teaching, and there are even important laws about, for example, teacher/student physical contact. But I also know that when a student is feeling desperately lost, the greatest gift I can give them (with consent, obviously) is a hug, and to hell with best practices.

Paul, then, is reminding us that laws are fine and dandy, but they're not in and of themselves mitzvoth, and following them does not inevitably create a healthy relationship with G-d. On paper Paul has everything, but remember that he goes on to say, "I regard everything as loss because of the surpassing value of knowing Christ Jesus my Guide." We are meant, Paul is reminding us, primarily to be *in love* with G-d, the Beloved of the vineyard, and to be in love also with each other, and with all of creation. Like Paul, we don't always—for that matter, we rarely—do this perfectly, or even moderately well, but, as Madeleine L'Engle said about prayer, it "is like playing the piano, or writing poetry; you don't do it well every single day, but unless you do it every single day, you're never going to do it well at all."[1] Paul is pressing on, like someone practicing piano, toward the goal of living in relationship with G-d and with others.

In the reading from Matthew, Jesus is almost certainly recalling the vineyard image from proto-Isaiah but is combining it artfully with other passages from scripture, including the quotation from Psalm 118. Here, however, the vineyard is not in relationship with G-d (in this story less erotically described simply as a landowner), but is nonetheless in relationship with humans, who will use it for either noble or nefarious purposes.

The story might be familiar, and is usually read simply as a prediction by Jesus of his own crucifixion ("the stone that the builders rejected" bit from Psalm 118), but I think there's more to be harvested (as it were) from this particular vineyard. Here we have the landowner who plants a vineyard, and leases it out to tenants in return for a share of the produce (as was common enough). The story goes that the landowner sends servants (to be read as the line of Hebrew prophets) to pick up the profits, if you will, and the tenants murder them, one by one. The landowner finally sends their own child (obviously to be read as Jesus, the Child of G-d), and

---

[1] Madeleine L'Engle, interviewed by John Alexander in *The Other Side* 73 (October, 1977): 20.

the tenants murder the child, too, in an effort to keep all the profits for themselves. When Jesus poses the frankly rhetorical question, "What will the landowner do to those tenants?" the people listening respond, "[The landowner] will put those wretches to a miserable death, and lease the vineyard to other tenants who will give him the produce at the harvest time." Only just, after all.

Again, it is perilously easy to simply read this as a presaging of the death of Jesus. I think, though, that—especially when we encounter this story in the context of our other readings—it is just as important as a reminder that we are in relationship not only with G-d but with all the earth. If we, as is all too common, see land merely as a source of profit for ourselves, then we have forgotten that G-d is the G-d of *all* creation, and that *all* the harvest belongs to G-d. Likewise, when we prioritize self-interest in our relationships with our human or nonhuman animals, and with the planet, we are not living fully into the mitzvoth, the blessings of relationship, even if we are technically obeying all the laws. The Pharisees in the story, who are *really* good at following the laws, are not, in fact, following The Law, and they, perhaps unsurprisingly, know (and are annoyed) that Jesus "was speaking about them."

As a queer theologian, I am convinced that I need to face up to and point out broken relationships of all kinds. Not just the broken relationships of a heteropatriarchal world with those who are diverse in sexualities or genders, but the broken relationships of racial or cultural diversity, or of truly working toward equal access to all spaces for the disabled, or, for that matter, the broken relationships of humanity and the entire created order. The story of the destruction of northern Israel, in this light, comes across not so much as a cranky G-d thwacking people for sucking up to G-d, but as the inevitable result of not pursuing justice in all of our relationships across the created and divine order. Relationships, whether with other humans, with the entire creation, or with the Divine, demand reciprocity and mutual thriving, and our lessons today remind us that the Covenant that binds us all together is not merely a set of laws, but are mitzvoth—blessings. And the blessings of this covenant are the goal toward which, with St. Paul, we must daily press on.

PROPER 23, THE SUNDAY CLOSEST TO OCTOBER 12

Dr. Peter Carlson

Track 1	or	Track 2
Exodus 32:1–14		*Isaiah 25:1–9*
Psalm 106:1–6, 19–23		*Psalm 23*
Philippians 4:1–9		*Philippians 4:1–9*
Matthew 22:1–14		*Matthew 22:1–14*

The lessons appointed to Proper 23 in the Sundays following Pentecost seem to point to experiences of the Divine that are alternately comforting and terrifying. It's all well and good to say blithely that G-d is love, in a kind of precious Hallmark-y way (as though love cannot be a completely daunting thing to face), but to leave it at that is not only far too easy, it is to be blind to the fact that vast swathes of scripture portray G-d behaving pretty badly apparently simply because, well, They're G-d. As a person who has experienced prooftexting developed for the express purpose of weaponizing scripture against me, I do not want to ignore passages that make me uncomfortable, whether they might appear to be anti-queer, or just telling stories where G-d acts in really shitty ways.

The infamous story of the Israelites fashioning and worshiping a golden calf at Mount Sinai (at the very moment that G-d is chatting with Moses up on the mountain) is probably familiar to many of us. The receipt of Torah, the Law, is observed in Judaism on Shavuot, fifty days after Passover, following the tradition that it was fifty days after the devastating final plague in Egypt that the Israelites made it to Sinai, where Moses once more chatted with G-d, who as always is represented by fire and smoke. The people down at the base of the mountain are, perhaps understandably, getting a little nervous that Moses has been gone so long. We, of course, as readers, are aware that G-d was giving some exceptionally detailed CC&Rs to Moses, taking up several chapters of time, but the people were getting anxious by the time Moses had been gone for forty days and forty nights (this number should be familiar; it should also not ever be taken literally—in ancient cultures the number forty is always metaphorical, essentially meaning "a lot"). So they convince Aaron (who, as Moses's brother, really should have known better) to make some visible god or gods for them, apparently being convinced that only things seen are actually real. Aaron famously forms a calf made of gold, and the people partied.

Now, we can perhaps understand why G-d would be pissed at the people. G-d has liberated them from slavery in Egypt, brought them miraculously through the Red Sea on dry land, fed them with manna and pigeons, and slaked their thirst at Meribah. Surely, they had seen enough to trust in G-d's reality! But to do the Israelites justice, this entire journey must have been terrifying as all hell. I regularly mention that, when they got sassy at the Red Sea, saying, "What? Weren't there any graveyards in Egypt? Was that the reason you brought us out here to die in the wilderness?" they really had some cause. The journey toward liberation is unnerving at best and probably as scary a thing as anyone will ever face. So, as cranky as G-d gets throughout this book, I find myself always wanting to side with the Israelites, who are, frankly, just wanting to stay alive and not be quite so bloody miserable.

But G-d is apparently a needy G-d and needs unwavering, if not slavish, devotion. And G-d lets Moses know exactly how furious G-d is: "I have seen this people, how stiff-necked they are. Now let me alone, so that my wrath may burn hot against them and I may consume them; and of you I will make a great nation." I love, incidentally, that G-d apparently wants to suck every bit of self-pity and woundedness out of the situation: "Let me alone!" which is, frankly, like a pouty three-year-old (or, to be honest, me on a pretty regular basis).

What happens next is extraordinary, if I think about it in the theological terms I was raised with: Moses fights back against G-d. Not only does he fight back, Moses gets G-d right where it hurts: G-d's ego. "Really, O Divinity of Bigness? Are you gonna drag your people out here, and then put them to death, so the Egyptians—the bad guys, remember?—can laugh and say, 'Ha! Look what kind of pathetic G-d *they* have, who "saves" them only to let them die in the desert!' Is that what you want, G-d?

Is that worthy of You?" It's notable that Moses is not making a case for the virtue of the Israelites, but a case for the virtue of G-d's own promises. And what is perhaps most remarkable about this whole story is that apparently G-d hadn't thought about that—that G-d had to be taught something by Moses. "And HaShem changed Their mind about the disaster that They planned to bring on the people."

Psalm 106, which follows the Exodus reading, is a psalm of penitence, that reviews the multitudinous ways in which the Israelites have failed the covenant, including the event at Sinai, but which finally concludes that G-d is always willing to protect them when they cry out, because of that very covenant. This psalm expressly omits Moses's intercessions for the people and gives all the credit to G-d, doesn't it? But in both readings, there is an important theme that relationships—covenants—may be broken but are always restorable.

The track 2 reading from Isaiah is a mind-bending mix of divine smash and divine comfort. It follows a disturbingly apocalyptic vision in the previous chapter in which the earth is laid waste in terms that feel all too real in these days of massive climate change: "The earth dries up and withers; . . . The earth lies polluted under its inhabitants, for they have transgressed laws, violated the statutes, broken the everlasting covenant. Therefore, a curse devours the earth, and its inhabitants suffer for their guilt." Chapter 25, however, changes the tune dramatically: This is the song of gratitude from those who have been rescued from the apocalypse, "the poor [and] the needy in [their] distress." It looks forward to the time of redemption, when "in this mountain, HaShem will make for all peoples a feast of choice pieces. . . . Then G-d will wipe away the tears from all faces, and the disgrace of Their people They will take away." Psalm 23, arguably the most famous of all the psalms, is assigned to this reading, and in it we are reassured that G-d, even in the shadow of death and in the presence of our enemies, will keep G-d's promise to us. Isaiah, then, like the authors of Exodus and the Psalms, provides a message of hope: Even if G-d has to be reminded occasionally of Their promise to Their people, G-d will remain in relationship with us, even if we aren't as faithful toward G-d.

Almost certainly, Paul's letter to the Philippians was written, or at least parts of it were written, while Paul was in prison (an experience that most modern-day evangelical Christians, claiming to be persecuted because someone says "happy holidays" or argues for equal religious protections for non-Christians, would scarcely begin to be able to cope with). And in that light, it might be forgivable to wonder if the epistle might actually have been written as a reminder to G-d, as Moses had to remind G-d, of who G-d is, and of Their promise. "Hey, G-d. Um. I'm in prison here, for your sake? Any chance you might have some tricks up your sleeve? You know, for Jesus's sake?"

But look at what Paul is saying! "All y'all are my beloveds, my joy and my crown! And I know things are challenging out there for us Jesus followers, but I'm gonna ask you to stand strong, just like I'm trying to do." And Paul goes on to name women (yes, women!) who have been leaders in the work of the Gospel, as well as others, commending them to the Philippians' care. "Rejoice!" Paul says. Stunning words, when you consider that being a Christian was illegal in the Roman Empire and could land you in prison, like Paul. And the final bit of advice in this passage is utterly countercultural, especially for me, living in an age when I am wondering if the rights I and my fellow queerlings have achieved might in fact be taken away, and wanting to fight hard for them: "Let your gentleness be known to everyone. [And] whatever is true, whatever is honorable, whatever is just, whatever is pure, whatever is pleasing, whatever is commendable, if there is any excellence and if there is anything worthy of praise, think about these things." The idea of fighting for justice through gentleness grates on my nerves, I'll be honest, because frankly I don't want to be gentle with hate-filled people. I want to slap them silly. But this is Paul's advice, written from a Roman prison. If he can bring himself to gentleness there, then I suppose I can at least attempt to follow his example. The world may be a shit-hole, Paul is reminding us, but G-d, as we were reminded in the passage from Isaiah, has not forgotten the poor and the needy, and has not given up on justice.

Justice seems a bit random in the parable from Matthew's Gospel for today. The story is one of a marriage feast—and I love stories about marriage feasts, because they are inevitably tangled up with embodiedness, with the promise of sumptuous food and the other promise that a couple is hopefully going to have some banging hot sex on their marriage night—to which all the "proper" people have been invited, though they all ignore their invitations. Remembering that Matthew is writing very much to a Jewish Christian audience, we can have no doubt that he is wanting us to identify these people with the first-century Jews themselves, a direct implication that they have, once again, ignored G-d's invitation to a covenantal relationship, and are, as it were, crafting golden calves that they'd rather worship, and the king destroys them for their snub. The irony, of course, is that this is clearly *not all Jews*, as it were. Matthew's audience is, I repeat, Jewish Christians. Nevertheless, the Gospeller at this point appears to be reminding his audience that the Good News of the reign of heaven is far bigger than Judaism, and that G-d fully intends to "invite everyone you find to the wedding banquet . . . both good and bad; so the wedding hall was filled with guests." Now, this sounds a bit more like the expansive, forgiving G-d that we all want to believe in these days, essentially absolving us not only from "being good," but also willing to welcome us even though—and perhaps ultimately especially *because*—we're not part of the in-crowd. Indeed, those aspects of my identity that are relegated to the margins rejoice at this point in the story: The outsiders are, in so many of the parables, the ones who become the insiders, welcomed into G-d's reign.

But there's one final reminder: The story of the person who showed up without a wedding garment. The king, seeing this social atrocity, has him cast out into outer darkness, where there will be "gnashing of teeth." My friend and mentor Fred Borsch, who was the diocesan bishop of Los Angeles, used to tell a story of an old man in church who, on hearing this one Sunday, shouted out, "What if we don't have any teeth?" to which the preacher responded without hesitation, "Teeth will be provided!" But seriously, this sounds not so much like Loving Inclusive G-d, as Judgy Cranky G-d. And it's really hard to reconcile them, even though they both show up in the same parable.

But I think that the story reminds us that the invitation might be wide open, and there's a banquet waiting for us, but we still have a responsibility to respond to that invitation in the right spirit, in the right, if you will, outfit. And this really is the story that stretches across all the readings for today: It is the story of a G-d who is enchanted with us and frustrated with us, perhaps simultaneously, but who most of all longs to be in relationship—in covenant—with us. And as in any relationship, there may be times when we have to give G-d a nudge, to remind Them of Their promises, and other times when G-d might get frustrated and screamy at us, to remind us of our promises. But in all times, even in prison, even in the valley of the shadow of death, all of us get glimpses of what is true, and honorable, and just, and beautiful. We will fuck up. But the opportunity to repair the relationship will always be there, gently pulling us back from our golden calves, holding us tight in the apocalypse, and inviting us profligately to the marriage banquet, where the G-d of peace will be with us.

PROPER 24, THE SUNDAY CLOSEST TO OCTOBER 19

Dr. Peter Carlson

Track 1	or	Track 2
Exodus 33:12–23		*Isaiah 45:1–7*
Psalm 99		*Psalm 96:1–9, (10–13)*
1 Thessalonians 1:1–10		*1 Thessalonians 1:1–10*
Matthew 22:15–22		*Matthew 22:15–22*

We have so many ruses, so many sneaky tricks, to avoid seeing G-d But that's perhaps not surprising. Gazing upon G-d is perilous work, and it hauls our asses out of the noiseless tenor of our way and forces us to reevaluate everything we've ever done.

In our entire goddam lives.

The reading from the Hebrew Bible (Exod. 33:12–23) is one of my favorites, both in its genuine distress and in G-d's hilarious response. How many of us have not, at some point or another, had a bitter conversation with G-d, saying something along the lines of, "Hey, Jerk. You said you'd be with me. You promised all sorts of cool shit if I follow You. You promised that You cared. You promised, whatever the hell it means, PEACE in my life. I've held up my end of the bargain, Dude. But it really seems like you're slacking. The justified might live by faith, but I can't do this for ever. I need to see you, you *G-d*. That is, if you even *are* a god at all. Start handing over some proof, Bucko."

We've all been there, I'm pretty sure. And I'm willing to bet that queer folk, people of color, the disabled, women—those who are outside of or only partially in systemic power structures—have been there more often than any of us cares to admit. In an unjust world, it is hard to view G-d, much less to see any kind of justice for us and our people. We scream to G-d, right there with Moses, "For how shall it be known to cis-het haters that I, faggy little me, have found favor in your sight, I and your queer people, unless you GODDAMN GO WITH US?!?" "For how shall it be known to our law enforcement and our gated white communities that I, unarmed black me, have found favor in your sight, I and all brown and black people who live in fear, unless you GODDAMN GO WITH US?!?" "For how shall it be known to predatory men that I, preyed-upon me, have found favor in your sight, I and all women who have posted, "Me too," unless you GODDAMN GO WITH US?!?"

Moses begs G-d to go with them, so that they can be "distinct, I and your people, from every people on the face of the earth."

Of course, the disabled, queers, asylum seekers, people of color, women . . . sometimes we wish we didn't have to be quite so fucking distinct. Certainly, we sometimes wish we weren't being quite so distinctly singled out. How many of us have wished that, sometimes, the world would just let us be . . . indistinct?

But that doesn't stop us from wanting to see G-d.

The problem is that seeing G-d is dangerous. Psalm 99 reminds that an experience of the unmediated divine causes the people to tremble and the earth to shake. We fall down before the footstool of G-d, because we cannot remain standing in G-d's presence (no wonder we've established a priesthood to approach G-d for us!). This is a G-d who will speak to the prophets and forgive them (us?), but who will not let them/us avoid responsibility for our evil deeds. G-d will forgive us our racist assumptions about the value of unarmed black lives, our transphobic assumptions about who can pee where, our patriarchal assumptions about a woman's right to live without sexual harassment; our homophobic assumptions about what kind of love is acceptable. But forgiveness does not mean being let off the hook. Our psalmist reminds us, "You were a forgiving God to them, but an avenger of their wrongdoings." Absolution is only the beginning of atonement.

I freely admit as a Protestant that there are days when the medieval understanding of purgatory makes a shedload of theological sense to me. Being purged of our sins, not merely having them blipped out, matters. Don't get me wrong—I understand the many challenges inherent in the economics of medieval atonement practice. But still. Being held accountable seems to be something we Protestant folk have kind of abandoned in our substitutionary sacrificial atonement theory.

The psalm and its warnings about being in the presence of G-d is perhaps the context that we need as we try to understand G-d's reply to Moses, which amounts to, "Okay, fine. I'm gonna hide you in this crevice here, and I'm gonna pass by, but y'all can't look at my face because, dude. You'd fry. So I'm gonna be RuPaul, and sashay on by, and when I've passed, you can peek, and take a look at my Divine Ass, girlfriend."

Because that's the view of the Divine that Moses gets to scope out: G-d's ass. "I will cover you with my hand until I have passed by; then I will take away my hand, and you shall see my back; but my face shall not be seen." Groove Armada comes to mind: "I see you, Baby, shakin' that ass." Go find her video and try not to dance. I dare you.

Hot as G-d's ass might be, however, and as much as G-d might have limited Moses's access to the divine presence to G-d's hinder parts, Christians believe in a G-d that literally *did* have an ass, a G-d who *wanted* a body, and a G-d who became in-bodied just as we are forced to be in-bodied every single day, and who presumably then can be seen in all G-d's bodyliciousness, just as we can be seen. Jesus was in-bodied and divine, and that meant that the people in power were trying to whoop his in-bodied ass all the time. Our Gospel reading (Matt. 22:15–22) is yet another example of the theological insiders threatened by Jesus's message of the radical and all-encompassing love of G-d, and the attempts that establishment orthodoxy will make to try to keep people they don't like away from G-d's embrace. The number of times that cis-het folk have tried to trap me with theological puzzles is legion. It is one of my dreams that I will someday be able to respond with the badassery that Jesus musters here.

It starts with the flattery. "Teacher, we know that you are sincere, and teach the way of G-d in accordance with truth, and show deference to no one; for you do not regard people with partiality." (No wonder Jesus was "aware of their malice"; he *totally* showed partiality against the rich and politically connected, and for the poor and oppressed.) I get similar stuff, believe it or not: "Oh, you're so thoughtful and wise. You have a PhD. You are so respectful of all your students. May I ask you a question about a theological nitpickiness that has been bothering me?" One tiny difference between Jesus and me is that I still fall for it, even though I've learned to be wary when I hear this kind of horseshit.

Sometimes the question is more obvious, having to do with one of the Clobber Passages (those few passages in scripture that are used to "clobber" queer Christians, whilst ignoring the rest of scripture). But sometimes the lead is more subtle: It will reflect a point of being "kind" to racists who just grew up that way; or of how queers might be less, well, *queer*, so as not to alienate potential allies. It might have to do with trying to understand a heterosexual white man's point of view in the interests of Christian charity. I'm getting better at recognizing when these are honest questions, and when they're just bait.

Because bait always has a "but."

If anyone is saying something that begins, "I know how fair you try to be, but . . ." or "I totally agree that justice is important, but . . ." that's a dead giveaway that this is a Pharisee speaking. I've done it myself, in all my own pharisaical talent.

The question the religious authorities put to Jesus is still with us today: Do we pay taxes to the government, when we absolutely disagree with so much that the government is doing? Conservatives worry: Do we pay taxes to support abortion? Or, on the so-called liberal side, do we pay taxes to support the military industrial complex? Do we support the economic and military imperialism that our country utilizes to maintain its place in the world? Do we give our hard-earned money to the fucking empire?

Jesus's response is still desperately important for us today: "Give to the secular world what belongs to it. Give to G-d what belongs to G-d." This is not cause to excuse ourselves from the democratic process, broken as it may be in this world, but to investigate our lives and ask what belongs to G-d. If indeed we believe that we have been created in the divine image, then we are stamped with the image of G-d in our very bodies, just as the coin shown to Jesus was stamped with the image of the emperor. We give ourselves, asses and all, wholly to G-d, and worship the Name with our sexy and wonderfully diverse bodies, and all they were created to enjoy and suffer.

Of course, it is possible that the right response is, "Everything belongs to G-d, so we should give everything to G-d." If that is what you truly believe, then you have a responsibility to make it so. So you should not only give your body to G-d, but your money and (yes) your vote. Ask how your vote affects the most desperately poor; ask whether it helps or hinders women who seek justice in the face of sexual harassment and abuse; ask if it protects and deeply loves the lives and bodies of trans people; ask if it will ensure that the next generation of black and brown people will not have to have "the talk" about how not to get killed when they're pulled over in a traffic stop. Ask if your vote works toward the reign of G-d, "lover of justice."

If you do that, you will be like the church in Thessalonica, who were chosen by G-d, "because our message of the gospel came to you not in word only, but also in power and in the Holy Spirit." You will be an example to all believers, because in giving to G-d what is G-d's, you will indeed have turned to G-d from the worship of idols; you will have turned—converted, dare I say?—to serve a living and true G-d.

And if you do that, you may even be lucky enough to see G-d's ass.

PROPER 25, THE SUNDAY CLOSEST TO OCTOBER 26

Dr. Peter Carlson

Track 1
Deuteronomy 34:1–12
Psalm 90:1–6, 13–17
1 Thessalonians 2:1–8
Matthew 22:34–46

or

Track 2
Leviticus 19:1–2, 15–18
Psalm 1
1 Thessalonians 2:1–8
Matthew 22:34–46

I crept out of the closet whilst I was at Wheaton College (the Evangelical Vatican). Some people have called this brave; others have called it insanity. All I knew was that honesty had been drilled into my moral code by my parents, and here I was, living at home (I grew up in Wheaton) with my parents, with whom I was not being honest. I could no longer live a lie, at least not with them.

I tell this story, not because of their response (it wasn't brilliant, but it wasn't hateful), but because part of that process of coming out included going, filled with faith and hope, to a counselor at the school, for the purpose of finding a way to bring together my entire identity—religious and sexual—in some kind of coherent way. The counselor was, I am now unafraid to claim, a self-proclaimed Religious Authority who flung bits of Bible at me as weapons. I should point out that a young man who has grown up in full-on evangelical Christianity is not the easiest adversary in this kind of fight; I can take the Bible out of context really fucking effectively. (Indeed, at one point, I recall asking him if he slept with his wife during menses, because if he had, he ought to be cut off from the community.) I look back on this episode of my life with sadness, not just because it was harmful to me as a Jesus follower, but because it was a Battle of the Bullshit, and love had no place in it—certainly love had no place in my own heart.

In the collect assigned for today, we pray for an increase of the gifts of faith, hope, and charity; and we pray that, in order to obtain what G-d promises, we will love what G-d commands. In both phrases, we tend to cherish the first bits but shy away from the latter bits. We all want to be known as people of faith and hope (even if, truth to tell, we may be hoping for different things), but when it comes to the practice of caritas? We're not great at that. The word comes from the Latin *carus*, which means "expensive," and this should give us an idea of what's involved: Love, if it is really love, costs us something dear. It's the same with the promises of G-d: We all want them. What we don't want so much is to love what G-d commands.

This unwillingness (that seems to be built into us—it's enough to make you believe in Original Sin) to accept an Entire Thing is part and parcel of our usual approach to scripture, which it seems to me Jesus is calling out in the Gospel of Matthew today (22:34-46): We cherry pick. We look for the bits that we can get on board with and conveniently ignore the bits that cut to the quick. It's natural, of course. But I'm going to be bold and state that prooftexting—the practice of pulling bits of the Bible out for the purpose of an argument—is inevitably bad theology. It is also, as we see in Matthew, an ancient practice. We see the religious leaders of the day laying a Purity Test on Jesus, and Jesus (who knows his scriptural texts as well as they do) shows that he can play that game too. The religious mucketymucks try to trap him into identifying a "greatest" commandment, perhaps hoping he'll pick one of the Big Ten (that some people in the United States seem so eager to post in courthouses, in defiance of the country's apparent separation of church and state). But he sidesteps it with a kicker that seems to us to be obvious: Love G-d. But even then he doesn't let it rest; he adds that the second most important commandment is actually directly related to the first: Love your neighbor. (The fact that our neighbor is almost always the person we are least inclined to like is something that he explains a couple of chapters later, in the infamous story of the Good Samaritan.)

So Jesus has weaseled his way out of that test; but then he poses his own sneaky question, asking whose son the Messiah should be, and when they respond that he is to be the son of David, quotes Psalm 110 at them, asking, "How is it then that David by the Spirit calls him Lord?"

I grew up being told that this is a sign of how clever Jesus was, and how savvy he was with the scriptures (and, it must follow, how I was to memorize tons of Bible so I could strive for a comparable level of cleverness). I am now convinced, however, that what Jesus was actually doing was demonstrating how fucking stupid it is to pull bits of scriptural texts out of context in order to score divine points. That's the path of legalistic, nitpicky, religious bullshit, and it has nothing to do with the Divine, who is not tallying points, but who is busy loving Their neighbor as Themself. And Their neighbor, shockingly, is us. G-d and we are neighbors.

But, to tweak the question asked by Francis Schaeffer, how shall we then love? Because we really do want to know how to love, even if we don't do it very well. At least, we think we do. The other lessons for the day have an answer to that question, I think.

We read in Deuteronomy the heartbreaking story of Moses being led to the top of Pisgah, where he gets to look at the land toward which he has, with G-d's guidance, been leading the Israelites after their escape from slavery in Egypt. But he is not allowed, finally, to go there. If you want to prooftext, and pull a passage out of scripture to show that G-d is an asshole, this is a really good one to choose: G-d basically forces Moses, who was living the good life as a shepherd in Midian, to go back to Egypt, to fight against the Pharaoh and the massed military might of that empire, and then to lead the Israelites (who were, let's be honest, understandably crabby, but it didn't make things any easier for Moses) for forty years in the wilderness. And now, when they're almost at their goal, G-d says, "You don't get to go in, because you got cranky once. Neener." In fact, though the Israelites duly mourned Moses, "No one knows his burial place to this day." The very location of his burial is forgotten. Some payback for a life of fucking hard work.

When I read this in conjunction with the Gospel today, though, I do not see it as an unfair G-d cutting Moses off for stupid reasons. Rather, I see it as an example of how we are to love: not with expectation of gain, but because it needs to be done. Moses gave everything he had, literally to the end of his life, simply because that's what it means to love G-d and neighbor.

Paul also has something to say to us about this in the first letter to the Jesus followers in Thessalonica, where he is making sure we know that he has "suffered and been shamefully mistreated" for preaching the Good News. To do Paul justice, he spent more time in jail than most of us ever will, and our traditions tell us that he was ultimately beheaded for his witness; so he arguably had reason to complain. But his point is that the only demands he ever made of the Christians were the demands of Christ himself. Love G-d? Love neighbor? Yes, said Paul, and here's how we modeled that for you: "We are determined to share with you not only the gospel of G-d but also our own selves." Paul is reminding the Thessalonians that Paul gave his very self for them.

We queers know a lot about giving our own selves to a cause, because it is our own, authentic selves we are trying to save, along with those of our fellow queers. It is the Marsha P. Johnsons at Stonewall, it is the lesbians who stepped up to care for their gay brothers dying of AIDS, it is the Harvey Milks, and it is the thousands of queerfolk who lived and died refusing to be anything less than a beloved of the Divine who have shared their own selves, and sometimes gave their very lives, so that we too could know the Good News of divine love.

Too often, like Moses, these queer prophets have not been able to make it to the Promised Land of Justice and Peace. A drag queen reading stories to children may never know that their public and ridiculed presence gave strength to a small child to dream of being their own fabulous self. A transman demanding equal access to health care may never achieve it for themself. A gay, somewhat-cis professor at a Lutheran University may never know if they saved a queer life because of their own determination to be relentlessly queer on campus.

Moses and Paul knew that love—charity—costs us dearly. Ultimately, they gave their own selves in an effort to love G-d and neighbor: the core of our scriptural texts. When I was prooftexting, however brilliantly, with the counselor at Wheaton, I was loving neither G-d nor him. I aced my scripture memorization exam, but I failed miserably at living out the scriptures. I've been trying ever since to make amends for that failure.

Join me.

ALL SAINTS' DAY

The Rev. Dr. Jay Emerson Johnson

Ecclesiasticus 44:1–10, 13–14
Revelation 7:9–17
Matthew 5:1–12
Psalm 34:1-10, 22

"Let us now sing the praises of famous men."

We could change that final word to "men and women," I suppose, or even better, *people*. But those linguistic adjustments don't soothe the greater discomfort I have with this passage from the Hebrew Bible, the one from Ecclesiasticus so frequently read for the celebration of All Saints' Day.

These famous ones worthy of sung praises apparently ruled kingdoms, lived with valor, spoke in prophetic oracles, and were endowed with great wealth.

None of those descriptive phrases apply even remotely to my own life. And that's the problem, because I have always wanted to be counted among that throng of saints, among the divinely sanctified, or in more common parlance, among all those who are truly *blessed*.

Of course, I could never quite measure up (or even come close) to the blessings of sanctity as a gay man who lives a bit effeminately around the edges. Certain sexual affiliations and nonstandard gender performance place one rather automatically outside the "blessing box."

The religious complexity of this feast day is compounded by the curious evolution of the notion of "blessing" itself in modern Western culture. Even as a priest and theologian, I scarcely notice how curious it is to think of myself as *blessed* by having a good car to drive (compared to those who have a junky one or none at all). What a *blessing*, I tell myself, to have a warm bed in a dry house as a chilling rain pours over those living without shelter on city streets.

There's certainly nothing wrong with claiming a blessing, especially when we've been told for so long that we can't have any.

But then Matthew's Jesus makes a big mess right in the middle of the blessings many of us were desperate to claim—and this turns out to be good news for everyone.

The All Saints' Day lectionary gives us "The Beatitudes" (either the version from Matthew or Luke), as if to scramble entirely how any of us should think of "saints."

Blessed are the poor in spirit, Matthew's Jesus says, and blessed are those who mourn, and blessed are the meek, too, and even all those persecuted because of righteous causes.

What in the world is a "blessing," anyway?

The crowds gathered around Jesus likely wondered the very same thing and whether they would ever be blessed. Matthew sets the stage for these enumerated "blessings" by describing the crowds who heard them as including those who were sick, *all* those, he writes, from the surrounding regions who were afflicted with various diseases and pains, those with deeply troubled spirits and plagued by seizures (4:23–25).

Those crowds, in other words, would never be described by most religious leaders as *blessed*; they were likely told, more than once, that they were not only living outside the "blessing box" but firmly ensconced in the "penalty box."

Contrary to the modern "prosperity gospel," the spurious approach to Christianity that makes material wealth synonymous with divine blessing, Matthew's Jesus invites that ragged and motley crowd to see—all evidence to the contrary notwithstanding—that their lives are a blessing.

Rather than the particular circumstances of our lives, what seems to matter to Jesus is the *way* we live in the midst of those circumstances. God doesn't *give* us a blessing; God calls us to *be* a blessing.

The word *blessing* emerged centuries ago from a gesture of setting something apart for special purposes. Historically, that "gesture" involved the ritual use of blood.

Prior to the arrival of Christianity in northern Europe, blood was thought to have cleansing properties—if it cleans all the interior spaces of the human body, in other words, then surely it could purify objects and places, ridding them of evil influences.

When those ancient cultural practices collided with Christian faith, the Old English verb *bloedsian* eventually became our word *blessing*, and it evokes that long and rich history of setting something apart, of making it sacred with blood.

That's not quite as strange as it sounds when we recall that human blood is mostly water and has a concentration of salts and other ions remarkably similar to sea water. Salty water actually does have the capacity to purify and preserve.

I began thinking about that history of blood in both tantalizing and poignant ways shortly after moving to Michigan and visiting the Ziibiwing Center in Mt. Pleasant, a place dedicated to the Anishinabe cultural and indigenous history of the Ojibwe, Odawa, and Potawatomi peoples of the Great Lakes.

In the center's exhibition space, I stumbled upon the Anishinabe notion of "blood memory." This refers to the emotional state, for example, of hearing one's native language spoken by one's relatives, or feeling the pulse of the planet in the rhythm of a drumbeat, or finding a home in the cadences of an ancient song.

Whatever grounds us and connects us to our ancestors and to earth itself stirs this blood memory.

I couldn't stop the tears from rolling down my cheeks as I encountered this powerful concept in a cultural center dedicated to the stories and rituals of a people that came so very close to being extinguished—the Ziibiwing Center was vibrating with *blood memory*.

The tears, I later realized, were surfacing other memories as well. More than a few gay men my age (and others of more recent generations too) still shudder at the thought of blood cleansing anything—for many of us, "blood memory" evokes instead something dirty, a viral infection caused by sexual intimacy. AIDS was the "penalty box" from which we could not emerge.

Even after so many years of wrestling with those old and terribly hurtful messages, I learned Gospel grace afresh from the history of a people my ancestors tried to erase, from those who were not *given* a blessing but who *lived* as a blessing—including, on that one day in a central Michigan cultural center, for me.

So hear, then, Matthew's Jesus for all those infected with HIV: Blessed are you who have lived with a virus in your blood; blessed are you who have cared for strangers with compassion and as if they were family because of your blood; blessed are you who marched in the streets for greater access to health care and demanded justice for the impoverished and created communities of care for the forgotten—*because of your infected blood.*

Modern Western sensibilities bristle at what sounds like a ghoulish ode to bodily fluids, and that is likely one of the vital reasons why the lectionary insists on having us hear from the queerest (which is not to say the gayest) book of the Bible, the last one.

In the vision from the Revelation to John assigned for this saintly celebration we see, not surprisingly, a great crowd, too many to count, from every nation, tribe, clan, and language—the vast Communion of Saints.

Who are all these dressed in dazzling garments?

A heavenly elder explains to John: These are the ones who have come through the time of great trouble and suffering.

These are the ones whose way of life God made a blessing for others.

These are the ones who have washed their robes in the *blood* of the lamb.

Saints are the ones washed in blood by the way they lived, and for some by the way they died. By telling their stories, whether of "famous men" or the "infamous queens" among us, we can better imagine how God is calling all of us to make our own way of life a blessing for the world.

This blood memory surely makes All Saints' Day one of the queerest on the church calendar. After all, more than a few of the stories of saints in Christian history are literally beyond belief—a headless bishop hiking across Europe; Thecla baptizing herself in a water tank with killer seals; Paul meeting a talking lion on one of his missionary journeys.

Aren't these stories just embarrassing? Why tell such tall tales? For that matter, why tell stories of men wearing sequins or a women in jeans and chaps (or no jeans and just chaps)?

I used to be embarrassed by these stories of wacky saints, just like I was embarrassed by "flamboyant fags" and "butch dykes" and even those gay men we saw on the news back in the 1980s who were wasting away on hospital beds from a virus they should have known better not to catch.

Then I stumbled on a great phrase from David Matzko McCarthy, who wondered much like I did how reasonable people can still belong to a religious tradition full of ludicrous legends. We embrace such stories, he argued, not naïvely or uncritically, but faithfully. We recognize in all those queer stories of queer people from Christian history the potential, as he put it, to *"disturb the world with God."*[1]

When the world needs troubling, in a world trapped by the smallness of its own visions and mired in the status quo, God calls God's people to live large, to expand our shared dreams toward bigger horizons where peace and justice kiss, as the psalmist declared (85:10), and where power serves not profit but only love and compassion.

More often than not, such expansions will mean flaunting the queerness God has called us to offer as a blessing—just like every other saint who has come before us and who disturbed the world with God.

I always appreciate celebrating All Saints' Day at the Eucharistic Table, where an ancient blood memory vibrates with hope: God calls queer people to live as witnesses to the Gospel, not in spite of our queerness but *because* of it—and that's a blessing.

---

[1] David Matzko McCarthy, "Desirous Saints," in *Queer Theology: Rethinking the Western Body*, ed. Gerard Loughlin (Blackwell Publishing Group, 2007), 307.

PROPER 26, THE SUNDAY CLOSEST TO NOVEMBER 2

Dr. Peter Carlson

Track 1	or	Track 2
Joshua 3:7–17		*Micah 3:5–12*
Psalm 107:1–7, 33–37		*Psalm 43*
1 Thessalonians 2:9–13		*1 Thessalonians 2:9–13*
Matthew 23:1–12		*Matthew 23:1–12*

This is one of those days when track 1 and track 2 seem to have no real way of being connected—and of course, I know that congregations generally have the choice of which track they will follow, but I'm trying really hard to reflect on everything we're given in the lectionary, and see where Miz Holy Spirit Thang leads me. And I know (Oh, my dears, who better?) that Miz Holy Spirit Thang sometimes leads us to really confusing, if not outright daunting, places. And today, as I read these lessons, I am hearing Miz Holy Spirit speaking to me about confidence: well- and misplaced confidence. In what, She is asking me, do I place my confidence? In my salary, and my 401(k)? In my status as a white, mostly male-presenting person in a society that will support that whiteness and maleness? In my career and reputation as a scholar of religion? Do I, perhaps more nobly, place my confidence in a community that I hope and pray will support me if life turns out to be a cesspool?

The thing is, I've placed my confidence in all those things and have been disappointed by them all. We live, after all, in an age that sees Social Security, into which many of us have been paying all our lives, as an "entitlement." We live in an age that is playing out Margaret

Thatcher's 1980s neoliberal "sado-monetarist" declaration that there is no such thing as society. We have watched corporations, desperate to maximize profits, collapse and take our savings with them. We have seen utterly unqualified white straight men win elections over highly qualified women of color.

None of the things that our world tells us are worthy of our confidence seem to be able ultimately to support us. In fact, they fail us miserably. And I'm gonna get dangerous here: Not even G-d seems ultimately to be able to support me some days.

I don't know absolutely for sure, but I'm willing to bet that G-d has been unable to make things better for you at various times too. We sob, with the psalmist in track 2, "You are the G-d of my strength; why have you put me from you?" We long for justice, and cry for comfort, because the very G-d that we have tried really, really hard to keep faith with has apparently wandered off to play poker with Their pals and forgotten about us, if not literally put us from Them.

Joshua seems, though, to have had no such experience. He is certain that G-d has called him to lead the Israelites, to command the priests, and generally be the Head Mucketymuck. In fact, in the first chapter, we read that G-d *commands* Joshua not to be "frightened or dismayed," because G-d "will be with you as I was with Moses." Oh. Would that be Moses, who you *didn't let enter the Promised Land*? That Moses, G-d? If I had been Joshua, I'd have had some trouble not being frightened or dismayed.

But this passage is the one that recounts bringing the Ark of the Covenant into the land, through the River Jordan. In what is obviously meant to recall the crossing the Red Sea in their escape from Egypt (the two safe passages bookending, as it were, the story of the Israelites wandering in the desert for forty years), we read a story that is meant, in addition to giving Joshua reason to feel confident, even though he was having to take up the mantle of leadership from Moses (who, admittedly, left some pretty big sandals to fill), to inspire confidence in G-d's promises and protection, even if (as we can read in the chapter immediately before this) G-d's promises and protection are fulfilled through a sex worker.

Psalm 107 talks more about the promises of G-d, which were given to the people, even though "some wandered in desert wastes." They cried to G-d, we read, and G-d answered them, giving them a city to dwell in, whilst destroying the livelihoods of those who lived there before. Setting aside for the moment the really problematic theology of a G-d who would arbitrarily hand the land of other peoples to another people (a theology that was literally used by white Europeans to dispossess Native Americans of their life and land), these readings tell us of the confidence we can have in G-d's promises, and are lovely.

The Prophet Micah, on the other hand, wields a different sort of confidence: This is the confidence required to speak out against the powers that be, and who have assumed that their occupancy of the land is a birthright, rather than part of a relationship with the Divine. Micah speaks scathingly toward those who cry "Peace!" when they have food. How often do we hear this today? It is those in positions of power and privilege who shout at us, "No violence! Stop being angry, Blackpeople! Stop being bitchy queens! Stop complaining, you disabled people who can't get into public spaces! Stop whining, poor people!" Is it any wonder that those who have no access to justice often feel that they have no recourse except violence, or at least nonviolent direct and disruptive action? "No peace, no justice," Micah is in essence crying. "I am filled with power!" Power, not necessarily to change hearts, but to speak the truth—a terrifying act in a world that kills truth-speakers.

The confidence of Micah is the confidence of a liberation theologian, or a womanist theologian, or a disability theologian, or a queer theologian. It is not a promise that the river will not flow over me and drown me, but that, even if I might die because of it, I have the strength and the fearlessness—the confidence—to stand before the political and religious authorities and speak the truth of what matters to G-d: the hungry, the oppressed, the folks who have not been given full access to basic human rights, or to G-d.

And Psalm 43 is the psalm of these theologians: "Vindicate me, O G-d, and defend my cause against an ungodly people." It is the confidence to claim G-d's promises as applying to one's self, even if the religious hoohahs have pretended to be G-d, and deny me those very promises.

We see this kind of confidence in Paul's letter to the Thessalonians too. He is making clear that he was not a preacher for profit, that he earned his keep, without allowing for even the potential accusation that he might have been "selling G-d" for cash (I'm always going to point out prosperity theology here). This is part of an ongoing theme in the letters of Paul: his need to convince people that he was, in fact, an apostle, despite his not ever having met Jesus when Jesus was still alive on earth. Paul notes in this letter that he might have used his status as an apostle to demand his keep, but that he earned his own way, apparently odd-jobbing in between preaching stints. But the key to our passage is Paul's gratitude that the Jesus followers in Thessalonica accepted the words Paul preached, that they had confidence in the promises of eternal life with Christ that Paul describes at the end of the letter. Almost certainly Paul was writing following the expulsion of the Jews from Rome, and as the fate of Jews and Christians were inextricably entwined before the destruction of the Jerusalem temple in 70 CE, that expulsion must have affected Christians too. Paul is writing to Christians who were clearly worried that Jesus had not yet returned, encouraging them (and perhaps himself?) to have confidence, like the ancient Israelites at the River Jordan, in the promises of G-d.

And so what does confidence have to do with the passage from Matthew's Gospel for today? I admit to some struggles with this story, particularly with Jesus saying, "Call no one your father on earth, for you have one Father—the one in heaven." I perhaps take this too literally, because my own biological father was an absolutely wonderful and even remarkable man, who taught me that telling the truth might be painful and even dangerous, but was always essential. Indeed, the fact that I have such a marvelous father is why I balk at titling clergy with parental terms: I already have a father and mother, thank you, and they were really grand. I know that many people (especially my queer siblings) have not had the privilege of supportive and loving parents. And quite frankly, both my own positive relationships with my parents and others' negative relationships with theirs are a reason I balk at using the metaphor of G-d as parent at all. It's a metaphor too fraught with our own experience, whatever that might be. Even so, it *is* a metaphor, not a literal thing, and the point here is that we are not G-d. The idea that I, as a university professor of religion, should hesitate to be called a teacher because G-d is the only true teacher is something that has the power to take me down a peg.

And that's the point. Echoing Micah, we see Jesus railing at the religious authorities, who are convinced that they stand in for G-d, and that they wield divine authority. But their confidence is misplaced, and the reason we can know that, Jesus is telling his followers, is because they are relishing their power too much. They say all the right words, but don't follow them. They tie up heavy burdens and make everyone else carry them. This is like the politicians who vote for yet another tax break for the fabulously wealthy, whilst telling the poor to lift themselves up by their own bootstraps. It is like the reigning monarch in England, who is worth, literally, billions of pounds, telling the everyday folk to be nice to poor people because it's Christmas. Once again, Jesus reserves his greatest disdain for hypocrisy.

So what are we to do?

Jesus has a suggestion: "The greatest among you will be your servant. All who exalt themselves will be humbled, and all who humble themselves will be exalted." Be a servant. Be genuinely humble. Assume that your job is to care for others, for the entire community. Embody the words of Dorothy Day, who reminded herself regularly of her priest's words, that "I really only love God as much as I love the person I love the least."[1]

Live into your servanthood, not your entrepreneurship. Not your fiscal savvy. Not your innovation. Not your scholarship. Not your influence. Not your C-suite. Not your retirement fund.

These are hard words, I get it. But the least we can do is wrestle with them honestly, rather than just trying to explain them away.

And maybe, in that wrestling, we'll find the confidence to cross the River Jordan.

---

[1] Dorothy Day, *By Little and a Little: The Selected Writings of Dorothy Day*, edited by Robert Ellsberg (Knopf, 1983), 229.

PROPER 27, THE SUNDAY CLOSEST TO NOVEMBER 9

Dr. Peter Carlson

Track 1	or	Track 2
Joshua 24:1–3a, 14–25		*Wisdom of Solomon 6:12–16* or *Amos 5:18–24*
Psalm 78:1–7		*Wisdom of Solomon 6:17–20* or *Psalm 70*
1 Thessalonians 4:13–18		*1 Thessalonians 4:13–18*
Matthew 25:1–13		*Matthew 25:1–13*

The book of Joshua is problematic reading for a number of reasons, not least of which is that it seems to lend divine countenance to genocide—a dangerous reading that, apparently, some are still using in the twenty-first century. But it's also problematic because, despite the divine command and the apparent willingness to follow it, the Canaanites continued existing, and other biblical evidence suggests that the Israelites did not so much conquer the land, as moved in and coexisted with the people who were already there. And finally, it's simply problematic if we want to consider it to be a historical text with any kind of factual grounding: Archeological evidence has demonstrated conclusively that the book is largely mythological, a story told to narrate the founding of a nation, much as the United States has created myths surrounding Plymouth Rock, or Jamestown, or George Washington and the cherry tree. This leaves us with the realization that the book must be read theologically, rather than literally, though even in such a reading, the idea that we would worship a god who would welcome the destruction of innocent people who were just trying to live their lives is distressing.

But Joshua is the first book in the Deuteronomistic History—the story of ancient Israel's vacillation between faithfulness to the covenant with HaShem and apostasy—and that history is ultimately perceived by its authors as providential history. G-d, it is made clear, controls everything. This means, if shit is happening, it's no accident; G-d made it happen, so you'd better look within to figure out why *you* fucked up. And this is the warning that Joshua is giving the Israelites in our passage today: You'd better be faithful, or G-d will have no cause to be faithful toward you. And the people are all, "Oh, yes! We'll be the faithfullest faithful G-d has ever seen! Yay G-d!" And Joshua basically asks them, "*Are you sure?* Because G-d has seen your lack of faithfulness in the wilderness after being brought out of Egypt. And, for that matter, in conquering the land where you stand right now. And G-d's not gonna put up with that crap." "No, really! Pinky swear! HaShem our G-d we will serve and obey!" So Joshua sets up a large stone under an oak tree, as a witness to their commitment, an action that seems to be similar to other ancient Middle Eastern land grants.[1]

But the stage is set: Obey G-d, and do fine; disobey G-d, and watch your life go down the sewer. It's not like G-d didn't provide fair warning. Remember, G-d says, what I've done for you, and behave accordingly. Indeed, the portion of Psalm 78 assigned to accompany the reading from Joshua is repeating this very theme: "G-d established a decree in Jacob, and appointed a law in Israel. . . . So that they should set their hope in G-d, and not forget the works of G-d, but keep God's commandments." Remembering and obeying kiss each other, like angels in a Botticelli painting.

The daunting reading from Amos that is an option in track 2 is continuing the theme set out in Joshua, but in the mid eighth century BCE. Amos was from the southern kingdom of Judah, preaching in the northern kingdom of Israel. Imagine someone from Mexico coming to the United States to tell us how we're all going afoul from G-d's ways, because the rich are getting richer and the poor are getting poorer. Probably wouldn't go over exceptionally well.

Those wealthy, who are going to all the right churches, and dutifully showing everyone how pious they are (I'm reminded of the white liberals

---

[1] K. Lawson Younger, Jr., "Joshua," in James D. G. Dunn and John William Rogerson, editors, *Eerdmans Commentary on the Bible* (Eerdmans, 2003).

that the Rev. Dr. Martin Luther King, Jr. critiqued), are always babbling in the streets about the coming Day of HaShem, to which Amos responds, "Why do you want the day of HaShem? It is darkness, not light! You've been worshipping false gods!" But, they protest, they *were* worshiping G-d! No, Amos reminded them: You're not worshiping G-d if you make all the appropriate sacrifices and then go to work and destroy people's lives with the stroke of a pen as you sign a contract. You're not worshiping G-d if you sing all the right hymns but kick the homeless on the way home from the temple. You're not worshiping G-d if you live in luxury while people are dying from poverty. So asking for the Day of G-d? You're asking for some deep shit. Be careful what you ask for.

Indeed, the passage from the Wisdom of Solomon is a warning, too, though prettified: "Concern for instruction is love of [Wisdom], and love of her is the keeping of her laws, and giving heed to her laws is assurance of immortality, and immortality brings one near to God." Do the wise thing, this passage is saying, and you will be eternally close to G-d. But the converse is right there, between the lines: Do the wrong thing? Disobey G-d? Behave unwisely? Prepare, as Inigo Montoya says in *The Princess Bride*, to die.

And it is the dead that are at issue in the first Epistle to the Jesus followers at Thessalonica. This is likely one of the earliest books of the Christian scriptures, and we can imagine Christians, eagerly awaiting the return of Christ and the establishment of his reign, becoming distressed that the first Christians are beginning to die off, when Jesus apparently had promised to return really promptly. When? they are asking. When will Jesus come back, and what will happen to the believers who have died? Paul, who has very possibly been wondering much the same thing, responds with hope that those who are alive when Christ returns will have to wait, because those who have died in faith will have first dibs. Then we'll get to join them all "in the air," and everything will be hunky dory.

But when? When will the parousia, the second coming, take place? How do we know when to get scrubbed up and pretty for Jesus?

Jesus himself seems to have something to say about that, in the reign of G-d parable from Matthew in today's Gospel. You think it's going to happen soon, right? Probably not. The bridegroom will in all likelihood be delayed. We "know neither the day nor the hour" in which the Child of Humanity is coming.

The story is a frustrating one in many ways, playing on themes of wisdom (with a connection to the Wisdom of Solomon reading), on preparedness (with a connection to Amos warning the Israelites to be prepared for the day of G-d) and on obedience (with a connection to Joshua). The "wise" and "foolish" virgins, who have apparently been appointed to lead a wedding procession, are gathered with their torches, or lamps, but only five of them have brought oil to light the torches with. They fell asleep after the bridegroom was delayed, and when the shout went up at midnight, the wise virgins filled their torches with oil, and told the foolish virgins to go find their own. The upshot is that the foolish virgins are shut out of the marriage feast, and Jesus warns everyone to "watch therefore."

So many problems with this parable: First of all, *all* the virgins fell asleep and weren't particularly watching, so none of them were technically following Jesus's command; second, the unwillingness of the wise virgins to share their oil goes against every kindergarten lesson about sharing that's ever been taught; third, the bridegroom's cruelty is hardly the depiction I would make of a loving G-d; fourth, Christians, despite Jesus's very plain words, have spent ridiculous amounts of time convincing themselves that they can, in fact, know the day and the hour in which Jesus shall return.

Unpacking all of this is well-nigh impossible in the space of a single sermon, but what strikes me in all of these stories is the threat, both implicit and explicit, that is running through them, and I will be completely honest in saying how uncomfortable that makes me. When I was a child, my family spent summers at our cottage at the Cedar Lake Bible Conference—a remnant of the old camp meetings of the nineteenth century. At the bookstore, there was a postcard for sale of a painting called *The Coming Rapture* by Charles Anderson. It shows a cityscape, with Jesus in the clouds above, and there are souls (in white, of course) rising joyfully, *à la* 1 Thessalonians, toward him. In the meantime, the vehicles those souls had been operating are crashing all over the place, including a plane flying into a building that eerily foreshadowed 9/11. The postcard terrified me as, I am sure, was intended. If you're not keeping the law, Joshua is screaming; if you're not wise, Solomon is chiding; if you're rich, Amos is yelling; if you're not ready, Jesus is shouting; you'll be tied up on the freeway in a pile of scrap metal that used to be your car, while the wise, the prepared, the obedient, will be floating in a white dress up toward White Jesus In The Sky.

The number of times I flashed on this image during those years as I was becoming uncomfortably aware of my sexuality are legion. The warnings from Mean Daddy G-d were always in my head. Joshua warning, "You cannot serve G-d, for They are a holy G-d. They are a jealous G-d; who will not forgive your transgressions or your sins or your homo-ness." Amos warning, "Why do you want the day of HaShem? It is darkness for queers, not light!" The Wisdom of Solomon warning, "The one who is vigilant (or straight) on Wisdom's account will be free from care" (while I was far from being free from care). Jesus warning, "Don't be a stupid, foolish, gay virgin!" All against the backdrop of Paul's rapturous (pun intended) image of the Good People floating up to Jesus, to feast eternally at some Wedding Banquet, where a virgin's cherry will be popped, but in a holy way that's okay.

And I had no idea if I could stop being gay in time for Jesus's return.

In the Protestant Reformations of the sixteenth century, the rejection of the doctrine of Purgatory mean that the reformers taught a death theology using trees as an image: "As ye fall, so shall ye lie."[2] In other words, if you died in a state of grace, you were saved; if you were unprepared, a foolish virgin, you were doomed—and this was all summarized visually on that fucking postcard. It was a shitty theology and a shitty thing to have to cope with as a kid. I'm sure if my parents had known earlier, they would have been willing to talk me through it, to help me understand it in a way that was less harmful, but how does a kid articulate that kind of theological abuse to their parents?

It took me, literally, years to come to a different way of thinking about the parousia. Instead of obsessing on my identity or even a particular act as a potential sin, I began to understand sin as separation from G-d. And this is the lesson of the covenant, of the seeking after wisdom, of the reminder that wealth is problematic in a society that doesn't care for the poor, of the hope that death doesn't bat last, and of the wise virgins.

---

[2] For a larger explication of Protestant effects on attitudes toward death and dying, see Peter Carlson, "The Art and Craft of Dying," in *The Oxford Handbook of Early Modern English Literature and Religion*, edited by Andrew Hiscock and Helen Wilcox (Oxford University Press, 2017).

We may not know the date or the hour of some fantastic parousia, but the Second Coming of Christ—the reign of Christ—is already happening all around us. It is found in the person who is doing what they can to save lives during yet another war in the Middle East. It is found in the person who provides a safe space for a queer kid who's been kicked out of their home. It is found in the legislator who seeks to enact laws that minimize the disparity between the obscenely wealthy and the desperately poor. It is found in the willingness to reach the top shelf in the grocery store, to get the last box of macaroni and cheese down for the person who can't reach it. It is found in churches that have made their spaces, including their altars, accessible to the disabled. It is found in ears that are willing to listen to women who speak of sexual assault, and to believe them. It is found in schools that are fully funded so education can in fact be an equalizer. It is found in judges who do not take bribes and are not influenced by personal gain. It is found in communities where weapons are melted down and turned into gardening implements.

It is found whenever we take the opportunity to let justice roll down like waters, and righteousness like an ever-flowing stream.

Be ready. Make sure you've got some oil with you.

The reign of G-d is now.

PROPER 28, THE SUNDAY CLOSEST TO NOVEMBER 16

Dr. Peter Carlson

Track 1	or	Track 2
Judges 4:1–7		*Zephaniah 1:7,12–18*
Psalm 123		*Psalm 90:1–8, (9–11), 12*
1 Thessalonians 5:1–11		*1 Thessalonians 5:1–11*
Matthew 25:14–30		*Matthew 25:14–30*

It strikes me as eminently sensible that the collect of the day should pray for discernment in reading Holy Writ, because these are some of the most awful lectionary lessons you can really imagine. It's no wonder so many people have pointed to the scriptures and said, "How can you Christians pretend this shit is even a tiny bit bearable?" I'm grateful, though, that the lectionary makes us cope with at least some of the hard bits, because if I don't, then I become just as dangerous as the prooftexters who use the Bible as a weapon, picking out the bits that seem to condemn the people they don't like. Utilizing scripture (or the sacraments, for that matter) solely for comfort is just as bad as utilizing it solely for condemnation.

Judges is a remarkable book, filled with all sorts of bloodshed and violence (why Hollywood hasn't made it into a movie is beyond me), and the fourth chapter of Judges is the one I have titled "Women Who Have Had Enough of Men's Shit," because today's bit about Deborah as judge and military hero is followed immediately by Jael and her Lethal Tent Peg. But even though women are the forces (literally) to be reckoned with here, the pattern is the same as in the rest of Judges. Note the first line: "The Israelites again did what was evil in the dight of HaShem." The entire book follows a cyclic pattern: Israel fucks up; G-d takes away G-d's hand of protection; a Judge calls Israel back to G-d, to repentance; G-d gets protect-y again; the Israelites fight back and win; everything is okay. Next chapter: rinse, repeat.

It's pretty macabre, actually, when you think about it: a G-d who takes revenge on you because you've fucked up in the relationship, but once you suck up to Them again, They'll let you pound the ever-living shit out of a neighboring country.

Even Psalm 123 is *begging* G-d for mercy, because "of the scorn of those who are at ease, of the contempt of the proud." This is one of the so-called Psalms of Ascent—perhaps recited as worshippers climbed the hill of Jerusalem toward the temple. But lurking behind the worshipful words are the assumption that G-d's mercy toward us will necessarily include G-d's wrath toward the indolent rich and the proud. And that G-d? We look to that G-d "as the eyes of servants look to . . . their master." G-d, then, is MASTER, and don't you forget it, and all you can do is beg for mercy. Please, please, please, please, G-d? With sugar on top? Destroy people I don't like because they're mean to me?

Paul's letter to the community of Jesus followers in Thessalonica is possibly the earliest of the Christian texts that we have—likely written in the reign of Claudius, and possibly even before the Jerusalem conference held around the same time. I bring this up because Claudius would certainly not have made any distinction between Christians and Jews at the time, and the eviction of the Jews from Rome as a result of the great famine during his reign would have included Christians as well. They were lumped together as dangerous monotheists who rejected Imperial divinity. These Jesus followers, then, were awaiting justice—"the day of HaShem"—and Paul is encouraging them, even as he reminds them that no one can exactly know what day it will be. The response, Paul says, to that lack of knowledge, is always to be on guard, always to be alert, and always to be ready to fight (hence the militaristic imagery of the "breastplate of faith and love," and the "helmet of the hope of salvation"). We, Paul reminds his fellow Jesus followers, are not destined for G-d's wrath, like Sisera was destined for a tent peg through his forehead, or like every last person of Sisera's army, poor suckers. We're destined for military victory! So I'll point out that Paul, despite his attempts to distinguish Christianity from Judaism, is still looking to a G-d that operates in the same way as the

Divine that we meet in the book of Judges. So we should encourage one another! We should build each other up! We're soldiers, dammit! We're gonna fucking go kill some fucking enemies! Salvation is ours, mofos!

This is really distressing to me, a Christian who believes that military might is the ultimate sign of a worldly lust for power, and that murdering people, even in so-called "just war" circumstances, is unjust, and anti-divine. Surely, *surely* I can look to Jesus for a better image of divinity than—well—wrathiness?

No such luck. At least not in the lectionary today.

Matthew's Gospel provides us with one of the nastiest visions of G-d that Jesus could possibly come up with: the parable of the talents. This is the ultimate G-d As Capitalist Robber Baron story you could dream of. If you're reading this sermon, I'm betting you've heard it: A Master/CEO is taking a bit of a holiday, and calls three of their slaves/employees, and gives each of them a different amount of money/resources to work with while they're gone. They return, and two of the employees/slaves have doubled their money, and the CEO/Master is all, "Dudes! You rock! I'm giving you promotions!" The third slave/employee hid their talent, fearing the Master/CEO, and gives it back. The CEO/Master is (understandably?) pissed; they clearly expected a return on their investment, and the poor employee/slave is fired, and thrown into "outer darkness."

I grew up hearing this parable interpreted in economic, capitalist terms: G-d is a CEO, and demands productivity from Their employee/slaves! It is your job to use your talents wisely and get a G-d-blessed *return* on them, assholes! And if you're not productive, you're unemployed! Thrown out—you're trash! (You can imagine how this felt to a child who was convinced that his talents were all negated by being queer, and who consequently spent his entire life proving how productive he could be.)

In reading, marking, and inwardly digesting this parable, however, I have come to see two deep problems with this interpretation. The first is that it continues the legalistic, nationalistic understanding of G-d that we see in Judges, and that is carried into Paul's letter. It assumes that we worship a G-d whose primary emotive state is one of wrath, because our primary experiential state is sin. The second is that it assumes that the Master in this story is an allegory for G-d.

I would like to suggest that the person we should be paying the most attention to in this story is not the CEO/Master, but Slave/Employee #3.

Look at what this employee/slave says: "I knew that you were a harsh man, reaping where you did not sow, and gathering where you did not scatter seed; so I was afraid." How on earth is the kind of injustice of taking someone else's crops a metaphor for a G-d who cares and loves Their creation? This isn't a G-d who cared so much about creation, and who was so delighted with bodies, that They became part of that creation, taking on a body, to experience enfleshment with us. No, this is a shithole robber baron, who then justifies their obscene wealth by salving their guilty conscience with an occasional Rockefeller Chapel, or a Carnegie Hall.

But back to Slave/Employee #3. The point that has struck me in reading the story this year is that, unlike the Rolling Stones classic song, this slave got exactly what they wanted: a terrifying, cruel G-d. Slave/Employee #3 cast themself into the outer darkness; they are gnashing their teeth, because they cannot imagine a G-d who gives talent in abundance, and wants them, not to be productive, but to be joyful, using those talents with abandon, and in profligate love.

The wrathful character in this story is not G-d. We don't have a "Master" who will cast us into outer darkness/unemployment if we don't produce enough in the factory; we have a cocreator who wants us to know ourselves as wonderfully and fearfully and queerfully made.

I'm convinced that the point we need to take from the Epistle is that when the "day of HaShem comes like a thief in the night," as Paul warns, we won't be sweating, worrying about how fucking much money we made for Jesus. We'll be rejoicing that we've been given the talents we've got, and are actually relishing them and having a jolly good time with them, and have "encouraged one another and built up each other" by clapping delightedly for each other's peculiar gifts.

Go play with your talents!

PROPER 29, THE REIGN OF CHRIST

The Rev. Naomi Gardom

Ezekiel 34:11–16, 20–24
Psalm 100 or *Psalm 95:1–7a*
Ephesians 1:15–23
Matthew 25:31–46

May I speak in the name of God, Holy Eternal Majesty, Holy Incarnate Word, Holy Abiding Spirit. Amen.

In the Picasso Museum in Antibes, there is a drawing of a she-goat by the great artist. It is about 120 cm by 150 cm, and the goat fills much of the space, so she is more or less life-size. It's a relatively realist drawing, for Picasso, reflecting his interest in anatomy and economy of expression: that is, the goat is immediately recognizable for what she is, but the outline of her skeleton and the planes of her skinny body are starkly depicted. She is far from being a well-fed specimen, and presumably reflects the scarcity of animal feed in Europe during the Second World War and in the aftermath of the Spanish Civil War. If you gave her a pat on the back, you'd be liable to cut yourself. The front half of her body is shaded in greater detail: Picasso has left the back half almost as an outline, with her udders sketched in with six short strokes of the pencil. And he has left a trace of a first attempt at her tail, visible beneath the finished outline, which gives the impression that she is wagging it cheerfully at us. This is the only touch of movement in the drawing: Other than this, our She-Goat is almost set in stone, one patient dark eye contemplating her viewer, contemplating the man drawing her, sardonic and amused.

Today is the feast of the Reign of Christ, a turning point in the Christian year when we celebrate Christ's power and Christ's majesty, the enthroning of Jesus as monarch of the universe, before we move into the penitential season of Advent. We're ending on a high, a moment of glitz and glamor, a fabulous party for Jesus, who sits resplendent in rhinestones, ornate as a drag queen. But today isn't just about celebration: It's also about looking ahead toward the season that's coming, this period of reflection and penitence that prepares us for Christmas. The Christ who reigns over us today is the Christ who was born into poverty and danger in a stable that smelled of animal muck. This is important, because when we seek to celebrate Christ's power and majesty, we are in perpetual danger of assuming that the things the world values are the things that Christ values. In short, we are in danger of proclaiming Christ as a patriarchal, power-hungry white male monarch, secure in his wealth and privilege.

This is why we have to pay attention to the actual depiction of Christ's reign that is portrayed in our readings. There's a definite theme that emerges from three of these four readings: one of a shepherd with sheep. This is a far cry from the power-hungry monarch I have just described. Shepherds, in Middle Eastern society in this period, were very far from being powerful, influential characters. They were nomadic or seminomadic, spending months of the year travelling with their flocks in search of good pasture. They were very much at the margins of society. And yet, throughout both the Hebrew Bible and the New Testament, the metaphor of a shepherd is used repeatedly to describe God's relationship with God's people. This relationship is one of hard graft on behalf of the shepherd, and it's one of dedication and commitment. A good shepherd, as Jesus says in John 10, knows his sheep and his sheep know him. He knows their needs, he sleeps close to them to keep them safe from wolves. He smells of them.

In today's psalm, Psalm 100, the singer presents us with a beautiful mixed metaphor. In verse three, they proclaim "It is he who made us, and we are his; we are his people and the sheep of his pasture." We are God's sheep and God is our shepherd: familiar, smelling like us, caring deeply for our daily needs. And then in the next verse, we are reminded of God's power and majesty: "Enter his gates with thanksgiving and his courts with praise." We are no longer in the fields, but in a court or a palace. But I like to think that, in the world of this psalm of praise, we are still sheep, pouring in through the magnificent gates and up the marble steps. We are the beloved, the cared for, the sometimes-useless, the often-helpless, sheep. We are his people, and the sheep of his pasture.

This relationship of love and care is also beautifully explored in our reading from Ezekiel, in which God promises to restore the scattered people of Israel following their exile. It's a promise of a personal search, not the impersonal policy of a king who can delegate such messy jobs to his subordinates. Listen again to the number of times the prophecy uses the word "I" in the first few verses: "I myself will search for my sheep . . . I will seek them out. . . . I will rescue them. . . . I will bring them out. . . . I will feed them on the mountains. . . . I will feed them with good pasture. . . . I myself will be the shepherd of my sheep, and I will make them lie down. . . . I will seek the lost," and so on! These are words of humility, of a promise of incarnate ministry, of being with the sheep.

But there is another side to this shepherding, just as there is another side to Advent. It's not just a cozy reminder of the wonder of Christmas: It's also a time to reflect on what we call the "parousia," or the Second Coming. This is the expectation that the ultimate destiny of the universe, of us and all creation, is to be delivered into Christ's power and judgement. And our reading from Ezekiel and our reading from Matthew don't skimp on this theme of judgement. In Ezekiel, the Lord says, "I myself will judge between the fat sheep and the lean sheep. . . . I will judge between sheep and sheep." And in Matthew, when the Son of Man is sitting on his throne of glory, his work is to "separate people from one another as a shepherd separates the sheep from the goats." The shepherd is on a throne now; the sheep have poured in through the magnificent gates and up the marble steps, and what they are faced with is judgement.

Judgement. Let's take a moment to let this word resound. It's a concept that progressive Christians are often shy of, and sometimes with good reason. After all, it has been weaponized again and again against people in the Church to force them to conform. It's been held as a sword of Damocles over the heads of queer people, compelling us to choose between two impossible positions: Either give up our so-called "sinful" ways and be a sheep, or be true to who we are and be labelled a goat, going away into eternal punishment. It's no wonder that we have preferred to talk of God's mercy and ease off on the rhetoric of judgement.

But for all this, it does a disservice to scripture and to ourselves to ignore the reality of judgement. The mistake we make is the same mistake

I mentioned earlier on: that of making Christ in the image of what the world values. If we project onto Christ all our own anxieties about our inadequacy, our fears about being unloved and rejected, our desire for affirmation from those in authority over us, then of course we end up seeing Christ as an autocratic arbitrary judge with fearful power. Of course we will go through life looking over our own shoulder to check that our behavior is abject enough. Of course we will end up as our own thought police, and also seek to police others because of our own anxieties.

But this is *not* what Christ is like, according to scripture. In our reading from Ephesians, another powerful description of Christ's enthronement, we're told that he is "far above all rule and authority and power and dominion and above ever name that is named." That is to say, Christ is totally removed from our human structures and expectations of power. He has completely transcended them, to the extent that they, too, are subject to his judgment. Just think about that: It's not just human beings, as individuals, who are subject to his judgment, but all the powers and structures and authorities of the world too. Colonialism, homophobia, the patriarchy, racism, ableism: All of these structures of sin are under his feet, and Christ tramples on them, just as he was subject to them in his earthly life. It's no coincidence that, in the reading from Matthew's Gospel, we again have a series of "I" statements: "I was hungry. . . . I was thirsty. . . . I was naked. . . . I was sick. . . . I was in prison." The Christ whose reign we celebrate today has authority over these powers precisely because of that birth in a stable, that life of poverty and marginality. His authority is the authority of a shepherd, who also knows what it is to be a lamb for the slaughter.

The good shepherd knows his sheep, and his sheep know him. So what does this say about individual judgement, then? For our Gospel reading does still seem to point toward an individual reckoning, for all that the powers and structures of the world are subject to it too. The Greek word for judgement is *krisis*, from the verb *krino*, meaning "I decide." But the noun, *krisis*, has a particular meaning. It was a medical word, used to describe the deciding moment in the course of an illness, the period of touch-and-go, before either an ultimate decline or an eventual recovery. A physician would have to pay total attention to a patient during the period of *krisis*, discerning from marginal signs which way they were heading, delicately adjusting their care to respond to changing conditions. In other words, *krisis* implies a careful, gentle, patient kind of intense watching. The kind of looking involved in the creation of a work of art, like Picasso's sketch of a goat.

C. S. Lewis describes the moment of judgement as "an absolute correct verdict—if you like, a perfect critique . . . on what each of us is."[1] This is something to be feared, for sure, but only because we are so well-practiced in self-deception now. We do not wish to be looked at, with the kind of careful, discerning gaze of love that Christ will turn on us, because we ourselves want to forget all the times when we have failed to feed the hungry, clothe the naked, visit the prisoner, and so on. We don't want to be looked at, because we can't imagine, in our heart of hearts, anything worse than looking at ourselves with that kind of clarity. We can only see our own inadequacies: our skinny goat necks and our starved-sharp vertebrae. This is the worst possible punishment for us, and it takes place in this seemingly endless knife-edge moment of *krisis*, as Christ's gaze burns away all that is unworthy, all that is unacceptable, all that has given into the powers of the world.

Perhaps there are some goats who are truly goats. Perhaps there are some people who, when Christ has finished burning away all that cannot enter the kingdom of heaven, have nothing left. But when I look at Picasso's goat, I see a sheep. I see a beloved animal, pared down to her bare essentials—a sturdy back leg and a sardonic eye. I see her as perhaps God sees me, and you: sometimes-useless, often-helpless, sheep. Loveable. Loved. We are his people, and the sheep of his pasture. Amen.

---

[1] C. S. Lewis, *The World's Last Night and Other Essays* (Harcourt, 1996), 112-13.

CONTRIBUTORS

The Rev. Phoenix Bell-Shelton Biggs is an ordained Unitarian Universalist minister. They are a committed advocate for social justice and spiritual care; and identify as Queer, BIPOC, and nonbinary person. Their ministry focuses on radical love and sanctuary movements, working to disrupt patriarchy and dismantle oppressive systems. They served as an intern minister at the Unitarian Universalist Fellowship of Fredericksburg, Virginia (2022–24), and have held or hold leadership roles in the UU Mental Health Network (UUMN), the UU Young Adult Revival Network (UUYARN), Transgender Religious-Professional Unitarian Universalists Together (TRUUsT), and others. They also completed a Spiritual Health Residency at Emory University Hospital in Atlanta, Georgia. Rev. Phoenix earned an MDiv from Meadville Lombard Theological School (2024), a BS in religious studies (2021), and an AS in media production (2018). This education empowers them to advocate for marginalized communities and provide inclusive pastoral care. Outside of their work, Phoenix enjoys nature, vegan food, theater, and coffee, seeking balance and grounding in their life. Their journey is dedicated to fostering a more just and loving world.

Dr. Gabrielle Bychowski, PhD, is the Anisfield-Wolf Fellow at Case Western Reserve University, where she leads seminars (such as "Queer Christianity," "Transgender Literature," and "Women of the Civil Rights Movement") on social justice movements from the Civil War to today. As a scholar, Gabby publishes a wide variety of research on the stories of medieval transgender people and people with disabilities. As a public intellectual, she has been invited to speak at a wide range of academic institutions, including Yale, Cornell, Johns Hopkins, Howard University,

Columbia University, and the University of the South. Growing up Catholic in Wheaton, Illinois, Gabby learned the challenges and complexities of being a neurospicy witchy trans woman in the Church. For the last ten years, Gabby has worked as sermon writer within the United Church of Christ and served on various church councils, communication teams, and executive boards on mental health in faith communities. Additionally, Dr. Bychowski has consulted for the Obama-era White House, the Cleveland Foundation, and the Michigan Disability Rights Coalition. On Trans Visibility Day 2024, the same day as Easter that year, Gabby won an award for Extraordinary Service to the Transgender Community from Margie's Hope in Cleveland.

The Rev. Alene Campbell-Langdell is a bivocational priest in the Episcopal Diocese of Los Angeles. Alene holds master's degrees in pastoral ministry (Boston College), divinity (Church Divinity School of the Pacific), and social work (Simmons University), but the smartest thing she did was to marry her wife, Melissa. Alene works as a clinical social worker/therapist during the week and serves as a supply priest on Sundays. Whether serving congregations in transition or living a queerly Christian life, Alene's theology is informed by liminal, in-between spaces.

(The Very Rev.) Melissa Campbell-Langdell is teasingly referred to as "The Extremely Reverend" by her brother, because siblings keep us honest. She loves serving in a bilingual, intercultural, and inclusive church setting at All Saints/Todos los Santos Episcopal Church in Oxnard, California, and as the area dean. Blessed to be married to Alene, who is also an author in this volume, she is thrilled to contribute to this series, as queer theology has been a passion ever since she took a class from the Rev. Dr. Jay Johnson. Her passion is bringing people together across all areas of different expression.

The Rev. Emily E. Ewing (they/them) is a pastor in the Evangelical Lutheran Church in America serving in Baltimore, Maryland. They combine creativity, spirituality, nerdiness, and the call to justice in many ways. Pastor Emily cohosts and coproduces the Nerds at Church podcast, a queer, feminist, indie podcast diving deep into faith, nerdery, and the Bible. They also cohost the Horror Nerds at Church podcast, a ridiculously queer podcast about horror movies and theology. Pastor Emily also consults with communities of faith for anti-oppression trainings, Praying in Color spiritual practices, and whatever the Spirit calls them to.

The Rev. Naomi Gardom was ordained in 2023 and is serving her curacy at the University Church in Oxford. Before this, she trained for ministry at Ripon College Cuddesdon, having previously worked as a pastoral assistant at St. Albans Cathedral and running a debt advice charity in Cambridge. Naomi's interests include medieval history, theology of the body, homiletics, and liturgy. She also has a passionate love for Golden Age detective fiction, which she refuses to call a guilty pleasure.

The Rt. Rev. Deon Kevin Johnson was consecrated as the eleventh bishop of the Episcopal Diocese of Missouri on June 13, 2020, becoming the first Black, gay, and immigrant to serve in this role. Born in Barbados, Johnson's faith was nurtured by his grandmother, whose prayers and teachings shaped his spiritual journey. After immigrating to New York at age fourteen, Johnson pursued degrees in English, history, and divinity. He served as associate rector in Ohio and as rector in Michigan before his election as bishop in 2019. Johnson's leadership, especially during the COVID-19 pandemic, is marked by a commitment to social justice, racial reconciliation, and pastoral care. Bishop Johnson and his husband, Jhovanny Osorio, are parents to two children, Lilohalani and Ja'Lon. He enjoys cooking, photography, and hiking.

The Rev. Dr. Jay Emerson Johnson is a priest in the Episcopal Church and a Christian theologian who serves as the rector of All Saints' Parish in Saugatuck, Michigan. Before moving to Saugatuck in 2020, Jay taught on the faculty at Pacific School of Religion and the Graduate Theological Union in Berkeley, California, for more than twenty years. During that time, he served as the programming director of the Center for Lesbian and Gay Studies in Religion at PSR and coordinated the school's Certificate of Sexuality and Religion program. Jay also served as a member of the steering committee of the Gay Men's Issues in Religion Group of the American Academy of Religion, eventually cochairing the group for nearly ten years. He continues to serve on the editorial board of the journal *Theology and Sexuality*. In addition to numerous journal articles and essays, he is also the author of three books, including *Peculiar Faith: Queer Theology for Christian Witness* (2014, Seabury Books). When not otherwise occupied, Jay enjoys volunteer crewing on a tall ship during the summer months and hiking with River, his Australian shepherd dog companion.

Pamela Lightsey, PhD has been a cutting-edge church and academic leader in many ways. She is currently the Vice President for Academic and Student Affairs and Associate Professor of Constructive Theology at Meadville Lombard Theological School in Chicago and serves as Site Pastor at Urban Village Church in the city.

Following service in the US Army and work as a civil servant, Dr. Lightsey received her academic and theological training at Columbus State University (BS), Gammon Seminary of the Interdenominational Theological Center (MDiv) and Garrett-Evangelical Theological School (PhD). After ordination, she served first as a United Methodist congregational pastor and then as a theological school educator, scholar, and administrator. Throughout her vocational life, she has been a leading social justice activist, working with local, national, and international organizations focusing primarily on the causes of peacemaking, racial justice, and LGBTQ rights.

Dr. Lightsey's publications include *Our Lives Matter: A Womanist Queer Theology* (Wipf and Stock), *Transforming Service: Reflections of Student Services Personnel in Theological Education* (Pickwick Publications), eds. Pamela Lightsey and Shonda Jones, "He Is Black and We are Queer" in *Albert Cleage Jr and the Black Madonna and Child* (New York: Palgrave Macmillan), "Reconciliation" in *Prophetic Evangelicals: Envisioning a Just and Peaceable Kingdom* (Wm. B. Eerdmans Publishing Company), and "If There Should Come a Word" in *Black United Methodists Preach!* (Abingdon Press).

River Cook Needham, MA, ThM (she/her/hers), is a graduate of and student at the Lutheran School of Theology at Chicago, working on her PhD focusing on transgender oral histories. As a queer, disabled, nonbinary, transgender woman and faith leader, she works to make progressive faith accessible with the diakonia.faith collective and St. Luke's Lutheran Church of Logan Square. River also gains deep meaning from ecumenical and interfaith work, particularly with humanist and Earth-based religious traditions.

The Rev. Melvin M. Soriano serves as an Episcopal priest at St. John's Cathedral in Los Angeles, and as the campus chaplain at Canterbury USC. An immigrant from the Philippines, he was raised Roman Catholic and studied psychobiology, business administration, British history, and divinity. Before turning to ministry, he built a software startup with clients worldwide. He turned to the Episcopal Church through All Saints Pasadena. He became active in multiple choral, liturgical, and pastoral roles, as well as serving on the board of a national Episcopal LGBTQ group and a diocesan ministry for Asian-American Pacific Islander spirituality.

Dr. Pace Warfield, PhD (they/them) is a graduate of the Graduate Theological Union in Berkeley, California, where their research interests are queer theology, Luther and Reformation history, and theological anthropology. They are the creator and cohost of Horror Nerds at Church, a podcast that examines the intersections of queerness, theology, and horror, and they are the director of faith formation shared between two ELCA congregations. They live in Minneapolis, MN.

The Rev. Jeremy S. Whitner, MDiv obtained a masters of divinity from Union Presbyterian Seminary and is ordained by the Christian Church (Disciples of Christ). He is an out and proud queer pastor in North Carolina. He currently serves Open Heart Gathering Christian Church (Disciples of Christ), an inclusive and justice-oriented faith community in Gastonia, North Carolina. He is a voracious reader of all things theological, mystical, and spiritual. When not doing ministry, he likes movies, reading, and doing queer art and iconography.

The Rev. Mollie Winninger is a trauma and death chaplain who was educated Lutheran and Presbyterian. A Word and Sacrament candidate within the ELCA, she considers herself an anxious albeit fervent theologian. Currently completing her PhD in disability studies and scriptural exegesis, Mollie is seeking to make connections from ancient Near Eastern ideologies of hysteria and chronic pain to the stories of modern women who continue to be gaslit, misdiagnosed, and dismissed. Their research interests include pharmacology, bioethics, New Testament healing stories, and the best recipe for an Arnold Palmer.

SCRIPTURE INDEX